Research Series on the C
and China's Developmen

MW00805773

Project Director
Xie Shouguang, President, Social Sciences Academic Press

Series Editors
Li Yang, Chinese Academy of Social Sciences, Beijing, China
Li Peilin, Chinese Academy of Social Sciences, Beijing, China

Academic Advisors
Cai Fang, Gao Peiyong, Li Lin, Li Qiang, Ma Huaide, Pan Jiahua, Pei Changhong,
Qi Ye, Wang Lei, Wang Ming, Zhang Yuyan, Zheng Yongnian, Zhou Hong

Drawing on a large body of empirical studies done over the last two decades, this Series provides its readers with in-depth analyses of the past and present and forecasts for the future course of China's development. It contains the latest research results made by members of the Chinese Academy of Social Sciences. This series is an invaluable companion to every researcher who is trying to gain a deeper understanding of the development model, path and experience unique to China. Thanks to the adoption of Socialism with Chinese characteristics, and the implementation of comprehensive reform and opening-up, China has made tremendous achievements in areas such as political reform, economic development, and social construction, and is making great strides towards the realization of the Chinese dream of national rejuvenation. In addition to presenting a detailed account of many of these achievements, the authors also discuss what lessons other countries can learn from China's experience.

More information about this series at http://www.springer.com/series/13571

Dikun Xie · Ye Chen
Editors

Chinese Dream and Practice in Zhejiang – Culture

Editors
Dikun Xie
Institute of Philosophy
Chinese Academy of Social Sciences
Beijing, Beijing, China

Ye Chen
Zhejiang Academy of Social Sciences
Hangzhou, Zhejiang, China

Published with support of Zhejiang People's Publishing House

ISSN 2363-6866   ISSN 2363-6874   (electronic)
Research Series on the Chinese Dream and China's Development Path
ISBN 978-981-13-7218-6   ISBN 978-981-13-7216-2   (eBook)
https://doi.org/10.1007/978-981-13-7216-2

Jointly published with Social Sciences Academic Press, Beijing, China
The print edition is not for sale in China Mainland. Customers from China Mainland please order the print book from: Social Sciences Academic Press.

Library of Congress Control Number: 2019935830

This Springer imprint is published by the registered company Springer Nature Singapore Pte Ltd.
The registered company address is: 152 Beach Road, #21-01/04 Gateway East, Singapore 189721, Singapore

Series Preface

Since China's reform and opening began in 1978, the country has come a long way on the path of Socialism with Chinese Characteristics, under the leadership of the Communist Party of China. Over thirty years of reform, efforts and sustained spectacular economic growth have turned China into the world's second-largest economy and wrought many profound changes in the Chinese society. These historically significant developments have been garnering increasing attention from scholars, governments, and the general public alike around the world since the 1990s, when the newest wave of China studies began to gather steam. Some of the hottest topics have included the so-called China miracle, Chinese phenomenon, Chinese experience, Chinese path, and the Chinese model. Homegrown researchers have soon followed suit. Already hugely productive, this vibrant field is putting out a large number of books each year, with Social Sciences Academic Press alone having published hundreds of titles on a wide range of subjects.

Because most of these books have been written and published in Chinese; however, readership has been limited outside China—even among many who study China—for whom English is still the lingua franca. This language barrier has been an impediment to efforts by academia, business communities, and policy-makers in other countries to form a thorough understanding of contemporary China, of what is distinct about China's past and present may mean not only for her future but also for the future of the world. The need to remove such an impediment is both real and urgent, and the *Research Series on the Chinese Dream and China's Development Path* is my answer to the call.

This series features some of the most notable achievements from the last 20 years by scholars in China in a variety of research topics related to reform and opening. They include both theoretical explorations and empirical studies and cover economy, society, politics, law, culture, and ecology; the six areas in which reform and opening policies have had the deepest impact and farthest-reaching consequences for the country. Authors for the series have also tried to articulate their visions of the "Chinese Dream" and how the country can realize it in these fields and beyond.

All of the editors and authors for the *Research Series on the Chinese Dream and China's Development Path* are both longtime students of reform and opening and recognized authorities in their respective academic fields. Their credentials and expertise lend credibility to these books, each of which has been subjected to a rigorous peer review process for inclusion in the series. As part of the Reform and Development Program under the State Administration of Press, Publication, Radio, Film, and Television of the People's Republic of China, the series is published by Springer, a Germany-based academic publisher of international repute, and distributed overseas. I am confident that it will help fill a lacuna in studies of China in the era of reform and opening.

                                                                          Xie Shouguang

Contents

Chapter 1
Zhejiang's Cultural Development: Experience and Achievements

Xiaoming Zhang and Ming Hui

Zhejiang is an economically large province and one of the forerunners of reform and opening-up in China. Since the reform and opening-up, with the advantage of a unique location and the entrepreneurial and innovative spirit of making unceasing improvements and blazing new trails, Zhejiang has rapidly grown from an ecologically weak province into one of the most developed provinces in China, and it has stayed ahead nationwide in the economic, political, cultural, social, ecological and other fields.

To fully summarize Zhejiang's developmental experience, the Chinese Academy of Social Sciences and Zhejiang jointly conducted a major survey on the national conditions in the "Zhejiang Experience and Its Implication for the Development of China" in 2006. As the members of the Culture Group, we had the opportunity to go deep into Zhejiang to carry out in-depth surveys on the achievements in and the internal impetus behind Zhejiang's cultural development. With these surveys, we found that Zhejiang endeavored to build a culturally large province under the guidance of the Zhejiang Spirit which features "pursuit of truth, pragmatism, integrity and harmony, open-mindedness and determination to become stronger" and the instruction, made by the then Secretary of the Party Committee of Zhejiang Province, Xi Jinping, of doing concrete work to stay ahead; this deeply impressed us. With the goal of building a culturally large province and the "Eight-Eight Strategies", the people of Zhejiang combined the outlook on culture with the outlook on development, intensified the reform of the cultural system through the Scientific Outlook on Development, adopted new modes for building a system of public cultural services and developed the cultural industry by the innovative spirit of starting from scratch, so that culture became the "absolute principle" for guaranteeing coordinated economic, social, political and ecological development across the province. In the book "The Zhejiang Experience and Its Implication for the Development of China—Scientific Development and the Building of a

X. Zhang (✉) · M. Hui
The Chinese Academy of Social Sciences, Beijing, People's Republic of China

© Social Sciences Academic Press and Springer Nature Singapore Pte Ltd. 2019
D. Xie and Y. Chen (eds.), *Chinese Dream and Practice in Zhejiang – Culture*,
Research Series on the Chinese Dream and China's Development Path,
https://doi.org/10.1007/978-981-13-7216-2_1

Harmonious Society in Zhejiang (Culture Volume)", a basic judgment made by us is that Zhejiang has stayed ahead nationwide in cultural development and has gained rich experience in cultural development for the rest of the country.

Eight years later, as the Culture Group under the Research Group of "The Chinese Dream and Zhejiang's Practice", we took a new perspective to examine the more than 10-period of Zhejiang's cultural development. We found that during this period, Zhejiang combined cultural development with the intrinsic requirement of economic and social development, strove to develop modern market ethics such as integrity and fairness, nurtured and aroused the regional cultural spirit of entrepreneurship and innovation, promoted the transformation of the economic growth mode and optimized the industrial structure across the province, and thus took a path of coordination and interaction between economic development and cultural development with Zhejiang's characteristics. In this survey, a high degree of cultural self-consciousness in Zhejiang extremely impressed us. Zhejiang's experiments in the localized developmental path and innovations in the cultural governance mode in cultural development made us excited. This cultural practice was the greatest bright spot in Zhejiang's cultural development and a major breakthrough which can serve as a reference for the rest of the country.

In September, 2014, when the Research Group concentrated on writing this book, we were informed of Alibaba's successful listing in the USA, and the whole world turned its attention to China. Alibaba is an enterprise growing out of Zhejiang, a fertile soil; with great symbolic significance, it brought China into an era of cybereconomy. In 2007, we focused on Zhejiang's cultural development, carefully studied and tapped the connotation of the Zhejiang Spirit and its self-consciousness in cultural development. Today, we once again turn our attention to Zhejiang and hope to further understand Zhejiang's economic transformation, especially the cultural impetus behind that transformation, after the global financial crisis broke out in 2008. We attribute this impetus to an s shift from cultural self-consciousness to cultural governance and we identify Zhejiang's cultural development in more than ten years as a process of unceasingly exploring the local path of cultural governance.

Zhejiang is situated in the Jiangsu and Zhejiang cultural circle and was the region of the ancient Wuyue kingdom, so Zhejiang enjoys rich historical and cultural deposits. Shangshan Culture, Hemudu Culture, Majiabang Culture and Liangzhu Culture, which have a history of 10,000 years, 7,000 years, 6,000 years and 5,000 years, respectively, are the important early sources of the Chinese civilization. At the cultural level, Zhejiang has been culturally prosperous and has been home to a galaxy of celebrities since ancient times. Litterateurs who are natives of Zhejiang and have been written into the annals of history since the Eastern Han Dynasty (25–220) account for 1/6 of all the litterateurs across the country. Zhejiang is hailed as a region giving birth to an immense number of articles. This is the cultural gene and humanistic advantage that is peculiar to the people of Zhejiang.

The humanistic advantage is a great advantage for Zhejiang's regional development. Since modern times, it has been difficult for Zhejiang to leverage its cultural advantages to promote regional development and modernization due to frequent wars. In the era of the planned economy, Zhejiang was always in the edge zone of the planning system; Zhejiang had no economic conditions and material foundation for turning its advantages of humanistic resources into cultural and economic strength.

Zhejiang has been outstanding nationwide in the development of the cultural industry. Since China established the national statistical system for the cultural industry for the first time in 2004, the added value of Zhejiang's cultural industry has grown by more than 20% most of the time except 2009 during which its growth rate was lower than 10% due to the impact of the financial crisis; in 2013, the total added value of the cultural industry accounted for 5.0% of the GDP, higher than the average national level, and it became the strategic pillar industry in leading Zhejiang's economic transformation and upgrading (see Table 1.1). Nevertheless, Zhejiang's cultural industrial development is interestingly associated with economic development. According to relevant data, in 2009 during which the impact from the financial crisis peaked, the growth rate of Zhejiang's economic development decreased to 8.9%, and that of the cultural industry fell to 9.87% for the first time, the lowest level in a decade. However, in 2010, the added value of the cultural industry soared to 30.71%, the peak level in a decade. If we say that the lowest growth rate of the added value of Zhejiang's cultural industry in 2009 was caused by the negative impact from the economic crisis which broke out in 2008, then the drastic growth in 2010 obviously ran counter to the opposite trend.

In more than 10 years, Zhejiang's cultural development has played an important role in its overall economic and social development and has also offered Zhejiang a sample for exploring the path towards modernization with Chinese characteristics. In terms of the rigid indicators or the look of the modern people of Zhejiang, Zhejiang is growing from a province of cultural relics in the premodern period into today's culturally large province, even a culturally strong province. In our view, Zhejiang is undergoing a real "cultural renaissance".

Undoubtedly, amidst Zhejiang's efforts in coping with the challenges from the financial crisis and creating glory again, cultural development and the integrative development of the cultural industry and the traditional economy have played an extremely important role. This phenomenon has aroused the attention and deep thoughts from the people, so that the people once again focus on the important role of culture in promoting economic and social development. As mentioned by comrade Xi Jinping, "The underlying reasons for Zhejiang's sustained, rapid and healthy economic and social development since the reform and opening-up lie in Zhejiang's profound cultural deposits and a combination of cultural tradition and the spirit of the current era, and in the fact that we have vigorously strengthened cultural development while promoting economic development, the people across the province have energetically carried forward the Zhejiang Spirit and have always kept their enterprising spirit."[1]

Zhejiang's cultural development has been pursued under the guidance of a clear strategic path. Since the 1990s, under the guidance of the guiding principles adopted by the Central Committee of the Communist Party of China, the Party Committee and the People's Government of Zhejiang Province have scientifically planned

---

[1]Xi (2006), p. 289.

Table 1.1 The growth of Zhejiang's cultural industry, 2004–2013

	2003	2004	2005	2006	2007	2008	2009	2010	2011	2012	2013
The added value of the cultural industry (100 million yuan)	312	377.61	442.24	501.72	595.93	735.4	807.96	1056.09	1290.01	1581.72	1880
The growth rate of the added value of the cultural industry	–	21.02%	17.12%	13.45%	18.77%	23.40%	9.87%	30.71%	22.15%	22.61%	18.86
The proportion in the GDP (%)	3.3	3.2	3.3	3.2	3.2	3.4	3.5	3.8	4.0	4.6	5.01

Note The data for the year 2003 cover sports; the data of the years 2012 and 2013 were compiled according to the new national industrial classification standard for the cultural and related industries
Source Zhejiang Provincial Bureau of Statistics

and rationally arranged cultural development. In 1999, Zhejiang put forward the strategy of building a culturally large province. In 2000, Zhejiang unveiled the *Plan of Zhejiang Province for the Building of a Culturally Large Province (2001–2020)*. In more than ten years, Zhejiang issued more than ten programmatic documents, including the *Decision of the Party Committee of Zhejiang Province on Accelerating the Building of a Culturally Large Province*, the *Decision of the Party Committee of Zhejiang Province on Earnestly Carrying Out the Guiding Principles Adopted during the 6th Plenary Session of the 17th Central Committee of the Communist Party of China and Vigorously Promoting the Building of a Culturally Strong Province,* and extensively carried out eight projects—including the cultural quality improvement project, the excellent cultural product project, the cultural research project, the cultural protection project, the project for the promotion of the cultural industry, the cultural front project, the cultural communication project, the cultural talent project—energetically built three main systems—the system of values with a socialist core, the public cultural service system, the system for the development of the cultural industry—to make Zhejiang embark on the path of a cultural renaissance. This introduction will attempt to roughly present Zhejiang' economic and cultural development in the previous more than ten years. We will take the usual perspective to classify the issues into the building of the core value system, the building of the public cultural service system, the reform of the cultural system, the development of the cultural industry, and cultural and artistic creations.

1.1 The Building of a System of Values with a Socialist Core

In 2006, the 6th Plenary Session of the 16th Central Committee of the Communist Party of China put forward, for the first time, the major issue and strategic task—the building of a system of values with a socialist core. The 17th National Congress of the Communist Party of China further stressed that the system of values with a socialist core was the essential embodiment of the socialist ideology. The 6th Plenary Session of the 17th Central Committee of the Communist Party of China further emphasized that a system of values with a socialist core was the soul for developing the country. The report delivered during the 18th National Congress of the Communist Party of China advocates a state of being prosperous, strong, democratic, culturally advanced and harmonious as well as freedom, equality, justice, the rule of law, love for the country, dedication, integrity and friendliness and an active cultivation of the socialist core values.

Zhejiang has actively explored the local path in building a system of values with a socialist core. Zhejiang has not only put it into practice, but has also successfully tailored it to local conditions, thus making fruitful achievements. As early as 2000, in the *Plan of Zhejiang Province for the Building of a Culturally Large Province (2001–2020)*, Zhejiang vowed to build a cultural and ethical system suitable for the development of a socialist market economy and improve the pattern of cultural development catering to the needs of economic and social development. Since 2006,

Zhejiang has taken the building of the system of values with a socialist core as the fundamental task for promoting Zhejiang's cultural and ethical development. In an effort to carry out the *Opinions on Cultivating and Practicing the Socialist Core Values* issued by the General Office of the Central Committee of the Communist Party of China, Zhejiang has focused on providing classified and layered guidance, making the socialist core values deeply rooted among the people.

Building a trustworthy Zhejiang in coordination with economic practice. Amidst increasing competition at home and abroad at present, the following factors present great challenges to Zhejiang's sustainable economic development: the underdevelopment of the system of market credit, the contrasts between Zhejiang's commercial culture based on a acquaintance society and modern economic ethics, between family-run management and the modern system of corporate governance, between economic growth and resources with environmental support. In response to these problems, in 2002, the People's Government of Zhejiang Province issued the *Several Opinions on the Building of a Trustworthy Zhejiang*, and vowed to do just that. In 2005, the People's Government of Zhejiang Province issued the *Administrative Measures of Zhejiang Province for the Collection and Release of Enterprise Credit Information*, extensively carried out moral education and fostered a credit culture. In 2012, the *Plan of Zhejiang Province for Civic Moral Construction* was unveiled, calling for making great efforts at building a trustworthy Zhejiang, giving priority to integrity-focused improvement, actively pushing forward improvements in government integrity, commercial integrity, social integrity, judicial credibility and personal integrity, strengthening the philosophy of integrity, carrying forward the spirit of integrity, and developing the quality of integrity and the social custom of valuing integrity.

Launching the great debate "Our Values" in line with the local experience. In practice, Zhejiang has extensively carried out moral education to promote the building of a system of social integrity and civic moral development in an integrative way. The most conspicuous ones are the appraisal and selection of the Most Beautiful People of Zhejiang which carries forward civic virtues, and the great debate "Our Values" which is aimed at building consensus on social values. The great debate "Our Values" started in 2012 and lasted for more than 4 months, with the participation for more than 10 million person-times, ultimately giving shape to the shared values of the contemporary people of Zhejiang: being pragmatic, trustworthy, advocating learning and upholding goodwill.

Building rural cultural auditoriums in coordination with the daily life in rural areas. The building of rural cultural auditoriums is a major project of innovation in the development of Zhejiang's primary-level public cultural services in recent years. Given underdeveloped facilities and a low degree of public participation in rural areas, Zhejiang has helped villages build new rural cultural auditoriums or turn the original auditoriums, movie theaters and meeting venues into rural cultural auditoriums. These rural cultural auditoriums serve as the public spaces where villagers can keep daily contact, conduct cultural and recreational activities, get together for communication, receive training, learn, take physical exercise, and even hold banquets.

These cultural auditoriums really become part of the farmers' daily life and the new homes where villagers can share ideas.

Carrying out the practical activity of "carrying forward fine family mottos, family traditions and folk customs" in line with local traditions. To utilize the mode of fine traditional moral education—family mottos handed down since ancient times, in 2014, the Civilization Office of Zhejiang Province issued the *Circular on Carrying Out the Activity of "Our Family Mottos—the People of Zhejiang Value Family Tradition"*. According to the circular, it is necessary to proceed from Zhejiang's fine historical and cultural traditions, conduct the activity of "Our Family Mottos—the People of Zhejiang Value Family Tradition" to guide the people to start from themselves, from their families, stress morality, foster family traditions, connect such principles as love for the country, dedication, integrity and friendliness with the local traditions of "behaving well, managing their homes and business affairs methodically", guide the people to value morality and family traditions, and thus develop good folk customs.

Conducting the activity of appraising and selecting the "Most Beautiful Phenomena" in coordination with the people's life. To practice the socialist core values, select and develop models to produce demonstration and driving effects, Zhejiang has carried out a series of activities of appraising and selecting the "Most Beautiful Phenomena".

Carrying out various educational activities with a moral theme in coordination with adolescent education. Zhejiang has promoted civic moral development by cultivating and carrying forward the socialist core values, and has conducted some practical activities focusing on integrity, friendliness, diligence, thrift, and filial piety. In the meantime, according to General Secretary Xi Jinping's requirements of "starting with children and schools to study and carry forward the socialist core values, introducing them into teaching materials and classrooms, making then rooted in the minds of the children", Zhejiang has studied and developed the *Implementation Opinions on Incorporating the Socialist Core Values into the Whole Process of School Education*, it has brought innovations to the ways and methods of teaching involving moral education at the primary and secondary schools and ideological and political theory courses at the institutions of higher learning; Zhejiang has carried out the educational activities on the themes of "My Chinese Dream" and "Striving to Become Zhejiang Youngsters Who Are Rich in Mind", and started with children to build the moral highland for the grass-roots groups.

Besides practical cultivation activities, Zhejiang has also taken practical actions in publicity, education and institutional development, making significant achievements. With regard to the publicity mode, besides traditional media, Zhejiang has also adopted new media and new channels, including mobile phone newspapers, WeChat, microblogs, micro films and micro videos, it has leveraged such publicity platforms as literary works and public service advertising to actively foster a social environment beneficial to spreading the socialist core values. Regarding institutional development, in order to build a mechanism of guarantees for fostering and practicing the socialist core values, Zhejiang issued and implemented the *Several Regulations of Zhejiang Province on the Welfare and Security for Moral Models (Provisional)* on September 18, 2014, further regulating the welfare and security for moral models, fostering the clear orientation that one good turn deserves another, and guiding more people to consciously practice the socialist core values.

Overall, there are more and more of "the Most Beautiful People" and "Good People"; the "potted landscape" has become "scenery", and "scenery" has been turned into "healthy trends".

1.2   The Building of a Public Cultural Service System

In 2005, China put forward the concept of the public cultural service system for the first time, and the level of public cultural service became an important indicator for examining the government's performance in serving the people and measuring the degree of the people's realization of cultural rights and interests. The increase in the level of public cultural services is closely related to the level of economic and social development; in the areas where there is a high level of economic and social development, the level of public cultural service facilities is also generally high. However, this does not mean that their utilization rate is necessarily high.

When conducting surveys in Zhejiang, we found that in recent years, Zhejiang has brought about some innovations to the construction of public cultural service infrastructures and has also greatly improved the performance in public cultural services.

Zhejiang has integrated and upgraded the primary-level public cultural service facilities and increased their rate of utilization to turn them into regular venues where the people can carry out cultural activities. In 2011, the 10th Session of the 12th Party Committee of Zhejiang Province identified "the building of the public cultural service system" as one of the six main tasks for promoting the building of Zhejiang into a culturally strong province, and vowed to improve network of public cultural facilities, enhance the capability for public cultural services and bring innovations to the mechanism of public cultural services.

Each year since the period of the 11th Five-Year Plan, Zhejiang has ranked no. 2 nationwide in total public cultural input, only second to Guangdong. In 2013, Zhejiang's expenditure on culture, sports and media was 10.6 billion yuan, accounting for 2.24% of Zhejiang's total public financial expenditure.[2] (There are survey materials and reports concerning Zhejiang.) According to the *Annual Report on the Development of Public Cultural Services in China (2012)*, Zhejiang has been listed among the top three nationwide in the composite index of public cultural services and the per capita composite index of public cultural services.

With more than 10 years of all-round development, in Zhejiang, significant achievements have been made in the construction of public cultural facilities, the level of public cultural services has increased gradually, the regional gap and urban-urban gap in public culture has narrowed progressively, a variety of public cultural service activities have been conducted, continuous innovations have been made in the

---

[2]See The Development of the Cultural Industry in Zhejiang Province, May, 2014.

public cultural service mechanism and an integrated urban-rural public cultural service system characterized by complementation of advantages, optimized allocation and rational layout has taken shape.

At present, in Zhejiang, there is 1 national public cultural service demonstration area, 7 provincial public cultural service demonstration areas, 27 advanced national cultural counties and 58 advanced provincial cultural counties, and a cultural facility network covering the provincial, municipal, county, town and village levels has been basically built. County-level cultural centers, libraries, town-level integrated cultural stations and cultural information sharing projects have basically provided full coverage. Radio and television have been made available to nearly 100% of Zhejiang's population. Zhejiang has also become the first nationwide to fully allow free admission to public cultural venues, including museums, libraries, art galleries, cultural centers (stations).

In the meantime, to deeply carry out the guiding principles adopted during the 18th National Congress of the Communist Party of China, according to the *12th Five-Year Plan of the Ministry of Culture for the Building of the Public Cultural Service System*, Zhejiang identified the year 2013 as the Year of Zhejiang Province for Promoting the Building of a Public Cultural Service System, and developed the *Plan of Zhejiang Province for Conducting the Activity of Promoting the Building of a Public Cultural Service System*, which marked Zhejiang's entry into a new stage of the development of public cultural services.

With a review of Zhejiang's achievements in public cultural services during a period of more than 10 years, the aspect which impresses us the most is that Zhejiang has made continuous innovations in the public cultural service system and mechanism, it has actively explored the local path of building a public cultural service system with Zhejiang's characteristics.

1. Focusing on the primary level, carrying out the projects for ensuring equal access to cultural services

Zhejiang has always given importance to allocating more public cultural resources to the primary level in urban and rural areas in building a public cultural service system and to the vulnerable groups in rural areas including poor people and migrant workers, so as to ensure equal access to public cultural services.

2. Focusing on guidance, guaranteeing efficient building of rural cultural auditoriums

In 2013, Zhejiang creatively put forward the idea of building rural cultural auditoriums, vowed to follow the requirement of "respecting the people's will, stressing characteristics and activities, promoting harmony" and the standard of "making available five factors and performing three functions",[3] and center on "building cultural auditoriums, turning them into the homes for communication" to build and put to use cultural auditoriums which feature the basic pattern of "two auditoriums and five galleries". As of late 2014, there were 3,447 cultural auditoriums.

---

[3]"Five factors" refer to venue, display, activity, team and mechanism; "three functions" refer to learning and teaching, etiquette, entertainment.

3. Focusing on cultivation, guaranteeing the endogenous activity of sowing cultural seeds

Each year since 2008, Zhejiang has allocated 15 million yuan in a special fund to carry out the activity of sowing cultural seeds in 1,000 towns and 10,000 villages, it has organized the training of tutoring groups of relevant departments for sowing cultural seeds in rural areas to towns and villages with a view to holding tutorial classes, forum and lecture activities covering dance, drama, science and technology and health; they have tutored and trained rural cultural teams, key cultural and artistic personnel for tens of thousands of person times.

4. Encouraging innovations, developing the distinctive public cultural service modes

The gap in the level of economic and social development is large among the different areas in Zhejiang. The per capita GDP in the most developed Hangzhou is more than three times that in the underdeveloped Lishui. Thus, the authorities in different areas should proceed from the local reality and make all the possible efforts within their ability to encourage independent innovation of the public cultural service modes and explore the local paths suitable for the local level of economic and social development and public cultural needs while first guaranteeing the provision of the basic public cultural services.

In order to make public cultural services really benefit the ordinary people, Zhejiang has actively explored the local paths in the philosophy of and concrete measures for development, and has vigorously developed the people's cultural rights and their awareness as main cultural players to fully arouse the people's cultural creativity. This should also be China's fundamental goal and developmental direction for developing public cultural services.

1.3 The Reform of the Cultural System and the Development of the Cultural Industry

Regarding the current development of Zhejiang's cultural industry, the most inspiring achievement and the one that the people of Zhejiang are the proudest of should be the upgrading of Zhejiang's economic form represented by the recent listing of Alibaba. During the initial stage of reform and opening-up, Wenzhou in Zhejiang initiated the Wenzhou Model, followed by the rise of the small commodity market in Yiwu. However, at that time, the merchants of Zhejiang generally lacked an awareness of innovation and integrity, Yiwu's commodities were basically low-end imitations, and they were subject to a great impact from the financial crisis. With the advent of the era of knowledge economy, as the result of combining high technology with high culture, the cultural industry has become the main engine for promoting economic development and transformation, the upgrading of traditional industries and it has played an increasingly prominent role in Zhejiang; Zhejiang has started to upgrade "Made in Zhejiang" to "Smart Manufacturing in China" or "Created in Zhejiang".

This volume expounds the reform of the cultural system and the development of the cultural industry at the same time because there has been an important line of thought for China's cultural development for which the reform of the cultural system is carried out to boost the development of the cultural industry, mobilize developmental levers, and arouse the enthusiasm for development to greatly enhance the efficiency of cultural development.[4] Zhejiang is the province which initiated the reform of the cultural system at the earliest and also the province becoming the first to make breakthroughs: in 2003, Zhejiang was identified as one of the two national pilot provinces for comprehensive cultural system reform. In 2006, Zhejiang became the first nationwide to merge the bureau of culture, that of radio and television and that of the press and publications below the prefecture-city level to establish the bureau of culture, radio, television, the press and publications. In the meantime, Zhejiang has set up an agency for comprehensive law enforcement on the cultural market so as to enforce laws on the cultural market in a unified and comprehensive way, producing good effects; Zhejiang has been listed among the top two in the national evaluation of administrative law enforcement on the cultural market by the Ministry of Culture for many consecutive years.

With the enormous vitality unleashed by deeply pushing forward the reform of the cultural system and the guidance of policies for earnestly developing the cultural industry, the cultural industry has developed robustly and its total scale has increased year by year in Zhejiang. According to the data from Zhejiang's relevant departments, in 2014, the operating income, total output and added value of the press and publication industry in Zhejiang were expected to reach 150,392 million yuan, 152,952 million yuan and 40,808 million yuan, with a year-on-year increase of 7%, 6% and 10%, respectively; the operating income of Zhejiang's radio, television and film industry exceeded 34 billion yuan, with a year-on-year increase of more than 10%. In 2014, there were more than 1,100 film and television program production institutions; 38 films, 62 TV plays (2,717 episodes) and 51 animated films (25,388 min) were produced in Zhejiang; Zhejiang ranked no. 2 and no. 3 nationwide in the output of animated films and TV plays.

Furthermore, Zhejiang has stayed ahead nationwide in the manufacturing of cultural products and cultural tourism. For the overall level of development of the cultural industry, Zhejiang enjoys extraordinarily outstanding advantages among the provinces and autonomous regions across the country. We hereby list several characteristics of Zhejiang's cultural industry which impress us the most.

The private cultural enterprises have shown prominent vitality and the state-owned cultural enterprises have grown steadily. The private economy has become developed since ancient times in Zhejiang, and Zhejiang has introduced a number of policies to support private capital in investing in the cultural field, thus the role of the private cultural enterprises as the fresh forces in the development of Zhejiang's cultural industry has been further improved. At present, in Zhejiang, there are about 70,000

---

[4]Liu (2014).

private cultural enterprises, the total scale of investments exceeds 200 billion yuan, and they employ more than 750,000 people.[5]

In the meantime, Zhejiang's state-owned cultural enterprise groups have made sustained improvements in their comprehensive strength and competitiveness. In 2014, the Zhejiang Daily Press Group realized 3.5 billion yuan in operating income and 520 million yuan in profits, up more than 30%. Zhejiang Wasu is currently the only cable network operator under cross-regional operations in China, extending cable TV service to 20 million households; its listed company, Wasu Media, has a market capitalization of 40 billion yuan and is one of the radio and television enterprises with the highest market capitalization in China. Overall, Zhejiang has witnessed the preliminary formation of a new pattern of a cultural industry in which public ownership is the mainstay and multiple forms of ownership develop side by side.

The cultural industry has distinctive regional characteristics and enjoys prominent advantages in differentiated competition. Zhejiang has always taken differentiated development of the cultural industry based on local conditions as an important principle. In the *Plan of Zhejiang Province for the Development of the Cultural Industry (2010–2015)*, Zhejiang put forward the massive characteristic layout of "one core, three poles, seven centers and four belts",[6] it vowed to more rapidly promote the industrialized development of regional characteristic cultural industrial resources and shape the pattern of the development of the cultural industry of "one product in one county". In 2014, the Hangzhou Base of the National Digital Publication Industry delivered 8,425 million yuan in operating income, with a year-on-year increase of 12.0%, among which the China Mobile Reading Base and the China Telecom Esurfing Reading Base delivered 6,208 million yuan and 235 million yuan in operating income. Dongyang City, being famous for the film and television industry in China, has leveraged the advantages of the national-level Hengdian Film and Television Industry Experimental Area to extend the cultural industrial chain, expand the cultural industrial fields and push forward the strategy for overarching development of the cultural industry.[7] As of 2013, the Hengdian Film and Television Industry Experimental Area, established in 2004, cumulatively

---

[5]See The Department of Publicity under the Party Committee of Zhejiang Province: The Development of the Cultural Industry in Zhejiang Province, May, 2014.

[6]"One core" lies in proceeding from Hangzhou's cultural industry which has rapidly risen in recent years to actively turn Hangzhou into Zhejiang's integrated cultural industrial development core and the national first-class cultural creative industrial center; "three poles" means the three highly competitive cultural industrial growth poles with outstanding advantages in the Ningbo city group, the Wenzhou city group and the city group in central Zhejiang; "seven centers" means the characteristic cultural industrial agglomeration centers which are built under the principle of characteristic advantageous development and by focusing on the cities divided into districts; "four belts" means the creative cultural industrial belt in northern Zhejiang, the industrial belt of film and television circulation in central Zhejiang, the marine cultural industrial belt in eastern Zhejiang and the ecological cultural industrial belt in southwestern Zhejiang which are built in light of regional cultural industrial development resources and common characteristics.

[7]See The Department of Publicity under the Party Committee of Dongyang City: Building a Famous Cultural City to Promote Industrial Development—Overarching Development of the Cultural Industry in Dongyang City.

realized nearly 30 billion yuan in operating income, made nearly 2 billion yuan in tax payments and provided more than 36,000 jobs. Dongyang has focused on Hengdian film and television cultural tourism to build a characteristic cultural tourism network which features "four horizontal lines and three vertical lines".[8]

Marked effects have been produced in making the culture "go global" and cultural trade has flourished. In recent years, Zhejiang has made notable achievements in stimulating Chinese culture to "go global" and in promoting the healthy development of cultural trade. In 2013, the total number of importations and exportations of cultural services in Zhejiang reached USD 533 million, among which the total number of exportations was USD 26 million, up 48.9% compared with the previous year. Zhejiang has also actively utilized the Yiwu Cultural Products Trade Fair, the China (Hangzhou) International Cartoon & Animation Festival, the Hangzhou Cultural Products Trade Fair and other international cultural exhibition platforms to promote external cultural exchanges and commercial and trade development.

The integrative developmental trend has become prominent and new forms of business have emerged. Zhejiang has vigorously promoted integration between culture and science, technology and related forms of business, and new forms of business have prospered and developed. Since 2013, eight projects in Zhejiang have received 70.08 million yuan in support from the national special fund for integration of science, technology and culture.

Overall, Zhejiang is intensifying the reform of the cultural system, is endeavoring to continuously optimize the structure of the cultural industry, and promote integrative development and coordination in the cultural industry; a good momentum of and prospects for development have emerged.

1.4 From Cultural and Artistic Creation to All-Round Prosperity

Since the 21st century, the people have no longer been the targets of cultural and artistic creation, and have gradually become one of the main forces in those creation. Such a change is closely related to the awakening of public awareness about cultural rights and the improvement of the cultural quality. The rise of popular culture means universal needs for cultural sharing, so the personnel engaged in cultural and artistic creation more consciously pay attention to the people's cultural needs; the cultural and artistic prosperity further promotes the awakening of public awareness about cultural rights and the improvement of the cultural quality. This is the modern path for cultural and artistic creation and is also one of the important indicators for measuring the all-round prosperity of cultural and artistic creation. If the development of Zhejiang's

---

[8]"Four horizontal lines and three vertical lines": the Hengdian film and television city, Luzhai ancient dwellings, the ancient tombs in the Western Zhou Dynasty (1046 B.C.–771 B.C.), and the dinosaur ruins are the horizontal lines; natural scenic spots, rural ancient buildings, and the three-town exotic line are the vertical lines.

cultural and artistic creation is examined on this basis, we can find that Zhejiang's cultural and artistic creation is developing towards all-round prosperity.

1. The private cultural and artistic performance groups have developed rapidly

In Zhejiang, there have been well-developed private performance activities since ancient times. Since the reform and opening-up, the private cultural performance activities have reappeared in large quantities in Zhejiang. In 2009, the Party Committee and the People's Government of Zhejiang Province issued the *Opinions of the General Office of the People's Government of Zhejiang Province on Accelerating the Development of Private Cultural and Artistic Performance Groups*, providing not less than 3 million yuan in subsidies to private troupes each year and incorporating the stage artists of private cultural and artistic performance groups into the scope of evaluation involving national artistic technical qualification. These private cultural and artistic performance groups often go deep into the primary level and rural areas to extensively develop the market; this further arouses the vitality in cultural and artistic creation.

2. Amateur cultural and artistic groups are vibrant

The rise and development of cultural and artistic creation has injected strong local characteristics into Zhejiang's cultural development. The primary-level cultural development cannot be achieved without cultural and artistic talents; they may be self-taught cultural and artistic enthusiasts or retired cultural and artistic workers. Moreover, in recent years, Zhejiang has continuously carried out the activity of sowing cultural seeds to cultivate a number of cultural and artistic personnel; these cultural and artistic talents have gradually become the planners and organizers of rural and community-level cultural and artistic creative activities. With their driving role, amateur cultural and artistic groups have been set up in large quantities, cultural and artistic activities have become rich and colorful; these amateur cultural and artistic groups and personnel have become the fresh forces for promoting primary-level cultural development.

We can find that Zhejiang has always actively explored the local path in the process of practicing the socialist core values, building a public cultural service system, promoting the reform of the cultural system and the development of the cultural industry, and developing cultural and artistic creation towards all-round prosperity. Only when the local path is taken can Zhejiang really embark on the path of a cultural revival.

References

Liu Yuzhu, Collaborative Innovation and Integrative Development are the Effective Ways to Transform and Upgrade the Cultural Industry, the Cultural Industry Channel at www.ce.cn, September 19, 2014.

Xi Jinping, Carrying out Concrete Work to Stay Ahead – Line of Thought and Practice in Promoting New Development in Zhejiang, The Party School of the CPC Central Committee Press, 2006.

Chapter 2
Successive Efforts in Pushing Forward the Strategy of Building a Culturally Large Culturally Strong Province

Jing Zhou

In November, 2002, the 16th National Congress of the Communist Party of China put forward the important task for intensifying the reform of the cultural system. On June 28, 2003, during the national conference on the pilot work relating to the reform of the cultural system, it was decided to initiate the pilot work on the reform of the cultural system in 9 provinces and municipalities, including Beijing, Shanghai, Chongqing, Guangdong, Zhejiang, Shenzhen, Shenyang, Xi'an, Lijiang and 35 publicity and cultural units. Zhejiang has become one of the two provinces for fully carrying out comprehensive pilot work on the reform of the cultural system; this marked Zhejiang's entry into a new stage of comprehensively promoting the building of a culturally large province after the implementation of the *Plan of Zhejiang Province for the Building of a Culturally Large Province (2001–2020)* in 2001. The year 2003 was the new starting point of the process in which the reform of the cultural system and the development of the culture industry evolved from points to plane, from the outside to the inside, and from quantity to quality.

2.1 Going with the Tide of the Times to Enhance Cultural Self-consciousness

"Culture is the soul of a nation, the bond for sustaining national unity and ethnic solidarity, and the epitome of national vitality, creativity and cohesion; cultural power is the fundamental power for a nation to survive and become strong."[1] This is a remark made by comrade Xi Jinping during the meeting on the reform of the cultural system and the building of a culturally large province after the special survey in

[1] Xi (2006a), p. 293.

J. Zhou (✉)
The Zhejiang Academy of Social Sciences, Hangzhou, China

© Social Sciences Academic Press and Springer Nature Singapore Pte Ltd. 2019
D. Xie and Y. Chen (eds.), *Chinese Dream and Practice in Zhejiang – Culture*,
Research Series on the Chinese Dream and China's Development Path,
https://doi.org/10.1007/978-981-13-7216-2_2

Hangzhou on July 18, 2003. After comrade Xi Jinping took office in Zhejiang in October, 2002, he went deep into the cities, counties and the departments directly under the provincial government to carry out some surveys; he set foot in 69 cities and counties in nine months. In the survey on the reform of the cultural system and the building of a culturally large province, he carried out field surveys on more than 20 cultural units and enterprises, listened to the reports from Hangzhou City and relevant departments, and held two special meetings on the film and television industry, troupe (theater) reform and the meeting on intensifying the reform of the cultural system and promoting the building of a culturally large province.

In this comprehensive meeting, the Zhejiang Spirit was included in the great cultural spectrum of the Chinese nation, and the power of culture was elevated to a historic height of helping the Chinese nation keep great vitality. The vitality of national culture (regional culture in a broad sense) in continuous self-renewal has become an objective description of the endogenous impetus of culture: "The Chinese nation has a long history, it has undergone great vicissitudes, many separations and reunions, invasions, but it is not split and does not vanish; it has always maintained great vitality; the fundamental reason is that the Chinese nation has long-standing profound cultural connotations; Zhejiang is a land of cultural relics, one of the birth-places of the Chinese civilization, it has a galaxy of cultural figures, a wealth of excellent cultural products, a variety of cultural forms and a long cultural tradition; they have made great contributions to enriching and developing the Chinese national culture and has vigorously promoted Zhejiang's economic and social development."[2] Therefore, the Zhejiang Spirit has a wide and deep historical and realistic foundation; it has brought about strong endogenous power for finding the deep cultural driving factors behind Zhejiang's economic development and shaping a new pattern of cultural, economic and political interaction.

2.1.1 Starting Point: The Plan of Zhejiang Province for the Building of a Culturally Large Province (2001–2020)

When Zhejiang reaches a certain stage of economic and social development, it is essential to refine the Zhejiang Spirit, further arouse the cultural self-consciousness of the whole society and fully understand the importance of cultural development. At this stage, the logical relationship between economic development and cultural development is that economic prosperity and development promotes cultural prosperity and development, in which an intermediary—cultural self-consciousness—is a must. In the *Plan of Zhejiang Province for Cultural Development (1996–2010)*, the Party Committee of Zhejiang Province realized that socialist cultural development played an important role in meeting the people's increasing cultural needs, in

---

[2]Xi (2006a), pp. 293–294.

improving the national quality and promoting economic development and all-round social progress.

In December, 1999, the 3rd Plenary (Enlarged) Session of the 10th Party Committee of Zhejiang Province put forward, for the first time, the goal of developing the cultural industry and building a culturally large province. In the meantime, Zhejiang's decision-makers and the theoretical circle quickly carried out the work on studying the Zhejiang phenomena, summarizing the Zhejiang experience and refining the Zhejiang Spirit, and ultimately identified the Zhejiang Spirit as "making unceasing improvements, being firm and indomitable, blazing new trails, stressing substantial results"; Zhejiang vowed to fully unleash the theoretical resources, from Zhejiang's non-governmental forces and traditions, conducive to the market economy, and became the first to promote the formation of the model of a local market economy.

As shown by the process of reform and development in Zhejiang, the original expression of that Zhejiang Spirit contains the special characteristics of the environment of Zhejiang's historical development at the turn of the centuries, between the 20th century and the 21st century. Since the reform and opening-up, Zhejiang has explored the Zhejiang Spirit to deeply understand the actual achievements, and discover the mindsets and thoughts of the people of Zhejiang behind the particular mechanisms, modes and practices; its significance lies in finding the cultural tradition—which comes from regional culture and adapts to the market economy—that allows the people Zhejiang to tenaciously overcome regional limitations for developing the economy, and also in seeking a strong intellectual impetus for Zhejiang to continue promoting all-round economic and social development. Therefore, the theoretical exploration and achievements made with respect to the Zhejiang Spirit in the year 2000 is a theoretical innovation brought about by the Party Committee of Zhejiang Province for continuing to seek breakthroughs and growth after a period of 20 years of rapid economic development; it is the prelude to the *Plan of Zhejiang Province for the Building of a Culturally Large Province (2001–2020)* systematically put forward by the Party Committee of Zhejiang Province, and it has played an important role in arranging for building Zhejiang into a culturally large province.

At the center of increasing integration between culture and economy in the 21st century, culture has brought about enormous creativity in economic development and has greatly promoted the emancipation and development of Zhejiang's productive forces. A more incisive expression is that Zhejiang's economy is "cultural", Zhejiang's culture is "economic". This is a new concept of Zhejiang's "cultural economy". Identifying and properly handling the relationship between economy and culture is the realistic starting point for studying Zhejiang phenomena, summarizing the Zhejiang experience and refining the Zhejiang Spirit; it is also the important goal of the *Plan of Zhejiang Province for the Building of a Culturally Large Province (2001–2020)* ("the Plan"); this suggests that during the initial stage of building Zhejiang into a culturally large province, Zhejiang closely followed the important trend of modern social development—economic and cultural integration, and also paid close attention to the source of the vitality for modern cultural development and the center of contrasts.

The Plan is the basic document concerning the strategy for building Zhejiang into a culturally large province. In the opinion of the outside world, Zhejiang has the financial capacity and the government is competent. The first basic principle specified in the Plan is that there should be coordination between economic development and cultural development, economic development provides the necessary material foundation for cultural development, and cultural development offers a great deal of strength to drive economic development. The second basic principle is that there should be coordination between social benefits and economic benefits, and the relationship between cultural programs and the cultural industry must be correctly handled and different policies and management measures must be adopted for different cultural forms while stressing that top priority must be given to social benefits in developing cultural programs and the cultural industry. It is thus pointed out that under a socialist market economy, the cultural industry is an integral part of the national economy, cultural products have the attribute of commodities, so it is essential to highly value the economic benefits from cultural products while maintaining social benefits, and to achieve the best combination between social benefits and economic benefits. Regarding the methodology, the Plan stresses equal emphasis on inheritance, use for reference, reform and innovation, it combines holistic promotion with breakthroughs in key fields, and the Plan calls for bringing about cultural innovations, carrying out bold reforms, developing the education of science and technology to lay a foundation and starting with developing the cultural industry.

Accordingly, the Plan presents the goal of forming a large scale and enhancing the competitiveness in Zhejiang's development of the cultural industry, it specially makes the goal be parallel to "developing cultural programs" and it arranges a special chapter, "Developing the Cultural Industry", to put forward developmental requirements; the Plan calls for more quickly shaping a pattern of cultural industrial development that is suitable for the drive towards modernization, and actively adjusting the cultural industrial structure, gradually optimizing the cultural industrial layout, vigorously supporting the key cultural enterprises, energetically cultivating and developing the cultural market. It also calls for vigorously fostering and developing key cultural sectors, and identifies media, tourism, performance, fine arts, convention and exhibition and sports as the key fields for developing the cultural industry. On this basis, the Plan dedicates a special chapter to stressing efforts to improve the cultural economic policy, adjust the structure of asset stocks of the cultural industry, intensify the adjustment of cultural industrial institutions, enhance the innovative vitality of cultural resources and promote the upgrading of the cultural industry. The Plan encourages individuals, enterprises and social groups to run cultural enterprises permitted by national policies, treats them as state-run cultural enterprises in planning, construction, land expropriation, reduction and exemption of charges, and professional title appraisal of the employed people.

2.1.2 Improvement: Cultural Soft Power as the Overall Competitiveness

The new outlook on cultural development is the outlook on the overall situation that the status, functions and tasks of culture are dealt with by focusing on "development" which is the first theme in China's reform and opening-up.

With economic and social development, increasing openness, Zhejiang's understanding of the important significance of cultural development is no longer limited to the development of the provincial economy and the inheritance of a regional culture. On December 11, 2001, China officially became a member of the WTO and entered a new stage of opening-up and modernization. As stressed by the report delivered during the 16th National Congress of the Communist Party of China, in modern development, culture increasingly interacts with the economy and politics, the status and role of culture in the competition of overall national strength has become increasingly prominent. China participated in the global competition involving the overall national strength while opening wider to the outside world. As Zhejiang was the forerunner of China's opening-up, Zhejiang's total amount of imports and exports reached USD 32.8 billion in 2001, up 17.8% compared with 2000; Zhejiang's total amount of imports and exports reached USD 42 billion in 2002, up 28% compared with 2001; Zhejiang's total amount of imports and exports reached USD 61.42 billion in 2003, up 46.2% compared with 2002.

On July 18, 2003, when he delivered a speech during the meeting on the reform of Zhejiang's cultural system and the building of a culturally large province, comrade Xi Jinping pointed out, "Culture is an important part of comprehensive strength and international competitiveness, and a productive cultural force is an important part of social productive forces; the fierce comprehensive strength of competition in today's world lies in not only economic, scientific and technological, national defense strength, but also in cultural power and the national spirit."[3] During the 8th Plenary Session of the 11th Party Committee of Zhejiang Province, held on July 28, he further stated that intense cultural interplay caused by world multipolarization and economic globalization presented severe challenges to us in economic development, and also made the ideological struggle more complicated. He stressed, "In order to more rapidly build a culturally large province, it is necessary to conform to the tide of the times, enhance cultural self-consciousness, always adopt the advanced culture to firmly occupy the ideological and cultural front, govern the ideological sphere, resolutely resist the political motive of hostile Western forces for westernization and division, various types of decadent and backward thoughts and cultures to ensure cultural security".[4]

Given the judgment on the situation and developmental expectations, not merely the economy serves as the coordinate system for improving Zhejiang's overall competitiveness. The cultural soft power reflects precisely the cultural power which falls

---

[3] Xi (2006a), p. 294.
[4] Xi (2006a), p. 290.

outside the economic field and is part of ideological appeal; it is the "booster" for economic development, the "navigational light" for political development and the "adhesive" for social harmony. According to the national conference concerning pilot work on the reform of the cultural system in 2003, the cultural soft power has two very clear dimensions: First, a national spirit. Culture nurtures and inherits a national spirit and it fosters national cohesion; the cultural power is the fundamental power for a nation to survive and become strong; second, the productive cultural force. Culture is an important part of productive social forces and has played an increasingly important role in the national economy; both dimensions combine the improvement of the cultural soft power with the practice in building a moderately prosperous society in all respects.

On July 29, 2004, when delivering a speech during the special study meeting on promoting Zhejiang's all-round coordinated, sustainable economic and social development, comrade Xi Jinping summarized the requirement of "giving great importance to the building of a culturally large province" as follows: more quickly building the soft power in Zhejiang's overall competitiveness. On July 28, 2005, when delivering a report at the 8th Plenary Session of the 11th Party Committee of Zhejiang Province, he once again stressed, "It is essential to examine cultural development by adopting the strategic line of thought, following the requirement of the times and taking the perspective of development, and further unify the line of thought, deepen the understanding of more rapidly building a culturally large province." He resolutely pointed out, "Zhejiang's ability to continue staying ahead in the process of building a moderately prosperous society in all respects, speeding up modernization in a certain period of time to come largely depends on our deep understanding of the cultural power, a high degree of self-consciousness about developing the advanced culture and great efforts in promoting the building of a culturally large province."[5] Therefore, studying the history and reality of Zhejiang's culture, enhancing the cultural soft power is the common cause for the people of Zhejiang, the important mission and responsibility of the Party committees and governments at various levels in Zhejiang.

Zhejiang has stayed ahead nationwide in a number of economic indicators, but the Party Committee and the People's Government of Zhejiang Province have still been keenly aware of the developmental pressure and have clearly understood that some existing problems have not yet been solved fundamentally, Zhejiang has encountered some new problems ahead of the rest of the country to varying degrees. "How to develop", especially in an all-round manner, coordinated and sustainable development among various fields, has become an overarching strategic issue.

---

[5] Xi (2006a), p. 289.

2.1.3 Expansion: The Zhejiang Spirit of Advancing with the Times

If change is made, Zhejiang will rise; otherwise, Zhejiang will decline. There is an urgent need for enhancing Zhejiang's overall competitiveness under the new situation, the Zhejiang Spirit should have a more universal connotation. According to the existing Zhejiang Spirit, merely the factors of impetus unleashed by a certain regional culture have been unable to fully adapt to the new situation. In 2005, the Party Committee of Zhejiang Province launched a great debate on the Zhejiang Spirit of Advancing with the Times. Ultimately, based on the original version, the Zhejiang Spirit was upgraded to the one characterized by "pursuit of truth, pragmatism, integrity and harmony, open-mindedness and determination to become stronger". Compared with the original version of the year 2000, the upgraded Zhejiang Spirit expands the realistic judgment, international perspective and future prospect regarding integrative economic and cultural development, and it introduces more modern mindsets, a value orientation, a psychological state and social moral standards.

On February 5, 2006, the front page of the *Zhejiang Daily* published a theoretical article written by comrade Xi Jinping entitled "The Zhejiang Spirit of Advancing with the Times". The article discussed the historical tradition and contemporary embodiment of the Zhejiang Spirit, and expounded the new spiritual value and realistic requirements. He stressed, "Pursuit of truth means that it is necessary to observe the inherent law of Zhejiang's economic and social development, maintain the characteristics of Zhejiang's development, do concrete work and also blaze new trails, create something new, always firmly hold the initiative in development; pragmatism means it is necessary to respect the reality, always proceed from the situation of the world, the country and the province, from the actual situation and tasks before us, from the actual will of the people across the province, clearly understand the new challenges and problems for Zhejiang as a forerunner and make the strategic choice consistent with Zhejiang's reality; integrity means that it is necessary to foster the mindset, in the whole society, that individuals cannot develop without integrity, enterprises cannot thrive without integrity, the government cannot become authoritative without integrity, the county cannot become strong without integrity, so that an awareness of modern integrity is deeply rooted among the people and it becomes the code of conduct for self-consciousness in the whole society; harmony means democracy, the rule of law, fairness and justice, integrity and fraternal love, great vitality, peace and order, harmonious coexistence between people and nature; open-mindedness means that it is necessary to continuously adapt our mindsets, living habits, way of acting and cultural quality to the open world and global competition, and go out of Zhejiang to develop Zhejiang, have the courage to actively participate in global cooperation and competition, engage in domestic and foreign economic and technical cooperation and competition on a wider scope, more fields and at a higher level, increase the degree of openness; determination to become stronger means that it is necessary to always keep an enterprising spirit, persist in goals, firmly seize opportunities, persevere in development, make Zhejiang better and stronger in various aspects and deliver a first-class performance which lives up to the times and to the people."[6]

2.2 Seizing Strategic Opportunities to Accelerate the Building of a Culturally Large Province

"Regarding the advancement in material, cultural and ethical respects, material advancement is substantive, while cultural and ethical advancement is virtual; with regard to the improvement in the quality of the people, the scientific and cultural quality is substantive, while intellectual and moral quality is virtual. It is easy to grasp the substantive things, while it is difficult to grasp the virtual things. Thus, virtual work must be carried out in a substantive way. Cultural and ethical advancement, especially intellectual and moral advancement, must be achieved by adopting a visible means, creating the real carriers, teaching through lively activities, making something deeply rooted among the people and gradually exerting a subtle influence. The principles should be clearly explained, but any principle must be deeply rooted among the people and cannot be expounded mechanically. The activity of "dual development, dual improvement" is a very good carrier; in such a large carrier, it is necessary to explore and create more concrete carriers so that the whole activity is closer to the reality, to the people and to life."[7] This is a passage in the review article " Virtual Work Must Be Carried Out in a Substantive Way" written by comrade Xi Jinping for the special column "Zhijiang Xinyu" on the front page of the *Zhejiang Daily* on December 30, 2004. This article revealed the working law of cultural development and clearly presented the reform line of thought that substantive carriers must be provided for building Zhejiang into a culturally large province in the future.

2.2.1 The Building of a Culturally Large Province Incorporated into the "Eight-Eight Strategies" and the Overall Strategy of Building a Safe Zhejiang

The Party Committee and the People's Government of Zhejiang Province have proceeded from economic, political, cultural and social development to take the building of a culturally large province as an important measure for carrying out the "Eight-Eight Strategies" and building a safe Zhejiang, and to link cultural development with Zhejiang's overall strategy of economic and social development. The building of a culturally large province is promoted from the political perspective and in light of

---

[6]Xi (2006b).
[7]Xi (2006a), p. 297.

the overall situation; it is supported by Zhejiang's overall reform and strategy of development; it is an indispensable practical measure under the new situation and the new strategy.

The "Eight-Eight Strategies" make up an extremely important strategic vision for Zhejiang's reform and development and a long-term plan for Zhejiang's economic and social development. When the "Eight-Eight Strategies" were systematically put forward, the strategic measure for more rapidly speeding up the building of a culturally large province became an important part of the advantages in 8 respects and the measures on 8 fronts. During the 4th Plenary Session of the 11th Party Committee of Zhejiang Province in July, 2003, comrade Xi Jinping, on behalf of the Party Committee of Zhejiang Province, completely and systematically put forward the "Eight-Eight Strategies": First, further giving play to Zhejiang's advantages regarding institutions and mechanisms, vigorously promoting the common development of the economy with different types of ownership while ensuring that public ownership remains dominant, continuously improving the system of a socialist market economy; second, further drawing on Zhejiang's locational advantage, proactively keeping in line with Shanghai, actively engaging in cooperation and communication with the Yangtze River Delta and constantly increasing the level of opening-up internally and externally; third, further leveraging the advantages of massive characteristic industries in Zhejiang, speeding up the building of advanced manufacturing bases and taking the path towards new industrialization; fourth, further giving play to Zhejiang's advantages in coordinated urban and rural development, thus quickening urban and rural integration; fifth, further utilizing Zhejiang's ecological advantage, turning Zhejiang into an ecological province and building a green Zhejiang; sixth, further exploiting the advantages of mountain and marine resources, energetically developing the marine economy, boosting leapfrog development of the underdeveloped areas, and making the development of the marine economy and the underdeveloped areas become the new economic growth point of Zhejiang Province; seventh, further utilizing Zhejiang's environmental advantages, actively pushing forward the main construction, mainly including five major projects worth ten-billion, practically strengthening legal construction and credit construction and improve the efficiency of organs; eighth, further leveraging Zhejiang's humanistic advantage, actively rejuvenating the province through science, technology and talents, stepping up efforts to turn Zhejiang into a culturally strong province.

Comprehensively building a safe Zhejiang is a major decision made by the 6th Plenary Session of the 11th Party Committee of Zhejiang Province according to the guiding principles adopted during the 16th National Congress of the Communist Party of China and in response to the new situation and new problems in development in May, 2004. When delivering a speech at this plenary session, comrade Xi Jinping pointed out that the "safe" in the safe Zhejiang was not the "safe" in a narrow sense; instead, it was the "safe" in a broad sense which was wide-ranging, extensive and multifaceted and covered the economic, political, cultural and social fields; the connotation of building a safe Zhejiang covered the overall goal of ensuring that politics became more stable, the economy developed further, culture became more prosperous, the society became more harmonious and the people's life became better;

the specific goals consisted of ensuring that the society and politics were stable, social order was good, economic operations were sound, work safety became stable and improved, and that the people lived and worked in peace and contentment. In the meantime, he published an article "Pushing Forward the Building of a Safe Zhejiang, Promoting Social Harmony and Stability" in the 7th issue of the *People's Tribune* in 2004. According to the article, upholding harmony, seeking stability, good governance, concordance and a safe society where the people live and work in peace and contentment is an important part of Chinese culture. The Party Committee of Zhejiang Province has always stressed that development is of overriding importance and is the key to solving all problems; maintaining stability is the rigid task and the prerequisite for reform and development. Zhejiang's practice has fully proved that only when the overall situation of reform, development and stability is grasped, the coordination among the intensity of reform, the pace of development and the bearing capacity of the society is properly managed can reform and development be really promoted amidst social stability, and can social stability be promoted through reform and development, and can material advancement, political advancement, cultural and ethical advancement really be pushed forward in a coordinated way while promoting social harmony and stability.[8] These theories reveal the internal relationship between the extensive safety and accelerated building of a culturally large province and the building of a harmonious society; they suggest that Zhejiang has incorporated cultural development into Zhejiang's overall strategy of economic development and social progress so that there is more solid and thicker grounds for policies for cultural development.

2.2.2 The Virtual Work Must be Carried Out in a Substantive Way

Conducting surveys is the first basic task for carrying out concrete work. On December 14, 2004, comrade Xi Jinping conducted a survey in Shengzhou City with respect to the activity of strengthening intellectual and moral development, the development of the cultural front, improving the cultural market and social trends ("dual development, dual improvement" in short). In early 2004, a workers' activity center in Shengzhou City was exposed by Topics in Focus, a CCTV program, due to a pornographic performance; after this center was rectified, a variety of activities covering physical fitness, skill training, reading, culture and entertainment were carried out in a healthy and positive way. As mentioned by comrade Xi Jinping, bad things became good things, it was possible to convert pressure into impetus and the effect of taking measures was different from that of not doing so; on any front, if we did not occupy it, some negative things would penetrate it; this was proved by our efforts on the front of cultural and ethical development: once we cracked down on

---

[8]Xi (2004).

something, our efforts could not be extended to every corner; only when we make positive things occupy the front can negative things be dispelled.

In the subsequent meeting, he took the perspective of strengthening socialist cultural and ethical development to put forward an especially realistic guiding principle for improving cultural work—the virtual work must be carried out in a substantive way. He pointed out that "substantive" was relative to "virtual"; regarding the advancement in the material, cultural and ethical aspects, material advancement was substantive, while cultural and ethical advancement was virtual; with regard to the improvement of the quality of the people, the scientific and cultural quality was substantive, while the intellectual and moral quality was virtual. It was easy to grasp the substantive things, while it was difficult to grasp the virtual things; some people often liked carrying out substantive work rather than virtual work; substantive work and virtual work were likened to the human brain and heart, both the brain and the heart are important and essential. Thus, both substantive work and virtual work should be carried out; in particular, the virtual work must be carried out in a substantive way; cultural and ethical advancement, especially intellectual and moral advancement, must be achieved by adopting visible means, creating the real carriers, teaching through lively activities, making something deeply rooted among the people and gradually exerting a subtle influence. The principles should be clearly explained, but any principle must be deeply rooted among the people and cannot be expounded mechanically; a very good carrier was needed, it was necessary to explore and create more concrete carriers which were closer to the reality, the people and life, so that the activity of promoting cultural and ethical development was carried out in a vivid and productive way.[9]

The year 2005 was the year of formulating the 11th Five-Year Plan and also the year of summarizing the comprehensive pilot work in the reform of Zhejiang's cultural system. The two-year reform experience involved a continuous shift to laws, regulations and policies and laid a good foundation for speeding up the building of a culturally large province and setting the cultural developmental goal for the next step. During the two days July 28–29, 2005, the 8th Plenary (Enlarged) Session of the 11th Party Committee of Zhejiang Province was held. During this session, comrade Xi Jinping delivered the report *Accelerating the Building of a Culturally Large Province to Provide Great Strength for Staying Ahead in the Process of Building a Moderately Prosperous Society in All Respects and Basically Achieving Modernization in Advance*. With a focus on the economic, political, cultural and social development, this session adopted the *Decision of the Party Committee of Zhejiang Province on Accelerating the Building of a Culturally Large Province* ("the Decision"), which marked continued rapid building of Zhejiang into a culturally large province.

On August 16, the 10th page of the *People's Daily* published the excerpt of the speech, delivered by comrade Xi Jinping during the 8th Plenary (Enlarged) Session of the 11th Party Committee of Zhejiang Province, which called for doing concrete work to speed up the building of a culturally large province. As stressed in the speech, the cultural cause is a cause which improves the people's will and sentiment; many

---

[9]Xi (2007).

things in culture are hardly measured by figures, and only when unremitting efforts are made can effects be produced; it is necessary to proceed from the reality, adapt measures to local conditions, strengthen classified guidance, observe the characteristics and law of cultural development, pursue development amidst accumulation, make innovations to development, prevent formalism and figure-focused performance in cultural development. On August 25, the first page of the *People's Daily · East China News* published a news report "Why Does an Ecologically Large Province Develop the "Cultural Engine"—An Analysis of the Strategic Arrangements for Accelerating the Building of a Culturally Large Province". This article also cited the remarks about cultural development made by comrade Xi Jinping, and stressed that cultural development was a project for the cultivation of the people focusing on development and a basic project which was not easy to help officials improve their performance; cultural development had its own law and characteristics, it entailed hard work and could not bring about instant benefits; it required painstaking efforts and inheritance from generation to generation; it could not deliver outcomes in a short time nor could it produce sensational effects; cultural work was a relatively "virtual" work and was measured in a relatively "subjective" way, it was expressed by means of various carriers, and might become useless if no sufficient energy was put into it. Therefore, in order to accelerate the building of a culturally large province, it was more necessary to be realistic and pragmatic, work with perseverance and in a down-to-earth manner.

2.2.3 Eight Projects: The Working Platforms for Accelerating the Building of a Culturally Large Province

In order to develop the soft power, it is necessary to take vigorous means, concrete measures and develop real skills. With regard to cultural development, it is essential to make the virtual work substantive, identify the overall goal when developing the strategic plan, divide it into the goals of specific stages, build the working platforms for guaranteeing manpower, financial resources and mechanisms, and seek vigorous external support in related developmental fields. These three points are embodied in the core content of the Decision and can be summarized as "three systems of impetus", "eight projects" and "a strong province in four respects". "Three systems of impetus" means the three systems of impetus for speeding up the building of Zhejiang into a culturally large province and they lie in enhancing the cohesion of the advanced culture, emancipating and developing the productive cultural forces and improving the capacity for public cultural services. "Eight projects" are aimed at putting into practice the first two out of three points of action—enhancing the cohesion of the advanced culture, emancipating and developing the productive cultural forces—including the cultural quality improvement project, the excellent cultural product project, the cultural research project, the cultural protection project, the project for the promotion of the cultural industry, the cultural front project, the cultural communication project and the cultural talent project; they are the necessary carriers and effective ways to more rapidly build a culturally large province. "A strong province in four respects" means a strong province of education, a strong province of science and technology, a strong province of health and a strong province of sports.

In 2005, Zhejiang's cultural research project—one of these important eight projects, advocated by comrade Xi Jinping, for Zhejiang's cultural development—was initiated; he led the steering committee for the project.

These eight projects offered diversified, multi-stage and multi-level working platforms and carriers for Zhejiang's cultural development during the periods of the 11th Five-Year Plan and the 12th Five-Year Plan. These eight projects have the following contents.

The cultural quality improvement project. Improving the people's quality in an all-round way is the main part of the efforts in accelerating the building of a culturally large province. It is necessary to focus on all of the citizens, enhance the intellectual and moral quality of the citizens, their scientific and cultural quality, and the quality of their health, and continuously increase the cultural level in the whole society.

The excellent cultural product project. The excellent cultural products are the important signs of a culturally large province. It is necessary to actively promote cultural innovations, support and push forward the creation, production and dissemination of excellent cultural products covering literature and art, social science, the press and publications, so as to meet the people's intellectual and cultural needs and incessantly increase the level of a culturally large province.

The cultural research project. Systematically studying Zhejiang's historical culture and contemporary development is of important significance for guiding Zhejiang's future development. It involves systematic research and the publication of series of books by focusing on researching Zhejiang's contemporary development and celebrities, conducting special research on Zhejiang's historical culture and reorganizing Zhejiang's historical documents. It promotes the building of research bases and sustainable research platforms.

The cultural protection project. It focuses on strengthening the demonstration in protection and utilization of cultural relics, the application to become a world cultural heritage, key scientific and technological development in protection of cultural relics, the construction of museums, the protection of famous historical and cultural cities, and building a relatively complete system of protection for immovable cultural relics, famous historical and cultural cities, historical and cultural blocks and towns, and basically building a network of museums with a rational layout and Zhejiang's characteristics.

The project for the promotion of the cultural industry. This project is aimed at fully leveraging regional cultural resources and the advantages of non-public sectors of the economy to cultivate a number of relatively powerful and competitive cultural industrial players; building a system of a cultural market with a variety of products, complete factors and well-regulated management; shaping an open pattern in which state-owned cultural enterprises are the mainstay and the cultural enterprises with different types of ownerships develop side by side.

The cultural front project. Full scope is given to the functions of cultural facilities including libraries, cultural centers, museums, broadcasting and TV stations, science and technology museums, sports venues, archives centers, workers' cultural palaces, youth activity centers and senior citizens activity centers; the construction of cultural facilities continues to be pushed forward. Culture is promoted in the countryside in a regular and institutionalized way.

The cultural communication project. Emphasis is placed on strengthening the development of cultural communication media, including newspapers, periodicals, radio, television, films, books, audio and video products, electronic publications and the Internet. Intensified efforts are made to develop cultural communication players and build cultural communication channels, make culture "go global" and "bring in" culture, build up some influential external publicity brands. Further actions are being taken to build cultural communication means, promote digitalization and online communication, and support the key websites for news.

The cultural talent project. According to the overall arrangement of making the province strong through talents, human resource advantages are being fully leveraged, and efforts are being made to cultivate a number of cultural celebrities and cultural masters who are highly influential at home and abroad in the cultural field, develop a wealth of talents in the theoretical, press, publication, artistic and cultural operation fields. Measures are being taken to establish and improve the mechanisms for talent cultivation, selection, utilization and management, and to build Zhejiang's cultural talent highland.

2.2.4 The 11th Five-Year Plan for Zhejiang's Cultural Development

The *Decision of the Party Committee of Zhejiang Province on Accelerating the Building of a Culturally Large Province*, issued in late July, 2005, required relevant departments, in coordination with the study and formulation of the 11th Five-Year Plan, to carry out the implementation opinions on the eight projects for cultural development, develop and improve concrete supporting measures, give prominence to developmental priorities and promote the implementation of the projects. The competent departments for cultural affairs at various levels and cultural units should develop the corresponding special plans for the development of cultural programs and the cultural industry, list a number of key developmental projects to guide the the direction of investments and form the bright spots of development.

On February 10, 2006, the People's Government of Zhejiang Province officially unveiled the *"Four-batch" Plan of Zhejiang Province for Cultural Development (2005–2010)* ("the Plan"), calling for building a batch of key cultural facilities, developing a batch of key industrial sectors, cultivating a batch of key cultural industrial blocks and growing a batch of key cultural enterprises during the period of the 11th Five-Year Plan, with a view to more rapidly promoting the building of Zhejiang into a culturally large province and enhancing the soft power in Zhejiang's overall competitiveness, covering the press and publications, radio, film and television, cultural arts, cultural tourism and sports fields across the province.

In order to build a batch of key cultural facilities, emphasis is placed on carrying out the "2345" project, namely, orderly building iconic cultural facilities at the provincial and municipal levels, strengthening the building of the primary-level cultural facilities at the county, community and rural levels, focusing on building the facilities for a network of cultural information in the fields of radio, film and television, press and publications, cultural art and cultural tourism; encouraging social capital to intensify investment in and operation of the for-profit cultural facilities covering cultural performance, leisure entertainment, physical fitness, cultural tourism, publications and distribution. In order to develop a batch of key industrial sectors, emphasis is placed on developing seven main advantageous cultural sectors, five main emerging cultural sectors and three main characteristic cultural sectors, namely, making Zhejiang's seven main advantageous cultural sectors—including publication, distribution, printing, cultural tourism, radio, film and television, conventions and exhibitions, the manufacturing of stationery and sporting goods—large and strong, developing five main emerging cultural sectors—online cultural services, animation, advertising, sports service and cultural brokering as well as actively supporting three main characteristic cultural sectors, including cultural performance, leisure entertainment and artwork operations. In order to cultivate a batch of key cultural industrial blocks, emphasis is placed on developing two new and hi-tech blocks, three traditional blocks and five advantageous blocks, namely, giving priority to cultivating the Hengdian Film and Television Industry Experimental Area and the Binjiang New and Hi-tech Cultural Industry Area; moreover, further support is being given to three types of traditional cultural industry blocks—including drama, arts and crafts, epigraphy, calligraphy and paintings, growing and enhancing five types of advantageous cultural industrial blocks—including modern media, the manufacturing of stationery and sporting goods, cultural tourism, publications, packaging decoration and printing, trade in stationery and sporting goods. In order to grow a batch of key cultural enterprises, actions are taken to make state-owned cultural groups large and strong, grow key state-owned cultural enterprises, develop the leading private cultural enterprises, cultivate outward-looking cultural enterprises, shape a pattern in which the cultural enterprises with various types of ownership, including state-owned, private and foreign-funded cultural enterprises, compete in an orderly fashion, interact benignly and develop together in Zhejiang.

With respect to the reform of the cultural system, the Plan required local authorities across the province to actively promote plan implementation, push forward innovations to institutions and mechanisms in the cultural sector, to more quickly develop the catalogue of cultural industrial investments, regulate access to the cultural market access, further expand the investment and financing channels, build a diversified investment and financing system for the cultural industry, increase support for the cultural industry and build some excellent platforms for developing the cultural industry. With full implementation of the "four-batch" plan, efforts are being made to more quickly build a well-functioning distinctive network of cultural facilities covering urban and rural areas across the province, bring together the modern cultural industrial blocks and leading cultural enterprises which are large-scale, powerful, competitive and can stimulate the development of others, and build a modern cultural industrial system with coordinated, integrative and common development of advantageous, traditional and emerging sectors.

2.3 "Three Main Systems" Lead Cultural Entrepreneurship and Innovation

During the period of November 6–7, 2007, the 2nd Plenary (Enlarged) Session of the 12th Party Committee of Zhejiang Province was held. The plenary session adopted the *Decision of the Party Committee of Zhejiang Province on Earnestly Implementing the Guiding Principles Adopted during the 17th National Congress of the Communist Party of China and Solidly Working on Making the People Rich by Starting Businesses and of Building a Strong Province through Innovation*. Making the people rich by starting businesses and the principle of building a strong province through innovation" make up the profound summary of Zhejiang's developmental experience since the reform and opening-up and the next chapter for continuing the "Eight-Eight Strategies". The decision called for earnestly cultivating the entrepreneurial and innovative players, actively carrying forward the culture of entrepreneurship and innovation, continuously enhancing the mechanism of entrepreneurship and innovation, more rapidly improving the policy of entrepreneurship and innovation, optimizing an environment of entrepreneurship and innovation, carrying out the work of "making the people rich by starting business and of building a strong province through innovation" in the economic, political, cultural and social fields and the building up of the Party and building a society of popular entrepreneurship and a fully innovative province, thus building up a moderately prosperous society in all respects and continuing to stay ahead nationwide.

On June 27, 2008, the Party Committee of Zhejiang Province held a working conference on studying and arranging the work on elevating the building of a culturally large province to a new level and promoting vigorous development and great prosperity of the socialist culture. In this conference, the *Plan of Zhejiang Province for Promoting Vigorous Cultural Development and Great Cultural Prosperity (2008–2012)* was adopted. During the period of June 28 to July 3, 2008, the front page of the *Zhejiang Daily* consecutively published five special comments on thoroughly carrying out the guiding principles adopted during the working conference of the Party Committee of Zhejiang Province; it published the news reports focusing on the building of Zhejiang into a culturally large province from the central media, including the People's Daily, the Xinhua News Agency, the Guangming Daily and the Economic Daily on June 28 and 29.

2.3.1 *"Three Main Systems" Become the Local Expression of the Cultural Soft Power*

Compared with the previous strategy of development for the building of Zhejiang into a culturally large province, the *Plan of Zhejiang Province for Promoting Vigorous Cultural Development and Great Cultural Prosperity (2008–2012)*, unveiled in 2008, gave prominence to the building of "three main systems", including the system of values with a socialist core, the public cultural service system and the system for the development of the cultural industry. These "three main systems" can be considered the deepened expression of the three points of action—enhancing the cohesion of the advanced culture, emancipating and developing the productive cultural forces, improving the capacity for public cultural services—in the *Decision of the Party Committee of Zhejiang Province on Accelerating the Building of a Culturally Large Province*, made in 2005; they are the local elucidation of the concept of the cultural soft power; they are consistent with the overall goal of promoting vigorous cultural development and great cultural prosperity and the reality of cultural development, so that the imported theory of "cultural soft power" can be carried out in China's practice of cultural development.

The building of the system of values with a socialist core is the priority in these "three main systems". It is necessary to carry out widespread publicity and education concerning the system of values with a socialist core and enhance the appeal and cohesion of socialist ideology; it is also necessary to actively explore the effective ways to adopt the system of values with a socialist core so that it can guide social trends and practically enhance the capability for guiding public opinion; it is also necessary to carry out the system of values with a socialist core in various respects of cultural development and make great efforts to develop harmonious culture, firmly grasping the correct direction for cultural development.

In order to build the public cultural service system, it is necessary to take it as the main way of realizing and safeguarding the people's basic cultural rights and interests, improving the people's cultural well-being, to promote the building of public cultural facilities and effective provision of public cultural products, innovate the modes of public welfare cultural activities and public cultural services, and actively make the achievements of cultural development benefit the people across the province.

In order to build the system for the development of the cultural industry, it is necessary to take it as the important means for transforming the economic developmental mode and pushing forward the optimization and upgrading of the industrial structure, focus on optimizing the cultural industrial structure, vigorously develop the private cultural industry, make the cultural industry more intensive, build a creative cultural industry and a modern cultural market system, and improve the overall strength of Zhejiang's cultural industry.

2.3.2 Promoting the Building of the System of Values with a Socialist Core

The *Decision of the Central Committee of the Communist Party of China on Some Major Issues Concerning Building a Harmonious Socialist Society*, adopted during the 6th Plenary Session of the 16th Central Committee of the Communist Party of China in October, 2006, specified, for the first time, the great issue and strategic task of building a system of values with a socialist core. The *Plan of Zhejiang Province for Promoting Vigorous Cultural Development and Great Cultural Prosperity (2008–2012)* stressed that the building of the system of values with a socialist core should be promoted mainly in the following five aspects.

The first aspect includes further arming the work with theories, requiring the leading cadres to strengthen their theoretical studies, giving full play to the roles of various reporting meetings and reading meetings, such as the Zhejiang Forum, establishing and improving the learning system, and making the theoretical study of the cadres more targeted and effective.

The second aspect includes prospering and developing philosophy and social science, establishing and improving a scientific and efficient management system, intensifying the reform of the system of philosophy and social science management and bringing about innovations to the mechanism of management, actively guiding and regulating the development of various non-governmental social science research institutions and groups, increasing the support for the philosophy and social science undertaking as well as further pushing forward the cultural research project, improving the operating mechanism, strengthening supervision and inspection, enhancing cooperation with famous institutions and universities, and delivering a number of research achievements with high academic value and social returns.

The third aspect includes carrying forward the national spirit that is focused on patriotism and the spirit of the times characterized by reform and that is focused on innovation. This aspect also includes reinforcing education towards patriotism, carrying out a variety of patriotism publicity and educational activities, intensifying the research on the Zhejiang Spirit, enriching and developing that spirit in response to the times and finally, further exploring the new forms and new carriers of typical publicity.

The fourth aspect includes strengthening intellectual and moral development, by extensively carrying out the practical activities relating to civic virtues, energetically advocating the Socialist Outlook of Honor and Dishonor, widely conducting education concerning social morality, professional ethics, family virtues and personal morality, strengthening education involving citizens' integrity, social responsibility and a scientific spirit, developing the social trends of making sound judgments about honor and disgrace, stressing uprightness and boosting harmony.

The fifth aspect includes deepening popular cultural and ethical development by further carrying out the activity of building culturally advanced cities, strengthening rural cultural and ethical development, thoroughly carrying out the project of "1,000-village demonstrations and 10,000-village improvements", and improving the rural living environment.

2.3.3 Promoting the Building of the Public Cultural Service System

The 5th Plenary Session of the 16th Central Committee of the Communist Party of China vowed, for the first time, to increase government input in cultural programs and gradually build a well-functioning public cultural service system covering the whole society. The *Plan of Zhejiang Province for Promoting Vigorous Cultural Development and Great Cultural Prosperity (2008–2012)* put forward, in details for the first time, the goal of and requirements for developing public cultural services: First, enhancing the capacity for production and provision of public cultural products, reinforcing the creation and production of cultural and intellectual products for the primary level and the people, giving full scope to the leading role of public welfare cultural units in public cultural services, supporting and encouraging cultural enterprises to make high-quality, inexpensive, healthy and suitable public cultural products and to participate in public cultural services, bringing about innovations to the mode of public cultural services, enhancing the service performance of important public cultural products, major public cultural service projects and public welfare cultural activities through government procurement and project subsidy, as well as actively pushing forward the project for providing a minimum of cultural security, supporting the development of private public welfare cultural institutions and earnestly carrying out public welfare cultural activities, by holding Zhejiang's cultural art festival.

Second, improving the network of public cultural services, strengthening the building of public cultural infrastructures, concentrating on reconstructing and building a number of important distinctive, well-functioning cultural sports facilities, moving faster to push forward key rural public cultural service projects, including the projects for extending radio and television to all of the villages, sharing cultural information resources, showing films in rural areas, building rural reading centers, strengthening the building of primary-level cultural fronts, including workers' cultural buildings, community-level cultural centers and village-level cultural activity centers, giving full play to the role of the existing cultural facilities, enhancing the efficiency of the utilization of various public cultural facilities, intensifying the protection and utilization of cultural heritages, extensively carrying out the cultural protection projects, building a network of museums at the provincial, municipal and county levels, supporting and guiding the construction of non-state-owned museums, further strengthening the protection of famous historical and cultural cities (blocks, towns and villages) and steadily pushing forward the application to become world cultural heritages.

Third, strengthening the protection and utilization of cultural heritages, strengthening the protection and utilization of historical relics, thoroughly carrying out the cultural protection projects, building a network of museums at the provincial, municipal and county levels, reinforcing the protection of famous historical and cultural cities (blocks, towns and villages), and reinforcing the protection and inheritance of intangible cultural heritages.

2.3.4 Promoting the Development of the Cultural Industry

The *Plan of Zhejiang Province for Promoting Vigorous Cultural Development and Great Cultural Prosperity (2008–2012)* shifted, for the first time, the work on making culture "go global" from cultural programs to the cultural industry. It called for expanding external cultural exchanges, extensively carrying out the activities with an external cultural exchange brand, including "Connect Zhejiang", "Go to the World · Zhejiang's Cultural Exhibition", especially promoting the exportation of cultural products and cultural services, cultivating a number of excellent external cultural product projects with Zhejiang's characteristics, participating in the international competition of cultural markets, expanding export trade, fostering a number of outward-looking leading cultural enterprises and enterprise groups in the fields of publication, distribution, films, television and performance, cultivating a number of external cultural intermediary bodies, developing a batch of cultural marketing enterprises, actively conducting international market surveys and providing information and marketing services, thus developing the international perspective of cultural development and cultural competition; in the meantime, identifying the key fields for development in the cultural industry, covering film and television, publication and distribution, cultural and artistic services, cultural services regarding tourism, conventions and exhibitions, animation, design art and artwork operations, as well as the manufacturing of stationery and sporting goods.

2.3.5 Pushing Forward the Overall Competitiveness of Mainstream Media

The *Plan of Zhejiang Province for Promoting Vigorous Cultural Development and Great Cultural Prosperity (2008–2012)* also separately listed the development of the news media in parallel to the building of the "three main systems", and focused on three requirements.

The first requirement involved enhancing the capability for guiding public opinion, which included firmly grasping the correct guidance of public opinion, developing strong mainstream forces in the public opinion field, actively studying and adopting new means of information and cultural services, including the Internet and mobile phones, promoting the development of the system of news releases and news spokes-people, strengthening the building of the mechanism for the handling of emergency news and firmly holding the initiative in the guidance of online public opinion.

The second requirement regarded speeding up the construction of media infras-tructures, enhancing the overall competitiveness of mainstream media, continuing to promote group-based construction, making the existing press groups, radio and television groups, publication groups across the province large and strong, form-ing groups of large enterprises with inter-regional development under multimedia operation, continuously improving the core competitiveness of the main newspa-pers and periodicals, promoting the building of key news websites, pushing forward brand-based development of online media, improving various networks of the press, publications and communication and increasing the level of digitization.

The third requirement involved strengthening the building of online media, making key news websites large and strong, increasing the provision of online cultural products and services, ensuring that the websites of governments at various levels release more authoritative government information, promoting the digitization and online communication of cultural products, reinforcing online cultural manage-ment, further improving the system and mechanism of online cultural management and developing and implementing Zhejiang's measures for the administration of online cultural information.

2.4 Building a Culturally Strong Province, Continuing to Stay Ahead

On October 18, 2011, the 6th Plenary Session of the 17th Central Committee of the Communist Party of China adopted the *Decision of the Central Committee of the Communist Party of China on Some Major Issues Concerning Intensifying the Reform of the Cultural System and Promoting the Vigorous Development and Great Prosperity of the Socialist Culture*. The proposition of culture was taken as the theme of the plenary session of the Central Committee of the Communist Party of China for the first time since the 17th National Congress of the Communist Party of China in 2007. The efforts in building a socialist culturally powerful country and promoting the vigorous development and great prosperity of socialist culture and the major policy trends in cultural development reflect the inevitable requirements of China's economic and social development and trigger a new round of changes in cultural mindset. To build a culturally powerful socialist country, it is necessary to push forward important developments in six fields which have a vital bearing on the overall situation and strategy of the socialist cause with Chinese characteristics: First, strengthening the building of the system of values with a socialist core; second, make cultural creation and production prosper; third, speeding up the development of public welfare cultural programs; fourth, accelerating the development of the cultural industry; fifth, carrying out reform and innovation to promote cultural development and prosperity; sixth, more rapidly cultivating high-caliber cultural personnel. The vigorous development and great prosperity of the socialist culture is reflected in three aspects: First, the important source of national cohesion and creativity; second, an important factor in comprehensive competitiveness; third, an important support in economic and social development.

2.4.1 From a Culturally Large Province to a Culturally Strong Province

The year 2011 was the first year of the 12th Five-Year Plan. Under the guidance of the *Decision of the Central Committee of the Communist Party of China on Some Major Issues Concerning Intensifying the Reform of the Cultural System and Promoting the Vigorous Development and Great Prosperity of the Socialist Culture*, Zhejiang's strategy for cultural development reached a new level. Zhejiang is the province which was one of the first provinces to take on the building of a culturally large province as a goal and a task in China; Zhejiang has always promoted cultural development by taking it as an overarching strategic task; this reflects the cultural self-consciousness and cultural self-confidence of the Party Committee and the People's Government of Zhejiang Province; in particular, comrade Xi Jinping made great efforts to promote the building of a culturally large province. Since the 16th National Congress of the Communist Party of China, the Party Committee and the People's Government of Zhejiang Province have adopted the building of a culturally large province as an important task for carrying out the "Eight-Eight Strategies" and the overall strategy of "making the people rich by starting businesses and of building a strong province through innovation"; they have developed and implemented the *Decision of the Party Committee of Zhejiang Province on Accelerating the Building of a Culturally Large Province* and the *Plan of Zhejiang Province for Promoting Vigorous Cultural Development and Great Cultural Prosperity (2008–2012)*, with a focus on building "three main systems", deeply carrying out "eight projects", more rapidly building "a strong province in four respects", enhancing Zhejiang's cultural cohesion, its capability for cultural innovation, a guarantee for the people's basic cultural rights and interests, the competitiveness of the cultural industry and cultural influence, and shaping the overall pattern of cultural work which conforms to Zhejiang's reality and has Zhejiang's characteristics.

The Party Committee and the People's Government of Zhejiang Province have taken the building of a system of values with a socialist core as the top priority in promoting cultural development, and they have promoted it on various fronts, including the work on arming Zhejiang with theories, intellectual and moral development, popular cultural and ethical development, news publicity, science, education, culture and health, art, publications and the popularization of science and laws. During the period of the 11th Five-Year Plan, the system of values with a socialist core was more deeply rooted among the people and civilian moral models emerged in

Zhejiang. Newspapers, periodicals, radio, television, publications and other media have actively offered public opinion platforms; a number of brands for the popularization of social sciences, including Social Science Popularization Week and the Humanities Lecture, have become the fronts for the mass communication of serious culture; public cultural institutions have carried out regular mechanisms to conduct education on a patriotism-focused national spirit and the education involving the reform and innovation-focused spirit of the times, carry forward the Zhejiang Spirit with entrepreneurship and innovation as the core, and give value to outstanding traditional culture. The building of a trustworthy Zhejiang and a "Zhejiang under the Rule of Law" has become the key project which has a vital bearing on the overall situation of Zhejiang's social development. The project for quality training concerning the rural labor force of 10 million people and the Spring Mud Program for the intellectual and moral development of juveniles have been carried out across the province. Zhejiang has solidly promoted the building of a moral educational system for the schools, the improvement of government conduct and the conduct in industries, education for the popularization of science, the education on combating corruption and building a clean government and the building of a culture of clean government. A social environment with good conduct has been fostered in various sectors across the province.

During the period of the 11th Five-Year Plan, the departments of finance at various levels in Zhejiang significantly increased support for culture and the input in the cultural field increased year by year, Zhejiang ranked no. 2 nationwide in annual total input in cultural programs, only second to Guangdong. Zhejiang has witnessed the basic formation of an integrated urban-rural regional public service system with complementation of advantages, staggered development, optimized allocation and rational layout.

According to statistics, during the period of the 11th Five-Year Plan, the added value of Zhejiang's cultural industry grew annually by an average of 19.0%, being 3.4 percentage points higher than the current-price GDP growth in the same period. In 2010, the added value of Zhejiang's cultural industry surpassed 100 billion yuan to reach 105.6 billion yuan for the first time, accounting for 3.8% of the GDP. Almost each year for 6 consecutive years, the added value of Zhejiang's cultural industry increased by 10 billion yuan, with its growth rate much higher than the growth rate of the GDP in the same period, the rate of its contribution to economic growth was on the rise.

Smooth progress has been made in restructuring the for-profit cultural units into enterprises across the province; the for-profit units in such sectors as publication, distribution and films have been basically restructured into enterprises. Zhejiang has basically completed the work on restructuring provincial art theaters and troupes into enterprises and the reform of the comprehensive law enforcement on the cultural market. During the period of the 11th Five-Year Plan, nearly 100 excellent works across the province were highly rated in domestic and foreign major activities of appraisal and selection. High-quality cultural personnel have been on the increase. So far, 23 people have been included in the national "four-batch" talent project in the publicity and cultural system, 279 people have been included in the provincial "five-batch" talent project, and nearly 100,000 people have engaged in social science teaching, research and management. In the meantime, there has been a group of full-time and part-time primary-level cultural workers consisting of professional cultural workers, personages from various sectors of the society and cultural volunteers.

2.4.2   Focusing on Promoting the Building of a Culturally Strong Province Through "Three Main Systems", Eight Projects and Ten Plans

The building of a culturally large province is the solid foundation for building a culturally strong province, while a culturally strong province is the inevitable direction for building a culturally large province. During the period October 20–21, 2011, the enlarged meeting and the leading cadre meeting of the Standing Committee of the Party Committee of Zhejiang Province conveyed the guiding principles adopted during the 6th Plenary Session of the 17th Central Committee of the Communist Party of China. In the following week, the leaders of the Party Committee of Zhejiang Province went to the primary-level units, enterprises and rural areas in Jiaxing, Yueqing, Jiaojiang, Anji, Yinzhou, Shaoxing, Suichang and Songyang to publicize the guiding principles adopted during the 6th Plenary Session of the 17th Central Committee of the Communist Party of China, surveying the overall situation of local cultural development, discussing the integrative development of a beautiful countryside, the industrial industry and the tourism industry, and the development of rural cultural fronts and personnel.

Special meetings were held in various cities, the cultural publicity circles and all sectors of the society across the province, offering ideas and suggestions for Zhejiang's further cultural development according to the 12th five-year development plans for various industries and sectors. During the period November 16–18, 2011, the 10th Plenary (Enlarged) Session of the 12th Party Committee of Zhejiang Province was held, making an in-depth study and implementing the guiding principles adopted during the 6th Plenary Session of the 17th Central Committee of the Communist Party of China, arranging the tasks for developing Zhejiang from a culturally large province into a culturally strong province, deliberating and adopting the *Decision on Earnestly Implementing the Guiding Principles Adopted during the 6th Plenary Session of the 17th Central Committee of the Communist Party of China and Vigorously Promoting the Building of a Culturally Strong Province* ("the Decision").

According to "the Decision", a culturally strong province should be built by enhancing the cohesion of the advanced culture, the capability for public cultural services, the competitiveness of the cultural industry, the capability for innovation for cultural development, regional cultural influence and the capability for the support of cultural talents. "The Decision" specified the main tasks for promoting the building of a culturally strong province: The first task was to vigorously build the system of values with a socialist core—adapt Marxism to the Chinese context, the times and the people's needs, firmly hold the common ideals of socialism with Chinese characteristics, carry forward the national spirit, the spirit of the times and the Zhejiang Spirit, strengthen civic moral development; the second task was to push forward the creation and production of excellent cultural products, actively make excellent cultural and artistic works and to develop philosophy and social science and make them prosper; the third task was to build a system of public cultural services—improving the network of public cultural facilities, enhance the capability for public cultural services, bring about innovations to the mechanism of public cultural services; the fourth task was to more rapidly build a system for the development of the culture industry—optimize the cultural industrial layout, increase the level of development of the culture industry and enhance the development of the modern cultural market; the fifth task was to promote innovations to the cultural systems and mechanisms—intensify the reform of state-owned cultural units and push forward the reform of the cultural management system; the sixth task was to reinforce the development of cultural personnel—cultivate high-level leading figures and high-quality cultural personnel, strengthen the development of the primary-level cultural personnel and bring about innovations to the working mechanism for cultural personnel.

Regarding concrete measures, "the Decision" called for, based on consolidating the achievements in building a culturally large province, continuing to push forward the building of the system of values with a socialist core, the public cultural service system and the system of cultural industrial development (the "three main systems"), thoroughly carry out the project for the improvement of cultural quality, the excellent cultural product project, the cultural research project, the cultural protection project, the project for the promotion of the cultural industry, the cultural front project, the cultural communication project and the cultural talent project (the "eight projects"), and to focus on carrying out the plan for the popularization of the system of the socialist theory with Chinese characteristics, the plan for civic moral development, the plan for the creation of excellent cultural and artistic works, the plan for the development of cyberculture, the plan for the construction of major cultural facilities, the basic public cultural service improvement plan, the cultural heritage inheritance plan, the plan for doubling the cultural industries, the external cultural development plan and the plan for the development of cultural celebrities (the "ten plans").

In April, 2012, Zhejiang's Leading Group for Cultural Development held a meeting. The meeting stressed that the year 2012 was the year of initiating Zhejiang's development from a culturally large province to a culturally strong province and also the year for concluding the stage tasks for cultural reform, and that it was necessary to push forward the building of a culturally strong province through the "three main systems", "eight projects" and "ten plans". The meeting deliberated and adopted the work priorities in the building of a culturally strong province and the "ten plans" for cultural development in 2012. The meeting emphasized efforts in carrying out the work regarding six aspects: First, deeply promoting the building of the system of values with a socialist core; second, comprehensively intensifying the reform of the cultural system; third, actively building a complete system of public cultural services to continuously meet the people's increasing cultural needs; fourth, vigorously developing the cultural industry—making efforts in improvement, integration and fusion, taking the plan for the doubling of the cultural industries as a means to extensively carry out the "122" project for developing the cultural industry, thus implementing the strategy for stimulating development through major projects; fifth, strengthening the creation and production of cultural and artistic works—bringing forth a great variety of excellent cultural and artistic works covering literature, drama, film and television, animation, choreography, folk literature and art, popular literature and art, developing the "Zhejiang forces" in the fields of film, television and culture; sixth, energetically cultivating high-caliber leading cultural figures and high-quality cultural personnel, strengthening the development of the primary-level cultural personnel and thus ensuring the healthy growth of cultural personnel.

2.4.3 The Building of a Culturally Strong Province Injects New Vigor into the Building of a Modern Zhejiang Which Is a Materially Affluent and Culturally Advanced Province, a Beautiful Province for a Good Life

Since the implementation of the "Eight-Eight Strategies", Zhejiang has obtained strong impetus from the reform of the cultural system, it has turned the good practices and excellent experience from the first-ever implementation of pilot programs into institutional design, proceeded from Zhejiang's reality to put forward a series of characteristic reform measures and take a pioneering developmental path which combines the inheritance of Zhejiang's culture and history with the advantages of contemporary development; this presents Zhejiang's characteristics. In November, 2012, the 18th National Congress of the Communist Party of China made the overall arrangement for promoting the socialist cause with Chinese characteristics in the new era and put forward the goal of doubling in two respects in reform and opening-up. In December, the 2nd Plenary Session of the 13th Party Committee of Zhejiang Province deliberated and adopted the *Decision of the Party Committee of Zhejiang Province on Earnestly Studying and Implementing the Guiding Principles Adopted during the 18th National Congress of the Communist Party of China and Solidly Promoting the Building of a Materially Affluent and Culturally Advanced Modern Zhejiang*; the session put forward the goal of building a materially affluent and culturally advanced modern Zhejiang, made the strategic arrangement for "doing a better job towards the goals set for the next 1, 3 and 5 years, doubling the value in four respects", and wrote a new chapter for the blueprint of the "Eight-Eight Strategies".

The *Decision of the Central Committee of the Communist Party of China on Some Major Issues Concerning Comprehensively Intensifying the Reform*, adopted during the 3rd Plenary Session of the 18th Central Committee of the Communist Party of China in November, 2013, serves as the program of action for comprehensively intensifying the reform at a new historical starting point; it offers the clear direction for Zhejiang to become the first to carry out reforms and stay ahead, especially in economic transformation and upgrading, the development of the private economy, urban and rural integration, the building of "Zhejiang under the Rule of Law", a safe Zhejiang and a beautiful Zhejiang. In late November, the 4th Plenary Session of the 13th Party Committee of Zhejiang Province deliberated and adopted the *Decision of the Party Committee of Zhejiang Province on Earnestly Studying and Implementing the Guiding Principles Adopted during the 3rd Plenary Session of the 18th Central Committee of the Communist Party of China and Comprehensively Intensifying the Reform to Foster New Advantages in Systems and Mechanisms*. According to the session, the "Eight-Eight Strategies" are the vivid practice of socialism with Chinese characteristics at the provincial level, the major strategy having a vital bearing on the overall situation of Zhejiang's modernization and also the pragmatic policy which conforms to Zhejiang's reality and can withstand practical testing. According to the rich connotation and essence of the "Eight-Eight Strategies", the decision put forward the roadmap of reform for "focusing on the work in eight respects", namely, letting the market play a decisive role in resource allocation, promoting structural adjustment and industrial upgrading, cultivating the new advantages of an open economy, pushing forward urban and rural integration and the building of marine power, reaching a new realm in cultural development, boosting the building of "Zhejiang under the Rule of Law" and a safe Zhejiang, building a beautiful Zhejiang, further leveraging advantages, intensifying reforms, and introducing innovative measures. The "work in eight respects" covers economic, political, cultural, social and ecological development, and is consistent with the "Eight-Eight Strategies"; it is the practical requirement of the "Eight-Eight Strategies" under the new historical conditions and concrete implementation of reforms; it is the working path for Zhejiang to comprehensively intensify reforms.

The *Decision of the Party Committee of Zhejiang Province on Earnestly Studying and Implementing the Guiding Principles Adopted during the 3rd Plenary Session of the 18th Central Committee of the Communist Party of China and Comprehensively Intensifying the Reform to Foster New Advantages in Systems and Mechanisms*, adopted during the 4th Plenary Session of the 13th Party Committee of Zhejiang Province, further specified the requirements for improving the systems and mechanisms for building a culturally strong province and divided the tasks into four parts.

The first part included deepening the building of the system of values with a socialist core. This meant thoroughly carrying out the publicity and education concerning the Chinese dream and socialism with Chinese characteristics, advocating and practicing the socialist core values, vigorously carrying forward the Zhejiang Spirit, deeply conducting the activity with the theme of "Becoming the Most Beautiful People of Zhejiang", and exploring the effective mechanisms of "turning the most beautiful potted landscape into scenery".

The second part included strengthening and improving cultural management. This meant promoting the reform of the cultural management system, further regulating the items subject to administrative examination and approval relating to cultural affairs, promoting functional merger and institutional integration at relevant departments in the cultural field, establishing the systems and mechanisms for cultural development conducive to bringing forth excellent works and talents and delivering returns, improving the modern cultural market system, cultivating and developing the cultural market players, improving the systems and mechanisms which uphold the correct guidance of public opinion, actively building a modern communication system, strengthening and improving the building of various media, especially new media such as the Internet and shaping a work pattern of online public opinion which combines correct guidance with law-based management.

The third task included improving the cultural industrial development system, which meant continuing to promote the restructuring of state-owned for-profit cultural units into enterprises, speeding up the corporate system and shareholding reform, exploring and carrying out a special system of share management in the important state-owned media enterprises which have been restructured according to regulations, speeding up the building of the system of investment and financing services for the cultural industry, encouraging the development of non-public cultural enterprises, actively cultivating the leading cultural enterprises, and pushing forward mergers, acquisitions and reorganizations of cultural enterprises.

The fourth task included reinforcing the building of the public cultural service system. This meant establishing a mechanism for coordinating the building of the public cultural service system, promoting the standardization of basic public cultural services and ensuring equal access to basic public cultural services, as well as encouraging social forces and social capital to participate in the building of the public cultural service system and promoting socialized development of the public cultural services.

On May 23, 2014, the 5th Plenary Session of the 13th Party Committee of Zhejiang Province adopted the *Decision of the Party Committee of Zhejiang Province on Building a Beautiful Zhejiang and Creating a Good Life*, presenting a new goal and a new vision for actively promoting Zhejiang's practice of the building of a beautiful China, speeding up the building of systems of ecological development and marching towards the new era of socialist ecological development. One of the main tasks for building a materially affluent and culturally advanced Zhejiang lies in carrying forward the humanistic spirit with Zhejiang's characteristics, it covers three parts and specially adds the specific requirements for actively cultivating ecological culture:

Inheriting excellent traditional culture. This means tapping the ecological philosophies and thoughts in Zhejiang's traditional culture, strengthening the protection and development of national major cultural and natural heritage sites, key culture relic protection sites, important revolutionary sites and ruins, famous historical and cultural cities, towns and villages, promoting the protection, inheritance and utilization of intangible cultural heritages and continuing its historical context.

Unceasingly improving the humanistic quality of citizens. This involves actively fostering and practicing values with a socialist core, advocating the shared value outlook of the contemporary people of Zhejiang—being pragmatic, trustworthy, advocating learning and upholding goodwill, energetically publicizing "the Most Beautiful Landscape", "the Most Beautiful People" and "the Most Beautiful Phenomenon" for building a beautiful Zhejiang and creating a good life, changing the "Most Beautiful" from "potted landscape" to "scenery" and generating positive energy in the society.

Positively cultivating ecological culture. This is in coordination with commemorative activities including the Zhejiang Ecology Day and the World Environment Day, presenting the achievements in ecological and environmental protection, popularizing the knowledge on ecological and environmental protection, and carrying forward an ecological humanistic spirit, as well as vigorously carrying forward the philosophy of respecting, conforming to and protecting nature and actively drawing upon the advanced philosophy of the developed countries for valuing ecological development.

References

Xi Jinping, Pushing Forward the Building of a Safe Zhejiang, Promoting Social Harmony and Stability, *People's Tribune*, 2004(7).

Xi Jinping, *Carrying out Concrete Work to Stay Ahead – Line of Thought and Practice in Promoting New Development in Zhejiang*, The Party School of the CPC Central Committee Press, 2006a.

Xi Jinping, The Zhejiang Spirit of Advancing with the Times, *Zhejiang Daily*, February 5, 2006b, p. 1.

Xi Jinping, *Zhijiang Xinyu*, Zhejiang People's Publishing House, 2007, p. 96.

Chapter 3
Outstanding Traditional Culture Brings Forth Developmental Path

Ye Chen

On November 29, 2012, when visiting the exhibition *The Road to Revival*, General Secretary Xi Jinping delivered a speech "Building on Past Successes to Further March towards the Goal of Achieving the Great Rejuvenation of the Chinese Nation". He pointed out, "Everyone is discussing the Chinese dream; in my opinion, achieving the great rejuvenation of the Chinese nation is the greatest dream of the Chinese nation since modern times; this dream represents the long-cherished wish of several generations of the Chinese people and reflects the overall interests of the Chinese nation and the Chinese people; it is the common aspiration of every Chinese person".

In the era and context of moving towards the Chinese dream of achieving the great rejuvenation of the Chinese nation, with his national feelings, classical virtues and political sagacity, comrade Xi Jinping comprehensively and profoundly elucidated and carried forward the contemporary value of excellent Chinese traditional culture. He pointed out, "There are no two identical leaves in the world; a nation, a country must understand its identity, origin and future, once this is understood in a correct way, it is necessary to firmly advance according to goals."[1] "With a long history, the Chinese culture contains the deepest cultural pursuit of the Chinese nation and represents the unique cultural sign of the Chinese nation, offers rich nutrition for the Chinese nation to exist forever and to develop."[2]

Such examination and understanding of historical tradition is a result of deep philosophical understanding, long-term experimentations and extensive practice. Since Zhejiang's implementation of the "Eight-Eight Strategies" in 2003, Zhejiang

---

[1] The speech delivered by Comrade Xi Jinping during the symposium with teachers and students of Peking University on May 4, 2014, Xinhuanet, http://news.xinhuanet.com/politics/2014-05/05/c-1110528066_2.htm, 2014-05-05.

[2] The speech delivered by Comrade Xi Jinping at the 13th collective learning of the Political Bureau of the Central Committee of the Communist Party of China on February 24, 2014, http://www.gov.cn/ldhd/2014-02/25/content_2621669.htm.

Y. Chen (✉)
The Zhejiang Academy of Social Sciences, Hangzhou, China

© Social Sciences Academic Press and Springer Nature Singapore Pte Ltd. 2019
D. Xie and Y. Chen (eds.), *Chinese Dream and Practice in Zhejiang – Culture*,
Research Series on the Chinese Dream and China's Development Path,
https://doi.org/10.1007/978-981-13-7216-2_3

has made continuous efforts to inherit and carry forward excellent traditional culture, has built Zhejiang's evident landscape of contemporary inheritance and promotion of excellent traditional culture, and presented Zhejiang's progressive path of that contemporary inheritance and promotion. With local characteristic practice and explorations, Zhejiang has advanced in response to the general situation of national development and the tide of the times, and has offered a vivid local sample for building the "root" and "soul" of the Chinese dream.

3.1 Spontaneous, Rich and Vivid Folk Cultural Inheritance

The Chinese culture has a long history, and Zhejiang enjoys a long-standing regional culture and a splendid civilization. A long-time development with great hardship has given birth to Zhejiang's profound cultural tradition and an impressive regional legend. The cultural creation and historical inheritance in the folk society constitute the foundation for Zhejiang's cultural tradition and also the source of vitality for the innovative development of Zhejiang's culture in the new era. In the past 10 years, the traditional culture has gradually recovered in Zhejiang's folk life and has reflected innovative development with the characteristics of the times.

3.1.1 Traditional Forms of Folk in Daily Life

The most vibrant cultural inheritance involves the outlook on common values from the production mode and lifestyle, the manner of entertainment, etiquette and folk customs in daily life. In the past 10 years, the abundant traditional cultural resources in the people's life in Zhejiang's urban and rural areas have been tapped and integrated; they have become the organic factors in a new life. In Xixi Village in Liandu District, Lishui City, which is a village established during the emperor Tang Xianzong's reign (806–820) in the Tang Dynasty (618–907), the traditional teachings from ancestors—etiquette and virtues—have nurtured the simple and honest folkway, there are about 10,000 m^2 of intact ancient dwellings. The villagers in Xixi Village have deeply tapped historical culture and transformed the ancestral temple in the village into an exhibition hall for ancient objects, villagers have also moved their treasured ancient objects from the Ming Dynasty (1368–1644) and the Qing Dynasty (1636–1912) to the exhibition hall. In June, 2006, Xixi Village was rated as the provincial historical and cultural village by the People's Government of Zhejiang Province. The rural traditional cultural activities similar to those in Xixi Village have been extensively carried out in Zhejiang's rural areas.

The traditional culture has local characteristics, and there are spaces and needs for promoting traditional culture in modern urban life. In the Zhu'er'tang Community in Gongshu District, Hangzhou City, traditional culture has become an important resource for building brands of family culture, there have been a number of calligraphy families, embroidery families, folk music families and antique families; the village has become an international tourist attraction.

With accelerated urbanization, the trend is for rural areas to become urbanized and villagers to become citizens. However, in this process, we can also find a tenacious continuity of rural traditional cultural contexts and the impact of rural culture on urban civilization. With the demolition of villages and the building of communities during urbanization, Luojiazhuang Stock Economic Cooperative in Xihu District, Hangzhou City has changed from a suburban rural area to a prosperous central community in the western part of the city. More than 20 years later, under the organizational structure of urban citizenship and the life of an urban community, the traditional lifestyle, way of entertainment and outlook on values still exert an impact on the life of the people of Luojiazhuang to varying degrees, even on that of the surrounding urban communities and residents. For instance, the people of Luojiazhuang still believe that they are villagers, and that identity is recognized among the villagers. In particular, the dragon boat race during the Dragon Boat Festival has been carried out for many years and has become a regular occasion for bringing all of the villagers together. This activity has attracted a large number of urban residents for enjoyment and participation, and has introduced the elements of traditional culture to the festival life of urban residents; rural traditional culture has been promoted to enrich the cultural life of urban residents.

3.1.2 The Continuity of Traditions in Folk Festival Activities

The time-honored folk festival activities carry rich connotations of the farming culture and contain the people's profound feelings of local friendship and humanity, they have everlasting traditional charm, cultural attraction and cohesion. In recent years, the traditional folk festival activities have been restored and carried out; there is an amazing interplay between the traditional culture and modern civilization. In 2008, for the first time, Zhejiang established 14 demonstration areas for the protection of traditional festivals. Such an establishment not only embodies Zhejiang's attention to and protection of the culture of traditional festivals, but it also mirrors a scenario in which traditional festival cultural resources are abundant, there are a variety of relevant activities, the atmosphere is animated and the demand is brisk in Zhejiang.

3.1.3 The Impartment of Traditional Folk Art

Zhejiang is a large province of folk art; there are a wealth of folk artists and a large number of excellent folk artistic works, including folk songs and dances, crafts, paintings and opera in rural areas. Take the Jinhua area as an example; there are poem-writing and reciting farmers in Wucheng; the Farmer's Art Festival in Yiwu; the "pavilion carrying activity", the "inheritance of opera melodies other than Kunshan and Yiyang melodies" and the "calligraphy and painting village" in Pujiang; the "water stage" and the "Huaxi Spring Tide" in Yongkang; "Treading on Fire", the "Wielding Flag" and the "ancient tea route culture" in Pan'an, all of which are highly popular and influential local cultural brands.

3.1.4   Extensive Rebuilding of the Genealogical Tree

The social form under the patriarchal clan system in ancient China is an important foundation of Chinese traditional culture and is still influential in today's rural society. In recent years, folk enthusiasm about rebuilding the genealogical tree has run high in Zhejiang. In Jinhua, Lishui and Wenzhou where there is always the tradition of rebuilding the genealogical tree, almost every household in many county towns, towns and villages has been included in the genealogical tree. This round of activities involving the rebuilding of the genealogical tree in Zhejiang has new characteristics in various respects, from the organization mode to the use of funds.

First, specialized folk genealogical tree associations were established. In September, 2012, the Zhuji Genealogy Research Society was officially established. It is a legal non-governmental organization approved by the department of civil affairs and also the first county-level genealogy association in China. Second, there are specialized genealogical tree rebuilding organizations and professionals, providing one package service for the clans with the needs for rebuilding a genealogical tree. Third, the costs for rebuilding a genealogical tree are high and range from hundreds of thousands of yuan to one million yuan; the costs are mostly borne by businessmen in the clans. Fourth, transnational rebuilding of the genealogical tree occurs thanks to high economic strength, easy access to information and a broad horizon.

It should be noted that the practices of becoming attached to celebrities, making blind comparisons, parading wealth and a popular surname, seeking improper gains and publicizing clan culture in the rebuilding of a genealogical tree are inadvisable. The government and the academic circle should intervene in a positive manner to regulate relevant behavior, ensuring that folk culture is promoted in a correct manner.

3.1.5   Private Museum: "Folk Cultural Banquet"

In Zhejiang, private museums emerged in the early 1990s. Zhejiang is one of the provinces where private museums were built at the earliest, where they have been available in the largest quantity and are the most influential in the country. According to the statistics of the year 2012 from the Zhejiang Cultural Relics Bureau, there were 92 private museums across the province, accounting for 36.5% of all the museums across the province. As of 2014, Zhejiang ranked no. 1 nationwide in the total number of private museums.

Private museums represent an innovation which shows that Zhejiang's folk culture has a long history and distinctive characteristics of the times, the awareness of innovation is strong and private capital actively participates in the cultural cause. With many years of development, Zhejiang's distinctive characteristics have gradually taken shape: First, they are mainly built by individuals and legal entities—individuals are mainly enthusiasts of the collection of cultural relics, and the building of private museums by individuals is based on folk collections; legal entities are mainly enterprises and public institutions, the museums built by legal entities are mostly related to the industries, sectors in which legal entities are engaged or to local economic and cultural characteristics, such as the Huqingyutang Traditional Chinese Medicine Museum. Second, each type of museum is dedicated to a particular type of collection; for instance, copper carving museums especially exhibit copper carving art, Ming and Qing furniture museums specially exhibit traditional ancient furniture. Third, museum collections involve many types, including vehicles, ships, bridges, clothing, glasses, stationery, badges, abacuses, post and telecommunications, securities, coins, Chinese herbal medicine, strange stones, locks, clocks, cameras, scissors, ceramics, brocade, calligraphy and paintings, paper cuttings, root carving, microscopic carving and pots; private museums have a record in Chinese museum history in terms of the types of collection and serve as an important supplement to state-owned museums.[3]

Private museums have played an active role in providing public cultural services to the general public. Five private museums in Ningbo are open for free for more than 315 days each year; they actively conduct public welfare activities to enrich the people's cultural life.

At present, as rural cultural auditoriums are common across the province, small venues which appear in the form of exhibition halls and exhibition galleries and reflect the tradition of "one product in one village" and contemporary cultural characteristics, are similar to private museums in nature and play the same roles as private museums, suggesting the gratifying extension of private museums from urban areas to rural areas.

The rise of private museums in Zhejiang is closely related to the fact that Zhejiang is economically developed, enjoys profound cultural deposits, has a long tradition of collection and folk cultural awareness is strong in Zhejiang. As a cultural form and social phenomenon, private museums inject new connotations and vigor into Zhejiang's cultural development; they are the private forces for protecting cultural heritages and also important windows for showcasing, carrying forward and inheriting outstanding Chinese traditional culture and Zhejiang's local culture, so they play a very good role in improving the cultural level.

3.1.6 Development of Excellent Historical Resources by Private Capital

Zhejiang has a long business tradition and a strong business atmosphere at the nongovernmental level. Since the reform and opening-up, the people of Zhejiang have blazed new trails and taken risks, worked hard and Zhejiang has witnessed rapid economic and social development. Zhejiang's private economy has played an enormous role in promoting development. Zhejiang's private entrepreneurs have unique insights and courage to tap the traditional cultural resources.

---

[3] Wen (2011).

The capital was founded in Hangzhou during the Southern Song Dynasty (1127–1279), stimulating vigorous economic, social and cultural development in Hangzhou and the entire province of Zhejiang; moreover, thanks to geographical advantages and the favorable conditions of natural mountains and waters, a cultural landscape mainly covering leisure, entertainment and tourism emerged, and both the rich and the poor enjoyed it. "The poor also frequently go on the spree and indulge in extravagant eating and drinking together with wives and children even if their budget is tight, and this custom has existed in this state since ancient times."[4]

This cultural characteristic and its value for commercial development in Hangzhou have been captured by Zhejiang's sharp-eyed private entrepreneurs, and the Songcheng Group has emerged accordingly. Songcheng Resort stimulates 10 billion yuan in consumption in the surrounding areas each year, promoting the structural upgrading of Hangzhou's tourism industry. Since the large-scale song and dance "The Romance of the Song Dynasty" was introduced, its performance has been staged more than 13,000 times, receiving audiences for 35 million person-times; it is currently the theatrical performance which is staged most frequently and receives the largest number of audiences each year in the world; it is the only work of cultural tourism performances that has been granted the national Five-Ones Project award. The Songcheng Group has been given the title of China's Top 30 Cultural Enterprises many consecutive times; it is the no. 1 share in cultural performances in China.

3.1.7 The Public Welfare Spirit of Loving Cultural Inheritance

In an article entitled "On Public Virtues", Liang Qichao said, "Virtues developed early in China, more emphasis is placed on personal virtues, but there are no public virtues." This view reveals an important feature of Chinese cultural tradition, but this is not absolutely true. For the teachings by sages and men of virtue, *The Book of Rites · Liyun* stresses that the people do not merely support their parents and raise their children, make the elderly people live a peaceful life, but the middle-aged people also realize their potential and children grow healthily, they make sure that the widower, the widow, the orphan and the childless and the disabled are supported. For the reality of the folk society, historically, Zhejiang had a large number of examples showing mutual assistance among neighbors, a love for public welfare, care for those in distress and aid for those in peril and they carry out joint efforts in tiding over the difficulties; this sufficiently proves that public care and a public spirit exist.

This kind of public care and public spirit have been embodied at the folk level in contemporary Zhejiang. In recent years, many individuals and groups have raised funds or made efforts to jointly carry out social public welfare programs, they have shown care for, paid attention to and participated in social public affairs.

In Yinjiang Town, Yinzhou District, Ningbo City, the retirees from 23 enterprises and public institutions, including government departments and electric power

---

[4]Wu (1984).

management stations, and the highly respected elderly personages have voluntarily established the Non-governmental Preparatory Committee for the Famous Historical and Cultural Town of Yinjiang. None of them receive any remuneration and they merely serve the people. Since its establishment, besides the daily work, the committee also carries out two major projects, the extension of the Tashan Temple and the rebuilding of the Yinjiang Bridge.

The inheritance of outstanding excellent culture in the contemporary folk society has been reflected in many fields. The above one is just one of the examples. The inheritance of traditional culture in Zhejiang's folk society in recent years broadly presents the following characteristics.

First of all, there is a profound foundation of inheritance and spontaneous historical inheritance behavior in Zhejiang's folk society; the people in Zhejiang display a natural cordial feeling and ardent love for traditional Chinese culture; this vividly demonstrates that traditional Chinese culture has an endless supply of blood and vitality and nourishes the people in their daily lives, it is the "root" and "soul" of the Chinese people.

Second, the historical inheritance of cultural traditions in Zhejiang's folk society covers extensive fields and has rich connotations; the people are highly enthusiastic about their inheritance, they are full of vigor and have great courage to take actions. The people are the most important and main practitioners of and innovators to their cultural inheritance.

Third, the spontaneous historical inheritance in the primary-level folk society is as primitive and plain as original ecology, the good and the bad are intermingled. It is often low, small and scattered; subject to a strong invasion of contemporary Western civilization and the interest-oriented environment in the market economy, it would be easy for it to disappear because it is belittled or weak, it is also vulnerable to alienation because it is used improperly or profits are sought after. Therefore, the Party and the government should strengthen top-level design, experts and scholars should leverage their expertise and strong points to lead and cultivate the inheritance of folk culture.

3.2 Rational Thinking and Theoretical Support for Traditional Cultural Value

Besides plain, passionate, vibrant and habitual cultural inheritance activities in the primary-level folk society, Zhejiang's thinkers and intellectual circles have also, through rational and rigorous thinking and research, from higher and deeper perspectives, actively explored the internal structure, basic elements and essential characteristics of Chinese cultural traditions, they have analyzed the relationship between Zhejiang's regional cultural traditions and the social development of contemporary Zhejiang, identifying the outstanding elements and active factors to expound its contemporary value.

3.2.1 Exploring the Contemporary Value of Traditional Culture Through Sagacious, Profound Rational Thinking

Comrade Xi Jinping has worked in Zhejiang as from October, 2002. He was deeply impressed by the long historical tradition, profound cultural deposits, unique cultural character, abundant resources, the enthusiasm and creativity in inheritance of traditional culture in the primary-level folk society in Zhejiang. In his general preface to *A Series of Books on the Achievements of Zhejiang's Cultural Research Project*, he pointed out that for thousands of years, the people of Zhejiang developed and inherited a profound cultural tradition, and that cultural tradition was unique thanks to remarkable creative wisdom and power.[5] He further understood and studied Zhejiang's historical cultural traditions, deeply explored the historical origin of the Zhejiang Spirit and its role in driving the economic and social development of contemporary Zhejiang; he put forward a number of creative and systematic views, philosophies and strategic thoughts about the contemporary value of traditional culture and Zhejiang's work on inheriting and carrying forward its outstanding traditional culture.

3.2.1.1 The Power of Culture is Integrated into the Vitality, Creativity and Cohesion of the Nation

Comrade Xi Jinping's line of thought regarding outstanding traditional culture and its contemporary value is first based on the understanding of culture and cultural tradition. Tradition is inherited continually, culture is all-inclusive. Long-standing inheritance and rich connotations have made cultural tradition extensive and profound. Comrade Xi Jinping had a deep understanding in this regard. He said, "Many elements, levels and types have arisen within different cultures during the evolution of human cultures, thus cultures are diverse and complex; the Chinese culture is extensive and profound thanks to its internal diversity; the everlasting nature of Chinese culture depends upon the strong innovative impetus generated through interaction, deconstruction and integration among various elements, levels and types in content and structure during the process of change." Therefore, cultural tradition shapes and nurtures the people's life: "Culture offers norms, modes and an environment for the life of groups, culture plays the basic role in making social progress through inheritance, culture promotes or hinders economic development and even the development of the entire society; the power of culture has been deeply rooted in the vitality, creativity and cohesion of the nation."[6]

The endless source of power for the Chinese nation lies in Chinese culture. "The Chinese nation has a long history, it has undergone great vicissitudes, many

---

[5]Xi (2006), p. 317.
[6]Xi (2006), p. 294.

separations and reunions, invasions, but it is not split and has not vanished, it has always maintained a great vitality; the fundamental reason for this is that the Chinese nation has long-standing profound cultural connotations".[7] Such an outstanding traditional culture has fostered the social living environment for the Chinese people and built a homeland for the Chinese nation to make cultural improvements; "it assimilates the people living in this environment, and thus it becomes an enormous power for sustaining the society and the nation; the cultural tradition shared by the Chinese nation enables us to have a strong sense of identity and a strong sense of belonging to the Chinese civilization".[8]

3.2.1.2   Zhejiang has Made Great Contributions to Enriching and Developing Chinese National Culture

For Zhejiang, comrade Xi Jinping was dedicated to studying and analyzing Zhejiang's historical tradition, humanistic advantages and cultural gene, thus identifying the contemporary value.

He is very familiar with Zhejiang's historical development and humanistic advantages. He said, "Zhejiang is a land of cultural relics, one of the birthplaces of the Chinese civilization, it has a galaxy of cultural figures, a wealth of excellent cultural products, a variety of cultural forms, a long cultural tradition; they have made great contributions to enriching and developing Chinese national culture and has vigorously promoted Zhejiang's economic and social development."[9]

For Zhejiang's historical cultural gene, he conducted in-depth research to make a comprehensive summary: "One outstanding feature of Zhejiang's culture is that it has a strong economic pulse. As Qiantang had been prosperous since ancient times, many great thinkers in ancient Zhejiang advocated the line of thought of placing equal emphasis on both righteousness and benefits and valuing industry and commerce; this is unique in Chinese cultural history and it has also deeply influenced the mindsets and behavioral styles of the people of Zhejiang as well as the fact that it has become an important source of Zhejiang's thoughts and culture. Chen Liang, the representative figure of the Yongkang School during the Song Dynasty (960–1279) developed the line of thought that commerce builds on agriculture while agriculture develops through commerce; Ye Shi, the representative figure of the Yongjia School, stressed that commerce should be promoted to develop industry, strength should be pooled at the national level to support merchants and the circulation of currency, agriculture and commerce should complement each other and a separation of righteousness and benefits should be opposed. Huang Zongxi, a great thinker of the late Ming Dynasty, put forward, for the first time, the line of thought that both industry and commerce are equally important, and opposed the mindset of discriminating against commerce. Another feature of Zhejiang's culture is that it integrates the

---

[7] Xi (2006), p. 293.
[8] Xi (2006), p. 293.
[9] Xi (2006), p. 2937.

characteristics of diverse cultures, contains the strong points of both inland culture and marine culture, the quintessence of both the Wuyue culture and the Central Plains culture, it reflects the interaction between Chinese culture and Western culture; living in an environment with mountains and sea, the people of Zhejiang are influenced by a number of cultural factors, so they demonstrate the tenacity of mountains and the breadth of the sea; they work hard and tenaciously under the influence of the inland culture; they dare to blaze new trails and take risks thanks to the marine culture."[10]

3.2.1.3   Zhejiang's Regional Cultural Tradition has Given Birth to the Zhejiang Spirit of Advancing with the Times

With an analysis of Zhejiang's historical tradition, humanistic advantages and cultural gene, comrade Xi Jinping expressed penetrating views on the cultural deposits of the Zhejiang Spirit: "As shown by the long-time historical practice, in ancient China, Dayu tamed the floods in light of local conditions; Goujian endured hardships and bode time to accomplish ambitions; King Qian Hongchu defended the border for the people's contentment and happiness and promoted national reunification; Hu Ze served the people wholeheartedly; Yue Fei and Yu Qian repaid the country with supreme loyalty and clean hands; Fang Xiaoru and Zhang Cangshui were upright and plainspoken, and sacrificed themselves for their country; Shen Kuo was learned and delved into matters; Zhu Kezhen saved the country through science and sought truth throughout his life; Chen Liang and Ye Shi acquired and applied knowledge suited to dealing with national affairs; Huang Zongxi placed equal emphasis on both industry and commerce; Wang Chong and Wang Yangming developed critical thinking and self-consciousness; Gong Zizhen and Cai Yuanpei were open-minded; the time-honored pharmacy Hu Qing Yu Tang always refrains from practicing deception and keeps good faith; merchants in Ningbo and Huzhou were diligent and kind; all of these facts demonstrate Zhejiang's profound cultural deposits." In such an excellent fertile cultural soil, the distinctive Zhejiang Spirit has emerged and developed, "as a result, the Zhejiang Spirit presents the philosophy of putting the people first and valuing the people's well-being; the reason is because the people are realistic, pragmatic and self-conscious; the broad mind of being all-inclusive, entrepreneurial and innovative; the vision of maintaining coexistence and achieving harmony between people and nature; the character of maintaining loyalty and faith, giving considerations to both righteousness and benefits; a great vigor and integrity, an iron will and lofty aspirations".[11]

Zhejiang's regional cultural tradition creates the Zhejiang Spirit, while the Zhejiang Spirit has always led and supported the people of Zhejiang on the road to a beautiful homeland, "the Zhejiang Spirit is different in form and focus in different periods; however, the connotations arising out of the above philosophy, reasoning, broad mindedness, vision, character, vigor and aspirations are vibrant in Zhejiang's

---

[10] Xi (2006), p. 316.

[11] Xi (2005), p. 2.

history like the flowing water. They accompany the historical life of the people of Zhejiang, the realistic life and future creation of the people of Zhejiang."[12] "It brings vitality to Zhejiang, enhances cohesion and arouses creativity in Zhejiang; it fosters Zhejiang's competitiveness and stimulates the people of Zhejiang to advance unceasingly, outdo themselves and make improvements in different historical periods."[13]

3.2.1.4 The Outstanding Cultural Gene Boosts Zhejiang's Rapid Economic and Social Development

The outstanding cultural gene does not merely exist in historical tradition, it is also inherited by the contemporary people of Zhejiang from generation to generation; it has laid a unique foundation for the development of contemporary Zhejiang.

Comrade Xi Jinping highly recognized the Zhejiang Spirit, identified by the Party Committee of Zhejiang Province, characterized by ceaseless self-improvement, grittiness, great courage in innovation and pursuit of substantial results; he specially proceeded from the outstanding cultural gene in the regional historical tradition to explain the underlying reasons behind the development of contemporary Zhejiang. In his view, Zhejiang's rapid economic and social development since the reform and opening-up is attributable to the excellent cultural gene of the people of Zhejiang—a vivid demonstration of the Zhejiang Spirit in modern times: "The long-standing Zhejiang Spirit always flows in the blood of the people of Zhejiang and constitutes the cultural gene inherited from generation to generation, it can thrive even in the presence of little rain and dew, sunshine. The sunshine and dew from the great practice in building socialism with Chinese characteristics have fully aroused such a cultural gene of the people of Zhejiang; they have greatly promoted rapid economic development and become economic creativity; they have immensely boosted full social progress and become the tremendous social cohesion; they have greatly pushed forward the building of a culturally large province and become the core cultural competitiveness".[14]

3.2.1.5 The Outstanding Traditional Culture Contains the Wisdom for Improving the Quality and Capability of the Leading Cadres

Adopting the outstanding traditional culture to enhance the cultural quality and capability for working of the Party members and cadres is an important aspect which comrade Xi Jinping pondered for a long time, paid high attention to and expounded on on many occasions. He fully and systematically called upon, for the first time, the leading cadres to learn about Chinese traditional culture and took it as an important

---

[12]Xi (2005), p. 2.
[13]Xi (2006), p. 317.
[14]Xi (2005), p. 2.

means for strengthening the development of the leading cadres.[15] The author read the brief comments made by him in the characteristic column "Zhijiang Xinyu" on the front page of the *Zhejiang Daily* from February 25, 2003 to March 25, 2007; the author found that more than 60 out of the 232 brief comments were related to traditional culture, they presented an analysis of tradition, or discussions of roles, or an exposition of the views from sages and men of virtue in the past, or cited the points of view of others. About 30 of them involved the Party members and cadres.

The Analects of Confucius stressed, "If politicians govern a county under the rule of virtue, the people are willing to accept their governance; one should cultivate his or her moral character and improve his or her conduct through virtues before entering politics; the measures for governing a country lie in soliciting more opinions from the people; reading helps develop more virtues". By adducing the above quotations from *The Analects of Confucius*, the article "Reading More to Foster Political Virtues" calls for improving the intellectual and moral quality of the Party members and leading cadres and making them more aligned with the Party's tenet, and it requires them to handle political affairs with virtues, be aware of the harm that comes from greed, practice self-discipline, be honest and clean and govern for the people. The article "To Be an Official, Be Sure to Bear in Mind the People" lauds the thoughts of several people of virtue in the ancient times—Fan Zhongyan: plan and worry ahead of the people, enjoy the fruits after the people; Zheng Banqiao: although we are low-ranking officials, we carefully observe and address the people's needs and sufferings; Du Fu: how to build tens of thousands of houses to provide shelter for poor scholars and make them happy; Yu Qian: no longer live in seclusion and take pains to become officials again in order to make sure that the people have enough to eat and wear—and then stresses that one should not be an official if he/she does not keep in mind the people, the Party's cadres are the people's servants and must show care for the people and serve the people wholeheartedly. The article "Power Is a Sacred Thing" presents the ancient philosophy that the state power is "magic" and sacred, it cannot be used by the ordinary people, and then requires that the leading cadres at various levels must deal with power carefully, use it prudently, properly and better, behave well and prevent others from using power and the influence of the post to seek unlawful interests. As mentioned in the article "Removing the Impure from the Pure, Give Priority to Righteousness", Gu Yanwu, a thinker during the Qing Dynasty, held, "In order to make officials upright, emphasis should be first placed on castigating the bad and extolling the good"; Mencius, a thinker and politician of the Warring States Period (the 5th century B.C.–221 B.C.), stressed, "Neither riches nor honours can corrupt him; neither poverty nor humbleness can make him swerve from principle; and neither threats nor forces can subdue him"; subsequently, the article calls on the leading cadres to act in a upright way, set a good example, endeavor to foster a good social atmosphere of praising righteousness, eliminate evil influences, uphold non-corruption and combat corruption. The article "The Delight of Life Matters" quotes two stories from ancient books to suggest that misconduct and unhealthy behavior in life often degenerate a leading cadre, require the leading cadres

---

[15]Dong (2014).

at various levels to, under the current complicated social environment, improve their intellectual and moral quality, cultivate a healthy lifestyle, correctly choose personal hobbies, prudently deal with friends, behave well in life and always preserve the political nature of the Communist. The article "In Theoretical Study, One Should Reach Three Realms" cites three realms in study put forward by the famous scholar Wang Guowei that require the leading cadres to study hard, be good at thinking, emancipate their mind, keep pace with the times, and apply the acquired knowledge to achieve something.[16]

There are a large number of examples, involving many aspects: handling political affairs with virtues, putting the people first, impartially using power, not being corrupt, restraining selfishness and acting carefully, developing a sense of responsibility, studying and thinking hard and being realistic and pragmatic. There is a deep affection for the people, a tireless zeal for teaching others, methodical and patient guidance, a strong sense of responsibility for the Party and the people, and strict requirements for the leading cadres.

3.2.1.6   Fostering a Good Atmosphere in Which the Whole Society Protects Cultural Heritage

The outstanding traditional culture has immense historical value and contemporary value, so we must treasure and protect it. Comrade Xi Jinping placed great importance on protecting and inheriting cultural heritage and developed a deep line of thought in this regard. In his opinion, as modernization is promoted, cultural heritage may be destroyed; as the rate of urbanization increases, the cultural characteristics of cities may be overlooked and even stifled, causing cultural discontinuity. Thus, government departments should correctly handle the relationship between the protection of cultural heritage and economic and social development, between the protection and inheritance of cultural heritage and its management and utilization. Zhejiang enjoys priceless historical cultural resources, and it is also a large province of tourism and home to a large number of historical cultural scenic spots and projects. How to properly deal with their relationship is an issue which should be addressed by Zhejiang as it seeks to develop the tourism industry. Comrade Xi Jinping resolutely stressed that cultural heritage should be protected by mainly taking it as a cause and then utilized from an industrial perspective, emphasis should be mainly placed on protection and rescue, and more considerations should be given to spending money rather than making money. "It is necessary to correctly handle the relationship between the protection of cultural relics and the development of tourism, put protection first and make it precede development, prohibit destructive development."[17] With regard to the relationship between the building of a new socialist countryside and the preservation of the original appearance of ancient villages, he also put forward the principle of putting protection first, "We should not turn the building of a new socialist

---

[16]Xi (2007).
[17]Xi (2006), p. 325.

countryside into the construction of new villages, not completely remove the historical buildings with cultural value and local characteristics during construction. Some new rural areas are the ancient villages whose original appearance needs to be preserved; for instance, Bagua Village in Lanxi should be dealt with by preserving its original appearance to embody its historical beauty and prevent its destruction".[18]

Protecting cultural heritage is not only the government's responsibility but it is also related to everyone. "Only when everyone shows care for and loves the wealth left to us by our predecessors can the spirit, unique aesthetic taste and distinctive traditional quality of our nation be inherited." In Xi Jinping's view, it is necessary to advocate the trend of treasuring cultural heritage in the whole society and foster a good atmosphere of jointly protecting cultural heritage, "thus becoming more familiar with Chinese history, inheriting Chinese civilization, carrying forward Chinese culture and arousing a sense of national pride and patriotic enthusiasm".[19]

Comrade Xi Jinping expounded many views on the value of the outstanding traditional culture in cultural diversity, in the education of traditional culture, in the intellectual and moral education of juveniles. Not all of these views are presented here due to a limitation of space. Overall, with an in-depth analysis of Zhejiang's historical tradition and its contemporary value, comrade Xi Jinping drew this conclusion: "Zhejiang's long-standing, profound and rich cultural tradition is the valuable wealth given to us by history and also an abundant resource and inexhaustible impetus for us to seek future development".[20]

The above views and unique insights of comrade Xi Jinping's on the inheritance and promotion of relevant outstanding traditional culture reflect his sincere feelings about the outstanding Chinese traditional culture; they represent systematic reorganization and an in-depth analysis of Zhejiang's historical tradition and contemporary value; they reflect his great vision for promoting Zhejiang's economic and social development under the new situation. In particular, he proceeded from analyzing regional cultural tradition to deeply explore the unique conditions in Zhejiang, the cultural gene and historical foundation behind Zhejiang's contemporary achievements, and the resulting distinctive developmental path, deepen the people's understanding of the potential power and contemporary value of their outstanding traditional culture, and identify the methods and routes for understanding, studying, inheriting and carrying forward that culture.

Since the 18th National Congress of the Communist Party of China, comrade Xi Jinping has delivered a series of important speeches on the inheritance and promotion of the outstanding traditional culture, deeply expounding the position and role of that culture in realizing the Chinese dream of the great rejuvenation of the Chinese nation. The line of thought developed and the theoretical achievements made by him when he worked in Zhejiang have elevated the work on the inheritance and promotion of Zhejiang's outstanding traditional culture to a new realm and they have also offered extensive experience for the Party to currently identify the cultural spirit, from the

---

[18] Xi (2006), p. 324.
[19] Xi (2006), p. 325.
[20] Xi (2006), p. 317.

outstanding Chinese traditional culture, of "spanning time and space, transcending the national boundaries, keeping eternal charm and presenting contemporary value", to understand and explain the historical logic that the socialist road with Chinese characteristics is rooted in the fertile soil of the Chinese culture, which reflects the Chinese people's will, and adapts to the needs of China and the times for achieving development and making progress, and to achieve the great rejuvenation of the Chinese nation.

3.2.2 The Traditional Cultural Gene in the Zhejiang Spirit of Advancing with the Times

In 2005, in response to the new challenges of globalization, the new practice in Zhejiang's development and the new expectations of the Central Committee of the Communist Party of China for Zhejiang's state of staying ahead, the Party Committee of Zhejiang Province studied the "Zhejiang Spirit of Advancing with the Times" on the basis of "the Zhejiang Spirit of ceaseless self-improvement, grittiness, great courage in innovation and pursuit of substantial results" in order to ensure that the people of Zhejiang have modern mindsets, a value orientation, a psychological state, social moral standards in an unremitting pursuit of building a moderately prosperous society in all respects and accelerating socialist modernization. Comrade Xi Jinping attached great importance to this study, and stressed, "The Zhejiang Spirit should be studied from the perspectives of Zhejiang's historical inheritance, socialist cultural and ethical development and the role of comprehensive cultural strength". According to the requirement of the Party Committee of Zhejiang Province for deeply studying the Zhejiang Phenomenon, substantiating and improving the Zhejiang Experience and enriching and developing the Zhejiang Spirit, the Department of Publicity under the Party Committee of Zhejiang Province, in conjunction with the General Office of the Party Committee of Zhejiang Province, the Zhejiang Academy of Social Sciences, the Zhejiang Federation of Humanities and Social Sciences Circles, and the Zhejiang Daily Press Group, carried out a study on the subject and an activity of soliciting articles involving the Zhejiang Spirit of Advancing with the Times, and more than 100 papers were received.

All-round examination of Zhejiang's cultural tradition was an important part of this study. Zhejiang's scholars intensively conducted studies and held discussions, they expressed a number of views from the perspectives of eastern Zhejiang's academic spirit, industrial and commercial culture, marine culture, Yue culture, eminent persons in history, folk culture and regional cultures in Zhejiang, they considered them as the traditional foundation and cultural deposits in order to identify "The Zhejiang Spirit of Advancing with the Times" which features a pursuit of truth, pragmatism, integrity and harmony, open-mindedness and determination to become stronger. In early 2006, the Party Committee of Zhejiang Province officially announced "The Zhejiang Spirit of Advancing with the Times" in the new period. In the same year, comrade Xi Jinping published a signed article "The Zhejiang Spirit of Advancing with the Times", recognizing the Zhejiang Spirit of ceaseless self-improvement, grittiness, great courage in innovation and pursuit of substantial results and deeply expounding "The Zhejiang Spirit of Advancing with the Times" which features "pursuit of truth, pragmatism, integrity and harmony, open-mindedness and determination to become stronger".

The Party Committee of Zhejiang Province has keenly understood the role of Zhejiang's culture in Zhejiang's economic development. "As there is increasing economic and cultural integration, when Zhejiang's economy is studied, it is essential to study Zhejiang's culture; otherwise, it is impossible to really understand Zhejiang's economy."[21] Therefore, the corresponding study should place more emphasis on the industrial and commercial spirit in Zhejiang's historical tradition; the views, within the Eastern Zhejiang School, that equal emphasis should be placed on both righteousness and benefit, on both industry and commerce, have become the main resources of thought for identifying the Zhejiang Spirit. According to relevant studies, such an academic thought is exactly the main cultural gene giving birth to the Zhejiang Spirit which features ceaseless self-improvement, grittiness, great courage in innovation and pursuit of substantial results,[22] rendering the people of Zhejiang highly capable of adapting to and developing the market economy, "with self-improvement and an indomitable will, the people of Zhejiang have blazed new trails in a pragmatic way to survive great vicissitudes within the market economy and they have nurtured the Zhejiang Spirit with distinctive characteristics of the times and a broad base among the masses, and this fully demonstrates the good look of the more than 40 million people of Zhejiang".[23]

However, after explaining the factors for driving economic development in a certain period of time, Zhejiang needs to more scientifically and rationally analyze and tap Zhejiang's historical tradition so as to obtain the impetus for stimulating Zhejiang to get better and go further. In Zhejiang's historical tradition, besides the Eastern Zhejiang School and the great skills in seeking substantial results in business and trade, there are more connotations and factors. With regard to academic thought, there are Shen Kuo, who was rated as "the coordinate in the history of Chinese

---

[21] See *The Decision of the Party Committee of Zhejiang Province on Deeply Studying and Implementing Comrade Jiang Zemin's Important Thought of Three Represents*, adopted during the 4th Plenary (Enlarged) Session of the 10th Party Committee of Zhejiang Province in July, 2000.

[22] The article entitled "Cultural Tradition and the Zhejiang Spirit", written by Lan Weiqing and other scholars, identifies five traditional factors giving birth to the Zhejiang Spirit—"the cultural tradition of valuing both industry and commerce gives birth to the awareness of doing business", "the value outlook on placing equal emphasis on righteousness and benefits gives birth to the down-to-earth character", "the interaction among diverse cultures shapes the awareness of taking pioneering and innovative actions", "an inherent shortage of resource conditions brings forth the enterprising spirit", and "the industrial tradition of developing diversified workmanship fosters intelligence and wisdom", see *The Zhejiang Spirit of Advancing with the Times*, Zhejiang People's Publishing House, 2005, pp. 3–11.

[23] See *The Decision of the Party Committee of Zhejiang Province on Deeply Studying and Implementing Comrade Jiang Zemin's Important Thought of Three Represents*, adopted during the 4th Plenary (Enlarged) Session of the 10th Party Committee of Zhejiang Province in July, 2000.

science and technology" and "the milestone in the history of Chinese science and technology" by British science and technology historian Joseph Needham, Wang Shixing, the founder of human geography in China, Gong Zizhen, an enlightenment thinker of modern times, Zhang Taiyan, a thinker, revolutionist, master of Chinese culture of the late Qing Dynasty and the early Republic of China and Cai Yuanpei, a revolutionist, educator, politician and a democratic progressive. Regarding regional folk customs, there are the temperate and mild style developed in the atmosphere of poem, calligraphy and painting in Huzhou and Jiaxing, the delicacy and elegance from the West Lake in Hangzhou, a pursuit of virtues and goodwill under the influence of the Nankong Culture in Quzhou and the emphasis on learning and teaching, part-time learning and part-time farm work in Jinhua. There are many other examples which cannot be elaborated on here. The trees of thought are luxuriant, the flowers of wisdom bloom in profusion. Therefore, Zhejiang can create brilliant achievements and display a fine historical tradition for thousands of years.

The article entitled "Vigorously Carrying Forward and Cultivating the Zhejiang Spirit of Advancing with the Times" presents seven characteristics of Zhejiang's traditional culture—which are the philosophy of putting the people first and valuing the people's well-being, the reason of being realistic, pragmatic and self-conscious, the broad mind of being all-inclusive, entrepreneurial and innovative, the vision of maintaining coexistence and achieving harmony between people and nature, the character of maintaining one's loyalty and faith, giving considerations to both righteousness and benefits, great vigor, integrity and an iron will and lofty aspirations[24]—and takes them as the historical foundation and traditional gene for "The Zhejiang Spirit of Advancing with the Times" which features "a pursuit of truth, pragmatism, integrity and harmony, open-mindedness and a determination to become stronger". Compared with the study in 2000, this summary more objectively, comprehensively and rationally captures the traditional scene of the Zhejiang area, including eastern Zhejiang and western Zhejiang, so it is more convincing.

It should be noted that in the article entitled "The Zhejiang Spirit of Advancing with the Times", comrade Xi Jinping stressed, "Zhejiang's unique geographical environment, production mode, lifestyle, many population migrations and cultural integrations throughout history have brought about the cultural characteristics of a farming civilization and a maritime civilization of the people of Zhejiang, their style of being all-inclusive and striving to become stronger and their character of stressing great virtues, culture, entrepreneurship and innovation."[25] "Stressing great virtues and culture" very accurately adds an important cultural gene, which should be possessed and comes from tradition, to the Zhejiang Spirit. In "the shared values of the contemporary people of Zhejiang "identified in 2012, "advocating learning and upholding goodwill" which expresses "stressing great virtues and culture" is recognized.

---

[24]The Department of Publicity under the Party Committee of Zhejiang Province (2005), pp. 11–16.

[25]The Department of Publicity under the Party Committee of Zhejiang Province (2005), p. 1.

"The Zhejiang Spirit of Advancing with the Times" is not only the exploration and innovation made by Zhejiang for cultural guidance and intellectual impetus under the new situation, but it is also the reexamination and evaluation of Zhejiang's historical tradition and outstanding cultural gene.

3.2.3 Providing Theoretical Support Through Reality-Focused Traditional Cultural Research

Zhejiang is hailed as the land of literature, and enjoys a solid historical literary foundation. In Zhejiang, there are more than 2,000 types of literature which date back to the Eastern Han Dynasty (25–220), covering 2,000 years. In Zhejiang, the learning style of valuing historical research, acquiring and applying knowledge suited to deal with national affairs has always been prevalent. The view of Zhang Xuecheng, a historian of the Qing dynasty, that all of the six ancient classics are historical, records has exerted a far-reaching impact. The famous scholar, Gong Zizhen, more directly elucidated the important relationship between history and national destiny: If someone hopes to understand the general principles which govern the world, it is essential to first gain insight into history.[26] In 1939, Mei Guangdi, the representative figure of the Xueheng School, was appointed dean of the School of Humanities, National Chekiang University by Zhu Kezhen; later, a large number of members of the Xueheng School joined the National Chekiang University. The Xueheng School believed that the quintessence of Chinese traditional culture had an eternal value and was the cornerstone for the national culture. They also proposed improving the old system and achieving a combination of Chinese and Western elements. With the support from the President of the National Chekiang University, Zhu Kezhen, with the National Chekiang University as the center, the Xueheng School brought together more than 100 personages to carry forward the spirit of seeking truth and to delve into traditional culture; as a result, they expanded the humanistic, academic and cultural influence of the National Chekiang University across the country, and with the status of the National Chekiang University in Zhejiang, they exerted a profound impact on the academic atmosphere in which Zhejiang's humanities and social science circle gave great importance to traditional cultural research.

The project on cultural research, put forward by Zhejiang in 2005, is currently one of the largest local cultural research projects in China. Three segments—"special research on Zhejiang's historical culture", "research on Zhejiang's celebrities", "reorganization of Zhejiang's historical documents"—are related to traditional cultural research; these segments cover multiple series of research, including "special history of Zhejiang's historical culture", "collections of Zhejiang's literature", "Zhejiang's historical and cultural celebrities", "research series involving the history of the Southern Song Dynasty", "research on Zhejiang's regional culture", "series

---

[26]Gong Zizhen, Demystifying Ancient History II, see *Ding'an Complete Works* (Vol. 17), Four Essential Classics.

research on Liangzhu culture", "research on the history of the development of the Qiantang River basin", "series of research projects on economic and social changes in Zhejiang's ancient towns and villages" and "a series of research projects involving Zhejiang's business culture". The cultural research project has produced strong demonstration effects. The cities (even counties) in Zhejiang have accordingly carried out relevant work to tap and study local historical culture; Wenzhou, Ningbo, Jinhua and Yiwu have reorganized and published local historical documents.

Zhejiang's scholars have conducted unremitting studies of local historical culture; in particular, multiple projects of special research conducted since the initiation of the cultural research project present a relatively comprehensive and systematic exploration of Zhejiang's cultural tradition, a vertical context in its key fields and internal structure, they also present the profound cultural deposits in Zhejiang and Zhejiang's historical resources which are available for being inherited in the contemporary era.

In recent years, Zhejiang's scholars have actively provided excellent traditional cultural resources to a number of cultural construction projects launched at the governmental and non-governmental levels, including "the beautiful countryside", rural cultural auditoriums, "the Most Beautiful Phenomenon in Zhejiang", cultural industry parks, characteristic cultural towns, former residences of celebrities and art galleries; they have carried out the transformation and design of ideas, as well as feasibility analysis and evaluation. They have played an active role in carrying out academic research and promoting the practical work in Zhejiang's building of the contemporary system of values with a socialist core, public cultural service system, cultural industry system and the system for the inheritance of outstanding traditional culture.

3.3 Careful and Consistent Layout of Macro Planning

Since the Party Committee of Zhejiang Province implemented the "Eight-Eight Strategies" in 2003, Zhejiang's inheritance and promotion of outstanding traditional culture has entered a new period of development. In cultural work, the Party Committee and the People's Government of Zhejiang Province have always focused on "inheriting outstanding culture and carrying forward the Zhejiang Spirit" in the strategic line of thought, macro layout and concrete measures, they have led the people across the province to make comprehensive, profound, extensive, vivid and fruitful innovative experiments and practical efforts in many fields in the province, giving rise to Zhejiang's characteristics.

3.3.1 Conducting Systematic Planning, Making All-Round Arrangements, Developing the Major Policies and Overall Framework for Inheriting and Carrying Forward the Outstanding Traditional Culture

"Further leveraging Zhejiang's humanistic advantage, actively rejuvenating the province through science, technology and talents, stepping up efforts to turn Zhejiang into a culturally large province" is a priority in the "Eight-Eight Strategies". The outstanding traditional Chinese culture and Zhejiang's regional historical tradition are the important foundation and kernel for Zhejiang's humanistic advantage, and they have an important position and roles in accelerating the building of a culturally large province.

In the *Decision of the Party Committee of Zhejiang Province on Accelerating the Building of a Culturally Large Province* ("the Decision"), a programmatic document which was issued in 2005 and identified the direction and path for Zhejiang's cultural development during the period 2005–2020, the inheritance and promotion of the outstanding traditional culture is fully valued and embodied in many fields and aspects, and the overall framework and path for the inheritance and promotion of the outstanding traditional culture have generally been put in place.

Enhancing the cohesion of the advanced culture is the important point of action for speeding up the building of a culturally large province. As an important bit of content, the Decision called for "carrying forward Zhejiang's outstanding historical cultural tradition, actively pushing forward cultural innovation, vigorously developing the advanced culture, supporting the healthy and beneficial culture, transforming the backward culture, resolutely opposing the decadent culture", "energetically carrying forward the patriotism-focused national spirit and the reform and innovation-focused spirit of the times, upholding and developing the Zhejiang Spirit of 'ceaseless self-improvement, grittiness, great courage in innovation and pursuit of substantial results', thus advancing with the times to advocate and carry forward the spirit which features 'the pursuit of truth, pragmatism, integrity and harmony, open-mindedness and determination to become stronger', providing strong cultural impetus for more rapidly building a moderately prosperous society in all respects and for basically achieving modernization in advance".

With regard to the project for the improvement of cultural quality, the Decision called for "strengthening the building of bases for education towards patriotism, developing red tourism, giving full scope to the important roles of revolutionary memorials, historical and cultural sites, museums and memorial halls". Regarding the project on excellent cultural products, the Decision called for supporting a number of cultural and artistic achievements which carry forward Zhejiang's outstanding traditional culture and are of significance to inheritance and innovation. With respect to the cultural research project, the Decision called for conducting special research on Zhejiang's historical culture, research on Zhejiang's celebrities, the reorganization of Zhejiang's historical documents, and a series of research projects on Zhejiang's regional historical culture. Regarding the cultural protection project, the Decision arranged a series of tasks on the protection and utilization of historical cultural heritage, called for making the rich historical cultural heritage really become important and unique valuable resources for building a culturally large province. Intensifying the reform of the cultural system is the necessary prerequisite and important guarantee for speeding up the building of a culturally large province. The Decision identified the correct direction of reform as follows: actively leveraging the advantages of traditional culture, national culture, revolutionary culture and regional culture, and making contributions to enhancing the competitiveness and influence of the Chinese culture.

Overall, the Decision stressed the inheritance and promotion of the outstanding traditional culture from the perspective of proving cultural impetus for more rapidly building a moderately prosperous society in all respects and basically achieving modernization in advance, and called for building a broad platform for fully inheriting and carrying forward the outstanding traditional culture in Zhejiang.

3.3.2 Carrying Through One Blueprint

As shown by the documents issued by the Party Committee and the People's Government of Zhejiang Province since the "Eight-Eight Strategies" was put forward in 2003 and the *Decision of the Party Committee of Zhejiang Province on Accelerating the Building of a Culturally Large Province* was adopted in 2005—including such documents as the *Plan of Zhejiang Province for Promoting Vigorous Cultural Development and Great Cultural Prosperity (2008–2012)* in 2008, the *Decision of the Party Committee of Zhejiang Province on Earnestly Carrying Out the Guiding Principles Adopted during the 6th Plenary Session of the 17th Central Committee of the Communist Party of China and Vigorously Promoting the Building of a Culturally Strong Province* in 2011, the *Decision of the Party Committee of Zhejiang Province on Building a Beautiful Zhejiang and Creating a Good Life* in 2014, the *Recommendations of the Party Committee of Zhejiang Province for the 12th Five-Year Plan of Zhejiang Province for National Economic and Social Development*, and the *12th Five-Year Plan of Zhejiang Province for Cultural Development*, since the "Eight-Eight Strategies" was put forward, Zhejiang has always carried through one blueprint in inheriting and carrying forward the outstanding traditional culture, and has made continuous experiments and enriched its practice in light of the times, the characteristics of the stages of Zhejiang's economic and social development and the actual needs of Zhejiang's cultural development.

3.3.2.1   Upholding and Carrying Forward the Chinese Culture is an Important Basic Principle for Promoting Vigorous Cultural Development and Great Cultural Prosperity

In the *Plan of Zhejiang Province for Promoting Vigorous Cultural Development and Great Cultural Prosperity (2008–2012)* ("the Plan") adopted by the Party Committee of Zhejiang Province in 2008, the inheritance and promotion of the outstanding traditional culture is further strengthened, "upholding and carrying forward the Chinese culture" is listed separately and becomes, together with "upholding the orientation of the advanced culture", "adhering to the people-oriented principle" and "putting social benefits first", one of the six basic principles in the Plan. The Plan also stressed these two aspects: "strengthening education involving the outstanding traditional culture" and "continuously enhancing the international influence of the Chinese culture".

On promoting the building of the system of values with a socialist core, the Plan called for actively carrying forward the Zhejiang Spirit, strengthening education on patriotism, taking the opportunities from major commemoration days, national traditional festivals, important festival activities and great events to conduct a variety of activities involving publicity for and education on patriotism as well as carrying out the development plan of Zhejiang Province for red tourism, giving full scope to the important roles of revolutionary memorials, historical and cultural sites, museums and memorial halls. The cultural research project has been expanded by supporting a number of research programs which are of great innovative significance, play an important role in carrying forward and inheriting national culture and exert an important impact on economic and social development.

With regard to public cultural services, the Plan called for thoroughly carrying out the cultural protection project, strengthening the protection and utilization of historical relics. The protection and inheritance of intangible cultural heritage is valued and stressed; promoting the "active" inheritance of intangible cultural heritage becomes a new bright spot.

Regarding the promotion of the development of the cultural industry, the utilization of traditional resources is mainly embodied in the cultural service industry for tourism; the Plan proceeded from the integrative development of the outstanding historical cultural resources and the tourism industry to call for leveraging Zhejiang's advantages of its tourism resources, building classic scenic spots for red tourism, developing excellent and distinctive cultural tourism blocks covering folk culture, ancient water towns, ecological culture, marine culture and the exotic style of She minority, carving out a number of excellent tourist itineraries and further promoting brands of cultural tourism at home and abroad.

3.3.2.2   Attaching Greater Importance to Leveraging the Contemporary Value of the Outstanding Traditional Culture

Given the international background of the expansion of world multipolarization, economic globalization and increasing cultural diversity, the *12th Five-Year Plan of Zhejiang Province for Cultural Development*, unveiled in August, 2011, further took "inheriting and carrying out the outstanding national culture, drawing upon the outstanding cultural achievements from various countries all over the world" as one of the basic principles specified in the Plan.

Regarding specific plans, "more rapidly transforming the manner of cultural development " and "strengthening cultural exchanges and cultural trade, stimulating Zhejiang's culture to go global" are two bright spots for planning the inheritance and promotion of the outstanding traditional culture. The former calls for "shifting from emphasis on the protection of cultural heritage to equal emphasis on both protection and utilization", which suggests the government's attention to fully leveraging the contemporary value of the outstanding traditional culture. The latter calls for strengthening research on the international cultural consumer market, and carefully cultivating a number of cultural brand enterprises and cultural brand products with international competitive advantages, which shows the attitude towards actively adopting the outstanding traditional culture to enhance Zhejiang's international cultural competitiveness.

3.3.2.3 The Outstanding Local Traditional Culture is an Important Part of the Internal Support for Building a Culturally Strong Province

The *Decision of the Party Committee of Zhejiang Province on Earnestly Carrying Out the Guiding Principles Adopted during the 6th Plenary Session of the 17th Central Committee of the Communist Party of China and Vigorously Promoting the Building of a Culturally Strong Province* ("the *Decision on Promoting the Building of a Culturally Strong Province*") in 2011 called for proceeding from a higher level, taking a wider perspective and making greater efforts to build Zhejiang into a culturally strong province with a lofty humanistic spirit, cultural prosperity, a developed cultural industry, a strong cultural atmosphere and a distinctive cultural image.

In coordination with the requirement of proceeding from a higher level, taking a wider perspective and making greater efforts, the attention from the *Decision on Promoting the Building of a Culturally Strong Province* to the outstanding traditional culture is embodied in the "realistic foundation and favorable conditions", "overall line of thought", "three main systems" and "eight projects". In the text, the word "traditional" relating to traditional culture appeared nine times and the word "historical" relating to traditional culture appeared four times; such a high frequency of appearance shows that Zhejiang has deepened its understanding of the contemporary value of the outstanding traditional culture and the important position of the outstanding traditional culture in the overall strategy for the building of a culturally strong province; this relies, to a certain extent, on tapping, converting and utilizing local profound traditional culture and abundant historical resources.

3.3.2.4   The Outstanding Traditional Culture is not Only a Resource, but also the Basic Mode and Important Means for Cultural Governance

The *Decision on Building a Beautiful Zhejiang and Creating a Good Life* in 2014 combined the inheritance and promotion of the outstanding traditional culture with ecological development and called for tapping the ecological philosophy and ecological thoughts in Zhejiang's traditional culture. Concrete measures are very novel: First, piloting the building of small ecological humanistic cities, proceeding from the characteristics of natural resources and humanistic characteristics to build a number of small towns with the exotic scenery south of the Yangtze River, demonstrating the unique charm of the area south of the Yangtze River. Second, actively building green towns and ecological demonstration villages, carefully building a number of residential dwellings in the Zhejiang style. Third, giving importance to inheriting native memories, making mountains and waters visible to the people, and ensuring that the native memories are retained.

As summarized, the layout of the plan and the line of thought regarding the decision-making developed by the Party Committee and the People's Government of Zhejiang Province for carrying forward and inheriting the outstanding traditional culture are governed by the following principles.

The first principle is fully understanding the adoption of scientific theory in order to lead cultural development, always giving consideration to China's reality. "Culture is a type of inheritance, if China's national conditions are not considered, there will be no soil for the existence of culture, it will be like a tree without roots and water without sources; therefore, considering China's reality is the requirement and vitality for being a characteristic of cultural development."[27]

The second principle regards always upholding the patriotism-focused national spirit and the spirit of the times that is focused on reform and opening-up, taking the building of the system of values with a socialist core as the fundamental task, grasping and improving the orientation of the path to take to obtain the contemporary inheritance of the outstanding traditional culture and its cultural quality, guiding the correct direction for inheriting and carrying forward the outstanding traditional culture for the people.

The third principle is that of paying attention to protecting, tapping and utilizing the outstanding traditional culture, especially the social needs in contemporary Zhejiang, converting, utilizing and innovatively developing multiple types of values of historical resources, so as to reflect the regional characteristics of traditional culture and the characteristics of the times.

---

[27]The Research Group of the Department of Publicity under the Party Committee of Zhejiang Province, Consciously Adopting the Scientific Theory to Lead Cultural Development, Promoting the Vigorous Development and Great Prosperity of the Socialist Culture, in: *Annual Report on Zhejiang's Development 2008 (Culture Volume)*, Hangzhou Publishing House, 2008, p. 21.

The fourth principle is fully respecting the status of the people as the main players and their pioneering spirit, preserving the folk soil for cultural inheritance, ensuring the participation of all the people, protecting the people's enthusiasm, and promoting innovation in cultural tradition in an "active" way in daily life.

3.4 The Practice of Pragmatic and Distinctive Experiments and Innovations

Only when the outstanding traditional culture enters the present life can it really be inherited in a dynamic way. On March 27, 2006, during the meeting of the commemoration of the 100th anniversary of the emergence of China's Shaoxing Opera, comrade Xi Jinping pointed out, "The course of the centenary development of China's Shaoxing Opera proves that China's Shaoxing Opera can go beyond regional and language limitations to create one-century brilliance because of its advancing with the times, blazing new trails, showing care for the people's well-being and learning and drawing upon the artistic elements of various outstanding cultures."[28] This reveals the essence of the innovative development of the traditional Shaoxing Opera and encapsulates the achievements made by Zhejiang through inheritance and promotion of the outstanding traditional culture. In more than 10 years, the people of Zhejiang considered the reality seriously, leveraged the rich endowment of historical resources and relied on full synergy among the Party, the government and the folk society, derived the Zhejiang Spirit of advancing with the times from local historical cultural tradition, and promoted extensive and vivid innovative practice to provide the strong power of the outstanding cultural tradition for exploring the developmental path with Zhejiang's characteristics.

3.4.1 Making the Excellent Historical Cultural Resources "Active"

The 20th century was a period during which Chinese cultural tradition and traditional cultural resources were subject to great impact and damage. This was mainly because wars caused damage and the eastward shift of Western style led to changes of the mindset in the first 50 years of the 20th century. In the later 50 years, first, political movements, including the Cultural Revolution and the elimination of the four stereotypes, occurred; second, after the reform and opening-up began, the market economy brought about the changes in the social system and structure, cultural concept and forms and rapid urbanization. As reported, in the past ten years, 900,000

---

[28] Xi (2006), p. 35.

natural villages disappeared in China.[29] That disappearance resulted from structural changes in the primary-level rural society on which the survival of traditional culture was based.

On December 30, 2013, in the 12th collective learning meeting of the Political Bureau of the Central Committee of the Communist Party of China, the General Secretary Xi Jinping pointed out, "It is necessary to systematically tap the traditional cultural resources, activate the cultural relics collected at the forbidden places, the heritages in the vast land and the words in the ancient books." Among Zhejiang's available historical resources, there are many excellent unique resources which have the value and role of contemporary inheritance, and they are regarded as the profound capital for building Zhejiang into a culturally strong province.

3.4.1.1   Cultural Heritage Resources

Zhejiang enjoys abundant cultural heritage resources and has stayed ahead nationwide in the protection of those resources.[30] In Zhejiang, there are 7 national-level famous historical cities including Hangzhou and Ningbo, 16 famous Chinese historical and cultural towns including Wuzhen, Nanxun and An'chang, 14 famous Chinese historical and cultural villages including Yuyuan, Guodong and Xinye, 231 key cultural relics sites under the protection of the State including the Shangshan Ruins and the Tianyi Pavilion, ranking Zhejiang no. 5 nationwide; the Liangzhu Ancient City Archaeology Project was granted the Field Archaeology (2009–2010) First Prize by the National Cultural Heritage Administration. In 2013, the first joint underwater law enforcement involving cultural heritage was conducted within the sea areas under the jurisdiction of Zhejiang Province, which was the first one in China. The Zhejiang Museum of National History, the China National Silk Museum and the Ningbo Museum have been rated as national first-level museums by the National Cultural Heritage Administration.

Based on protection, the development and utilization of cultural heritage has been continuously promoted. Since all of the museums in Hangzhou were open to the public for free in 2003, the Zhejiang Provincial Museum, the China National Silk Museum and more than 20 municipal and county-level museums across the province have been open for free, keeping Zhejiang ahead nationwide in the number of audiences annually received by museums. The cultural relic circle of the province has interactively conducted a series of activities called the Cultural Heritage Day since 2006, during which all of the displayed and exhibited items in the state-owned museums across the province were open to the public for free, fostering a good social atmosphere for the protection of cultural heritage. Over the years, 12 national

---

[29]Feng Jicai, Nearly 100 Villages Disappear in China Each Day, http://www.chinanews.com/cul/2012/10-21/4263582.shtml.

[30]For Zhejiang's work on the protection and utilization of intangible cultural heritage, see Sect. 8.1 in Chap. 8 "Folk Culture: Cultural Belongingness and the Source of Impetus for Social Cohesion" in this volume; relevant content is not repeated here.

bases for the demonstration of education on patriotism, including the Zhenhai Coast Defence Site and the Nanhu Revolutionary Memorial Hall, were built. A provincial network of educational bases teaching patriotism with the national and provincial bases as the backbone and the municipal and county-level bases as the foundation has preliminarily taken shape, providing the front guarantee for promoting the building of the system of values with a socialist core. Zhejiang has built the first batch of 8 provincial parks of archaeological sites and 19 national key scenic spots with traditional culture as the element of the human landscape. Among 78 cultural scenic spots above the level of Grade 3A scenic spots across the province recorded in the *12th Five-Year Plan for the Development of Zhejiang's Tourism*, more than 70 scenic spots focus on traditional culture as a resource or a landscape. Eleven museum displays and exhibitions, including "Baiyue Area Long Song—Zhejiang's Historical and Cultural Display" in the Zhejiang Provincial Museum, have been granted the National Top 10 Excellent Museum Exhibits Award, ranking Zhejiang no. 1 nationwide.

3.4.1.2 Humanistic Resources of Mountains and Rivers

On August 24, 2005, in the special column "Zhijiang Xinyu" in the *Zhejiang Daily*, comrade Xi Jinping pointed out, "We pursue harmony between people and nature, between the economy and the society, in other words, we need clean, clear waters and lush mountains, and the 'gold and silver mountain'."[31] As Zhejiang's clean, clear waters and lush mountains become the "gold and silver mountain", the excellent natural environment is suitable for the people to live in, the ecological economy is developed to deliver economic benefits, and there is a rich historical and humanistic connotation.

Zhejiang is situated in the region of mountains and rivers south of the Yangtze River and has a large number of mountains and rivers. There are Tianmu Mountain, Mount Mogan, Siming Mountain, the Yandang Mountains, Mount Putuo, West Lake, South Lake, the Beijing-Hangzhou Grand Canal, the Qiantang River, the Fuchun River and the Nanxi River; they are grotesque, picturesque, refreshing and dreamy, they fascinate countless men of letters who write poetry and paint pictures about them; they are a repository of inexhaustible cultural resources. For the Chinese people, mountains and rivers bring inspirations, a higher aesthetic realm, a cultural implication and a cultural spirit, and the mountains and rivers south of the Yangtze River and in Zhejiang are typical representatives of all mountains and rivers, and they become the Chinese cultural symbols with the most classic significance.

Abundant mountain, river and human resources have been fully utilized in Zhejiang's contemporary cultural development. There are Su Shi, Bai Juyi, Yang Mengying, Ruan Yuan and three causeways and one pier in the West Lake in Hangzhou, the father of scenic poetry, Xie Lingyun, mountain and river cultural tourism along the Nanxi River, the development of Lake Jianhu, the Yanxi River, Lake Wozhou, Tianlao Mountain, Tiantai Mountain, and the Tang Poetry Road in

---

[31]Xi (2007).

eastern Zhejiang; moreover, there is the misty rain and the Red Boat spirit in Lake Nanhu in Jiaxing, the anti-Japanese base area and red tourism at Siming Mountain; all of these are examples of folk culture harmoniously existing among natural mountains and rivers. All of them show the close connection between Zhejiang's mountains and rivers and virtues, wise thoughts, wisdom, sentiment, nostalgia and the homeland, and they are embodied in contemporary cultural development. The *Dwelling in the Fuchun Mountains* painted by Huang Gongwang has brought creative inspiration to artists; it has also promoted a cultural exchange by means of a joint exhibition across the Taiwan Straits. On June 24, 2011, the West Lake Cultural Landscape of Hangzhou was included in the World Heritage List. On June 22, 2014, the Grand Canal of China was successfully included in the World Heritage List through application; as the southernmost point of the Beijing-Hangzhou Grand Canal and the starting point of the East Zhejiang Canal, Hangzhou is an important node of the Grand Canal of China; Hangzhou is at the forefront among the cities across the country in the number of points and sections covered by heritage application. These world cultural heritages demonstrate the fine quality and worldwide influence of Zhejiang's humanistic resources of mountains and rivers, and they bring honor to Zhejiang.

3.4.1.3   The Resources Represented by Folk Opera

Zhejiang is the birthplace of Chinese opera. In the history of the development of Chinese opera, the first mature opera form was the Nanxi Opera which originated in Wenzhou during the Northern Song Dynasty (960–1127). The Shaoxing Opera, one of the top 10 operas in China, originated in Zhejiang. Zhejiang is reputed as a large province of opera. According to current statistical data, Zhejiang has 17 types of opera, including the Peking Opera, the Kunqu Opera, the Shaoxing Opera, the Wu Opera, the Shao Opera and the Yong Opera.[32] Throughout history, there have been many opera celebrities, including Li Yu and Hong Sheng, excellent operas, laying a solid foundation of cultural resources for the development of Zhejiang's contemporary performing arts. The above-mentioned operas with Zhejiang's characteristics are characterized by many theaters and troupes, large audiences, a lot of excellent works and frequent external exchanges. The projects of intangible cultural heritage relating to operas have been vigorously protected, orderly inherited and extensively spread. In 2014, the protection of the project of intangible cultural heritage—traditional opera "Zhejiang Good Tune"—was fully initiated, laying a good foundation for unveiling the provincial plan for the revitalization of traditional operas and holistically protecting the projects of intangible cultural heritage relating to traditional operas.

---

[32] Wang (2014).

3.4.1.4   Diversified Workmanship Resources

In history, Zhejiang had a regional industrial tradition and cultural deposit with diversified workmanship. The famous industries include muddy water woodwork and wood carvings in Dongyang, small hardware in Yongkang, reeled silk fabrics in Huzhou, lace in Xiaoshan, and ceramics in Longquan. The diversified workmanship with regional characteristics is the important foundation for Zhejiang's intangible cultural heritages and has given birth to the Sword of Goujian, brocade, embroidery, fan art, silk parasols, celadon ware, treasured swords and other traditional arts and crafts, and such famous brands as Dujinsheng and Wangxingji. On September 30, 2009, Longquan's traditional firing technique for celadon ware, mulberry silk weaving technique, seal cutting, paper cutting, and traditional wooden arch bridge building technique in Zhejiang were included in the List of the Intangible Cultural Heritage of Humanity by UNESCO, ranking Zhejiang no. 1 nationwide in the number of projects included in the list. The diversified workmanship has become a valuable resource for Zhejiang's contemporary cultural industrial development, and has given rise to characteristic cultural industry parks and bases. According to the *Introduction to Zhejiang's Cultural Industry (2012–2013)*, 12 out of 20 cultural industry parks are based on Dongyang's wood carvings, Qingtian's stone carvings, Longquan's celadon ware, Longquan's treasured swords and other traditional techniques.

3.4.1.5   The Resources of Calligraphy and Painting Art

Zhejiang is a land of literature and art. Wang Xizhi, Zhao Mengfu, Huang Hongwang, Xu Wei, Wu Changshuo, Huang Binhong, Lin Fengmian and others have shone out in China's history of calligraphy and painting art. The tradition of Chinese art stresses that "writings are for conveying truth". Overall, that "truth" shows kindheartedness, good manners and righteousness at the level of aesthetic thought; it presents moral virtue, conformance to nature and unconstrained style; it also embodies humanistic care in the realistic life amidst the tide of the times, social change, national development and improvement of the people's well-being. Zhejiang's painting and calligraphy art better reflects various aspects of the unique "truth" from Chinese culture and art, and demonstrates the subtle observation of the reality and fearlessness in life.

3.4.1.6   The Resources of Good Customs

Zhejiang enjoys profound folk cultural deposits and is full of good customs, including revering nature, respecting life, upholding culture and education, doing good works, helping those in distress and aiding those in peril, loving one's country and one's hometown. There are Cao'e, a filial girl who moves the heaven and earth in a folk legend; Zhengshi Yimen, the no. 1 family south of the Yangtze River which stressed filial piety and uprightness and was renowned; the rural tradition of studying hard while doing farm work; the philosophy of doing business with good faith; Zhejiang merchants who show great affection for and repay their hometown; there are many non-governmental charitable organizations throughout Zhejiang; the overseas Chinese who never forget their hometown and offer mutual assistance.

The historical good customs are the precious resources for contemporary Zhejiang to base their building of the system of values with a socialist core, and helps carry forward the shared values of the contemporary people of Zhejiang, cultivate healthy social trends and build a moral highland.

3.4.1.7 Resources of Academic Thought

Zhejiang is a land of masters of academic thought with an innovative spirit. Throughout history, the innovations to Zhejiang's academic thought have played the vanguard role in making breakthroughs for China on countless occasions. Chen Liang and Ye Shi's pragmatist school, Wang Yangming's philosophy of the mind, Huang Zongxi's political theory, Zhang Xuecheng's view that all of the six ancient classics are historical records, Gong Zizhen's enlightenment thought regarding change, and Lu Xun's unyielding and critical spirit are the examples of Zhejiang's cultural innovations. Huang Zongxi, reputed as one of the three greatest Chinese thinkers, vehemently criticized and negated the absolute monarchy of feudal times, and his contributions to the critical spirit and creative thought have inspired and influenced Zhejiang's modernization. Lu Xun, the initiator of the New Literature Movement and the leader of the May 4th New Culture Movement, carried out social and cultural criticism; with great tenacity, he carved out a new path for Chinese culture and also left a valuable wealth of thought for the people in his hometown.

3.4.2 Adopting the Outstanding Traditional Culture to Enrich and Promote the Building of the System of Values with a Socialist Core

To build the value system and core values for contemporary Chinese people, it is essential to proceed from the historical background of the Chinese people to explore the deposits and connotations, thus identifying the historical logic and basis for inheritance and promotion. In an effort to build a system of values with a socialist core, Zhejiang has always given importance to combining the outstanding traditional elements with the new social life and the spirit of the times, and developing them into a new cultural homeland for the contemporary Chinese people.

3.4.2.1 Giving Importance to Ensuring that Red Resources Play the Role of Education and Guidance

With a history of more than 90 years, the Communist Party of China has developed the Party historical culture with a complete system, rich connotations and great significance, and has gathered abundant red resources. The Party historical culture and red resources are an important part of the cultural wealth for cultivating and carrying forward the system of values with a socialist core. Zhejiang has attached great importance to adopting various means to thoroughly tap red resources, extensively carry out a distinctive kind of education to patriotism, and carry forward the national spirit and the Zhejiang Spirit of advancing with the times.

In recent years, with the educational bases to teach patriotism at various levels as platforms, Zhejiang has utilized the major festival activities and commemoration days to extensively display, publicize and carry forward the history of the Party and the people's development, and the heroic deeds of revolutionary martyrs. Zhejiang held exhibitions, commemorative activities and activities regarding publicity on Party history for 135, 368 and 2,399 times, respectively. For instance, in order to commemorate the 85th anniversary of the founding of the Party, based at the Nanhu Revolutionary Memorial Hall in Jiaxing, the Party Committee of Zhejiang Province held "The Creation of the World—Photo Show Commemorating the 85th Anniversary of the Founding of the Communist Party of China" in the National Museum of China, with the exhibition tour in Hangzhou, Harbin, Chongqing and Nanjing, during the period June 23 to July 3, 2006. In October, 2006, in order to commemorate the 70th anniversary of the victory of the Long March and earnestly carry out the great spirit of the Long March, the Department of Publicity under the Party Committee of Zhejiang Province, in conjunction with 11 cities across the province, conducted the activity of "Carrying Forward the Spirit of the Long March from Generation to Generation—Zhejiang's Red Base Tour". In more than a decade, led by the Department of Publicity under the Party Committee of Zhejiang Province, patriotic educational reading activities were conducted among primary and middle school students across the province with one theme for each year, educational materials were prepared in light of Zhejiang's reality, which were well received by primary and middle school students across the province, and more than one million primary and middle school students participated in those activities each year.

As of September, 2010, in Zhejiang, 2,443 important sites during the new period of the democratic revolution were registered by means of a general survey, 59 provincial educational bases for the teaching of Party history, 340 municipal and county-level educational bases for the teaching of Party history were rated and selected, and more than 230 Party history memorial venues were newly built or rebuilt and expanded. Since 2008, an amount of 30.50 million yuan has been allocated from provincial finances to conduct special surveys on and protection of revolutionary sites. As of late 2013, local authorities in Zhejiang had allocated a total of 199 million yuan for building relevant red memorial facilities. Zhejiang has stayed ahead nationwide in the protection of revolutionary sites.

Regarding the communication of the Party history culture, Zhejiang has produced 329 film and television works (episodes). The television documentary films "Forerunner—Zhejiang's Progressives and the Founding of the Communist Party of China", "Epic Farewell", "The Secretary of a Provincial Party Committee" and "Fierce Battle in Yijiangshan" were shown on CCTV and provincial and municipal TV stations, exerting an extensive impact. Moreover, Zhejiang has also made the *Map of the Red Tour*, introduced the "Online Red Map" and some books relating to the Party history to rural cultural auditoriums and the people from various sectors of the society across the province without charge.

3.4.2.2   Actively Conducting the Activity on the Theme of "Our Festivals"

Traditional festivals are the depositories and expression of the Chinese nation's long-time and profound historical culture in the people's daily life; they contain our national characteristic, spirit and character, and they have a strong appeal. Therefore, the activity of "Our Festivals" is the effective carrier for inheriting the outstanding traditional culture. Zhejiang has paid a great amount of attention to, during the traditional festivals of the Chinese nation, including the Spring Festival, the Tomb-Sweeping Day, the Dragon Boat Festival, the Mid-Autumn Festival and the Double Ninth Festival, tapping the folk culture and the connotations of a spirit of festivals, and has deeply carried out readings of popular classics, festival customs, cultural, entertainment and physical fitness activities, so that the people, especially adolescents, can become familiar with and love the classics, and the long-standing etiquettes and outstanding folk customs of the Chinese nation are once again rooted among urban and rural residents.

Ningbo City has incorporated "Our Festivals" into the 12th five-year plan of the government and the building of a culturally advanced city, the responsibility for the evaluation of the annual targets of various departments, and has taken "Our Festivals" as an important part of the efforts at building a culturally strong city. Each year, the city sets aside nearly one million yuan in special funds and allocates more than 5 million yuan from the funds involving the development of the cultural industry and the building of a culturally strong city to carry out activities.

3.4.2.3   Promoting the Outstanding Traditional Culture in Popularizing the System of Values with a Socialist Core

The activity of "Our Values" is an important carrier for promoting the building and popularization of the system of values with a socialist core, while one of its priorities lies in inheriting and carrying forward the outstanding traditional culture. According to the Party Committee of Hangzhou City, carrying out the practical activity with the theme of "Our Values" is essential for carrying forward and inheriting the outstanding traditional culture of the Chinese nation, and it is necessary to "conduct that activity in order to deal with the outstanding Chinese traditional culture with respect and pride, so that citizens earnestly learn ethical, historical, philosophical and literary classics and other excellent traditional culture books, actively carry out traditional Chinese virtues, including loyalty, filial piety, benevolence, righteousness and politeness and correctly deal with the important relationships between righteousness and benefits, between self and others and between material enjoyment and cultural enjoyment; therefore, it is necessary to cultivate good taste through learning, nourish the mind through outstanding culture, broaden the horizons through social practice, cultivate the noble spirit and character to unceasingly improve the cultural quality, reach a higher ethical realm and increase the level of urban culture".[33] With considerations given to the important festivals, great historical events and Chinese traditional festivals, Hangzhou City has identified the keywords for defining the theme activities, including the people's well-being (January), etiquette (February), integrity (March), gratitude (April), dedication (May), care (June), faith (July), responsibility (August), science and technology (September), patriotism (October), innovation (November) and harmony (December)—which is a great innovation—with a view to tenuously incorporating the values with a socialist core into the people's work, learning and life through monthly activities.

3.4.2.4 Leveraging the Classics of Chinese Studies to Popularize the System of Values with a Socialist Core

The classics of Chinese studies are the quintessence of the Chinese civilization and carry the cultural power of the Chinese nation; they are the important depositories and support for the current building of the system of values with a socialist core. Various points for inheriting the classics of Chinese studies are built at the provincial, municipal and county levels to popularize the outstanding traditional classics; this is an important part of Zhejiang's efforts in popularizing the system of values with a socialist core and it has produced good effects. Hangzhou has cultivated and built about 100 primary-level points for inheriting the classics of Chinese studies, including the citizens classroom and the Chinese studies classroom, to conduct a series of activities for carrying forward the ancient Chinese civilization and to guide and foster a learning atmosphere in which the people are eager and pleased to learn the outstanding traditional culture.

Furthermore, in the building of cities with a learning basis and daily cultural work in primary-level towns, communities, sub-districts and rural areas, Zhejiang's primary-level organizations and people actively experiment with and take bold actions to tap the traditional cultural resources, carry forward national traditions, revitalize the national spirit, and build a cultural homeland, thus producing marked effects.

---

[33] Weng Weijun's Speech in the Working Conference on the Practical Activity with the Theme of "Our Values", in: *Move towards the Cultural Highland*, Hangzhou Publishing House, 2012, p. 90.

3.4.3 Inheriting the Outstanding Farming Civilization, Building the New Rural Culture

Throughout history, China has based its development on agriculture, as the Chinese cultural tradition was built on the farming civilization, rural areas and villagers were the main forces for generating and inheriting the cultural tradition. At present, rural areas lag far behind urban areas in the degree of promoting modern civilization, and the traditional cultural forms with original ecology are still retained in rural areas. The transformation of the mindset is a long process; villagers' mindsets based on the traditional social soil has not yet changed thoroughly; a certain triviality in the traditional culture still exists among villagers. In general, the level of the villagers' cultural knowledge is relatively low; this is a fact in the rural society. All of these factors hinder the building of a new socialist countryside and the growth of the new generation of young farmers. Therefore, a priority in Zhejiang's cultural development lies in inheriting and carrying forward the traditional culture, continuing rural culture and drawing upon modern civilization in rural areas.

So far, Zhejiang's rural areas, especially mountainous areas, still have strong local living customs and a profound social foundation for cultural inheritance. In parallel to respecting the people's willingness and pioneering spirit, the Party Committee and the People's Government of Zhejiang Province have given great importance to regulating and guiding relevant practices, and, subject to the inheritance of a rural cultural context, radically removing something bad and transforming social customs, so as to build a new cultural homeland in the rural living atmosphere familiar to the people.

Experimenting in utilizing old rural ancestral temples to build rural cultural activity centers is a rural cultural task to which Zhejiang has always given importance. In 2004, after surveying Pujiang County's rural cultural facilities, the county's local authority learnt about the following facts: the village-level cultural facilities were seriously inadequate, only 106 out of 430 villages across the county had cultural activity centers; 159 old ancestral temples were unused. Therefore, with the enthusiasm of the villagers about renovating ancestral temples and continuing their genealogy, the culture department guided local villagers to conduct cultural activities at the renovated ancestral temples. In 2006, Pujiang saw the renovation of nearly 100 old ancestral temples and took a new path of introducing new culture at the old ancestral temples.

Restoring folk customs, including traditional temple fairs, is also an effective way of guiding villagers to increase cohesion and improve their quality. The Fangyan/Hugong temple fair in Yongkang of Jinhua originated from the worshiping activity of commemorating the famous official Hu Ze in the Song Dynasty, and the people, male or female, old or young, participate in it. In June, 2011, the Fangyan/Hugong temple fair was listed among the third batch of national intangible cultural heritages, and became a large platform for carrying out folk cultural, artistic and sports activities.

In Zhejiang, a province which abounds in historical and cultural resources, there are many examples of utilizing the outstanding historical and cultural resources peculiar to villages to enhance the villagers' cultural self-confidence, provide resources for economic development and enrich the cultural life. Huanxi Village in Tonglu, inhabited by the descendants of Zhou Dunyi, a great litterateur of the Northern Song Dynasty, the author of the *Ode to the Lotus Flower*, has fully leveraged the characteristic advantages of resources to renovate the time-honored ancestral temple, the "Ode to the Lotus Flower" Temple, establish the "Ode to the Lotus Flower" Book Center, the only book center with the qualification of a legal person in the county, the "Ode to the Lotus Flower" cultural square and corridor for showcasing the traditional culture of "Ode to the Lotus Flower", and conduct the photographic exhibition and contest "Ode to the Clear Lotus", junior "Ode to the Lotus Flower" recitation contest, a farmers forum and other activities for the masses.

Similar rural cultural activities have helped tap, recover and carry forward local culture, draw upon and introduce modern urban civilization, so rural bad habits have been massively removed, the new rural culture has been fostered, rural customs have improved, the cultural level has increased, villagers' recognition and participation have greatly improved.

3.4.4 Utilizing the Outstanding Traditional Culture to Enhance the Overall Quality and the Professional Quality of the Leading Cadres

As a Chinese saying goes, to govern a country, officials' conduct must be regulated. The Communist Party of China has always given great importance to improving the Party conduct to enhance cohesion among the Party members and the people, and make the government carry out folk customs better. The rich thoughts and wisdoms in the outstanding traditional culture are the high-quality resources for educating cadres. As mentioned by comrade Xi Jinping, "the leading cadres at various levels and positions should learn more about history to deepen their understanding of the law which governs the development of human society, the law of socialist construction and the law of the Communist Party of China's governance, thus acquiring more historical knowledge; only in this way can the leading cadres broaden their horizons and become open-minded, greatly improve their cognitive ability, reach a higher cultural realm and enhance their leadership."[34] In "Zhijiang Xinyu", he adopted the outstanding traditional culture to strengthen the education of the Party members and cadres, setting a good example in Zhejiang. Since 2003, Zhejiang has always paid high attention to tapping historical resources to conduct the education of a non-corrupt government culture among the leading cadres, so as to improve the overall quality and professional quality of the leading cadres.

---

[34]The speech delivered by Comrade Xi Jinping during the opening ceremony of the fall semester of the year 2011 at the Party School of the CPC Central Committee.

3.4.4.1 Drawing Upon Historical Resources to Promote the Education of a Non-corrupt Government Culture

In 2005, Zhejiang People's Publishing House published six books concerning clean governance, including the *Explanatory Notes to Ancient and Modern Articles about Clean Governance* and the *Chinese Historical Narrative of Clean Governance*. The *Chinese Historical Narrative of Clean Governance* systematically presents the history of Chinese clean governance from the pre-Qin period (the 21st century B.C.–221 B.C.) to the period of the Republic of China (1912–1949) and has a special chapter for expounding the clean governance under the Communist Party of China (1921–1949). The *Explanatory Notes to Ancient and Modern Articles about Clean Governance* includes the ancient and modern articles involving clean governance; it is divided into the chapters "Working Diligently for the People", "Being Upright and Clean", "Treating the People of Virtue Well, Soliciting Opinions", "Cultivating a Moral Character for Governing", "Clean Governance by the Leaders of the Communist Party of China" and an appendix, "Celebrated Dictums and Aphorisms on Clean Governance".

3.4.4.2 Systematically Popularizing and Studying the Outstanding Traditional Culture

In 2010, in order to carry out the guiding principles adopted during the 4th Plenary Session of the 17th Central Committee of the Communist Party of China and finish the task of building a political party with a Marxist learning base, Zhejiang Ancient Books Publishing House published *The Chinese Ancient Civilization Reader for the Leading Cadres*. The first part, "Political Virtues", is divided into 14 categories, such as "the ways of dealing with affairs", "understanding virtues", "regulating the family", "governing the country", "putting the people first", "integrity and thrift", "the rule of law", "appointing the able people" and "soliciting opinions", and it covers the virtues and good conduct which the leading cadres and administrators should have. The second part, "Culture and Art", focuses on poems, tunes, calligraphy, painting, music, opera and other ancient culture and art. The third part, "Chinese Studies", presents key books, ancient relics, the capitals of past dynasties, ancient appellations and six other aspects to help readers understand ancient society, history and culture.

In 2013, in order to carry out the instruction of comrade Xi Jinping that the leading cadres should read some history, the Department of Publicity under the Party Committee of Zhejiang Province and the Zhejiang Academy of Social Sciences published *The Reader of Zhejiang's History and Humanities*, covering 8 volumes and 644 articles, which presents Zhejiang's humanistic splendor to readers and is aimed at making the leading cadres learn from their predecessors and martyrs and draw lessons from experience in governance, and thus obtain better achievements in realizing the Chinese dream.[35]

3.4.4.3 Conducting the Activity of Learning the Outstanding Traditional Culture in the Party School Training, Cadre Education and Relevant Activities

Hangzhou has profound historical and cultural depositories and a good atmosphere of inheritance and promotion, while that atmosphere also exists in education and learning about care. An interesting example is that in 2011, Shangcheng District thoroughly tapped Chinese traditional cultural resources and energetically carried out activities on the theme of education, such as "learning *Disciple Gauge* to behave well", as the important means for carrying out the practical activity on the theme of "Our Values" and the important part of efforts in building the urban areas for learning.

Zhejiang's work on inheriting and carrying forward the outstanding traditional culture is embodied in various fields involving daily life in urban and rural areas. Not all of the examples are described here due to a limitation of space; the above examples are only some examples with Zhejiang's characteristics in key fields and key groups. With pragmatism, perseverance and distinctive experiments, Zhejiang has activated the outstanding traditional culture in daily life, routine work and the inner world, connecting it with today's life and the present era, developing the spirit and character of the people of Zhejiang and deepening the connotation of Zhejiang's economic and social development. Zhejiang has made effective innovations in realizing the contemporary value of the outstanding traditional culture.

3.5 Conclusions

Since the 18th National Congress of the Communist Patty of China, the Party's attention to the outstanding traditional culture has become more prominent. Comrade Xi Jinping got familiar with, valued and applied the outstanding traditional culture; in particular, he stressed, on many times, the important significance of the outstanding traditional culture for the great cause of building socialism with Chinese characteristics, which constituted a unique style of his governance. On October 13, 2014, in the 18th collective learning meeting of the Political Bureau of the Central Committee of the Communist Party of China, comrade Xi Jinping stressed, "China's problems are solved only by seeking the path and solutions from China which are suitable for China; for thousands of years, the Chinese nation has taken a path towards the

---

[35]See Xia Baolong's Preface to *Zhejiang's History and Humanities Readings*, Zhejiang Ancient Books Publishing House, 2013.

development of civilization which is different from that in other countries and nations; the socialist path with Chinese characteristics carved out by us is not occasional and is determined by Chinese historical inheritance and cultural traditions."[36]

The long-standing outstanding Chinese cultural tradition is the valuable wealth left to us by our ancestors and it has shaped our thoughts, spirit, character and power, our roots and our path. Therefore, we should not only understand that the contemporary value of the outstanding traditional culture lies in the "cultural" level—enriching the cultural life and building a cultural homeland, but we must also realize that it is closely associated with major issues, such as the choice of a path under the new situation, economic development, environmental governance, social management and well-regulated construction of order. The resources which can be inherited and utilized are available in many aspects, including participating in building the system for interpretation of social self-evident truth and a system of regulation, establishing a new social order and rules, reshaping the framework of customs in folk social life, building the new-type social relations with Chinese characteristics, enhancing the nationals' national collective awareness, the sense of identity and cohesion involving national culture. In the final analysis, the Chinese people have the desire to ultimately take their own path and live their own life. Historical wisdom, patriotism and a national spirit are the strong cultural power for achieving the great rejuvenation of the Chinese nation. This is the necessity for safeguarding the Chinese cultural tradition and is the responsibility for maintaining the world's cultural diversity. In particular, against the background of globalization, the exchange, integration and interaction among various cultures become more intense and the challenges are greater. The world's situation is changing, various trends are emerging, so it is necessary for us to stand firm, identify our own path, our direction to make our dream come true. Therefore, the contemporary inheritance and promotion of the outstanding traditional culture is of cultural value and practical significance, it is both soft power and hard power.

As China has a vast land and territory, China's unique cultural tradition, historical destiny, basic conditions and developmental path are largely related to the distinctive historical traditions in different areas. Zhejiang's rational line of thought, theoretical research and extensive practice in inheriting and carrying forward the outstanding traditional culture in nearly 10 years conform to the historical tide of the great rejuvenation of the Chinese nation in the 21st century, and they offer active experiments with local characteristics, vivid experience and inspirations, at the provincial level, for "seeking the path and solutions from China which are suitable for China", they are of far-reaching practical value and historical significance with rich connotations.

---

[36]The speech delivered by Comrade Xi Jinping at the 18th collective learning meeting of the Political Bureau of the Central Committee of the Communist Party of China, Xinhuanet, http://news.xinhuanet.com/politics/2014-10/13/c-1112807354.htm, 2014-10-13.

References

Dong Genhong, On Xi Jinping's Outlook on Traditional Culture, *Ideological and Political Work Research*, 2014(9).

Wang Xianghua, A New Line of Thought of Zhejiang's Performing Art Industry – A Study Based on the Perspective of the Diamond Model, *Annual Report on Zhejiang's Development 2008 (Culture Volume)*, Zhejiang People's Publishing House, 2014, p. 163.

Wen Yue, The Construction of Private Museums is in Full Swing in Zhejiang, *Zhejiang Cultural Monthly*, 2011(3).

(The Southern Song Dynasty) Wu Zimu, *Menglianglu – Narration of an Ancient Cityscape* (Vol. 1), Zhejiang People's Publishing House, 1984, p. 8.

Xi Jinping, *Carrying out Concrete Work to Stay Ahead – Line of Thought and Practice in Promoting New Development in Zhejiang*, The Party School of the CPC Central Committee Press, 2006

Xi Jinping, The Zhejiang Spirit of Advancing with the Times, in: *The Zhejiang Spirit of Advancing with the Times* compiled by the Department of Publicity under the Party Committee of Zhejiang Province, Zhejiang People's Publishing House, 2005.

Xi Jinping, *Zhijiang Xinyu*, Zhejiang People's Publishing House, 2007, p. 153.

Chapter 4
Promoting the Building of the System of Values with a Socialist Core

Hongling Zhang and Ye Chen

During the reform and opening-up, Zhejiang has given importance to creating material wealth and has stayed ahead nationwide in economic aggregate for 10–20 consecutive years. Zhejiang has also paid a great amount of attention to creating cultural and ethical wealth—including the Zhejiang Spirit and the shared values of the contemporary people of Zhejiang—and creatively pushing forward the building of the system of values with a socialist core.

Comrade Xi Jinping made a correct judgment about Zhejiang's development in 2004: Zhejiang would be in "six periods", including the period of economic development and take-off, the period of the transformation of the growth mode, the period of making breakthroughs in reforms, the period of increasing openness, the period of social structural transformation and the period of salient social contrasts.[1] The characteristics of Zhejiang's stages of development in this period determined that Zhejiang's tasks for building a harmonious society were arduous, so there was an urgent need for valuing cultural development; in particular, it was necessary to rebuild the leading values, moral order and ethical norm in the new period. Building the system of values with a socialist core catering to the needs of social development was a very important strategic task for Zhejiang during a period of nearly ten years. Therefore, the successive Party Committees of Zhejiang Province gave great importance to the cultural and ethical development, firmly grasped the period of opportunities for Zhejiang's rapid development and the objective reality of salient contradictions, actively built the system of values with a socialist core, adopted Marxism in development to guide Zhejiang's practice, carried forward the national spirit and the spirit of the times, developed the Zhejiang Spirit in response to the times, utilized the socialist core values to lead social trends, promoted healthy trends and cultivated good customs.

H. Zhang (✉) · Y. Chen
The Party School of the Zhejiang Provincial Party Committee,
The Zhejiang Academy of Social Sciences, Hangzhou, China

[1] Xi (2006), pp. 31–35.

The course of Zhejiang's building of the system of values with a socialist core during the period 2004–2014 covers three stages.

2004–2007, before the 17th National Congress of the Communist Party of China was convened. During this period, the Central Committee of the Communist Party of China deliberated and put forward the building of the system of values with socialist core; this period was an important period for Zhejiang in promoting the building of an advanced culture and carrying out the strategic arrangement of the Central Committee of the Communist Party of China for building the system of values with a socialist core.

In September, 2004, the 4th Plenary Session of the 16th Central Committee of the Communist Party of China adopted the *Decision of the Central Committee of the Communist Party of China on Strengthening the Building of the Party's Governance Capacity*. In November, Zhejiang Province issued the *Opinions of the Party Committee of Zhejiang Province on Earnestly Implementing the Guiding Principles Adopted during the 4th Plenary Session of the 16th Central Committee of the Communist Party of China and Strengthening the Building of the Party's Governance Capacity*, making the strategic arrangements for consolidating the cultural foundation for the Party's governance and comprehensively promoting the building of a culturally large province, incessantly enhancing the capability for building an advanced socialist culture, and making specific arrangements for consolidating the guiding role of Marxism and strengthening cultural, ethical, intellectual and moral development.

In August, 2005, Zhejiang made the *Decision of the Party Committee of Zhejiang Province on Accelerating the Building of a Culturally Large Province,* identifying "enhancing the cohesion of the advanced culture" as the no. 1 point of action among the three points of action for building a culturally large province, and making specific arrangements for upholding the guiding role of Marxism, grasping the correct guidance of public opinion, carrying forward the national spirit and the spirit of the times, developing the Zhejiang Spirit in response to the times, and strengthening intellectual, moral, cultural and ethical development.

In March, 2006, the Central Committee of the Communist Party of China put forward the Socialist Concept of Honor and Disgrace focusing on eight honors and eight disgraces, deepening the understanding of the socialist intellectual and moral development and the criterion for ethical values. In October, 2006, the 6th Plenary Session of the 16th Central Committee of the Communist Party of China adopted the *Decision of the Central Committee of the Communist Party of China on Some Major Issues Concerning Building a Harmonious Socialist Society*, putting forward, for the first time, the major issue and strategic task of building a system of values with a socialist core. In 2007, the Central Committee of the Communist Party of China called for energetically building that system of values and consolidating the foundation of development of common thought for the whole Party and the people across the country. The system of values with a socialist core covers four basic parts: a Marxist guiding thought, a common ideal with Chinese characteristics, the patriotism-focused national spirit and the reform and innovation-focused spirit of the times, as well as the Socialist Concept of Honor and Disgrace.

After the 6th Plenary Session of the 16th Central Committee of the Communist Party of China in 2006, the Party Committee of Zhejiang Province adopted the *Opinions on Earnestly Implementing the Guiding Principles Adopted during the 6th Plenary Session of the 16th Central Committee of the Communist Party of China and Building a Harmonious Socialist Society*, making specific arrangements for building a system of values with a socialist core, carrying forward the Socialist Concept of Honor and Disgrace, fostering an active and healthy atmosphere of public opinion and increasing the intellectual and moral forces for building a harmonious socialist society. This is the specific work on the major issue and strategic task of "building a system of values with a socialist core" put forward by the Central Committee of the Communist Party of China, with the building of that system of values as the means for promoting socialist cultural and ethical development.

At this stage, Zhejiang actively carried out the guiding principles adopted during the 16th National Congress of the Communist Party of China, the 3rd, 4th, 5th and 6th plenary sessions of the 16th Central Committee of the Communist Party of China, and with a focus on the "Eight-Eight Strategies", the building of a safe Zhejiang and a trustworthy Zhejiang, Zhejiang achieved transformation from cultural and ethical development dominated by the development of the advanced culture to the building of a system of values with a socialist core. Regarding the building of a system of values with a socialist core, Zhejiang expanded the publicity and education relating to the latest achievement in adapting Marxism to the Chinese context, the Scientific Outlook on Development and the basic lines, principles and policies of the Party; Zhejiang learned and practiced the Socialist Concept of Honor and Disgrace and actively carried forward the national spirit and the spirit of the times; Zhejiang responded to the times to identify the Zhejiang Spirit which features "a pursuit of truth, pragmatism, integrity and harmony, open-mindedness and determination to become stronger"; Zhejiang gave importance to the intellectual and moral education of juveniles, carried out the projects regarding the moral education of juveniles including the front project, the excellent works project, the green network project, the purification project and the assistance project; Zhejiang pushed forward the work on "dual development, dual improvement", carried out the project of "double-10,000 paired joint constructions", initiated the publicity activity on the "Civic Virtue Awareness Day", and extensively conducted the activity of civic cultural quality improvement and cultural and ethical development; Zhejiang introduced the systems for strengthening the work on the publicity of news, public opinion, news releases and online publicity in the new period, creating a good mainstream public opinion and oral social order for Zhejiang's reform and development.

From the 17th National Congress of the Communist Party of China in 2007 to the 18th National Congress of the Communist Party of China in 2012. In October, 2007, the 17th National Congress of the Communist Party of China put forward the line of thought that held that a system of values with a socialist core was the essential embodiment of socialist ideology, and made new strategic arrangements for building that system of values. In November, the Party Committee of Zhejiang Province adopted the *Decision of the Party Committee of Zhejiang Province on Earnestly Implementing the Guiding Principles Adopted during* the *17th National Congress of the Communist Party of China and Concretely Working on Making the People Rich by Starting Businesses and of Building a Strong Province through Innovation*, calling for adopting the system of values with a socialist core to lead social trends, taking the building of the advanced culture as an important support for making the people rich by starting businesses and of building a strong province through innovation, promoting vigorous cultural development and great cultural prosperity, and making strategic arrangements for Zhejiang's building of the system of values with a socialist core.

In July, 2008, Zhejiang developed and implemented the *Plan of Zhejiang Province for Promoting Vigorous Cultural Development and Great Cultural Prosperity (2008–2012)*, comprehensively planning Zhejiang's cultural development. The Plan put forward, for the first time, the building of three main systems, including the building of the system of values with a socialist core, the innovative building of the public cultural service system, and the innovative building of the system for the development of the cultural industry.

In October, 2011, the 6th Plenary Session of the 17th Central Committee of the Communist Party of China stressed that the system of values with a socialist core was the soul for developing the country and the building of that system of values was the fundamental task for promoting vigorous cultural development and great cultural prosperity. In November, the Party Committee of Zhejiang Province adopted the *Decision of the Party Committee of Zhejiang Province on Earnestly Carrying Out the Guiding Principles Adopted during the 6th Plenary Session of the 17th Central Committee of the Communist Party of China and Vigorously Promoting the Building of a Culturally Strong Province;* the Decision upgraded the strategic goal of building a culturally large province to the building of a culturally strong province, and it had the special chapter for arranging the building of a system of values with a socialist core.

This stage was between the 17th National Congress of the Communist Party of China and the 18th National Congress of the Communist Party of China; it was an important period for Zhejiang in carrying out the guiding principles adopted during the 17th National Congress of the Communist Party of China, the 3rd, 4th, 5th and 6th plenary sessions of the 17th Central Committee of the Communist Party of China, and in promoting the building of a system of values with a socialist core in light of Zhejiang's reality. At this stage, Zhejiang shaped the strategic layout of its cultural development dominated by "three main systems" and started systematically promoting the development of the advanced culture, cultural and ethical development, intellectual and moral development and public opinion work led by "the building of the system of values with a socialist core". At this stage, Zhejiang deeply studied and publicized the Scientific Outlook on Development and the guiding principles adopted during the 17th National Congress of the Communist Party of China, adopted the latest achievement of developing Marxism to guide Zhejiang's practice, and pushed forward the "Eight-Eight Strategies" and the overall strategy of "making the people rich by starting businesses and of building a strong province through innovation"; Zhejiang vigorously carried forward the national spirit and the spirit of the times, and developed "the Zhejiang Spirit mainly characterized by entrepreneurship and innovation" in response to the times; it actively coped with the new challenges from new media to the publicity of the news, brought about innovations to the ideological work in the new period, continuously expanded and renewed the publicity and public opinion front, introduced modern media science and technology, publicized the mainstream values, carried out the great debate on "Our Values", identified the shared values of the contemporary people of Zhejiang, consolidated the guiding role of Marxism, strengthened civic moral development, carried forward new moral trends, and pressed ahead with cultural and ethical development, thus providing thought-based cohesive forces and a strong cultural impetus for Zhejiang's economic and social transformation and upgrading.

From 2012 to the present. The 18th National Congress of the Communist Party of China, convened in November, 2012, put forward new requirements for building a system of values with a socialist core, and called for advocating a state of being prosperous, strong, democratic, culturally advanced and harmonious; it also called for freedom, equality, justice, the rule of law, love for the country, dedication, integrity and friendliness and an active cultivation of core socialist values; this was the latest summary of core socialist values. In December, 2013, the General Office of the Central Committee of the Communist Party of China issued the *Opinions on Cultivating and Practicing the Socialist Core Values*, putting forward the socialist core values with the basic part consisting in "advocating a state of being prosperous, strong, democratic, culturally advanced and harmonious; freedom, equality, justice, the rule of law; love for the country, dedication, integrity and friendliness"; this tallied with the developmental requirement for socialism with Chinese characteristics, the outstanding Chinese traditional culture and the excellent achievements of human civilization; this was the important judgment made by the Party in building a consensus among all Party members and throughout the society.

With a focus on the strategic arrangement of the Central Committee of the Communist Party of China, Zhejiang actively learnt and publicized the guiding principles adopted during the 18th National Congress of the Communist Party of China, carried out the guiding principles from the 18th National Congress of the Communist Party of China, the 3rd and 4th plenary sessions of the 18th Central Committee of the Communist Party of China, deeply learned the Chinese dream and the principles from General Secretary Xi Jinping's addresses, and adopted the latest achievement in adapting Marxism to the Chinese context and the guiding principles adopted by the Central Committee of the Communist Party of China to guide Zhejiang's reform practice. Zhejiang thoroughly learned and implemented General Secretary Xi Jinping's strategic arrangement for ideological work, including cultural publicity, and brought about innovations to the public opinion work in response to new media changes. Zhejiang energetically made the core socialist values rooted in Zhejiang, and vigorously strengthened the popularization of those values. In 2012 and 2013, Zhejiang conducted themed publicity and educational activities regarding "Our Values" and "the Shared Values of the Contemporary People of Zhejiang ", thus making the values with a socialist core greatly responsive to the times and highly popular.

This period was an important period for Zhejiang in carrying out the guiding principles adopted during the 18th National Congress of the Communist Party of China and during the 2nd, 3rd and 4th plenary sessions of the 18th Central Committee of the Communist Party of China, the principles from General Secretary

Xi Jinping's addresses and the "Eight-Eight Strategies", in continuing to carry through one blueprint, and widely promote the building of the system of values with a socialist core. In this period, Zhejiang continuously carried out the work on learning, publicity and education concerning the guiding principles adopted at the 18th National Congress of the Communist Party of China, at the 3rd and 4th plenary sessions of the 18th Central Committee of the Communist Party of China, adopted the Party's latest theoretical achievements to arm all Party members in Zhejiang, guide Zhejiang's reform practice, carried forward the national spirit, the spirit of the times and the Zhejiang Spirit, developed thoughts and built consensus through the Chinese dream, brought about innovations to the Party's work on publicity and public opinion, cultivated the core socialist values, carried forward the "Most Beautiful Phenomena", and identified the shared values of the contemporary people of Zhejiang, thus providing the strong cultural cohesive force and moral guidance for Zhejiang to comprehensively intensify the reform and become the first to achieve modernization.

4.1   Adopting Developing Marxism to Guide the New Practice

The system of values with a socialist core needs to be built by giving priority to upholding and developing Marxism because, with respect to the system of values with a socialist core, it is necessary to uphold the basic positions, viewpoints and methods of Marxism, its worldview, outlook on life, and values, adopt the "latest achievement in adapting Marxism to the Chinese context" to guide China's reform practice and lead the basic direction for China's drive towards modernization.

To uphold and realize the guiding role of Marxism in the ideological field, it is essential to promote the innovative development of Marxism in light of the new practical development and the issues of the new era, make Marxism adapt to the Chinese context and to the times.

Regarding Zhejiang's reform and developmental practice during the period 2004–2014, the adoption of developing Marxism for guiding Zhejiang's practice involved the adoption of the socialist theoretical system with Chinese characteristics for guiding Zhejiang's practice. With regard to a time node, concretization meant that it was necessary to adopt the Important Thought of Three Represents, the Scientific Outlook on Development and the principles from General Secretary Xi Jinping's addresses to guide Zhejiang's reform practice.

Furthermore, when working in Zhejiang even the Central Committee of the Communist Party of China, comrade Xi Jinping pointed out on many occasions, "with regard to learning Marxism's guiding thoughts, and the theoretical achievements in adapting Marxism to the Chinese context, it is essential to deepen the understanding of the background to the era, the practical foundation, scientific connotations, essence and historical status of these important thoughts, and earnestly study, really understand, believe in and apply them, get a good grasp of and put into practice theories and thoughts and bring about innovations in work".[2]

4.1.1 Deeply Publicizing and Studying the Important Thoughts of Three Represents

The 16th National Congress of the Communist Party of China established the Important Thoughts of Three Represents as the Party's guiding thoughts. In 2003, according to the arrangements made by the Central Committee of the Communist Party of China, the Party Committee of Zhejiang Province vowed to study in an in-depth way, blaze new trails and do concrete work, earnestly study, really understand, believe in and apply the Important Thoughts of Three Represents, solidly conduct themed education concerning the guiding principles adopted during the 16th National Congress of the Communist Party of China, and arouse a new wave of studying and implementing the Important Thoughts of Three Represents.

1. Strengthening study

The study of the Party's theories was strengthened mainly through study in the central groups and in the form of seminars, study classes and reading classes. In 2003, the Central Group for Theories under the Party Committee of Zhejiang Province organized study groups 8 times, and held seminars on the Important Thoughts of Three Represents and theories and reading classes of the leading cadres, training 24,000 cadres at the county division level. In 2004, the Central Group under the Party Committee of Zhejiang Province organized special study groups ten times, carried out special study activities including "carrying forward the spirit of being realistic and pragmatic, vigorously promoting the style of being realistic and pragmatic", and held the theoretical seminar and symposium "Deng Xiaoping Theory and Zhejiang's Practice". In 2005, the Party Committee of Zhejiang Province conducted special study groups 30 times.

2. Strengthening publicity

The news units at various levels stepped up publicity, introduced high-quality articles and special programs, and for instance, provincial media opened special columns including "The New Tide in Zhejiang". Publicity groups were organized within the primary-level units for publicizing the Party's latest theories.

3. Strengthening research

Zhejiang intensified research on the Party's latest theoretical achievements by compiling special teaching materials, holding special theoretical seminars and organizing relevant research subjects. For instance, in 2005, Zhejiang organized

---

[2]Xi (2006), p. 14.

and implemented the major research project "Zhejiang's Practice of the Important Thoughts of Three Represents since the 16th National Congress of the Communist Party of China", and systematically summarized Zhejiang's efforts in carrying out the Important Thoughts of Three Represents and promoted Zhejiang's development since the 16th National Congress of the Communist Party of China.

Overall, Zhejiang turned the Important Thoughts of Three Represents into a thought-based cohesive force and cultural guidance by strengthening study, publicity and research on them.

4.1.2 Deeply Studying and Publicizing the Scientific Outlook on Development and the Socialist Theoretical System with Chinese Characteristics

After the Central Committee of the Communist Party of China put forward the Scientific Outlook on Development in 2004, Zhejiang actively conducted publicity and educational activities to foster and implement the Scientific Outlook on Development and to study the Party's latest achievements in theoretical innovation. After the 17th National Congress of the Communist Party of China in 2007, the Central Committee of the Communist Party of China put forward the socialist theoretical system with Chinese characteristics. During the period 2005–2012, Zhejiang publicized and popularized the Scientific Outlook on Development and the socialist theoretical system with Chinese characteristics, creatively adopted the Scientific Outlook on Development to solve the problems in Zhejiang's development, and made the corresponding developmental strategy and developmental arrangements to lead Zhejiang's reform and developmental practice.

To really adopt the Scientific Outlook on Development to guide Zhejiang's practice, it is essential to earnestly study it. The successive Party Committees of Zhejiang Province gave great importance to studying, publicizing and researching the basic theories of Marxism and the socialist theoretical system with Chinese characteristics, they urged the leading cadres across the province to solidly and earnestly study theories and really understand the guiding principles adopted by the Central Committee of the Communist Party of China. The Party committees at various levels in Zhejiang established study systems to promote the advancement of the Party organizations devoted to learning. In 2010, the General Office of the Party Committee of Zhejiang Province issued the *Opinions on Promoting the Building of the Party Organizations Devoted to Learning*, summarizing the previous study systems and institutionalizing the building of the Party organizations devoted to learning.

The Party organizations at various levels focused their studies on the socialist theoretical system with Chinese characteristics, the guiding principles adopted and work arrangements made by the Central Committee of the Communist Party of China, and the major issues in China and Zhejiang's reform and development.

In response to these issues, the Party Committee of Zhejiang Province built the carriers and platforms for studying the theories. For instance:

(1) The study systems of the central groups under the Party committees at various levels. The Party Committee of Zhejiang Province led the study group at the Central Group under the Party Committee of Zhejiang Province. In 2005 alone, the study group at the Central Group under the Party Committee of Zhejiang Province was conducted 30 times—the Zhejiang Forum was held to invite the experts from relevant fields to deliver reports 8 times.

(2) Intensifying publicity and education concerning the Scientific Outlook on Development and the socialist theories with Chinese characteristics. The publicity groups of the Party committees at various levels were assigned to further publicize the guiding principles adopted by the Central Committee of the Communist Party of China and Marxist theory. In 2008 alone, the Party committees at various levels in Zhejiang organized 4,959 publicity groups to publicize the socialist theoretical system with Chinese characteristics on 100,000 occasions.

(3) Continuously intensifying special research and discussion of the socialist theories with Chinese characteristics and the Scientific Outlook on Development. Each year, the Party Committee of Zhejiang Province held academic seminars to discuss the major issues concerning the socialist theoretical system with Chinese characteristics.

(4) Introducing a number of research achievements in the socialist theoretical system with Chinese characteristics. In the process of studying the Scientific Outlook on Development and the socialist theories with Chinese characteristics, Zhejiang turned research achievements into the study materials for the cadres and the people. Each year, Zhejiang introduced the research achievements and publicity teaching materials concerning Marxist theory, the socialist theoretical system with Chinese characteristics and the Scientific Outlook on Development.

Overall, as the Party committees at various levels incessantly worked on publicity and study of the Scientific Outlook on Development and the socialist theories with Chinese characteristics, the cadres and the people in Zhejiang deeply understood the theoretical quintessence of the Scientific Outlook on Development, and greatly improved their ability to adopt the Scientific Outlook on Development to guide Zhejiang's practice.

4.1.3 Adopting the Principles from General Secretary Xi Jinping's Addresses to Guide Zhejiang's Practice

After the 18th National Congress of the Communist Party of China, the strategic arrangements and theoretical innovations made by the Central Committee of the Communist Party of China became embodied in the report delivered at the 18th National Congress of the Communist Party of China, the guiding principles adopted at the 3rd and 4th plenary sessions of the 18th Central Committee of the Communist

Party of China and the guiding principles specified in relevant documents issued by the Central Committee of the Communist Party of China, while they are most concentrated in the principles from General Secretary Xi Jinping's addresses. The principles from General Secretary Xi Jinping's addresses are the theoretical innovations made by the new central collective leadership in light of the issues of the new era and are the theoretical guideline for comprehensively intensifying the reform at present. Zhejiang continued to strengthen the study of the socialist theoretical system with Chinese characteristics and its latest theoretical achievements, and further adopt developing Marxism to guide Zhejiang's practice.

4.1.3.1 Deeply Studying the Guiding Principles Adopted at the 18th National Congress of the Communist Party of China and the Principles from General Secretary Xi Jinping's Addresses

After the 18th National Congress of the Communist Party of China, Zhejiang conducted publicity and educational activities concerning the guiding principles adopted during the 18th National Congress of the Communist Party of China, at the 3rd and 4th plenary sessions of the 18th Central Committee of the Communist Party of China, and the principles from General Secretary Xi Jinping's addresses. In 2012 alone, the Central Group under the Party Committee of Zhejiang Province organized special study groups 20 times, and publicized the socialist theoretical system with Chinese characteristics on 100,000 occasions, attracting audiences of more than 10 million person-times. Zhejiang also brought about innovations to the mode of studying and publicizing the socialist theoretical system with Chinese characteristics, and launched Zhejiang WeChat as an online theoretical study platform; Zhejiang became the first nationwide to establish microblog groups for theories.

In an effort to publicize and study the guiding principles adopted during the 18th National Congress of the Communist Party of China, during the 3rd and 4th plenary sessions of the 18th Central Committee of the Communist Party of China, and the principles from General Secretary Xi Jinping's addresses, Zhejiang strengthened theoretical research and discussions, held theoretical seminars and symposiums involving the guiding principles adopted at the 18th National Congress of the Communist Party of China, the 3rd Plenary Session of the 18th Central Committee of the Communist Party of China, and the principles from General Secretary Xi Jinping's addresses, and carried out relevant training classes on theory and special training classes at the Party schools and cadre training institutes. The above publicity efforts stimulated the cadres and the people in Zhejiang to further study and understand the latest theoretical achievements in adapting Marxism to the Chinese context after the 18th National Congress of the Communist Party of China. In the process of studying Marxist theory and its latest achievements, Zhejiang compiled relevant works and introduced a number of theoretical achievements.

As Zhejiang made efforts to organize and conduct the series of activities involving the study of Marxist theory and the socialist theoretical system with Chinese characteristics, especially its latest theoretical achievements, these efforts enabled the cadres and the people in Zhejiang to further understand the strategic arrangements made by the Central Committee of the Communist Party of China, especially laying a foundation for Zhejiang to adopt the most important theoretical achievements made after the 18th National Congress of the Communist Party of China—the principles from General Secretary Xi Jinping's addresses—to guide Zhejiang's practice.

4.1.3.2 Adopting the Guiding Principles from the 18th National Congress of the Communist Party of China and the Principles from General Secretary Xi Jinping's Addresses to Guide Zhejiang's Practice

Based on deeply studying the guiding principles from the 18th National Congress of the Communist Party of China and the principles from General Secretary Xi Jinping's addresses, Zhejiang further carried out the "Eight-Eight Strategies", carried through one blueprint via successive Party Committees and the People's Government of Zhejiang Province, vowed to "do a better job towards the goals set for the future 1, 3 and 5 years, double the value in four respects", arranged "three renovations and one demolition" to continuously promote the rule of law in Zhejiang, and made the strategic arrangement of governing "five waters" in tandem to continue the building of a beautiful Zhejiang. These concrete arrangements and measures are the important achievements made by Zhejiang in deeply studying the guiding principles from the 18th National Congress of the Communist Party of China and the principles from General Secretary Xi Jinping's addresses, and creatively combining the arrangements of the Central Committee of the Communist Party of China for comprehensively intensifying the reform with the prominent issues in Zhejiang's development, thus demonstrating Zhejiang's pioneering spirit.

Overall, in 10 years, Zhejiang adopted developing Marxism to creatively analyze Zhejiang's realistic issues, develop Zhejiang's developmental strategy, turned the macro strategy, guiding thought and theoretical innovations for Zhejiang's development into the cultural wealth for promoting and guiding Zhejiang's reform and development. This cultural wealth vividly shows Zhejiang's fundamental principle of always adopting Marxism to guide its practice in an effort to promote the building of the system of values with a socialist core.

4.2 Carrying Forward the Zhejiang Spirit of Advancing with the Times

Carrying forward the Zhejiang Spirit in response to the times is an important effort with Zhejiang's characteristics made by Zhejiang in building the system of values with a socialist core.

Since the reform and opening-up, the people of Zhejiang have developed the distinctive Zhejiang Spirit on the basis of profound traditional culture and in light of the requirements of the new era. When serving as the Secretary of the Party Committee of Zhejiang Province, comrade Xi Jinping vowed to carry forward the Zhejiang Spirit in response to the times, and published articles in important domestic publications, including *Philosophical Researches* and the *Zhejiang Daily*, to explain the course of the development of the Zhejiang Spirit and its essential connotations. The Zhejiang Spirit is the vivid embodiment, in Zhejiang, of the patriotism-focused national spirit and the reform and innovation-focused spirit of the times. Reinforcing patriotism; this is the valuable cultural wealth created by the people of Zhejiang in the tide of reform and opening-up and the great practice of entrepreneurship and innovation.

4.2.1 The Zhejiang Spirit: Concentrated Embodiment of the National Spirit and the Spirit of the Times in Zhejiang

The national spirit and the spirit of the times are placed in a very important position in the building of the system of values with a socialist core. This at least has two implications.

4.2.1.1 The Building of a System of Values with a Socialist Core Must Be a National Attribute

The system of values with a socialist core must contain and embody the quintessence of the national spirit. It is necessary to inherit and carry forward the quintessence of the national spirit through the building of the system of values with a socialist core. If there is no inherent requirement for inheriting and rebuilding the national spirit, the building of a system of values with a socialist core fails to inherit the outstanding Chinese traditional culture, bring about cultural cohesion among 1.3 billion Chinese people and lead the great rejuvenation of the Chinese nation.

4.2.1.2 The Building of the System of Values with a Socialist Core Must Embody the Times

To promote socialist modernization with Chinese characteristics in response to the times, it is necessary to ensure that the building of its core value system internally tallies with the spirit of the times and the development tide all over the world. Tapping and vigorously carrying forward the spirit of the times is conducive to promoting Zhejiang's reform and opening-up, integrating China's development into the world's developmental tide and making the building of a system of values with a socialist core embody the requirements of the development of an era.

After the 16th National Congress of the Communist Party of China, the Central Committee of the Communist Party of China identified the patriotism-focused national spirit and the reform and innovation-focused spirit of the times. The word "focused" in both spirits means that in the building of the system of values with a socialist core, it is necessary to focus on patriotism in carrying out the national spirit but go beyond patriotism, and carry forward and develop the reform and innovation-focused spirit of the times but go beyond reform and innovation.

For Zhejiang, the national spirit and the spirit of the times are most concentrated in the Zhejiang Spirit. The Zhejiang Spirit is the result of Zhejiang's regional historical and cultural development, and also the inherent cultural factor contributing to "The Zhejiang Phenomenon", "The Zhejiang Experience" and "The Zhejiang Miracle" created by the people of Zhejiang and the state of the people of Zhejiang in reform and opening-up over the years. The Zhejiang Spirit of advancing with the times is distinctively regional and special, and is also common and universal under the condition of the socialist market economy. It epitomizes the national spirit and the spirit of the times in Zhejiang.

4.2.2 "Advancing with the Times" is the Inherent Requirement of the Zhejiang Spirit

In the great practice of reform and opening-up, Zhejiang has stayed ahead nationwide in various respects including economic and social development. "The Zhejiang Phenomenon", "The Zhejiang Experience" and "The Zhejiang Model" have drawn widespread attention. From the late 20th century to the first ten years of the 21st century, the people of Zhejiang summarized the cultural gene and humanistic tradition for Zhejiang's development, tapped and developed the mindsets, value orientation, psychological state and social moral criterion which can lead Zhejiang's modernization drive. The Zhejiang Spirit emerged against such a background and became the cultural power for stimulating Zhejiang's reform and development.

The Zhejiang Spirit is based on Zhejiang's profound cultural deposits; it is the result of Zhejiang's long-standing regional cultural tradition, and its cultural and ethical development. It is also a state of entrepreneurship and innovation presented by the people of Zhejiang in the new era of reform and opening-up. As mentioned by Xi Jinping in 2006, advancing with the times is the theoretical quality of Marxism and also the inherent requirement of the Zhejiang Spirit.[3] As the Party Committee of Zhejiang Province led the people of Zhejiang to summarize and identify the Zhejiang Spirit, there was a process of several important stages in doing so, which resulted in identifying the basic part of the Zhejiang Spirit which developed in response to the times in the new period.

---

[3] Xi (2006).

Since the beginning of the new century, the Party Committee of Zhejiang Province has made a theoretical summary of the Zhejiang Spirit as follows: The 4th Plenary (Enlarged) Session of the 10th Party Committee of Zhejiang Province, held in July, 2000, officially put forward the Zhejiang Spirit and identified "ceaseless self-improvement, grittiness, great courage in innovation and pursuit of substantial results" as the basic connotation of the Zhejiang Spirit; in 2006, the Party Committee of Zhejiang Province further identified the Zhejiang Spirit as "pursuit of truth, pragmatism, integrity and harmony, open-mindedness and determination to become stronger". Both versions are consistent, show the cultural power in Zhejiang's reform and development and reveal the cultural factor contributing to the Zhejiang Model.

The raising of the Zhejiang Spirit: In the late 20th century, with more than 20 years of reform and development, Zhejiang stayed ahead nationwide in economic aggregate, the per capita income and the level of social development, "The Zhejiang Phenomenon" received wide attention at home and abroad. The Party Committee of Zhejiang Province started to ponder and summarize the spirit and cultural factor behind the "Zhejiang Phenomenon". On December 21, 1999, the then Secretary of the Party Committee of Zhejiang Province, comrade Zhang Dejiang, called, on behalf of the Party Committee of Zhejiang Province, on the social science workers across the province to summarize the Zhejiang Spirit and the Zhejiang Experience to create Zhejiang's future. The 4th Plenary (Enlarged) Session of the 10th Party Committee of Zhejiang Province, held on July 24, 2000, officially put forward the Zhejiang Spirit and identified it as "ceaseless self-improvement, grittiness, great courage in innovation and pursuit of substantial results". This was the first summary statement and expression of the Zhejiang Spirit since the reform and opening-up.

The Zhejiang Spirit of advancing with the times: After the 16th National Congress of the Communist Party of China, new challenges in globalization, new practice in Zhejiang's reform and development, the new requirement of the Central Committee of the Communist Party of China for Zhejiang's state of staying ahead provided the new mindsets, value orientation, psychological state and social moral criterion for the Zhejiang Spirit in the new period. The Party Committee of Zhejiang Province gave great importance to summarizing the Zhejiang Spirit in the new period. In 2006, the then Secretary of the Party Committee of Zhejiang Province, comrade Xi Jinping, vowed to deeply study the "Zhejiang Phenomenon", substantiate and improve the "Zhejiang Experience", and enrich and develop the "Zhejiang Spirit". With multiple theoretical research projects, discussions and surveys on cities, relevant departments solicited opinions from experts, scholars, primary-level cadres and the people, conducted repeated research and discussions to finally determine the new expression of the Zhejiang Spirit of advancing with the times as "pursuit of truth, pragmatism, integrity and harmony, open-mindedness and determination to become stronger".

In 2007, the 2nd Plenary Session of the 12th Party Committee of Zhejiang Province adopted the *Decision of the Party Committee of Zhejiang Province on Earnestly Implementing the Guiding Principles Adopted during the 17th National Congress of the Communist Party of China and Concretely Working on Making the People Rich by Starting Businesses and of Building a Strong Province through Innovation,* stressing that the Zhejiang Spirit is the vivid embodiment of the national spirit and the spirit of the times in Zhejiang and also the valuable cultural wealth created by the people of Zhejiang in the great practice of entrepreneurship and innovation; it is necessary to adopt the entrepreneurship and innovation-focused Zhejiang Spirit to gather strength, arouse vitality and inspire actions.

The Zhejiang Spirit is summarized consistently, improved and developed, suggesting that the inherent requirement of the Zhejiang Spirit of advancing with the times is that the connotation of the Zhejiang Spirit is continuously enriched in light of the development of the era and the Zhejiang Spirit is given the new era implication, so that it serves as the cultural impetus for leading Zhejiang's development.

4.2.3 *"Local Spirits" Derived from the Zhejiang Spirit*

The discussions about the Zhejiang Spirit have given rise to the "Local Spirits" of Zhejiang's cities. The discussions and summary of the Zhejiang Spirit have deepened the reflections and cultural self-consciousness of the Party and government organs and the people from various sectors of the society regarding the Zhejiang Experience and the Zhejiang Model. The research, discussions and summary of the Zhejiang Spirit have produced a very strong "spillover effect" on Zhejiang's regional cultural development. It has stimulated Zhejiang's cities, counties, county-level cities and districts to summarize regional spirits and industrial spirits, ponder and summarize the shared values with local characteristics.

Local authorities in Zhejiang have summarized urban spirits or regional spirits in light of local characteristics. For instance, Hangzhou City realized early on in the country that the urban humanistic spirit was the soul and root of a city in urban development, and with discussions, Hangzhou City summarized its humanistic spirit as "exquisite, harmonious, magnificent and open-minded". Ningbo City summarized the Ningbo Spirit as "trustworthy, pragmatic, open-minded, innovative".

Overall, the Zhejiang Spirit is the concentrated embodiment of the national spirit and the spirit of the times in Zhejiang; it also represents the ethical summarization and cultural reflection of "the Zhejiang Phenomenon", "the Zhejiang Experience" and "the Zhejiang Model" which emerged over the years; it reflects the core factors of the shared values of the contemporary people of Zhejiang; it is an important part of Zhejiang's building of the system of values with a socialist core.

4.3 Consolidating and Expanding the Mainstream Ideology and Public Opinion

The cultivation of the system of values with a socialist core cannot be achieved without the guidance of the mainstream public opinion. The mainstream public opinion is fostered to provide important carriers and forms for the people to develop, accept, disseminate and practice the socialist core values. Following the latest developmental situation, including the information revolution and new media changes, to bring about innovations to the Party's work on mainstream ideology and public opinion is the inherent requirement for the Party in firmly holding the leadership in the ideological field. In the field of ideology and public opinion, Zhejiang has upheld the guiding role of Marxism, actively disseminated and practiced the socialist core values, brought about innovations to the systems and mechanisms of the guidance of mainstream public opinion, Zhejiang has also intensified the publicity of mainstream values in response to new challenges from the Internet to the guidance of mainstream public opinion, providing strong public opinion support and a guarantee of publicity for the building of the socialist core values.

4.3.1 The Basic Requirements for the Party's Work on Ideology and Public Opinion in the New Period

Since the beginning of the 21st century, modernization and IT application have been promoted rapidly, and dramatic changes have taken place in the media amidst the deepening information revolution in China. In this era, will the Party's work on ideology and public opinion change greatly? How can we understand such change? How does the work on ideology and public opinion adapt to the era of new media? These issues have drawn widespread attention from the press and public opinion circles.

As early as 2004, the then Secretary of the Party Committee of Zhejiang Province, comrade Xi Jinping, gave great importance to the publicity in the mainstream public opinion, he chaired the working conference on press publicity and put forward the basic principles for the work on ideology and public opinion. In 2013, after General Secretary Xi Jinping delivered the "August 19 Speech" on the Party's work on ideology and public opinion, the Party Committee of Zhejiang Province made specific arrangements for the work on ideology and public opinion according to the new requirements put forward by General Secretary Xi Jinping for ideological work, including the press and public opinion.

When working in Zhejiang, comrade Xi Jinping put forward the very explicit requirements for the work on mainstream public opinion, which are summarized as "ensuring that the press is run by politicians"; this is the most important principle for the work on ideology and public opinion. Moreover, his requirements also include the awareness about the overall situation, a sense of responsibility and a sense of innovation.

4.3.1.1 Ensuring that the Press is Run by Politicians

"Ensuring that the press is run by politicians" is the most important requirement put forward by comrade Xi Jinping and the successive Party Committees of Zhejiang Province for the work on ideology and public opinion. "The press and public opinion are important parts of superstructure and ideology; once publicity in the press becomes problematic, public opinion tools are not really controlled by Marxists, public opinion is not guided according to the Party and the people's will and interests, severe harm and huge loss will occur".[4] This is the fundamental reason why Zhejiang's work on ideology and public opinion must be governed by the principle of "ensuring that the press is run by politicians".

As stressed by comrade Xi Jinping, in order to uphold the principle of "ensuring that the press is run by politicians", it is necessary to always take the socialist theoretical system with Chinese characteristics as a guide, really enhance the self-consciousness and determination in carrying out the Party's basic theory, line, programme and experience; regarding publicity in the press, it is essential to firmly hold the correct direction, carry forward the main theme, advocate diversity, actively publicize all thoughts and spirits that are beneficial to patriotism, collectivism, socialism, reform, opening-up and modernization, thus fostering a good atmosphere for reform, opening-up and modernization. It is necessary to criticize the view that the press falls outside ideology, oppose the act of preaching the so-called freedom of the press, oppose the cancellation of pres management and the negation of the Party's principles relating to the press, further identify and resist the invasion of the Western liberal outlook on the press, take a clear-cut stand to uphold the Marxist outlook on the press and the Party's principles relating to the press.[5] It is essential to oppose the erroneous views and news reports and resist various erroneous trends. It is necessary to be politically keen and be able to discern with regard to political affairs, take a clear-cut stand and stand firm on the issues having a vital bearing on political direction and fundamental principles. In the field of publicity in the press, we must never cause political errors, provide channels for spreading erroneous thoughts and views, publicize the views and practices inconsistent with the Party's policies, or one-sidedly and incorrectly publicize the Party's policies.[6] Regarding publicity in the press, it is essential to keep political alignment with the Central Committee of the Communist Party of China, and ensure that the leadership over the Party's news agencies at various levels is firmly held by the personnel loyal to Marxism, the Party and the people.[7]

This is the most important political requirement put forward by Xi Jinping for Zhejiang's work on ideology and public opinion under the new situation.

---

[4]Xi (2006), p. 307.
[5]Xi (2006), p. 308.
[6]Xi (2006), p. 309.
[7]Xi (2006), p. 308.

4.3.1.2   Having the Awareness of the Overall Situation and a Sense of Responsibility

The second important principle put forward by comrade Xi Jinping for the work on ideology and public opinion lies in having an awareness of the overall situation and a sense of responsibility; this is an extension of the principle of "ensuring that the press is run by politicians". For the concrete connotation of the awareness of the overall situation and a sense of responsibility, he expounded, "Zhejiang's press must proceed from the overall situation, correctly deal with the relationship among reform, development and stability, arrange tasks according to the province's overall work, create an atmosphere in light of the key work carried out by the Party Committee of Zhejiang Province".[8] Regarding the reporting of the news, it is essential to determine the contents of the report and the focus of publicity according to the overall situation[9]; the work on ideology and public opinion should focus on making explanations to dispel doubts, enhancing understanding, intensifying publicity and guidance, persuasion, unifying thoughts and gathering strength; it should also focus on rousing rather than dampening enthusiasm, offering help rather than making troubles.[10] The main media directly under the provincial departments must actively keep coordination with the central tasks of the Party Committee of Zhejiang Province, intensify publicity and reporting on important issues. The press cannot merely pursue economic benefits and local benefits, it must put social benefits and global benefits first. The leaders on the press and public opinion front must exercise strict control, focus on the publicity and reporting relating to the central tasks of the Central Committee of the Communist Party of China and the Party Committee and the People's Government of Zhejiang Province.

These requirements for having an awareness of the overall situation and a sense of responsibility were put forward by comrade Xi Jinping with respect to Zhejiang's work on ideology and public opinion; they can play a very strong role in guiding Zhejiang's work on ideology and public opinion.

4.3.1.3   Having a Sense of Innovation

The third important principle put forward by comrade Xi Jinping for the work on ideology and public opinion lies in having a sense of innovation, proceeding from the development of the era to bringing about innovations to the press carriers and the mode of publicity in the press. This is mainly embodied in three aspects: First, making innovations to philosophy. Renewing press philosophies, adopting the achievements of new technologies and new media revolutions to bring about innovations to publicity platforms and modes. Second, making innovations in practice. Enriching communication means, improving the ability of various media

---

[8]Xi (2006), p. 309.

[9]Xi (2006), p. 309.

[10]Xi (2006), p. 309.

to attract, inspire and fight in communication. Third, working on the front line of Zhejiang's reform and development, further going deep into social life, discovering publicity materials from the people and practice, and bringing about innovations to the content of publicity in the press.

Given the new situation and new issues in the work on ideology and public opinion, comrade Xi Jinping always gave great importance to the ideological work including the mainstream public opinion, summarized the basic principles for guiding Zhejiang's, and even the national, work on ideology and public opinion and put forward the core requirements—"the Marxist outlook on the press" and "ensuring that the press is run by politicians"—to guide Zhejiang's, and even the national, work on ideology and public opinion. These thoughts laid a foundation for Zhejiang to keep a correct political direction in the work on ideology and public opinion, and served as the guiding thoughts for Zhejiang to explore innovations to the systems and mechanisms involving the guidance of the mainstream public opinion and to address the rapid development of the Internet.

4.3.2 Bringing Innovations to the Channels and Modes for Publicizing the Mainstream Values

For the work on ideology and public opinion in the era of new media, only when system and mechanism innovations are promoted along with the deepening information revolution can the Party's leadership over the ideological field be consolidated and can the ideology and public opinion under the Party's leadership really ensure that the power of the mainstream public opinion guides and leads.

In nearly ten years, Zhejiang brought about continuous innovations to the systems and mechanisms involving the guidance of the mainstream public opinion, intensified the publicity of the socialist core values and renewed the publicity mode, thus Zhejiang acquired much valuable practical experience in the innovations relating to ideology and public opinion.

Comrade Xi Jinping, when working in Zhejiang, and the subsequent Party Committees of Zhejiang Province gave importance to the work on ideology and public opinion in the new period, actively coped with the new situation and new issues from new media to the work on ideology and public opinion. On May 26, 2004, comrade Xi Jinping specially wrote an article to discuss the issue of ideological and public opinion oversights in the new period. He pointed out, "It is necessary to keep improving the publicity in the press, focus reports on central tasks and major issues, increase the level of public opinion oversights, improve the reporting on major emergencies, enhance the rapid response and emergency coordination mechanism involving reporting in this regard, earnestly carry out and improve the news release system and firmly hold the initiative in news information communication. News reports should give prominence to the main theme of solidarity, stability and encouragement, promptly and accurately convey the Party's voice, actively and effectively give explanations to dispel doubts and foster a good atmosphere conducive to promoting social harmony and stability".[11]

In the above remarks, comrade Xi Jinping vowed to improve the mechanism of response to public opinion crisis in case of major emergencies, carry out and improve the news release system, give prominence to the main theme, and promptly and accurately convey the Party's voice. These requirements represent the new line of thought and new arrangements for the work on ideology and public opinion under the condition of the new media. Zhejiang's explorations and innovations in the systems and mechanisms involving the work on ideology and public opinion are mainly embodied in the following aspects.

4.3.2.1   Bringing About Innovations to the Systems and Mechanisms of Public Opinion and the Media

The Party Committee of Zhejiang Province specially set up the Office of Internet Information according to the new situation in the Internet era. In 2005, the Party Committee of Zhejiang Province established the Leading Group for Internet Administration, and developed the *Implementation Opinions on Further Strengthening Internet Administration*, built and improved the working system for online monitoring, online reading and appraisal, and online comments, and built the team of full-time and part-time online commentators. Regarding the development of the mainstream public opinion front, Zhejiang brought about innovations to the systems and mechanisms to guide traditional media to develop into modern media.

4.3.2.2   Universally Establishing the System of the News Spokesman

In nearly ten years, Zhejiang widely established the system of the news spokesman; this is an important measure taken by the Party committee and the government for enhancing information disclosure and transparency in the period of frequent news events. In 2003, Zhejiang developed and implemented the *Opinions of the Department of Publicity under the Party Committee of Zhejiang Province and the News Office of Zhejiang Province on Further Improving News Releases*. In 2004, Zhejiang started cultivating news spokesmen and initiated the building of the system of the news spokesman, holding the first news spokesmen training class, thus the system of the news spokesman was gradually established at the provincial, municipal and county levels and in various functional departments.

---

[11] Xi (2007).

4.3.2.3   Establishing the Mechanism for the Management of Public Opinion Crises

Zhejiang endeavored to build the systems and mechanisms for the management and handling of public opinion crises. In 2003, Zhejiang issued the *Implementation Measures for Further Improving and Strengthening the Work on News Reporting Concerning Emergencies within the Province* and the *Implementation Measures for Strengthening the Administration of Short News on Internet Websites*. In 2004, the Department of Publicity under the Party Committee of Zhejiang Province developed and issued the *Opinions on Strengthening and Improving the Reporting for Internal Reference* and the *Circular on Exercising Strict Control over Publicity Discipline to Ensure the Correct Guidance of Public Opinion*. In 2009, Zhejiang reinforced the research and training on the handling of public opinion crises. With these measures, Zhejiang built a systematic mechanism for the handling of public opinion crises so that Zhejiang's mainstream public opinion front was further consolidated.

4.3.2.4   Continuously Renewing the Online Release Platform

When working in Zhejiang, comrade Xi Jinping pointed out, "Regarding the public opinion publicity, it is essential to foster a strong sense of front and realize that with respect to any front, if we did not occupy it, some negative things and hostile forces would penetrate it; only when we let Marxism occupy it can negative things and hostile forces be dispelled and can the responsibility for preserving the front be really assumed".[12]

4.3.3   Intensifying the Publicity of the Mainstream Values

Zhejiang renewed the publicity channels and routes in response to the new media revolution and the times, providing an important condition for carrying forward the main theme and reinforcing the publicity of the socialist core values. Strengthening the publicity of the mainstream values is the basic responsibility for Zhejiang's work on ideology and public opinion, mainly covering: First of all, the new publicity of the annual guiding principles from the Central Committee of the Communist Party of China and the Party Committee of Zhejiang Province, the annual major strategic arrangements of the Central Committee of the Communist Party of China and the Party Committee of Zhejiang Province, namely, the publicity of the annual major issues; second, intensified publicity of education on integrity and moral models; third, the publicity of new social trends.

---

[12]Xi (2006), p. 312.

4.3.3.1 Actively Publicizing the Important Principles and Strategic Arrangements from the Central Committee of the Communist Party of China and the Party Committee of Zhejiang Province

Major annual publicity can be divided into two categories: First, the publicity of the latest strategic arrangements made by the Central Committee of the Communist Party of China and the Party Committee of Zhejiang Province. Publicity focused on the annual guiding principles and strategic arrangements from the Central Committee of the Communist Party of China, and the guiding principles and strategic arrangements from the important meetings convened by the Party Committee of Zhejiang Province. It included publicity reporting on the annual sessions of the NPC and the CPPCC, on the plenary session of the Central Committee of the Communist Party of China, the annual sessions of the provincial people's congress and the provincial CPPCC, and the plenary session of the Party Committee of Zhejiang Province. For instance, in 2004, Zhejiang determined the publicity theme focusing on fostering the Scientific Outlook on Development, carrying out the "Eight-Eight Strategies", building a safe Zhejiang, and strengthening the building of the Party's governance capacity. In 2005, Zhejiang carried out the themed publicity activity of "doing solid work to stay ahead".

Second, the publicity of the major anniversary commemoration activities, such as the publicity reporting on the 100th birthday of Deng Xiaoping and the 55th anniversary of the founding of the new China in 2004; commemoration of the 70th anniversary of the victory of the Long March in 2005.

4.3.3.2 Strengthening the Publicity of Education on Integrity and Moral Models

Regarding the publicity of the mainstream values, Zhejiang stepped up education on integrity and actively carried out the building of a trustworthy Zhejiang arranged by comrade Xi Jinping when working in Zhejiang, advocated the moral trends of stressing integrity and trustworthiness in families, schools and the society; Zhejiang also focused on typical reporting on the trustworthy enterprises, units and individuals to foster models of integrity and thus lead the social moral trends. Moreover, Zhejiang promoted publicity reporting on moral models, special publicity of the "Most Beautiful Mother", the "Most Beautiful Driver", the "Most Beautiful Zhejiang People" and other typical characters.

4.3.3.3 Publicizing the New Trends in Social Progress, Including Learning Lei Feng, a Role Model Ready to Help Others, and Fostering New Customs

Publicizing the civilized mindsets and civilized behaviors to develop the new trends in social progress is an important part of the press and public opinion work. In nearly ten years, Zhejiang unremittingly carried forward the new social trends and publicized the new civilized behaviors, for example, introducing "civilized travel", "civilized etiquette", "taking care of zebra crossings", "becoming a virtuous person" and "learning Lei Feng, fostering new trends", extensively carrying out the themed publicity activities "stressing civility, health, science, fostering new trends", carrying forward the scientific spirit, removing bad habits in the society, advocating a culturally advanced life, popularizing scientific knowledge, improving the cultural quality, and carrying forward the active new moral trends.

Overall, comrade Xi Jinping, when working in Zhejiang, and the subsequent Party Committees of Zhejiang Province gave great importance to the work on the mainstream public opinion, upheld the Party's basic requirements for the work on ideology and mainstream public opinion in the new period, brought innovations to the channels and modes for publicizing the mainstream values, intensified the publicity of the socialist core values and gave full play to the role of the mainstream values in the value orientation and morality in the whole society. With efforts made to consolidate and expand the mainstream ideological and public opinion front, Zhejiang fostered a good mainstream public opinion and greatly promoted the cultivation and dissemination of the system of values with a socialist core in Zhejiang.

4.4 The "Most Beautiful Phenomena" and the Building of Our Shared Values

When working in Zhejiang, comrade Xi Jinping gave great importance to the building of values, advocated and carried forward the Zhejiang Spirit of advancing with the times, incorporated "integrity" into the expression of the Zhejiang Spirit. He also took charge of and arranged the building of a trustworthy Zhejiang, advocated and carried forward the outstanding traditional culture, and cultivated the socialist core values. As from 2004, the successive Party Committees of Zhejiang Province paid a great deal of attention to the cultivation of the system of values with a socialist core, vigorously carried forward the Socialist Concept of Honor and Disgrace, and made arrangements—in the "Eight-Eight Strategies" and the overall strategy of "making the people rich by starting businesses and of building a strong province through innovation"—for the building of the socialist core values and moral development; they creatively promoted the building of moral rules and values in the new period in light of Zhejiang's regional characteristics. The implementation of such strategic arrangements as a safe Zhejiang, a trustworthy Zhejiang, a culturally large province, a Zhejiang under the rule of law, and a materially affluent and culturally advanced Zhejiang provided great impetus for Zhejiang to foster a healthy and positive cultural and moral atmosphere in the whole society and build a moral system suited to a socialist market economy.

4.4.1 Enhancing the Moral Support for the Development of Zhejiang's Transformation

Those nearly ten years were crucial for the development of Zhejiang's transformation. During the period 2004–2013, in Zhejiang, the economic aggregate increased from 1164.9 billion yuan to 3756.8 billion yuan, the per capita GDP increased from a level higher than USD 4,000 to a level higher than USD 10,000 and the rate of urbanization rose from 53 to 64%. For Zhejiang, this period was an important golden period of development, the period of salient social contrasts and a crucial period of strengthening the building of the social credit system and moral ethical order suited to a socialist market economy. The cultivation and development of the social credit system, moral order and ethical rules can provide vigorous moral support for the development of Zhejiang's transformation and also offer strong cultural impetus and value guidance for Zhejiang's further economic and social development and the building of a materially affluent and culturally advanced Zhejiang.

4.4.1.1 Comprehensively Improving the Civic Intellectual and Moral Quality

According to the arrangements made by the Central Committee of the Communist Party of China and the Party Committee of Zhejiang Province for moral civic development, Zhejiang thoroughly carried out the *Implementation Plan for Civic Morality*, and proceeded from Zhejiang's reality to develop and implement the *Civic Moral Rule of Zhejiang Province*, the *Implementation Plan of Zhejiang for Civic Morality* and the *Plan of Zhejiang for Moral Civic Development*, providing an institutional guarantee for Zhejiang to comprehensively improve civic morality.

Zhejiang reinforced education of social morality, professional ethics and family virtues. Each year, Zhejiang carried out the Civic Morality Day activity under the theme of "Zhejiang's Good Person, Going Far with Virtues", and conducted the civic moral publicity education among the entire population. Zhejiang extensively and thoroughly carried out the activity of learning Lei Feng in the whole society, took feasible measures to routinize and institutionalize the activity of learning Lei Feng, and increased the breadth and depth of moral civic development. Zhejiang pushed forward the activity of "stressing civility, fostering new trends", organized the moral themed reading activity and deepened the moral model appraisal and selection activity. Each year, Zhejiang carried out themed moral practical activities including the themes of "Zhejiang's Good Person", "Becoming a Civilized, Polite Zhejiang Person" and "Becoming a Virtuous Person".

4.4.1.2 Systematically Building a Working System for Intellectual and Moral Development of Juveniles and University Students

Zhejiang has always given importance to the intellectual and moral development of juveniles. Juveniles are the future of a country, thus it is essential to develop good moral mindsets and behaviors of juveniles. Xi Jinping said, "The intellectual and moral development of juveniles is a systematic project and involves various aspects, and the participation of the whole society and strong synergy are needed".[13]

In 2004, in coordination with the guiding principles adopted by the Central Committee of the Communist Party of China and Zhejiang's reality, the Party Committee and the People's Government of Zhejiang Province issued the *Implementation Opinions on Further Strengthening and Improving the Intellectual and Moral Development of Juveniles*, specially making arrangements for the intellectual and moral development of juveniles. With a focus on this, Zhejiang gradually set the "3510" work goal for all juveniles—"3" means improving the network for the intellectual and moral education of juveniles covering schools, families and the society; "5" means thoroughly carrying out the front project, the excellent works project, the green network project, the purification project and the assistance project for the intellectual and moral development of juveniles; "10" means doing substantial work in ten aspects, including the creation, production and dissemination of cultural products, showing care for rural juveniles and juveniles as special groups, each year. The establishment of the "3510" work goal for the intellectual and moral development of juveniles greatly promoted the improvement of the intellectual and moral education of juveniles in Zhejiang.

With a focus on the intellectual and moral development of university students, Zhejiang actively carried out the university student tutorial system, extended the network of ideological and political work and the work on the intellectual and moral development of university students to apartments and student organizations, improved the system of the education, management and services for university students, Zhejiang also incorporated the learning and practice of the Socialist Concept of Honor and Disgrace and moral civic development into the courses of intellectual and moral cultivation and the fundamentals of law at the institutions of higher learning. Each year, the provincial leaders and provincial lecturer groups were invited to the institutions of higher learning to deliver special reports and speeches on the situation. Zhejiang strengthened moral education at schools, the development of online intellectual and moral cultural fronts, improved the management of cyberculture at campuses, and adopted various means to improve the intellectual, moral and cultural quality of university students.

In nearly ten years, Zhejiang gradually built a working system for the intellectual and moral development of juveniles and university students, greatly enhancing the intellectual, moral and cultural quality of juveniles and university students across the province and providing strong moral power for Zhejiang's future development.

---

[13]Xi (2006), p. 303.

4.4.1.3 Intensifying the Intellectual and Moral Development of Special Groups

Zhejiang has always given importance to the intellectual and moral development of special groups and carried out different intellectual and moral work on different groups, so that the intellectual and moral quality of the people in different industries and different groups across the province improved. For instance, Zhejiang carried out the Spring Mud Program for the intellectual and moral development of rural juveniles, and promoted the intellectual and moral development of the migrant population in some areas with a large migrant population in Zhejiang.

In order to strengthen and promote the intellectual and moral development of rural juveniles and create a good healthy growth environment for rural juveniles, in 2008, the Civilization Office of Zhejiang Province issued the *Circular Concerning the Pilot Work on the Spring Mud Program in Rural Areas across the Province*. In 2009, the Civilization Office of Zhejiang Province issued the *Circular on Further Implementing the Spring Mud Program*, resulting in implementation of the Spring Mud Program across the province. The Spring Mud Program specially caters to the characteristics of the intellectual and moral development of rural juveniles; with the village as a unit, the Spring Mud Program has enriched the extracurricular life of rural juveniles and improved their intellectual and moral development; it has become one of Zhejiang's major projects to strengthen the intellectual and moral development of the special groups—rural juveniles.

In the meantime, Zhejiang carried out special practical moral activities, including "double-10,000 paired joint construction", to intensify the intellectual and moral development of special groups, such as the migrant population and stay-at-home people in rural areas. Such intellectual and moral development of special groups has greatly improved the intellectual and moral development of the people across the province, creating a good moral order and social atmosphere for Zhejiang's harmonious and stable development.

With efforts in promoting the intellectual and moral development and improving the moral civic quality, moral models, good people and good deeds mushroomed in Zhejiang. Zhejiang has stayed ahead nationwide in economic and social development, and has also drawn national attention in cultural, ethical and moral development. Zhejiang has a great deal of innovative practice in intellectual moral development, and the most conspicuous practice is as follows: First, the "Most Beautiful Phenomena" have emerged one after another and have played an active role in leading and inspiring at the moral level. Second, Zhejiang has energetically conducted the "Our Values" activity to foster the shared values of the contemporary people of Zhejiang and carry forward the socialist core values and the shared values of the contemporary people of Zhejiang, thus greatly promoting the modernization of Zhejiang.

4.4.2 The Emergence of the "Most Beautiful Phenomena" in Zhejiang

In recent years, based on long-term cultivation of the socialist core values, the moral civic quality of the people of Zhejiang has improved continuously, new moral trends have arisen, healthy social trends and positive energy have been earnestly carried forward, and a large number of the "Most Beautiful Phenomena" have emerged. These "Most Beautiful Phenomena" are the achievements made by Zhejiang in cultivating the core value system and rebuilding a moral order in response to the needs of the development of social change and they reflect the great achievements made by Zhejiang in moral development and the building of values in nearly ten years.

4.4.2.1 The "Most Beautiful Phenomena" in Zhejiang

The "Most Beautiful Mother", the "Most Beautiful Driver", the "Most Beautiful Police", the common heroes who put out fires to save people in Hangzhou's June 7 bus arson case, and other moral models and moving deeds have sprung up in recent years; these are the "Most Beautiful Phenomena" in Zhejiang which are influential nationwide.

The "Most Beautiful Phenomena" in different areas, different industries and different sectors of Zhejiang demonstrate the moral sentiment and spirit of the people of Zhejiang in the new period. They are too numerous to mention one by one.

With the "Most Beautiful Phenomena" in various parts of Zhejiang, the expansion and derivation of the expression "most beautiful" make the "Most Beautiful Phenomena" in Zhejiang multidimensional and stereoscopic and they present the new moral trends and new spiritual coordinates in Zhejiang.

4.4.2.2 The Multidimensional "Most Beautiful Phenomena"

The "Most Beautiful Phenomena" are not isolated, but multidimensional and sustainable.

1. Stereoscopic

From the "Most Beautiful Phenomena", we can find that the greatest characteristic is that they are stereoscopic; "stereoscopic" involves the new moral trends presented by the "Most Beautiful Phenomena" and means that there are the "Most Beautiful" people and deeds among men and women, old and young, regardless of area, profession and position.

2. Multidimensional

A further characteristic of the "Most Beautiful Phenomena" is that they are multidimensional; they cover family virtues, including professional ethics and social morality; they may be minor matters and ordinary things; they may be great feats or magnanimous acts which embody dedication and new socialist moral trends.

3. Sustainable in time

An additional characteristic of the "Most Beautiful Phenomena" is that they are sustainable in time. Over the years, the "Most Beautiful Phenomena" have not been discontinuous, like the spring water.

These "Most Beautiful Phenomena", "Most Beautiful People" and "Most Beautiful Deeds" demonstrate Zhejiang's continuous improvement in moral, cultural and ethical development in its drive towards modernization. These "Most Beautiful Phenomena" have also provided the strong moral power and spirit for Zhejiang's development in the new era.

4.4.3 The Building of "Our Values"

In recent years, Zhejiang has given great importance to incorporating the building of the system of values with a socialist core into the practice of intellectual, moral, cultural and ethical development, Zhejiang has combined its historical and cultural inheritance with the spirit shown by its people in reform and opening-up, conducted the great debate "Our Values" and thus identified the shared values of the contemporary people of Zhejiang on the basis of summarizing the Zhejiang Spirit of advancing with the times.

4.4.3.1 The Great Debate of "Our Values"

Zhejiang is an eastern province as a forerunner, it has witnessed rapid economic development, its urbanization rate is higher than the national level, and it has a large external population, so Zhejiang meets with many problems in social and cultural change. Zhejiang's building of "Our Values" is an active response to these problems.

The great debate of "Our Values" originated in Hangzhou and was promoted across the province. The important achievement from the great debate is the shared values of the contemporary people of Zhejiang which guide Zhejiang's building of the socialist core values in the future and have Zhejiang's regional characteristics.

1. The "Our Values" themed practical activity in Hangzhou

In July, 2011, Hangzhou extensively conducted practical activities in summarizing the keywords under the theme of "Our Values" across the city. With the "Our Values" themed activities, Hangzhou widely solicited opinions from the people and summarized and interpreted the socialist core values in a popular way, thus promoting the great debate of "Our Values" across the province.

2. The great debate of "Our Values" across the province

In 2012, Zhejiang, based on summing up the experience from the "Our Values" themed practical activities in Hangzhou, arranged and conducted the great debate of "Our Values" across the province. The Party Committee of Zhejiang Province specially set up a leading group for the work, and collected the core words relating to "Our Values" through traditional media and online platforms and the cadres and the people throughout the province participated in the great debate. Zhejiang held more than 8,000 symposiums, public lectures and seminars, with extensive participation in discussions for more than 10 million person-times. With careful study and discussions, the Standing Committee of the Party Committee of Zhejiang Province finally adopted these core words: being pragmatic, trustworthy, advocating learning and upholding goodwill. The subsequently-held 13th Party Congress of Zhejiang Province vowed to actively advocate the shared values of the contemporary people of Zhejiang with the connotation of "being pragmatic, trustworthy, advocating learning and upholding goodwill".

With extensive public participation, discussions in the academic circles, online collection and decisions made by the Party Committee of Zhejiang Province, the great debate of "Our Values" has promoted the province's cultural reflection and values examination of its development and brought about innovations to the manner of dissemination and the carrier of activities relating to the socialist core values. The great debate of "Our Values" also represents public participation in building the system of values with a socialist core, and has led to the summarization of the moral rule, value standard and code of conduct to be jointly observed, making the socialist core values localized and popular in Zhejiang.

4.4.3.2   The Theoretical Perspective for the Shared Values of the Contemporary People of Zhejiang

With the great debate of "Our Values", Zhejiang has summarized the shared values of the contemporary people of Zhejiang, which are of important innovative significance for building the socialist core values.

1. Summarizing the shared values of the contemporary people of Zhejiang reflects an urgent need of the development of Zhejiang's economic and social change

In an effort to build the socialist core values, Zhejiang creatively proceeded from Zhejiang's reality to identify the shared values of the contemporary people of Zhejiang with the connotation of "being pragmatic, trustworthy, advocating learning and upholding goodwill"; this showed an examination of cultural reflection and values regarding Zhejiang's development and catered to the urgent need of the change in Zhejiang's economic and social development.

The period of 2004–2014 was an important period for the change in Zhejiang's economic and social development, during which the most important building of values in the cultural soft power became very pressing. As early as 2005, comrade Xi Jinping gave great importance to the role of culture as the soft power and worked on strengthening the building of values. When delivering a speech in 2005, he pointed out, "The power of culture, or the cultural soft power considered as part of the overall competitiveness by us is always subtly integrated into economic, political and social forces and becomes the'booster' for economic development, the'navigational light' for political development and the'adhesive' for social harmony".[14] Zhejiang experienced the process from developing the Zhejiang Spirit in response to the times, upholding the Zhejiang Spirit which features "pursuit of truth, pragmatism, integrity and harmony, open-mindedness and determination to become stronger" to upholding and carrying forward the entrepreneurship and innovation-focused Zhejiang Spirit, and then identifying the shared values of the contemporary people of Zhejiang; these practical innovations catered to the needs of Zhejiang's economic and social change, and really integrated the power of spirit and that of values into economic and social development.

2. Exploring the basic path for rebuilding the contemporary values

In "Our Values" and "the Shared Values of the Contemporary People of Zhejiang", the words "us" and "shared" are the most conspicuous. The "us" and "shared" also suggest that the building of the socialist core values needs to be based on "us" and "shared", and that only in this way can they become popular and be rooted in the people's lives. Only when they come from the people can the core values be given strong internal vitality; this is a basic path explored by Zhejiang for rebuilding contemporary values. The path is suitable to and universal for Zhejiang's cities, and even for the whole country.

3. The shared values of the contemporary people of Zhejiang belong not only to Zhejiang but also to China

The great debate of "Our Values" originated in Zhejiang and led to the summarization of the shared values of the contemporary people of Zhejiang, they have Zhejiang's characteristics. However, they certainly contain two basic implications: They are the result of adapting the socialist core values to Zhejiang's context and also that of adapting the shared values of the people of Zhejiang to the Chinese context.

The view that "Our Values" summarized by Zhejiang are the result of adapting the socialist core values to Zhejiang's context means that they embody not only the essential requirements of the socialist core values but also Zhejiang's regional characteristics, so they are the values expressed in Zhejiang's way. The view that "the shared values" summarized by Zhejiang are the result of adapting to the Chinese context means that these core words indicating "value coordinates" have the internal implication of adapting to China's socialist modernization and embody the universal pursuit of values by the Chinese people.

Overall, in 10 years, Zhejiang catered to the urgent requirements of the development of economic and social change for the building of values to actively build and cultivate the system of values with a socialist core, deepen the publicity and education concerning the Socialist Concept of Honor and Disgrace, comprehensively improve the moral civic quality, carry forward the "Most Beautiful Phenomena" and build

---

[14]Xi (2006), p. 289.

"Our Values", thus making great achievements in the cultural and ethical development; they embody the achievements of the innovation brought about by Zhejiang in promoting the building of the system of values with a socialist core, they provide strong cultural support, moral rule and values guidance for Zhejiang's reform and development, and they offer an endless thought-based cohesive force and cultural impetus.

4.5 The Building of Rural Cultural Auditoriums Defined as the Homes for Meeting the People's Cultural Needs

Rural cultural auditoriums are the rural homes for meeting the people's cultural needs in the new era and they are built by the Party Committee and the People's Government of Zhejiang Province in light of the increasing cultural needs of Zhejiang's farmers and the reality of rural cultural development and for the purpose of consolidating and carrying forward the socialist core values; they serve as the new platforms, new carriers and new fronts for making the socialist core values rooted in rural areas. Cultural auditoriums have been fully recognized by leaders, well received by the people and have drawn close attention from the media. With cultural auditoriums as the basis, Zhejiang has been designated by the Ministry of Culture as the national pilot province for the building of primary-level integrated cultural service centers. The central media, including the People's Daily, the Xinhua News Agency, CCTV and the Guangming Daily, have publicized and reported the building of cultural auditoriums.

4.5.1 The Rise of Rural Cultural Auditoriums

Zhejiang has a permanent resident population of 54 million, including a rural population of 20.88 million, accounting for 38%. For a long time, rural areas were the main part of rural China. Even at present, agriculture, farmers and rural areas remain the focus of China's development. In the environment of an era of social change, agriculture, farmers and rural areas are subject to the impact from new mindsets and new things.

Since the reform and opening-up, as the forerunner in the market economy, Zhejiang has been early and more obviously subject to the impact of the market force on agriculture, farmers and rural areas than some other areas in China. Under the household contract system in the economic institution, farmers can independently carry out production activities in the capacity of individual workers; with the improvement of economic conditions,[15] their living conditions have gradually developed towards standalone buildings, televisions, telephones, mobile phones,

---

[15]In 2014, the per capita disposal income of Zhejiang's rural permanent residents was 19,373 yuan, being 8,884 yuan more than or 0.5 times higher than 10,489 yuan, the level of the national average,

computers, network and other modern communication modes have entered ordinary rural households; as individuals enjoy an increasingly rich life, the relatively closed from of life has emerged, so like urban residents, and there has been an atomic state of social connection. As farmers' needs for material life are met, their cultural needs are on the increase, but public facilities, spaces and cultural life in rural areas are lacking and hardly meet their cultural needs; as a result, in some rural areas, social evils, including distortion of values, feudalistic superstition, pornography, gambling and drug abuse, occur to varying degrees; external religions have spread in some rural areas. Therefore, the Party committee and the government have always given importance to the building of homes in order to meet the farmers' cultural needs, especially that of enhancing their cultural identity and the integration of values.

Over the years, the successive Party Committees and the People's Governments of Zhejiang Province have given great importance to basic rural public cultural services and to the building of the socialist core values; in the process of carrying out the project of meeting the people's cultural needs and the project of "1,000-village demonstrations and 10,000-village improvements" and building a beautiful countryside, they have endeavored to incorporate the socialist core values, enrich the farmers' cultural life and promote the cultural and ethical development of rural areas in Zhejiang.

In the meantime, we should also be aware of the spontaneous new forces of cultural development in rural areas. The farmers in the new era, especially young farmers, have been influenced by modern civilization and have a high degree of cultural quality and strong modern awareness. They are willing and able to participate in activities for their rural cultural development, and they are the main participants in rural cultural development. Under the long-term influence of the outstanding traditional culture, there has been profound national cultural identity and value identification in rural areas, and villagers have a high degree of cultural judgment and cognitive ability.

In 2011, in some rural areas of Lin'an City, Zhejiang, local people spontaneously built public cultural spaces in villages and carried out cultural activities in villages. In an effort to build a beautiful countryside, excellent villages, a green homeland, magnificent mountain villages and other characteristic villages, villagers used the original auditoriums, book halls and ancestral temples in villages to actively develop public activity spaces and seek the collective venues for cultural life. Thanks to addressing the cultural folk needs and respecting the pioneering spirit of the farmers, the building of cultural auditoriums was well received by villagers. There have been venues for conducting public cultural activities, including villagers meetings, public lectures, commendation activities, cultural and artistic activities, summer training programs, the showing of films and performances; villagers can freely take part in a variety of activities, developing a sense of a big family.

The cultural auditorium activities in Lin'an City which produced preliminary results drew attention from the Party Committee and the People's Government of Zhejiang Province. Based on adequate surveys and repeated discussions, the Party

ranking Zhejiang no. 2 among 31 provinces (autonomous regions, municipalities) and no. 1 among provinces (autonomous regions) across the country.

Committee and the People's Government of Zhejiang Province decided to arrange and conduct the building of cultural auditoriums in administrative villages across the province in early 2013; they designated it as the practical project of the provincial government for three consecutive years, vowed to build cultural auditoriums in more than 50% of the administrative villages, basically build cultural auditoriums in the central villages and make cultural auditoriums cover more than 80% of the rural population across the province by 2020, with a view to making cultural auditoriums become the homes for inheriting the traditional culture and carrying forward advanced culture, an important brand of primary-level cultural publicity and an important front for building a beautiful countryside in Zhejiang, through "1,000-village demonstrations, 10,000-villages reaching the standard", so that rural people can universally enjoy the achievements in building cultural auditoriums.

4.5.2   The Line of Thought of Building Rural Cultural Auditoriums and Their Operational Management

With pilot exploration and demonstration for two years, Zhejiang has gradually developed the line of thought, a system of institutional guarantees and the basic components for building rural cultural auditoriums, it built the corresponding organizational guarantee system and preliminary institutional framework, and developed an integrated method for operational management covering building, management and use.

1.   The line of thought and standard for building rural cultural auditoriums

There is clear thinking regarding the building of rural cultural auditoriums in Zhejiang, which is as follows: focusing on the overall requirement of "arousing a new wave of socialist cultural development" and "enhancing the rural developmental vitality, promoting the common prosperity of rural and urban areas", by first making plans, determining the scientific layout, promoting the work in a layered way to build a number of cultural front complexes under the theme of "cultural auditoriums and homes for meeting the people's cultural needs" and marked by cultural auditoriums, improve a new system of public cultural services integrating the municipal and county-level key cultural facilities, town-level integrated cultural stations and cultural auditoriums, build a new rural cultural system which guides, educates and inspires the people, provide solid cultural guarantee for scientific rural development, harmony and stability.

Based on the above thoughts regarding the building, repeated discussions, continuous explorations and adjustments in practice, as the competent department for the building of cultural auditoriums, the Department of Publicity under the Party Committee of Zhejiang Province has carefully designed explicit standards for building: adopting the standard of "making available five factors and performing three functions"—five factors refer to venue, display, activity, team and mechanism; three functions refer to learning and teaching, etiquette, entertainment—to build the rural cultural complexes integrating intellectual and moral development, cultural, sports and entertainment activities, popularization of knowledge and skills. In practice, this means acting according to local conditions, promoting the work in a classified way, giving prominence to characteristics, integrating the existing cultural facilities of administrative villages, adopting the means of new construction, reconstruction and expansion to build the rural cultural complexes, thus integrating intellectual and moral development, cultural, sports and entertainment activities, the popularization of knowledge and skills and creating the homes for meeting farmers' cultural needs in the new period.

2. The organizational guarantee and institutional system for rural cultural auditoriums

Regarding the system of organizational guarantees, a leading group consisting of the people in charge of 20 departments—including the Department of Publicity under the Party Committee of Zhejiang Province, the Department of Culture, the Rural Work Office, the Department of Finance, the Department of Construction of Zhejiang Province—was specially set up at the provincial level, and the corresponding leading groups at various levels were established; many counties (county-level cities, districts) also established the system under which the leaders of the Party and the government contact the villages for building cultural auditoriums. The village-level Party organization or village committee was required to determine one village cadre responsible for the work on cultural auditoriums. The full-time (part-time) management personnel were assigned for cultural auditoriums.

With respect to the institutional system, in 2013, the General Office of the Party Committee of Zhejiang Province and the General Office of the People's Government of Zhejiang Province jointly issued the *Opinions on Promoting the Building of Rural Cultural Auditoriums*, specifying the work goals, basic principles and main tasks for cultural auditoriums. Such departments as the Department of Publicity under the Party Committee of Zhejiang Province issued the *Circular Concerning the Establishment of the Expert Guidance Group of Zhejiang Province for the Building of Rural Cultural Auditoriums* and the *Circular Concerning Strengthening the Instructor, Administrator, Volunteer Teams for the Work on Rural Cultural Auditoriums*. To normalize and standardize the building of cultural auditoriums, the Department of Publicity under the Party Committee of Zhejiang Province organized experts, scholars and relevant personnel to compile the *Operating Manual for Cultural Auditoriums*, specifying the criteria and requirements for facility construction and exhibition setting at cultural auditoriums, especially the procedures for ritual activities.

To guarantee the funds for the building of cultural auditoriums, the Department of Publicity under the Party Committee of Zhejiang Province and the Department of Finance of Zhejiang Province issued the *Measures of Zhejiang Province for Appraisal, Rewards and Subsidies Involving the Advanced Counties (County-level Cities, Districts) in Building Rural Cultural Auditoriums*, calling for arranging 30 million yuan from provincial finances in 2013 and 50 million yuan each year as from 2014 as subsidies in place of rewards for supporting the building of cultural auditoriums. Each year, the Department of Publicity under the Party Committee of Zhejiang Province allocates 30 million yuan to subsidize the underdeveloped areas in building cultural auditoriums, while the Department of Culture of Zhejiang Province allocates more financial resources from working funds to support the building of cultural auditoriums. The cities, counties (county-level cities, districts) earmark a special fiscal fund ranging from millions of yuan to tens of millions of yuan to support the building of cultural auditoriums, arousing the enthusiasm of administrative villages for the building of cultural auditoriums.

3.   The facility carriers and content carriers at rural cultural auditoriums

The building of rural cultural auditoriums is based on the construction of facilities and focuses on the construction of content. The work mainly covers the following aspects.

(1)   Building the venue facilities in a coordinated way. Venue facilities include an auditorium on a certain scale, which is provided with a stage and can meet the farmers' needs for holding cultural festivals, cultural ceremonies, cultural and sports activities, gatherings and discussions of issues; moreover, these facilities include a lecture room for conducting intellectual and moral education, introducing the situation and policies, etiquette, popularizing scientific and legal knowledge among farmers, developing their production skills and carrying out physical training as well as a well-functioning cultural activity center, a rural library, a broadcasting room, the activity room for the Spring Mud Program, a facility for mass sports activities, primary-level points under the cultural information resource sharing project, which are built according to relevant national and provincial requirements. Online cultural auditoriums are concurrently built in the counties (county-level cities, districts) where conditions permit.

(2)   Rationally arranging exhibitions. Exhibiting photos, written materials and objects to introduce village history and conditions, customs, virtues, the people of virtue, current affairs and policies.

(3)   Carefully organizing cultural ritual activities. Conducting various cultural ritual activities, including "Our Festivals", to attract farmers for extensive participation, enhance the farmers' sense of affinity towards, identity and belonging to cultural auditoriums. Regularly carrying out the activities of introducing the Party's theories, the situation and policies, intellectual and moral development, scientific knowledge, healthy life, and cultural, sports and entertainment activities.

(4)   Building and improving the working team. Designating one village cadre responsible for the work on cultural auditoriums, assigning the full-time (part-time) management personnel for cultural auditoriums, and the personnel for publicity and introduction, establishing various amateur cultural and artistic groups, building cultural volunteer groups, giving play to the roles of various organizations, including rural senior citizen associations, in managing and serving cultural auditoriums.

4.5.3   The Effects and Significance of the Building of Rural Cultural Auditoriums

At present, in Zhejiang, an extensive consensus that cultural auditoriums conform to the people's will and warm the people's hearts has been gradually built, farmers have increasingly recognized cultural auditoriums, local authorities have no longer passively accepted the building of cultural auditoriums and have volunteered to build them, villagers have actively participated in the activities at cultural auditoriums, and a sense of belonging to the daily life in villages has gradually developed.

From the process, practices and effects in Zhejiang's building of rural cultural auditoriums, we can find that the Party and the government have introduced many fresh elements into the working philosophy, method and path, and have achieved a demonstrative value of this work.

1. Addressing the needs of the times

In the final analysis, the building of rural cultural auditoriums largely has a deep intrinsic connection with China's traditional farming civilization. The tradition of ancient Chinese civilization is built on the farming culture, it relies on ethic kinship, it follows the acquisition of experience and stresses ritual education. Rural culture is an important part of it and sustains the endless Chinese cultural tradition. Since modern times, social changes have exerted a huge impact on rural civilization; the disappearance of the patriarchal clan system and the patriarch and the improvement of farming techniques have boosted the change in the manner of production; material abundance has changed the lifestyle; the entry of external forces has changed the state of the rural society and social relations; population movement has broken the closed state of villages and led to inhabitation by people with different surnames; all of these factors have broken the old order and rules in rural areas. Amidst drastic changes, farmers have been subject to disintegration and so confusion is unavoidable. It is easy for farmers to adapt to the changes at a material level, while it is often hard to cope with the dilemma at a cultural level. Rebuilding new rules and a new order is the intrinsic appeal for self-renewal and development of rural civilization. Rural cultural auditoriums, positioned as the homes for meeting farmers' cultural needs and as a cultural landmark, cater to such needs of the times, the society and farmers' living and cultural needs, so farmers warmly welcome and passionately take part in the building of cultural auditoriums.

2. Building the homes for meeting cultural needs

The greatest breakthrough in Zhejiang's rural cultural auditoriums lies in making improvements in nature and function through their positioning as "the homes for meeting cultural needs" on the basis of pure entertainment on the previous cultural fronts. The rural primary-level cultural life is the foundation for continuing the Chinese culture; farmers are the most important members in the shared home for meeting the Chinese nation's cultural needs; as the integrated service platforms for rural cultural life, cultural auditoriums are bound to serve as the homes for enhancing the power to unite all villagers and their sense of belonging, and they are a cultural landmark for rural public life.

Simply speaking, the building of the homes for meeting cultural needs is the work on increasing cohesion and building shared values; it is embodied in an emotional and spiritual attachment to parents, family, hometown and motherland, and to a higher degree, national feelings, a cultural identity and shared values. The philosophy from cultural auditoriums to auditorium culture reflects the builders' deepening understanding based on practice: on the one hand, further upholding the positioning of cultural auditoriums as the homes for meeting cultural needs, carrying forward the socialist core values, adopting the "most beautiful" elements, elements of civility and modern elements to lead the cultural life of the villagers and enrich their cultural world; on the other hand, placing more emphasis on continuing the traditional rural context, respecting the status of farmers as the main players, valuing cultivation through education and exquisitely integrating the socialist core values into daily life.

We cannot belittle the profound significance of these daily folk activities. According to the *Recommendation on the Safeguarding of Traditional Culture and Folklore* issued by UNESCO in 1989, folklore (or traditional and popular culture) is the totality of tradition-based creations of a cultural community, expressed by a group or individuals and recognized as reflecting the expectations of a community in so far as they reflect its cultural and social identity; its standards and values are transmitted orally, by imitation or by other means. Its forms are, among others, language, literature, music, dance, games, mythology, rituals, customs, handicrafts, architecture and other arts.[16] The folk cultural activities are a "deep sea" with deep feeling, expectations, standards and values; they contain the profound cultural identity, value judgment and spiritual orientation of the people; they shape our code of conduct; they serve as an important bond for sustaining the shared homes for meeting cultural needs.

3. Rebuilding public spaces

In Binhu Village of Changxing County beside Lake Tiahu, when the evening lights are lit at cultural auditorium in summer, the cultural night life of the villagers begins: films are shown, dancers come on stage, and villagers sing the Shaoxing Opera, which receive a loud applause. Since the cultural auditorium was built, villagers have the opportunity and reason to get together, while such an opportunity and reason come from the public spaces within the cultural auditorium.

Villages are organic community settlements, bringing together various interpersonal relations and social interactions to constitute the village-based public spaces. Rural cultural auditoriums are of the nature of a "public space" in the sense of sociology; they provide the platforms for villagers to offer mutual assistance and engage in cooperation; more importantly, they shape a public spirit and shared values. "In rural areas, face-to-face communication is preferred among the villagers, between the villagers and the cadres; rural cultural auditoriums create a public space for

---

[16]Wu (2007).

meeting such needs, we must better use them to persistently conduct publicity and education."[17]

The corridor of village history, that of folk customs, the list of filial piety, the list of the god of longevity and the list of contributions at the cultural auditorium also provide a list of revolutionary martyrs, model workers, dutiful sons and daughters-in-law, the god of longevity as well as able and virtuous personages from the villages; this presents the common historical memory and good customs of villages in a popular way; this is a kind of public communication and interaction, and arouses the emotional identity of the village community and the value identification of upholding virtues and goodwill.

4. Continuing the rural cultural tradition

An outstanding traditional culture is an important resource for building cultural auditoriums, and cultural auditoriums provide a large number of platforms and opportunities for conducting activities concerning outstanding traditional cultural inheritances. Zhejiang has given great importance to adopting the outstanding traditional culture to enrich auditoriums and keep villagers closely-knit. For instance, the traditional cultural festival and ritual activities in various forms are carried out to make it possible for farmers to participate in great numbers, and enhance their sense of affinity, identity and belonging.

Rural areas are the birthplace of the Chinese culture and important inheritance areas; they have given birth to rural China. The elements and information from rural cultural tradition have a natural affinity and appeal for the Chinese people. With their excellent resources as construction capital, cultural auditoriums cater to farmers' vital needs, and arouse the awareness of urban residents of native places, bringing the source of vitality for sustained development of cultural auditoriums.

5. Addressing farmers' needs

"How can we sow the seed of 'civilization' into the hearts of the farmers? A piece of successful experience tells us: The guidance of civilization is certainly based on understanding and respecting rural areas and farmers, it should come from the people and the things on this land and should be accompanied by a strong fragrance from the soil; only under a subtle influence can the cultural level in rural areas be increased gradually."[18] Understanding and respecting rural areas and farmers and valuing the subtle influence are two aspects of Zhejiang's understanding of the ways to build cultural auditoriums, and reflect the people-oriented philosophy and the professional level of the government in work.

Among the four principles for building cultural auditoriums put forward in the *Plan of Lin'an City for the Building of the Village-level Cultural Auditoriums* unveiled by the Office of the Party Committee of Lin'an City and the Office of the People's Government of Lin'an City, two principles are related to farmers: The first one is

---

[17]Ge (2004).
[18]Ge (2004).

being close to farmers and life; the second one is pooling wisdom from villagers, thus giving prominence to the main players.

Ritual activities are important and conspicuous elements at cultural auditoriums. The success of these activities lies in villagers' enthusiastic participation and active innovations. Villagers have created new rituals, including collective inauguration of village cadres and farewell to new recruits, and they have also inherited traditional rituals, such as getting married and establishing a business at the age of 30 at Longmen Town in Fuyang, the celebration among the people who are 50 years old at Shifu Village in Tonglu. These ritual activities originate from the original ritual folk traditions, and are derived from meeting the daily living and cultural needs of the farmers; they have the endogenous foundation for primary occurrence, and reflect the farmers' enthusiasm for participation in the building of cultural auditoriums and activities, and the ability of their independent creation.

References

Ge Huijun, The Speech in the Provincial On-the-Spot Meeting on the Building of Rural Cultural Auditoriums, 2014-03-21, http://whzt.zjcnt.com/201405_whlt/9160.htm.

Wu Bing'an, Several Theoretical and Practical Issues Concerning the Definition and Recognition of Intangible Cultural Heritage, *Journal of Henan Institute of Education* (Philosophy and Social Science), 2007(1).

Xi Jinping, *Carrying out Solid Work to Stay Ahead – Line of Thought and Practice in Promoting New Development in Zhejiang*, The Party School of the CPC Central Committee Press, 2006.

Xi Jinping, The Zhejiang Spirit of Advancing with the Times, *Philosophical Researches*, 2006(4).

Xi Jinping, *Zhijiang Xinyu*, Zhejiang People's Publishing House, 2007, p. 55.

Chapter 5
Accelerating the Building of the Public Cultural Service System

Lixu Chen

According to the report delivered during the 18th National Congress of the Communist Party of China, it is necessary to intensify efforts in carrying out major public cultural projects and cultural projects, and to improve the public cultural service system and the efficiency of the services. As stressed by the *Decision on Some Major Issues Concerning Comprehensively Intensifying the Reform* adopted during the 3rd Plenary Session of the 18th Central Committee of the Communist Party of China, it is essential to establish a coordinating mechanism for the building of the public cultural service system, build a network of service facilities in a coordinated way, promote the standardization of and equal access to basic public cultural services, and establish a mechanism for public evaluation and feedback to connect cultural projects with the people's cultural needs. When serving as the Secretary of the Party Committee of Zhejiang Province, comrade Xi Jinping proceeded from putting into practice the overall requirement of staying ahead, put forward by the Central Committee of the Communist Party of China for Zhejiang, to assume the great responsibility for making early experiments for developing a socialist culture with Chinese characteristics; he had all-round in-depth experiments and a strategic line of thought regarding the issue of actively developing the public welfare cultural programs in the practice of leading Zhejiang's cadres and people to speed up the building of a culturally large province. Since the implementation of the "Eight-Eight Strategies", Zhejiang has gradually increased its input in public cultural services, started with integrating resources, improving the network of services, bringing about innovations to the service mechanism, adding more service means and enriching the forms of activities to actively bring about innovations to the contents and modes of public cultural services so as to meet the people's cultural needs. In the meantime, the Party committees and governments at various levels in Zhejiang have energetically changed and brought about innovations to the input mode, the method of management and the operating mechanism, and it explored the law which governs the building of the public cultural

L. Chen (✉)
The Party School of the Zhejiang Provincial Party Committee, Hangzhou, China

© Social Sciences Academic Press and Springer Nature Singapore Pte Ltd. 2019   125
D. Xie and Y. Chen (eds.), *Chinese Dream and Practice in Zhejiang – Culture*,
Research Series on the Chinese Dream and China's Development Path,
https://doi.org/10.1007/978-981-13-7216-2_5

service system under the condition of the market economy, established a better public cultural service governance structure to improve the efficiency of providing public cultural products and services. These successful practices in Zhejiang have effectively improved the cultural level and also present the direction for the development of public cultural services in China against the background of a market economy .

5.1 The Course of Theoretical and Practical Development of Public Cultural Services Since the Implementation of the "Eight-Eight Strategies"

Since the implementation of the "Eight-Eight Strategies", profound changes have taken place in domestic and foreign environments, there is an urgent need for Zhejiang to timely adjust and renew its strategy for cultural development in response to the changes in the overall strategy for economic and social development. In the meantime, Zhejiang has entered a new historical stage of economic and social development, the socialist market economy has shifted from the formative period to the mature period, economic and social development has changed from freed pursuit of development dominated by GDP growth to the historical period of consciously practicing the Scientific Outlook on Development. The Scientific Outlook on Development must be practiced by increasing the people's material standard of living on the one hand and effectively meeting the people's cultural needs on the other hand. This requires Zhejiang to adopt the spirit of "doing concrete work to stay ahead" to plan the building of the public cultural service system, strengthen the effective provision of public cultural services, and comprehensively enhance the quality of the cultural life of the people in urban and rural areas.

5.1.1 Carrying Out the Reform of the Cultural System to Unleash the Vitality of the Development of Public Cultural Services

The formation of a well-functioning public cultural service system covering the whole society always accompanies the birth and development of a market economy, the emergence of its "advantages", and occurrence of its "failure". In the period of the planned economy, almost all of the Chinese cultural products and services were included in the traditional developmental mode of "cultural programs" and were provided solely by the government; the cultural service function was mainly performed by the units engaged in "cultural programs", and there was no distinction between the "public welfare cultural programs" and the "for-profit cultural industry". The market-oriented reform certainly exerted an impact on this traditional mode. Zhejiang, a province as a forerunner, encountered great challenges for rebuilding the cultural developmental mode under the condition of a market economy ahead of most provinces across the country, Zhejiang also met the special opportunity for breaking the traditional mode of cultural development pursued solely by the government ahead of the rest of the country. At the turn of the century, with the implementation of the strategy for building a culturally large province, Zhejiang became the first nationwide to strip the "public welfare cultural programs" and the "cultural industry" from the traditional developmental mode of "cultural programs", and adopt the principle of classified guidance and classified development. However, this merely meant that innovations began to appear in the cultural developmental mode. The main drawbacks in the traditional developmental mode of public welfare programs are as follows: the provision channels were not diverse, the level of guarantee was not high, the capital gap was large and the rate of utilization was low, and the efficiency of provision was low. To innovate and rebuild the public cultural service developmental mode against the background of a market economy, there is an urgent need for making greater breakthroughs in theory and in the guiding thought.

In June, 2003, a year during which the Party Committee of Zhejiang Province initiated the implementation of the "Eight-Eight Strategies", Zhejiang was designated as the national pilot province for the comprehensive reform of the cultural system. In the process of leading the pilot work on that reform, the Secretary of the Party Committee of Zhejiang, Xi Jinping, deeply and comprehensively expounded the strategic line of thought of reforming and developing the public welfare cultural programs. In July, 2003, when attending the meeting on the reform of the cultural system and the building of a culturally large province, comrade Xi Jinping proceeded from the goal of continuously enhancing vitality to expound the priorities in the reform and development of the public welfare cultural programs from the perspectives of increasing input, transforming the mechanism and improving services. "Increasing input means that the leading role of the governments at various levels is upheld and social donation is encouraged to increase input into cultural infrastructures such as museums, cultural centers, libraries and art galleries, the construction of the supporting cultural facilities including communities and residential quarters, the construction of rural cultural fronts including town-level cultural stations and village-level cultural rooms. It is also necessary to value the layout plans for the construction of major cultural facilities, prevent excessive premature and repeated construction from causing resource wasting." "Transforming the mechanism means that the systems of cadres, personnel and distribution within cultural units are further reformed to build an enterprise-based management mode under which personnel can enter and exit cultural units, cadres can be promoted and demoted, income can be increased and decreased, so as to enhance the vitality of development." "Improving services means that the cultural public institutions are guided and encouraged to adopt multiple means to become people- and market-oriented, fully leverage the market mechanism to increase the level of serving the people."[1] This presents the direction, tasks and path for reforming and developing the public welfare cultural programs.

---

[1] Xi (2006), p. 326.

In August, 2003, the *Master Plan of Zhejiang Province for Pilot Comprehensive Reform of the Cultural System* was unveiled, which marked the full implementation of pilot comprehensive reform. The Plan adopted the words "relatively strong", "vibrant" and "competitive" to describe the players in the cultural industry and also made them become part of the main players in the public welfare cultural programs; it stressed that it was necessary to adopt a reform-minded line of thought to increase government input, and absorb social capital to more quickly build a number of the technologically advanced, well-functioning key cultural facilities with massive investments, including the West Lake Cultural Square, the Zhejiang Art Museum, the Zhejiang Science and Technology Museum, the Zhejiang Museum of Natural History, the Hangzhou Grand Theatre and the Ningbo Grand Theatre; it was also necessary to bring about innovations to the cultural facility operational mode and adopt a market mechanism to turn them into operators able to pursue market-oriented self-development. This indicates that the requirement for solving the problem concerning the efficiency of development in Zhejiang's public welfare cultural programs was highlighted in an unusual way; the pilot work on the reform of the cultural system created an important opportunity for bringing innovations to the public welfare cultural program developmental mode and improving the efficiency of development.

First, innovation to the public welfare cultural program developmental mode under the condition of a market economy cannot be made without rebuilding the Party and the government's macro cultural management mode. For a long time, in China, the departments and systems under the central government performed separate managerial functions, local governments conducted level-to-level administration according to administrative divisions, namely, a segmented cultural administrative management system was carried out. Because of excessively dense multi-departmental management, functions overlapped, multiple departments exercised the management of the same aspect, department operations went beyond the specified limits, and were in the wrong position and were absent, the efficiency of the departments was low, thus hindering cultural development.

In the meeting on the reform of the cultural system and the building of a culturally large province in July, 2003, comrade Xi Jinping pointed out, "Culture is of a clear ideological nature, thus the reform of the cultural system must be conducted by taking into full account China's national conditions, focusing on managing the direction, introducing a flexible mechanism, making management result-oriented and improving the quality of management ". He stressed that it was necessary to shift focus to social management and market supervision, manage the orientation, principles, planning, layout, the market and order, focus on planning, coordination, service, supervision and optimization of the developmental environment. He required the competent department for cultural affairs to change its functions, correctly deal with the relationship between "action" and "inaction", make continuous improvements in the leadership method and managerial mode, focus more on mobilizing active factors, regulating the interest relationship, and adjusting the code of conduct; he pointed out, "It is necessary for the competent department for cultural affairs to gradually achieve transformation from running cultural affairs to managing cultural affairs, from micro control to macro control, from management mainly focusing on the units directly under the competent department for cultural affairs to management covering the whole society and to separate government functions from enterprise management and public institutions; it is essential to adopt legal, economic and administrative means, give scope to the role of economic policy as a lever, improve the macro control system, more rapidly establish a macro management system under which the Party committee exercises leadership, moderate control is exercised, orderly operations is performed to boost the development".[2] This presents the fundamental direction, basic line of thought and goal for reforming the system of macro cultural management—establishing a new system under which the Party committee exercises leadership, the government performs management, the industry practices self-discipline, and enterprises and public institutions operate according to laws; this also shows the basic principles for reforming the system of cultural management against the background of a market economy: in the areas where the market works, scope is given to the basic role of the market in resource allocation; in the areas where the market fails to work, the government under the leadership of the Party committee plays its due role.

During pilot comprehensive reform, Zhejiang took "further solving the problem of no separation between the government and public institutions, between the government and enterprises, and between public institutions and enterprises" as a very important reform task, sought a new management system and operating mechanism which cater to the developmental needs, and gradually built a new macro cultural management mode under which the Party committee exercises leadership, the government performs management, the industry practices self-discipline, and enterprises and public institutions operate according to laws. This created a favorable environment with a macro system and mechanism for exploring and building a new developmental mode for public welfare cultural programs under the condition of a market economy.

The innovation to the mode of development of the public welfare cultural programs under the condition of a market economy cannot be made without reshaping the micro cultural players. Although multiple adjustments and reforms were carried out since the reform and opening-up, the public cultural institutions still had many salient problems. The public welfare cultural institutions had prominent problems: the system of internal management, the personnel system, the distribution system were underdeveloped, reform policies were not complete, bad practices, including equalitarianism and "the big rice bowl", were deep-seated, and it was difficult to resettle redundant staff, especially the "old people". During reform, some departments and units gave more considerations to addressing fiscal and investment issues and reducing government management functions, but took insufficient account of a possible lack of efforts during the post-reform period in assuming public responsibility, thus there were no actions taken to assume the responsibility for further meeting the people's cultural needs. Therefore, the Central Committee of the Communist Party of China put forward opinions on the reform of the cultural system at the micro level in the pilot areas for comprehensive reform, and stressed that the focus of reform consisted in transforming the cultural public institutions into micro players.

---

[2]Xi (2006), p. 328.

Being consistent with this requirement, Zhejiang took all cultural institutions as market players, and thus explored a combination of the government and the market, multiple modes involving production and provision of cultural products, and built "four-batch" players, including for-profit cultural units and public welfare public cultural institutions. Zhejiang took different reform measures for different types of cultural players, including "restructuring into an enterprise", "separation and enhancement in press publicity services and operations", "intensifying the reform of cultural and artistic theaters and troupes", "building state-owned cultural groups" and "guiding the private cultural industry".

Zhejiang identified "innovating the system, transforming the mechanism, being market-oriented and enhancing the vitality" as the direction of reform for the for-profit state-owned cultural units, and required the adoption of the principle of "transforming the nature of units, labor relations and the property rights structure" to restructure them into enterprises in a classified and step-by-step way. Accordingly, Zhejiang identified "increasing input, transforming the mechanism, enhancing the vitality and improving services" as the direction of reform for the public welfare state-owned cultural units, and based on the reform of the labor, personnel and distribution systems which started at the beginning of the century, continued intensifying the reform of the internal management system and operating mechanism involving personnel, distribution and incentives, fully carried out an all-staff appointment system and cadre appointment system, explored multiple employment modes including the personnel agency system, the contract-signing system and the labor contract system, broadened developmental channels to increase the service level, and more extensively and effectively serve the people. Obviously, the post-reform public welfare micro cultural players have tended to engage in the public welfare cultural programs under the philosophy of "governance".

5.1.2 More Rapidly Enhancing the Capability for Public Cultural Services

Since the implementation of the "Eight-Eight Strategies", Zhejiang has entered a new historical stage of economic development. In 2004, Zhejiang became the 4th province in China with a GDP higher than one trillion yuan. In 2005, Zhejiang's urban per capita disposable income and rural per capita net income reached 16,294 yuan and 6,660 yuan, respectively, being 1.55 times and 2 times the average national levels. In the same year, Zhejiang became the first province in China with per capita GDP higher than USD 3,000; measured by this indicator, Zhejiang was ahead of the whole country in economic development for 10 years or longer. Rapid economic and social development certainly required Zhejiang to act ahead of the rest of the country to speed up urban and rural integration of the public cultural service system, strengthen effective provision of public cultural services, comprehensively improve the people's well-being in the cultural field in urban and rural areas, and make it possible for culture to benefit the people.

In 2004, the National Development and Reform Commission issued the *Opinions on the Reform of the Economic System in 2004*, calling for intensifying the reform of the labor personnel, income distribution and social security systems involving the public welfare public institutions, establishing and improving the public cultural service system, in which the new concept of "public cultural service system" appeared for the first time. The 5th Plenary Session of the 16th Central Committee of the Communist Party of China, convened in October, 2005, further put forward the new philosophies of "gradually building a system covering the whole society" and "well-functioning" concerning a public cultural service system, and stressed that it was necessary to actively develop cultural programs and the cultural industry, increase government input in cultural programs, and gradually build a well-functioning public cultural service system covering the whole society. Against such a background, in July, 2005, the 8th Plenary Session of the 11th Party Committee of Zhejiang Province adopted the *Decision of the Party Committee of Zhejiang Province on Accelerating the Building of a Culturally Large Province*, explicitly adopted, for the first time, the new words "social public service" and "public cultural service system" to build the framework for expressing "public welfare cultural programs". "Enhancing the capability for public social services", in parallel to "enhancing the cohesive force of the advanced culture" and "emancipating and developing the productive cultural forces", was regarded as one of the three points of action for accelerating the building of a culturally large province. The issue of accelerating the building of the public cultural service system was considered as having a vital bearing on accelerating the building of a culturally large province and so received unprecedented attention. The core of the strategy and task, in this document, for accelerating the building of a culturally large province can be summarized as "three points of action", "eight projects" and "a strong province in four respects".[3] Among the "three points of action", "enhancing the cohesive force of the advanced culture" and "enhancing the capability for public social services " are directly associated to the building of the public cultural service system, while "emancipating and developing the productive cultural forces" include emancipating and developing the productive forces of the cultural industry and that of the public welfare cultural programs. As mentioned by scholars, "emancipating and developing the productive cultural forces" covers two levels: "emancipating the productive cultural forces" focuses on the cultural industry, while "developing the productive cultural forces" focuses on cultural programs; the former focuses on the state-owned for-profit cultural units fettered by the original system, while the latter focuses on the public welfare public cultural institutions.[4] In particular, among the "eight projects" which are considered as the core of efforts in

---

[3] It means a strong province in education, science and technology, health and sports; since the Central Committee of the Communist Party of China put forward the overall layout of making progress in the economic, political, cultural and social fields, a considerable part of the contents concerning "a strong province in four respects" has been included in the scope of social development.

[4] Zhao (2007).

accelerating the building of a culturally large province, except for the cultural industry promotion project, the remaining seven projects can be included in the scope of the public cultural service system. In this programmatic document, Zhejiang's blueprint for building a well-functioning public cultural service system covering the whole society was clearly presented for the first time.

More importantly, thanks to innovative practice in various parts of the province and the extensive practical experience that had been gradually gathered, the second programmatic document concerning the building of a culturally large province adopted more accurate words to express the new philosophies and new modes involving the building of the public cultural service system amidst the development of the market economy, the transformation of government functions and the rise of non-governmental social forces, namely, "giving full scope to the supporting role of public finance, exploring and building a new pattern of the development of public programs led by the government and with social participation under market operations."

Since the *Decision of the Party Committee of Zhejiang Province on Accelerating the Building of a Culturally Large Province* was issued, the philosophies and strategy for accelerating the building of that system have been further clarified and concretized in relevant documents and practice of the cultural management department of Zhejiang Province and the Party committees and governments of Hangzhou, Ningbo, Wenzhou, Jiaxing, Huzhou, Shaoxing, Taizhou, Jinhua, Zhoushan, Quzhou and Lishui. Hangzhou stayed ahead across the province in the practice of accelerating the building of the public cultural service system. In November, 2007, Hangzhou unveiled the *Plan of Hangzhou City for the Building of the Public Cultural Service System (2008–2010)*; this is the first special plan for the building of the public cultural service system in Hangzhou City, and even in all of Zhejiang Province. The unveiling of the plan suggested that Hangzhou City had the self-consciousness to safeguard the basic cultural rights and interests of urban and rural residents and meet the public needs for basic public cultural services; the unveiling also indicated that the Party committees and governments at various levels across the province, represented by Hangzhou City, had started with improving the network of public cultural service facilities and the capacity for public cultural product provisions and building the public cultural service brand to comprehensively and step by step consider and plan the building of the public cultural service system.

As from the implementation of the "Eight-Eight Strategies", the financial input from public finance at various levels in Zhejiang into the public welfare cultural programs increased year by year: it was 593 million yuan, 848 million yuan, 892 million yuan, 1,240 million yuan and 1,726 million yuan in 2001, 2002, 2003, 2004 and 2006, respectively, an average annual increase of 23.82%. During the period of the 10th Five-Year Plan, Zhejiang ranked no.2 nationwide in total expenditure on culture, Zhejiang's per capita expenditure on culture was 7.8 yuan, ranking Zhejiang no. 1 among the provinces (autonomous regions, municipalities) across the country. During the period of the 11th Five-Year Plan, Zhejiang's expenditure on culture further increased. Zhejiang's expenditure on cultural and cultural relics programs—it refers to the fiscal input, including special funds but excluding capital construction investment—in 2006, 2007 and 2008 was 6.53 billion yuan, up 3,006 million yuan or 1.85 times compared with the end of the period of the 10th Five-Year Plan. More importantly, as from the implementation of the "Eight-Eight Strategies", Zhejiang increased its expenditure on culture in rural areas. The financial input from provincial special funds into the rural cultural field was 82 million yuan in 2006, up 4.5 times compared with the annual input level of 15 million yuan during the period of the 10th Five-Year Plan. As from 2007, the financial input from provincial special funds into the rural cultural field across the province increased to an annual 109 million yuan, among which the special fund for building the rural cultural facilities (libraries, cultural centers and cultural stations) reached an annual 38 million yuan, which was mainly used to build rural cultural facilities in the underdeveloped areas across the province. With increasing financial input, a (public welfare) a network of the systems of cultural facilities covering the provincial, municipal and county levels has gradually taken shape across the province. In the meantime, the network of Zhejiang's public cultural services has gradually improved, the service items have been on the increase, continuous innovations have been made to the service mode, and service means have increased. Zhejiang has stayed ahead nationwide in the building of public cultural facilities in urban and rural areas and in the level of its public cultural services.

5.1.3 More Rapidly Building the Public Cultural Service System Covering the Whole Society

In August, 2007, the General Office of the Central Committee of the Communist Party of China and the General Office of the State Council issued the *Several Opinions on Strengthening the Building of the Public Cultural Service System*, specifying the guiding thought, goals and tasks, working means and requirements for building the public cultural service system. The 17th National Congress of the Communist Party of China vowed to build the public cultural service system covering the whole society. The orientation of the policies of the Central Committee of the Communist Party of China presented a new strategic opportunity for Zhejiang to speed up the building of the public cultural service system.

As from the 17th National Congress of the Communist Party of China, Zhejiang's public finance became better, residents became wealthier, and their ability to consume cultural products and services generally improved. Against such a background, accelerating the building of Zhejiang's public cultural service system was naturally put on the more important agenda. In June, 2008, the working conference of the Party Committee of Zhejiang Province adopted the third programmatic document concerning the building of a culturally large province—the *Plan of Zhejiang Province for Promoting Vigorous Cultural Development and Great Cultural Prosperity*, further improving the important status of the public cultural service system, taking it as one of the three main systems for Zhejiang's cultural development including the system of values with a socialist core and the system of cultural industrial development. The Plan specified the overall goal of building Zhejiang's public cultural service system, namely, further improving that system, becoming the first to build a well-functioning public cultural service system covering the whole society, ensuring coordinated development between urban and rural areas and among regions, significantly increasing the level of the public cultural services of the public welfare cultural units, gradually ensuring equal access to basic public cultural services, guaranteeing the people's basic cultural rights and interests, including watching television, listening to the radio, reading books and newspapers, appreciating public culture, participating in mass cultural sports activities, and enriching the cultural social life. The Plan also specified the main task for building the public cultural service system, namely, enhancing the capacity for producing and providing public cultural products, improving the public cultural service network, and strengthening the protection and utilization of cultural heritage.

In 2011, Zhejiang's per capita GDP surpassed USD 9,000, the pace of change was significantly quickened in the economic structure, social structure, urban and rural structure, consumption structure and the people's cultural needs grew rapidly and became multi-faceted, multi-level and diverse; this presented higher requirements for public cultural services and injected new impetus into the building of the public cultural service system. Against such a background, in October, 2011, the 6th Plenary Session of the 17th Central Committee of the Communist Party of China put forward the strategic task of intensifying the reform of the cultural system and promoting vigorous cultural development and great cultural prosperity, incorporated the building of the public cultural service system into the overall layout of building a culturally powerful socialist country. The plenary session stressed that it was essential to uphold the leading role of the government, follow the requirement of "focusing on public welfare and basic needs, ensuring equal access and convenience" to strengthen the construction of cultural infrastructure and improve the public cultural service network, so that the people can enjoy free or preferential basic public cultural services. In November, 2011, the 10th Plenary Session of the 12th Party Committee of Zhejiang Province adopted the *Decision on Carrying Out the Principles Adopted during the 6th Plenary Session of the 17th Central Committee of the Communist Party of China and Promoting the Building of a Culturally Strong Province*, identifying "building the public cultural service system" as one of the six main tasks for promoting the building of Zhejiang into a culturally strong province, and making new arrangements for "building the public cultural service system amidst the building of a culturally strong province" from the perspective of the following five aspects: "improving the network of public cultural facilities", "enhancing the capability for public cultural services", "innovating the mechanism of public cultural services", "strengthening the building of the modern communication capacity" and "strengthening the inheritance and utilization of cultural heritages".

This programmatic document concerning the building of a culturally strong province further expounded the line of thought of adopting a new philosophy and mode to build the public cultural service system against the background of a market economy. It stressed, "the public cultural institutions for public welfare, professional ensembles or troupes, radio, film and television institutions, publishing enterprises, literary federations, federations of social science circles, writers associations and other cultural groups should fully play the role of main actors in providing a greater number of better public cultural products for the people", "the main public cultural products and service items, public welfare cultural activities are incorporated into the recurrent expenditure budget of public finance", "it is necessary to adopt such policy measures as government procurement, project subsidies, loan interest subsidies, tax reduction and exemption to encourage cultural enterprises to participate in public cultural services", "the public finance at various levels should guarantee sufficient financial input, it is necessary to improve free admission to public cultural venues at various levels, including public libraries, museums, art galleries, cultural centers and memorial halls and gradually promote free admission to exhibition halls, science and technology museums, workers' cultural buildings and youth buildings" and "it is necessary to leverage the advantages of Zhejiang's private economy, encourage social forces to participate in the public welfare cultural development, support the development of private museums, art galleries and other non-governmental cultural institutions". The key point of these expressions lies in combining the government authority with market advantages, changing the mode of public cultural service provision from the conventional mode of single-center provision to the multi-center, multi-level and cooperative mode of provision and building an efficient governance structure with many supply items, broad objects and an optimal mode, so as to better meet the people's public cultural needs.

In October, 2013, the 3rd Plenary Session of the 18th Central Committee of the Communist Party of China adopted the *Decision on Some Major Issues Concerning Comprehensively Intensifying the Reform*, calling for establishing a coordinating mechanism for the building of the public cultural service system, building a network of the service facilities in a coordinated way, promoting the standardization of and equal access to basic public cultural services, establishing a public evaluation and feedback mechanism and effectively connecting the cultural projects with the people's cultural needs, integrating the facilities involving primary-level cultural publicity, the education of the Party members, science popularization and physical fitness and building the integrated cultural service centers; moreover, it called for specifying the functional orientation of different cultural public institutions, calling for establishing the corporate governance structure, improving the mechanism for the evaluation of performance, promoting the establishment of the board of governors in public libraries, museums, cultural centers, science and technology museums, involving relevant representatives, professionals and the people from various sectors in management, introducing the mechanism of competition, promoting the socialized development of public cultural services, encouraging social forces and social capital to participate in the building of the public cultural service system and cultivating the non-for-profit cultural organizations. This further specified the goals and tasks for building a modern system of public cultural services and bringing innovations to the public cultural service development system and mechanism. In November, 2013, the 4th Plenary Session of the 13th Party Committee of Zhejiang Province adopted the *Decision on Earnestly Studying and Implementing the Guiding Principles Adopted during the 3rd Plenary Session of the 18th Central Committee of the Communist Party of China and Comprehensively Intensifying the Reform to Foster New Advantages in Systems and Mechanisms*, calling for establishing a coordinating mechanism for building the public cultural service system, building a network of service facilities in a coordinated way, promoting the standardization of and equal access to basic public cultural services and improving the mechanism for the management and utilization of the network of cultural facilities, promoting the building of a network of cultural facilities covering urban and rural areas in a classified and layered way; this Decision also called for implementing the basic public cultural service improvement plan, continuing to push forward major cultural projects focusing on rural areas and the underdeveloped areas and extensively carrying out mass cultural activities as well as deepening the building of rural cultural auditoriums and building the homes for meeting the people's cultural needs in rural areas. More importantly, the Decision once again called for encouraging social forces and social capital to participate in the building of the public cultural service system, cultivating the non-for-profit cultural organizations, promoting the socialized development of public cultural services, bringing about innovations to the public cultural service mechanism and exploring the mode for the co-building and sharing of public cultural facilities.

The Decision further specified the direction and task for Zhejiang's public cultural service system and also further stressed that an inevitable trend in building the public cultural service system under the condition of a market economy was that the single responsibility system in which the government solely carries out cultural programs under the conventional mode shifted to a diversified pattern in which government security plays the leading role with participation of the government, enterprises, third parties, and individuals. Against the background of a market economy, the government is no longer the only body monopolizing public cultural affairs; it is necessary for the government to transfer a large number of public cultural affairs to various types of social players, and make the things which the government should not do or cannot do better be undertaken by various types of social players, so as to transform the mode of public cultural product and service provision from the conventional single-center provision mode to the multi-center, multi-level and cooperative mode of provision, improve the efficiency of building the public cultural service system and better meet the people's public cultural needs.

5.2 Increasing Input into the Building of the Public Cultural Service System

Since the beginning of the 21st century, especially the implementation of the "Eight-Eight Strategies", with the accelerated building of a culturally large province, the governments at various levels across the province have gradually allocated more resources to supporting the public cultural programs, and thus laid a solid material foundation for building a well-functioning public cultural service system covering the whole society; they have also gradually optimized the structure of the input to the public cultural services, thus allocating the limited financial resources of the government to provide the public cultural services most needed by the people.

5.2.1 The Fund Guarantee System: The Blood of Public Cultural Services

As a kind of public goods, public cultural services have an obvious externality and are hard to be produced and provided completely through the market mechanism, so it is necessary for the government to adopt fiscal means to make up for the deficiency in market functions. Since the reform and opening-up, the proportion of the expenditure on public services in the public finance of the Chinese Government has been noticeably low; the economic expenditure dominated by government investments and the maintenance expenditure dominated by administrative management experience has made up an excessively large proportion of the expenditure on public services, while the social expenditure dominated by the expenditure on education, culture, medical services and health and social security has not grown rapidly. In the area of China's public social services, public cultural services are the part in which more government input was not put in place in the past. Moreover, the for-profit cultural industry which should be market-oriented relied on government input for a long time, so some for-profit state-owned cultural units operated outside the market economy for a long time, they were less competitive and diluted the limited public financial resources, aggravating the shortage of funds for the public welfare cultural development.

Like the rest of the country, the public cultural programs had long been the area that showed a lack of a good deal of government input in Zhejiang's economic and social development. Zhejiang saw rapid economic growth, but for a long time, the expenditure on culture did not increase along with rapid economic development, and Zhejiang once lagged far behind in the development of public cultural programs. According to the *Blue Book of Zhejiang's Economic and Social Development in 1998–1999*, at the end of the period of the 8th Five-Year Plan, there were only 5 municipal public libraries with house areas reaching the standard specified by the Ministry of Culture across the province, accounting for 45.5%, and there were only 30 county-level public libraries reaching the standard, accounting for 43.5%, among which 5 county-level public libraries had no houses, accounting for 6.2%.[5] During this period, some local authorities and departments indiscriminately made all cultural units market-oriented, they tried to make up for the deficiency in culture through culture or help cultural development through multiple industries, and "seek self-help through production". These practices mitigated the fiscal burden and provided opportunities for the for-profit state-owned cultural units to be market-oriented and for developing the cultural industry, but these practices also caused some problems. In particular, as all cultural units were indiscriminately encouraged to perform paid services, many public welfare public cultural institutions were largely no longer of public welfare and no longer had a public nature, making it difficult to really serve the people and socialism.

---

[5] Yang and Ge (1999).

In July, 2003, when attending the meeting on the reform of the cultural system and the building of a culturally large province, comrade Xi Jinping pointed out, "The prosperity of socialist culture cannot be achieved without fiscal input from the government; the reform of the cultural system is aimed at developing culture better, and it cannot be simply understood as relieving the government of burdens and financial input; the overall principle is that the government should continue to increase its input".[6] This made it clear that against the background of a market economy, the government cannot fully make the public welfare cultural units market-oriented, and so the government must assume the responsibility and allocate more resources to support the public welfare cultural programs. In November, 2005, when delivering a speech at the 6th Congress of the Zhejiang Provincial Federation of Literary and Art Circles, Xi Jinping stressed, "It is necessary to increase government input into cultural programs, and gradually build a well-functioning public cultural service system covering the whole society".[7] This shows that the government's fiscal input is the blood for the building of the public cultural service system.

5.2.2 Increasing Government Input in the Public Cultural Programs

Since the beginning of the 21st century, especially since the implementation of the "Eight-Eight Strategies", Zhejiang has seen increasing cultural awareness of the cadres and people, and the Party committees and governments at various levels in Zhejiang have gradually reached a consensus on increasing their input to change the situation in which the public welfare cultural development has lagged behind economic development and for-profit cultural development, and progressively build a public cultural service system covering Zhejiang's regional society. In the meantime, the total fiscal revenue in various parts of the province further increased, economic strength improved rapidly, and local authorities also created the conditions for increasing input into public cultural services. Zhejiang's input in culture increased year by year, and Zhejiang's advantages regarding economic development began to gradually turn into cultural developmental advantages.

During the period of the 10th Five-Year Plan, the total expenditure from the public finance at various levels in Zhejiang on culture grew at an average annual rate of 24.57%, higher than the annual growth rate of total fiscal budget expenditure, the growth trend was obvious, the total expenditure on culture (excluding the capital construction investment) reached 4,952 million yuan, up 3,393 million yuan or 2.2 times compared with the period of the 9th Five-Year Plan. During the period 2001–2005, 500 million yuan in a special fund was arranged from provincial finance to support the construction of the Zhejiang Art Museum, the Zhejiang Science and Technology Museum and the Zhejiang Museum of Natural History;

---

[6]Xi (2006), p. 329.
[7]Xi (2006), p. 336.

each year, 50 million yuan in special subsidies for cultural programs was arranged to promote primary-level cultural development, protect national folk art and support the development of the cultural industry. During the period of the 10th Five-Year Plan period, Zhejiang stayed ahead nationwide in main indicators concerning the input in the cultural field. For comparison with the developed areas across the province, the total expenditure on cultural programs from the public finance at various levels in Zhejiang was higher than that in Jiangsu and Shandong, ranking Zhejiang no. 2 nationwide, following Guangdong; the proportion in the total fiscal budget expenditure and the per capita expenditure on cultural programs were higher than those in Jiangsu, Shandong and Guangdong. The total expenditure on rural cultural programs and the proportion in the expenditure on cultural programs were lower than those in Guangdong, but higher than in Jiangsu and Shandong; the rural per capita expenditure on cultural programs measured by rural population was the highest among these four provinces. Thanks to a significant increase in input, during the period of the 10th Five-Year Plan, the construction of public cultural facilities was promoted steadily in Zhejiang, "in Zhejiang, there were 92 public libraries above the county level, with a building area of 453,000 m^2; 12 mass art centers, 87 county-level cultural centers, with a building area of 266,000 m^2; the coverage rates of county-level cultural centers and libraries reached 97 and 87%. A total of 1,493 out of 1,525 towns in Zhejiang were under the system of building cultural stations, accounting for 97.9%; 837 of them had station houses, accounting for 56% of the towns under the system of building cultural stations; 439 towns (sub-districts) had provincial-level 'Zhejiang East Sea Cultural Pearls', accounting for 29.34% of all towns (sub-districts). A total of 19,072 out of 35,061 administrative villages in Zhejiang had village-level cultural activity rooms, accounting for 56%".[8]

The total expenditure from the public finance at various levels in Zhejiang increased significantly during the period of the 11th Five-Year Plan compared with the period of the 10th Five-Year Plan. According to statistics, Zhejiang's expenditure on cultural and cultural relics programs—this refers to the fiscal input, including special funds but excluding capital construction investments—was 6.53 billion yuan during the period of 2006–2008, up 3,006 million yuan or 85.3% compared with the end of the period of the 10th Five-Year Plan. The expenditure from the public finance at various levels in Zhejiang on culture (mainly culture in a narrow sense) totaled 13,516 million yuan during the period 2008–2011, including 9,762 million yuan in appropriation for cultural programs, 2,382 million yuan in appropriation for cultural relics programs and 1,372 million yuan in other appropriations. The expenditure from the public finance at various levels in Zhejiang on culture was 2,857 million yuan, 3,006 million yuan, 3,644 million yuan and 4,008 million yuan in 2008, 2009, 2010 and 2011, respectively. Zhejiang ranked no. 1 nationwide in the proportion of the expenditure on cultural programs in fiscal expenditure for 9 consecutive years. During the period of the 11th Five-Year Plan, the total building area of public cultural facilities increased steadily in Zhejiang. In Zhejiang, there were more than 300 cultural squares and cultural centers above the county level;

---

[8]Wang (2009).

such large provincial facilities as the new branch of the Zhejiang Museum of Natural History, the Zhejiang Art Museum, and the Wulin Branch of the Zhejiang Provincial Museum (the Zhejiang Revolutionary History Memorial Hall) were built; a number of large high-end modern cultural facilities, including the Wenzhou Grand Theatre, the Huzhou Grand Theatre, the Hangzhou Library, the Ningbo Museum, the Lishui Cultural and Art Center and the Liangzhu Museum, were built, so the main framework of public cultural facilities was preliminarily built.

Since the beginning of the 21st century, especially the implementation of the "Eight-Eight Strategies", the governments at various levels in Zhejiang have increased their input in culture, thus the long-standing cultural underdevelopment compared with economic development has been changed greatly, the deficiency in the building of the public cultural service system has been overcome fundamentally, and main indicators have been at the forefront nationwide. According to the *Result of the Special Audit Survey on the Cultural Expenditure of Zhejiang Province* released in March, 2013, Zhejiang came out in front nationwide in main indicators and comprehensive strength involving cultural development at the end of the period of the 11th Five-Year Plan. This conclusion was proven and supported by the *Annual Report on China's Public Cultural Service Development 2012* released by the Urban Culture Research Center of Shanghai Normal University—a key research base under the Ministry of Education, and Shanghai University and College Urban Culture E-Institute in May, 2013. According to the report, in China, the top three in the composite index of public cultural services were Guangdong, Jiangsu and Zhejiang, and the top three in the composite index of per capita public cultural services were Shanghai, Beijing and Zhejiang.

5.2.3   Optimizing the Structure of Expenditure on Public Cultural Services

For a long time, public expenditure was irrational in many areas in China: the structure was not scientific, the proportions of various types of expenditure were irrational; relevant decisions were not made through scientific appraisal but were based on the will of leading officials; the sequence of public expenditure was often reverse or improper, luxury-type public expenditure caused extravagance and waste, while the expenditure on the general public goods was excessively low; there was a severe imbalance in the development of public services between urban and rural areas; the government's administrative costs were too high and the fiscal expenditure on official business was excessive. Obviously, one key to overcoming the irrationality in public expenditure lies in determining the priorities of expenditure, and allocating the limited financial resources of the government to support the public services most needed by the people.

For a long time, because of insufficient public expenditure, the county, village and community-level primary-level cultural institutions in China were generally in poor conditions regarding the infrastructures and were less able to provide services; they were the weaknesses in public cultural services. According to the principle of equality, public cultural services must benefit everyone, and they must be made available in urban and central developed areas, rural areas and remote underdeveloped areas. This means that the expenditure on public cultural services must be allocated to the lower levels, and more fiscal funds must be earmarked to the weal fields; it is necessary to provide more guarantee for main expenditure items, allocate more resources to rural areas and the economically underdeveloped areas, and ultimately ensure that everyone enjoys the achievements of cultural development.

Since the implementation of the "Eight-Eight Strategies", how to optimize the structure of expenditure while increasing public expenditure on culture, gradually transform the public financial policy and allocate more funds to the fields with fewer public cultural services has become a significant issue for the Party committees and governments at various levels in Zhejiang. In a certain period of time since the reform and opening-up, the expenditure on culture was at a low level and the structure of expenditure was severely unbalanced in Zhejiang. When serving as the Secretary of the Party Committee of Zhejiang Province, comrade Xi Jinping pointed out, "Cultural development was unbalanced between Zhejiang's urban and rural areas, most cultural activity venues were concentrated in the cities above the county level, many rural cultural fronts lacked facilities, funds, talents and content in Zhejiang, some remote rural areas still cannot get access to broadcasting and TV programs, the provision of cultural products was less effective, the cultural life of the farmers was not rich."[9] Overall, in the economically developed areas, the construction of cultural infrastructure was better, while cultural infrastructure was underdeveloped in the economically backward areas.

Since the implementation of the "Eight-Eight Strategies" especially the strategy for accelerating the building of a culturally large province, optimizing the structure of expenditure on culture has been put on the agenda of the more important issues. When serving as the Secretary of the Party Committee of Zhejiang Province, comrade Xi Jinping stressed, "In order to enhance the capability for public cultural services, it is necessary to focus on developing the public welfare cultural programs, the primary-level, especially rural, cultural programs".[10] "We should give full expression to the requirement of urban-rural integration and coordinated development, give more consideration to coordinated cultural development between urban and rural areas, place more emphasis on rural areas in the layout of cultural facilities, the usage of cultural funds, the arrangement of the cultural life and the production of cultural products, so as to greatly improve the rural cultural environment."[11] This presented the priorities and points of action in the development of Zhejiang's public welfare cultural programs. The *Plan of Zhejiang Province for Promoting Vigorous Cultural Development and Great Cultural Prosperity (2008–2012)*, unveiled in June, 2008, stressed, "It is necessary to optimize the structure of expenditure on the public cultural

---

[9]Xi (2006), p. 331.

[10]Xi (2006), pp. 330–331.

[11]Xi (2006), p. 331.

service system, improve the efficiency of making expenditures, and allocate more financial resources to the primary level, rural areas, especially the underdeveloped areas, in order to promote coordinated cultural development between urban and rural areas and among regions".

During the period of the 10th Five-Year Plan, the expenditure from the public finance at various levels in Zhejiang on rural cultural development was 1,123 million yuan, ranking it no. 2 among the provinces (autonomous regions, municipalities) across the country. The rural per capita cultural expenditure was 7.8 yuan, ranking Zhejiang no. 1 among the provinces (autonomous regions, municipalities) across the country. Zhejiang's expenditure on rural cultural programs increased year by year; during the period of the 10th Five-Year Plan, the cumulative special funds from provincial finance for the development of the primary-level cultural facilities reached 65 million yuan, and the supporting funds allocated by local authorities across the province for the development of the primary-level cultural facilities reached 1,005 million yuan.

During the period of the 11th Five-Year Plan, Zhejiang further allocated more financial resources to support cultural development in rural areas and the under-developed areas. The expenditure from provincial special funds on culture in rural areas reached 82 million yuan in 2006, up 4.5 times compared with the annual expenditure of 15 million yuan during the period of the 10th Five-Year Plan. As from 2007, the expenditure from provincial special funds on culture in rural areas across the province further increased to an annual 109 million yuan, among which the special funds for building rural cultural facilities (libraries, cultural centers and cultural stations) reached an annual 38 million yuan, which was mainly used to build rural cultural facilities in the underdeveloped areas across the province. In 2008, Zhejiang initiated the implementation of the *Action Plan for Ensuring Equal Access to Basic Public Services (2008–2012)*. "The network of urban and rural public cultural services would further improve. Zhejiang would comprehensively achieve the goal of building cultural centers and libraries in each county, integrated cultural stations in each town, and cultural activity venues in more than 85% of the administrative villages; Zhejiang would intensify its efforts to carry out the project for staging 10,000 performances in rural areas, the project for delivering 1 million books to rural areas and the project for showing films on 10,000 occasions in rural areas; it would also make efforts to make wired radio available to 80% of the rural households, extend cable TV networks to more than 95% of the administrative villages, ensure that the natural villages with more than 20 households would account for more than 50%, and the overall population coverage by radio and television in rural areas would exceed 98%."[12] Obviously, the plan can play an important role in promoting equal access to public cultural services across the province.

Since the period of the 12th Five-Year Plan, Zhejiang has further increased its resource input to strengthen and improve the construction of cultural facilities in rural areas, communities and municipal districts, it has combined the construction of cultural landmarks with the coverage of a network of primary-level facilities it

---

[12] Action Plan for Ensuring Equal Access to Basic Public Services (2008–2012) (2008).

has built a number of iconic rural and primary-level public cultural facilities and promoted "cultural poverty alleviation" in the economically underdeveloped areas, provided more public cultural products to the primary-level and remote areas, the vulnerable groups, thus further effectively narrowing the urban and rural gap in public cultural facilities. In particular, in early 2013, the building of 1,000 rural cultural auditoriums was written in the *Zhejiang's Government Work Report*. The provincial government identified the building of cultural auditoriums as one of the ten substantive tasks relating to the people's well-being in 2013 and 2014; the provincial leading group for the building of rural cultural auditoriums made great organizational and coordinating efforts, while member units actively cooperated in this process; input was guaranteed, the Department of Finance, the Rural Work Office, the Department of Culture of Zhejiang Province, the Department of Publicity under the Party Committee of Zhejiang Province and other departments increased their special input of resources, while the Zhejiang Daily Press Group and other enterprises and public institutions also provided financial support for the building of cultural auditoriums. As of late 2014, there were 3,447 cultural auditoriums in Zhejiang's rural areas. These facts fully prove that the policy of the Party Committee and the People's Government of Zhejiang Province for allocating more fiscal resources to the primary level and rural areas, especially the underdeveloped areas, and promoting coordinated development between urban and rural areas and among regions has been steadily carried out in practice.

5.3 Making Public Cultural Services More Accessible to the People

When serving as the Secretary of the Party Committee of Zhejiang Province, comrade Xi Jinping pointed out, "Our culture is a socialist culture, the fundamental goal of cultural development is to meet the people's cultural needs and help realize the people's cultural rights; besides the creation of excellent cultural products, we should place more emphasis on the creation, production and dissemination of cultural products for the primary level and the people, build and improve the system of public welfare cultural program services, enhance the capability for public cultural services and really serve the people and socialism".[13] This made it clear that in order to more rapidly develop the public welfare cultural programs, it is essential to ensure that the people fully enjoy the right to participate in cultural creation, that they share cultural achievements and express cultural views, so as to improve the people's well-being through cultural development.

---

[13]Xi (2006), p. 330.

5.3.1 Innovating the Rural Public Cultural Service Content and Mode

China's system of rural public cultural services is subject to two salient problems: on the one hand, the input is insufficient, causing short supply; on the other hand, supply is not diversified, so supply does not cater to demand. Since the implementation of the "Eight-Eight Strategies", local authorities in Zhejiang have significantly increased input into rural public cultural services for addressing the problem of short supply, and they have actively innovated the service content and mode to solve the problem of supply not catering to demand. These moves reflect equality and convenience, and the new philosophy of public cultural services which is result-oriented and driven by the people's needs.

5.3.1.1 Innovating the Content and Mode for Delivering Culture to Rural Areas

At present, delivering culture to rural areas has become the project for the provision of rural public cultural services which has been generally carried out in various parts of the country. The Party committees and governments at various levels in Zhejiang have also always taken "delivering culture (books, operas and films)" as a priority in doing substantive work for the people, and has vigorously carried out the following projects for delivering culture to rural areas: the project for staging 10,000 performances in rural areas, the project for showing films on 10,000 occasions in rural areas and the project for delivering 1 million books to rural areas. Since the implementation of the "Eight-Eight Strategies", especially the strategy for accelerating the building of a culturally large province, Zhejiang has intensified its efforts to deliver culture to rural areas each year, effectively mitigating the difficulties in reading books, watching films and seeing operas, and greatly enriching the cultural life of farmers. The bright spots of Zhejiang's delivery of culture to rural areas lie in not only maintaining large quantities of performances, films and books delivered to rural areas each year, but also in bringing about innovations to the organizational and activity modes for delivering culture to rural areas.

In the process of delivering culture to rural areas, Zhejiang carried out a number of characteristic and popular demonstration activities for doing that, including a rural performance tour of the Qianjiang Langhua Art Troupe, an excellent child play performance tour under the Eyas Program, and the rural cultural activities of the "Singing a Paean of Civilization" vocalist tutorial group, as well as an outstanding singer show and performance group. These activities introduced many innovations in content and form, and also broke through, in the organizational mode and operating mechanism, the conventional framework in which public cultural services are performed solely by the government; they combined, to a certain extent, the functions and advantages of the government with those of the market, and provided beneficial experience for changing the mode of providing public cultural services from the conventional single-center mode to the multi-center, multi-level and cooperative mode.

At present, the mode of the Qianjiang Langhua Art Troupe has become a nationally influential famous brand of rural public cultural services in Zhejiang. From 2005, when it was established, to 2012, each year, the Qianjiang Langhua Art Troupe provided more than 200 cultural and artistic performances to the people in towns, communities and schools in Zhejiang's rural areas, the troupe traveled for nearly 70,000 km and staged more than 1,200 performances to an audience of more than 3 million. The mode of the Qianjiang Langhua Art Troupe contains a number of achievements in the reform of Zhejiang's cultural system, cultural innovation, and cultural science and technology. Its typical characteristics are embodied in the innovative practices of its cultural service content and mode, and its operating mechanism.

First, adopting the manner of intermediary integration which combines "cultural express" with the art troupe. The Qianjiang Langhua Art Troupe was jointly established by the Department of Publicity under the Party Committee of Zhejiang Province, the Department of Culture of Zhejiang Province, th Zhejiang Guangsha Holding Investment Co., Ltd., the Zhejiang Daily Press Group Co., Ltd. and the Zhejiang Radio & TV Group. It adopts the mode based on the leading role of the Party committee and the government, participation of social forces and the company-based operation of art troupes to integrate artistic resources and performance market resources. It is a cultural service intermediary organization under the shareholding system; it is neither a state-owned asset organization nor merely a private asset organization, it combines both types of organization; it adopts the intermediary integration mode which combines "cultural express" with the art troupe; it is also a new public cultural service form which meets the primary-level rural cultural needs, is highly mobile and flexible and can integrate various types of resources.

Second, bringing about innovations to the expenditure mode in order to provide public cultural services for mere public welfare with zero charges. As a public cultural service group, the Qianjiang Langhua Art Troupe has the characteristics of public welfare, including "mere public welfare with zero charges", "publicity through entertainment", "zero distance dual interaction", "frequent performance in rural areas and full coverage" and "versatile talent and a highly capable team", among which "mere public welfare with zero charges" is the most prominent. The art troupe stages performances in rural areas without charges, the boarding, lodging, travel and other costs for performers and staff are fully borne by the art troupe. The activity funds for the art troupe mainly come from two channels: The first one is that the government procures the program through performance allowance; second, the art troupe receives social sponsorship.

Third, adopting the "meal ordering system" and the "extra meal system" to better meet diverse cultural needs in rural areas. The "meal ordering system" breaks the previous conventional mode under which one troupe is the dominant actor, and enables program purchase mainly from the troupes directly under the provincial department and supplemented by other troupes within and outside the province; under the "meal ordering system", a repository of programs is built for the people in rural areas to make choices and orders before the performance. Under the "extra meal system", appointments are made in advanced and special programs are arranged according to the special needs of towns for cultural activities.

Fourth, establishing the performance-oriented evaluation system. In order to arouse performers' enthusiasm, with the "expansion of the system of management of cultural and artistic troupes" as an opportunity, Zhejiang's cultural management department has specially developed incentive measures, linking the number of troupe performances with performance evaluation, linking performers' participation in performances with professional title appraisal and performance evaluation and linking the number of performances and audience scale with allowance.

The activities of delivering culture to rural areas have been conducive to enriching the rural cultural life and improving the scientific and cultural quality of the farmers. In 2013, Zhejiang entered the crucial developmental stage for modernization at which the per capita GDP reaches USD 10,000. Apparently, as an important part of social modernization, rural modernization or the construction of the new countryside cannot be achieved without the modernization of the people—farmers. From this perspective, the activities of delivering culture to rural areas which make educational efforts through entertainment are of great significance. If farmers do not undergo a change from the traditional mentality, mindset, attitude and behavioral mode to the modern ones, without residents as main participants, the most perfect blueprint for the construction of the new countryside will become a pile of waste paper. The cultivation of the new-type farmers is certainly an integrated project involving various aspects, while practice shows that delivering culture to rural areas is an important way to achieving this end.

5.3.1.2 From "Delivering Culture to Rural Areas" to "Sowing Cultural Seeds by Farmers"

"Sowing cultural seeds by farmers" reflects the farmers' initiative and creativity in culture; it indicates that farmers are not the passive consumers of culture, instead, they are the producers and creators of culture. Since the reform and opening-up, the market-driven mode, spontaneous mode and self-organization mode have been carried out in various aspects of Zhejiang's economic development, such as the rise of the individual private economy, specialized markets, the shareholding cooperative system and the regional economy, in other words, the folk entrepreneurial forces have played the main role. However, in the past rural cultural life, farmers' autonomy was not fully embodied. With an increasing awareness by farmers of participation and the awareness of farmers as main participants, they have a stronger desire to participate in cultural activities, and hope that they can be free to choose cultural products and services, autonomously take part in rural cultural activities, and change from cultural bystanders to participants, from audiences to performers.

Against such a background, Zhejiang's cultural management department and local governments gave prominence to the autonomous right of farmers and the role of farmers as main participants in rural cultural activities, and combined the activities of delivering culture with the activities of sowing cultural seeds, making the cultural seeds take root, bloom and bear fruit in rural areas just like planting crops. To be specific:

First, improving the activities of delivering culture, laying stress on the farmers' right to choose programs and the role of farmers as main participants in programs. This has been embodied in the "meal ordering system" and the "extra meal system" of the Qianjiang Langhua Art Troupe. A more typical example in this regard is the rural activity of "showing films on 10,000 occasions and staging 1,000 performances" in Ningbo which was initiated in 2005.[14]

Second, the practices adopted by some art troupes in the activities of delivering culture to rural areas also reflect a combination of "delivering cultural products and services" and "developing the ability to make cultural creations", a combination of "delivering culture" and "sowing cultural seeds". For example, when delivering culture to rural areas, the Qianjiang Langhua Art Troupe invited rural artistic personnel to perform the programs which were created by them and had local characteristics, fostered an atmosphere in which professional performance was combined with amateur performance, troupe performers and rural artistic personnel performed on the same stage, thus supporting and cultivating rural characteristic cultural and artistic groups, enhancing the farmers' ability to create cultural products and services.

Third, supporting farmers in independently conducting the public cultural activities or the activities of sowing cultural seeds. Since the beginning of the 21st century, especially the implementation of the "Eight-Eight Strategies", on the initiative of the Party committees and governments at various levels, the people in Zhejiang's rural areas have been increasingly active in independently carrying out the public welfare cultural activities. According to statistics, as early as 2005, the village-level amateur cultural and sports groups across the province conducted various types of activities for about 316,717 times, with activities carried out for 9.03 times at each village on average. At present, the primary-level rural mass cultural activities in various parts of Zhejiang are produced and provided mainly in the following ways: the government directly provides them, the government purchases and provides them, the people spontaneously produce and provide them, the non-profit organizations produce and provide them and enterprises produce and provide them.

It is worth mentioning that the activities of sowing cultural seeds by farmers are organized by farmers. Compared with the conventional mode under which they are carried out solely by the government, this reflects an innovation to the public cultural service development mode. The organizations arising out of the activities of sowing cultural seeds, such as the farmers' cultural and artistic groups and rural culture associations, are highly voluntary and are not subject to administrative orders in operations, they take root in rural communities and have the characteristics of the non-profit organizations, such as "non-profit" and "self-governing". The practice of sowing cultural seeds by farmers shows that the non-governmental social organizations can produce better effects than administrative means in many areas of public cultural services.

Apparently, the extensive activities of sowing cultural seeds by farmers in various parts of Zhejiang are the result of "folk inducement", are distinctively autonomous, and have been supported and "enhanced" by the Party committees and governments

---

[14]Li and Luo (2005).

at various levels in Zhejiang. For instance, in 2011, given the actual cultural needs in rural areas, the Civilization Office of Zhejiang Province assigned relevant personnel to 20 counties (county-level cities, districts) in Zhejiang to carry out the training and coaching demonstration activity relating to sowing cultural seeds in rural areas, directly training more than 3,000 people.

In the past, culture was delivered from urban areas to rural areas. With the expanding activities of sowing cultural seeds in Zhejiang's rural areas, some farmers have delivered culture to urban areas. In 2007, Yinzhou District in Ningbo City organized the "Starlight Grand Stage" performance activity to build the primary-level mass cultural and artistic performance brand. In less than one year, 28 rural amateur cultural and artistic performance groups came on the stages on which many stars once performed or many large cultural and artistic performances were held. With a variety of rural cultural activities held by farmers and with government support, the level of rural amateur performance groups has been on the increase and performing talents have emerged. As a result, farmers can deliver culture to urban areas.

5.3.2   Bringing About Innovations to the Urban Public Cultural Service Content and Mode

Besides increasing the provision of rural public cultural services, local authorities in Zhejiang have also actively started to bring about innovations to the service mechanism, thus increasing service means and improving the network of services to provide more urban public cultural services, enrich the public cultural life and guarantee the cultural rights and interests of the people, especially the primary-level vulnerable social groups.

5.3.2.1   Integrating Urban and Rural Cultural Resources, Building the Network of Public Cultural Services

The key to integrating regional, urban and rural public cultural resources lies in cities. Modern cities have the characteristics of agglomeration and diffusion, which means that the coordination and integration of public cultural resources must be achieved by leveraging the cities' function of agglomeration; balanced distribution and rational allocation of public cultural service resources among the groups in urban and rural areas must be based on giving play to the diffusion and radiation functions of cities. In recent years, some local governments in Zhejiang have made beneficial attempts and experiments in coordinating and integrating public cultural resources, leveraging the functions of cities in public cultural resource agglomeration and public cultural service diffusion, increasing the systematic level of the public cultural services and the rate of public cultural resource utilization, promoting the balanced distribution and rational allocation of public cultural service resources between urban and rural areas, among regions. A typical example is Cixi City.

In early 2013, Cixi Public Cultural Service Center was officially established. The service center adopts the basic operational line of thought of "addressing supply and demand in a people-oriented way, making products market-oriented and performing services through a network", and it integrates the city's resources of public cultural services and product supply, so that the service center makes these resources available to the primary-level units and people for choice by building a connection between supply and demand and enabling menu-based distribution. After the establishment of the public cultural service center, Cixi will also actively explore the public cultural service operational mode under which products are distributed according to public recognition, the government supports service delivery, and management is strengthened under market operations, and Cixi will comprehensively build a network for the city's public cultural product supply service by carrying out a number of people-oriented cultural projects, including popular classrooms, popular exhibition halls, popular stages, popular variety show venues, the activity of performing operas on 100 occasions, showing films on 1,000 occasions in rural areas, the activity of staging 100 cultural and artistic performances at and delivering 1 million books to the primary level, and the issuance of cultural love cards. "Integration and activation", "chain distribution" and "two-wheel drive" are the keywords in this new operational mechanism[15]: "integration and activation": taking stock in a hierarchical and classified way, integrating the city's public cultural service resources; "chain distribution": building a "center-station (point) institutional framework"; "two-wheel drive": establishing and improving an efficient operational mechanism covering the public welfare mechanism and the market mechanism.

Obviously, in order to establish this new public cultural service mechanism with "integration and activation", "chain distribution" and "two-wheel drive", it is necessary to first remove administrative barriers and break up institutional obstacles. Only in this way can "integration and activation" be conducted, the public cultural service resources be coordinated, various forces be brought together, the advantages in various respects be leveraged, the systematic level of the public cultural services and the rate of public cultural resource utilization be increased to achieve "chain distribution" and "two-wheel drive", and promote the balanced distribution and the rational allocation of public cultural service resources among the groups in urban and rural areas.

5.3.2.2 Allowing Free and Low-Charge Admission to Urban Public Cultural Facilities

Such public cultural service institutions as libraries and museums directly serve individuals to improve their civic cultural quality, thus indirectly serving the whole society; they have the general characteristics of public welfare programs, including "public", "sharing" and "common". The public cultural institutions follow the principle of public welfare, they are the measures which the government should take to

---

[15]Liu (2013).

make up for market failure and also the measures necessary for the public sector to repay taxpayers, create cultural welfare for the entire population.

During the period of the planned economy, almost all of the cultural products and services in Chinese cities were provided to the public without charge or with a low charge. Free or low charges under the planning system also reflected the principle of "public welfare", but the level and efficiency were low, the varieties of public cultural services were available only in small quantities, the service level of cultural institutions was low. Since the reform and opening-up, with the transition of the economic system, subject to financial strain, some public welfare cultural sectors sought "self-help through production" in a market-oriented way. Some urban public welfare cultural venues which were originally free of charge or at a low level of charges gradually collected charges and progressively increased their prices. This practice mitigated the shortage of funds and to a certain extent increased the income of workers, but it ran counter to the purpose of safeguarding the people's basic cultural rights and interests and the principle of equality. Charges, especially excessively high charges, "excluded" the vulnerable social groups, so that these social groups could not participate in cultural activities due to inability to pay, and citizens were subject to inequality in enjoying cultural rights. Zhejiang realized the deficiency in the previous practices early on. Since the beginning of the 21st century, especially since the implementation of the "Eight-Eight Strategies", with a gradual improvement in public finances and an increasing cultural awareness, Zhejiang has become the first to adopt the policies of free of charge and low charge for the urban public cultural service facilities for which charges were originally collected.

Zhejiang is the province becoming the first nationwide to provide free admission to museums. On May 18, 2003—the International Museum Day in the same year, the China National Tea Museum, the Southern Song Dynasty Guan Kiln Museum, the Hangzhou History Museum, the Zhang Taiyan Memorial Hall, and the Su Dongpo Memorial Hall, around the West Lake in Hangzhou, announced free admission for the public, while the Memorial Temple to Yu Qian, the Yuquyuan Memorial Hall, the Lin Fengmian Former Residence Memorial Hall, and the Zhejiang Revolution of 1911 Memorial Hall, around the West Lake in Hangzhou, were already previously open to the public for free. In 2004, the Zhejiang Provincial Museum and the China National Silk Museum became the first among provincial museums across the country and national museums to allow free admission throughout the year, respectively. In 2007, the Zhejiang Library became the first among national and provincial public libraries to allow free admission, became the first to launch online libraries, and started to build the "all-purpose card" project for the integrated urban-rural public library system. In 2012, the Department of Culture and the Department of Finance of Zhejiang Province jointly issued the *Implementation Opinions on Further Promoting the Work on Free Admission to Art Galleries, Public Libraries and Cultural Centers (Stations)*, fully enabling barrier-free and zero-threshold admission to art galleries, libraries and cultural centers (stations) at various levels in the charge of the competent provincial department for cultural affairs, free admission to all public spaces, facilities and venues, and making all of their basic service items provided free of charge.

These practices undoubtedly further reflect the cultural self-consciousness of Zhejiang as the province at the forefront nationwide. They have restored the characteristics of public welfare which public cultural institutions have, including the aspects of "public", "sharing" and "common". With free admission, these public cultural institutions can be better integrated into the society, more audiences can enter museums, libraries and art galleries and have more opportunities to understand history and experience civilization. After free admission, the Zhejiang Provincial Museum, the China National Silk Museum and most museums in Hangzhou have witnessed a steady growth in the number of audiences. Before free admission, the Zhejiang Provincial Museum received audiences for 400,000–500,000 person-times each year. Since free admission was introduced in 2004, the Zhejiang Provincial Museum has annually received audiences for an average of more than 1.40 million person-times; the China National Silk Museum has annually received audiences for about 400,000 person-times, two times the number before free admission was introduced.

Of course, free charge and low charge at public cultural institutions does not merely "return to" the practices in the period of the planned economy; instead, it is a higher-level "return" based on the achievements and experience of reform and opening-up.

First, "returning" on the basis of improving the public cultural facilities. Free admission has made museums, libraries and art galleries really open to the society and has also posed huge challenges to the protection and management of collection. As audiences have increased greatly, the problems concerning crowded houses and underdeveloped hardware facilities have become more prominent, affecting the effect of public participation. Since free admission, Zhejiang has increased its financial input to improve the supporting facilities, and more rapidly renovate and build the public cultural facilities open to the public for free.

Second, "returning" on the basis of intensifying internal reform of the public cultural service institutions, increasing the level of management, and improving the efficiency of services and the service attitude. After free admission, the public's requirements for the quality of services provided by the public cultural institutions have not decreased. Museums, libraries and art galleries have continuously intensified their reforms to enhance vitality, improve services and seek development, they have worked on the goal of providing better services to the public, standardized the work in various aspects, and improved the quality of services to meet the needs of the audiences.

Third, "returning" on the basis of bringing about innovations to the service mechanism, increasing service means, and improving the service network. Under the planned economic system, the public cultural service mechanism was rigid, service means were not diverse, and the service network was not complete. As the governments at various levels in Zhejiang have changed their managerial functions, there have been sufficient conditions for bringing innovations to the public cultural service mechanism, increasing service means and improving the service network. With the goal of providing equitable, free and barrier-free public cultural services to urban and rural residents, Jiaxing City has built an integrated mode for an urban-rural system of public library services mainly characterized by government-led efforts, centralized management and resource sharing. The above innovative practices epitomize the philosophy of the "Hangzhou Library Model" for public cultural services: equitable, free, barrier-free, namely, open to all.

5.3.2.3 Bringing About Innovations to the Urban Public Cultural Activity and Service Modes

Apparently, the free charge and low charge policy for the urban public cultural service facilities for which charges were originally collected mainly reflects "stock" reform for making these facilities and institutions "return" to the characteristics of public welfare and guaranteeing the public's basic rights and interests. In the meantime, Zhejiang has also acted in an "incremental" way to enrich the methods of urban public activities and to meet the public's cultural needs. The urban festival activities in various parts of Zhejiang are "increments" for enriching the manners of urban public cultural activities.

Since the beginning of the 21st century, especially since the implementation of the "Eight-Eight Strategies", the urban festival activities have always been available in a large number in Zhejiang; as a famous historical and cultural city, Hangzhou has always carried out a variety of cultural festival activities; each year; Hangzhou has the tea festival, the women's wear festival, the beer festival, the tourism shopping festival, and the arts and crafts festival. Hangzhou has always tried to break up the conventions of festival activities in other cities, give prominence to its humanistic characteristics, and give expression to the characteristic of co-building and sharing by the people. Since 2005, Ningbo has been rated as one of China's Top Ten Festival Cities for many consecutive years.

Besides cultural festival activities, the Party committees and governments at various levels in Zhejiang have also, through multiple channels—including cultural and ethical development activities and the building of corporate culture, campus culture, corridor culture, wall & door culture, family culture and garden culture—brought about innovations to the service mechanism, increased service means to enrich the modes of urban public cultural activities, meet the public's cultural needs and improve the cultural quality of the public. These government-led urban cultural activities are welcomed by citizens because they serve as the effective carriers for citizens to find the "significance" of production and circulation, "pleasure" and "social identity"; "sharing" of a cultural activity means sharing a significance and pleasure. "Sharing" is one of the essential characteristics of public cultural activities. With participation in cultural activities including festival culture, corporate culture, campus culture, corridor culture, wall & door culture, garden culture, citizens share a common "significance", "pleasure" and "social identity". Therefore, from a certain perspective, these urban cultural activities are the good medicines for treating "the illness of urban cultural poverty" and also effective adhesives for urban social solidarity and social harmony.

5.3.3 Bringing About Innovations to the Mode of Safeguarding the Cultural Rights and Interests of Rural Migrant Workers

The rural migrant workers make up a huge social group. The service for meeting cultural needs of rural migrant workers is one of the weakest parts of public cultural services. According to the national research group for the survey on the cultural life of rural migrant workers, the marginalization of rural migrant workers under a dual economic structure has substantively affected and restricted the consumption of cultural products and activities of rural migrant workers. Moreover, many local governments do not perform the public cultural service function and the cultural service supply channels are unsmooth, which are also important causes of the cultural marginalization of rural migrant workers. Therefore, in order to overcome generally insufficient effective supply in the cultural life of rural migrant workers, less willingness to take part in cultural activities and asymmetry between supply and demand, comprehensive improvement must be made.[16]

Zhejiang is a large province of rural migrant workers. With the rapid economic development since the reform and opening-up, Zhejiang has not only transferred a rural labor force of more than 10 million people in the province to the secondary and tertiary industries, but it has also received a large number of rural migrant workers. As of June 30, 2011, Zhejiang's registered migrant population totaled 22,151,000, ranking Zhejiang no. 2 nationwide for 12 consecutive years—the population migrating across provinces accounted for more than 90% of that migrant population. In recent years, Zhejiang's migrant population has further increased. As of January, 2013, it totaled 24.03 million. Rural migrant workers have worked hard at promoting economic development and increasing resident income in Zhejiang. Massive migration of rural migrant workers has optimized the combination of Zhejiang's regional production factors, increased the rate of the utilization of resources, reduced industrialization costs and promoted national economic growth. In the meantime, their massive migration has also effectively controlled labor costs, thus enhancing the competitiveness of Zhejiang's products on the international market.

Obviously, in Zhejiang, a province with a large number of rural migrant workers, the ability to promote scientific development and social harmony largely depends upon the ability to effectively improve the well-being of rural migrant workers, properly deal with the relationship between new and old people of Zhejiang, establish a responsibility mechanism, a long-term mechanism and a service system to help rural migrant workers seek employment and safeguard their rights and enhance their sense of identity and sense of belonging. Against such a background, making rural migrant workers share the achievements of urban cultural development is of special significance. Providing basic public cultural services to rural migrant workers is an important way to make rural migrant workers develop a sense of identity and a sense of belonging regarding urban culture.

---

[16]Fu et al. (2007).

As shown by the surveys on the cultural life of rural migrant workers carried out by a number of research institutions across the country over a period of more than ten years, it was common knowledge that the level of cultural consumption of rural migrant workers was low, their cultural life was deficient and monotonous; even if rural migrant workers participated in some cultural activities, these activities were basically recreational activities. In the meantime, rural migrant workers had great expectations and needs for a cultural life. According to the field interview and questionnaire survey on the cultural life of Zhejiang's new generation of rural migrant workers carried out by the Zhejiang Cultural Center in 2010,[17] the most urgent cultural needs of the new generation of rural migrant workers were as follows: watching a film (48.38%), surfing the Internet (45.53%), watching artistic performances (40.65%), reading books and newspapers (33.78%), singing karaoke (29.75%), playing cards and Mahjong (18.86%), and playing chess (18.47%).

Since the beginning of the 21st century, especially since the implementation of the "Eight-Eight Strategies", the Party committees and governments at various levels in Zhejiang have increasingly realized that rural migrant workers are entitled to enjoy public cultural services, that such enjoyment can make them develop a sense of integration and a sense of identity, thus the whole society has a greater cohesion and stronger bonds of attachment. The *Decision of the Party Committee of Zhejiang Province on Accelerating the Building of a Culturally Large Province*, made in 2005, stressed, "It is necessary to extensively carry out mass cultural sports activities at the primary level and for the people, actively promote the development of corporate culture, campus culture, community culture, village culture, square culture and military camp culture, and incessantly enrich the people's cultural life; moreover, it is necessary to address the multi-level and diverse cultural needs of different social groups, so that the achievements of civilization are shared by the whole population". Rural migrant workers are not mentioned above, but such requirements as "extensively carry out mass cultural sports activities at the primary level and for the people" and "address the multi-level and diverse cultural needs of different social groups" do in fact cover rural migrant workers and their cultural needs. The *Plan of Zhejiang Province for Promoting Vigorous Cultural Development and Great Cultural Prosperity*, unveiled in 2008, called for paying attention to rural and special juvenile groups, really safeguarding the rights and interests of orphaned and disabled children, rural stay-at-home children, the children of rural migrant workers, the juveniles of urban households in difficulty, vigorously pushing forward the project of providing a minimum cultural security, intensifying the provision of free cultural services to the primary level, especially the low-income and special groups. These expressions of "rural migrant workers" appeared in the programmatic document concerning cultural development issued by the Party Committee of Zhejiang Province for the first time. The *Decision on Carrying Out the Principles Adopted during the 6th Plenary Session of the 17th Central Committee of the Communist Party of China and Promoting the Building of a Culturally Strong Province*, made in 2011, further called for expanding the scope of the public welfare cultural products and services covered by

---

[17] Wang and Zhou (2012).

government procurement to ensure that such groups as the households in financial difficulty, rural migrant workers and the handicapped enjoy public cultural services. These expressions mean that Zhejiang has started paying attention to the cultural life of rural migrant workers. In practice, the Party Committee and the People's Government of Zhejiang Province and some local Party committees and governments in Zhejiang started experimenting in increasing the public cultural service supply for rural migrant workers, bringing about innovations to the content and mode of public cultural services for rural migrant workers, enriching the cultural life of rural migrant workers and the ways to safeguard the basic cultural rights and interests of rural migrant workers.

During the period of the 11th Five-Year Plan, Zhejiang carried out the project for providing a minimum cultural security, and subsidized the cultural activity centers for rural migrant workers. The Zhejiang Federation of Trade Unions, the Department of Culture of Zhejiang Province and other departments started taking safeguarding the cultural rights and interests of rural migrant workers as their responsibilities, exploring the ways and methods of improving and enriching the cultural life of rural migrant workers. In 2006, the Zhejiang Federation of Trade Unions initiated the action of delivering culture to rural migrant workers, and jumpstarted efforts in delivering films, performances, books, newspapers, training, radios, color TVs and health with a view to enriching the cultural life of those workers. In the same year, the Zhejiang Federation of Trade Unions also initiated the following training activity: each year delivering 1,000 performances to rural migrant workers, delivering films to them on 10,000 occasions, delivering 10,000 newspapers to them, adopting various means to train rural migrant workers for one million person-times; this offered a cultural entertainment platform for rural migrant workers and also provided them with an important channel for understanding the society, acquiring knowledge and improving the quality of their lives. On May 30, 2007, the Department of Publicity and Education under the Zhejiang Federation of Trade Unions and the Zhejiang Radio and News Station officially launched the special program "Rural Migrant Workers Online", which is aimed at listening to rural migrant workers by such means as news information and hotline interviews and providing them with services for consultation and the safeguarding of their rights.

In the meantime, the needs of rural migrant workers regarding their cultural life drew increasing attention from local Party committees and governments at various levels in Zhejiang. In an effort to enrich the cultural life of rural migrant workers, some local authorities gave full considerations to the characteristics of their work and life as well as their ability to consume, they adopted convenient means and channels to provide rural migrant workers with as many public welfare cultural services as possible, they built cultural facilities in the areas inhabited by rural migrant workers to facilitate their participation; regarding the form, they organized and carried out a variety of cultural activities on a small scale in a scattered, convenient and highly feasible way.

The cultural activity centers and cultural homelands for rural migrant workers which have emerged in some areas of Zhejiang in recent years are the venues which are more able to make rural migrant workers develop a sense of belonging to their homeland. In 2006, three villages in which rural migrant workers were concentrated, including Yangjia Village, Wumatang Village in Baiyun Sub-district and Datiantou Village in Nanshi Subdistrict, Dongyang City, became the first to build the cultural activity centers for rural migrant workers. Dongyang City also actively experimented in bringing about innovations to the construction and operation mechanisms involving the cultural activity centers for rural migrant workers, and the city built the cultural activity centers for rural migrant workers by adopting the new philosophy of government-led efforts, enterprise co-building and social participation. As of late 2013, there were 243 provincial cultural homelands for rural migrant workers in Zhejiang. The Zhejiang Federation of Trade Unions donated 600 books to each provincial cultural homeland for rural migrant workers and supported the building of 60 provincial cultural homelands for rural migrant workers in the areas inhabited by rural migrant workers, such as development zones, towns and communities; it also provided a subsidy of 40,000 yuan for the building of each provincial cultural homeland for rural migrant workers where there was financial difficulty in its building.

Some local authorities not only provided public cultural services to rural migrant workers but also involved them in participating in the development of public culture. For instance, Yinzhou District of Ningbo City extensively involved new and old people of Yinzhou in cultural and ethical development and the building of a beautiful homeland. Given that there were large numbers of rural migrant workers in the villages planned for building beautiful homelands, the district built a platform for communication between old villagers and new villagers—the association for co-building 381 beautiful homelands—to assist the leading group in building beautiful homelands.

Cultural entertainment is an important part of the public cultural service supply for rural migrant workers in various parts of Zhejiang Province. For rural migrant workers, cultural entertainment brings physical and mental pleasure, and also conveys a particular significance and value. Cultural entertainment embodies a new lifestyle, a new "industry" and new economic and social development; it involves the daily life experience of the ordinary people, new interpersonal relationships and social relationships. With participation in the cultural entertainment activities in cities and enterprises, rural migrant workers can realize that they belong to particular cities and understand the sentiment, value and significance that their identity as city members brings to them, thus enhancing their sense of identity and sense of belonging regarding the cities and communities where they live and the enterprises where they work. Besides cultural entertainment, local authorities in Zhejiang also took, as an important part of the public cultural services, the professional skill training aimed at improving the scientific and cultural quality of rural migrant workers.

5.4 Innovating the System and Mechanism for the Building of the Public Cultural Service System

When serving as the Secretary of the Party Committee of Zhejiang Province, comrade Xi Jinping truly realized that current development of the public welfare cultural programs cannot deviate from the general background of a market economy. The development mode of public welfare cultural programs under the condition of the market economy is different from the cultural program mode, in a planned economy, under which the government solely undertakes cultural programs, so it is essential to introduce the market mechanism and social forces, adopt the well-proven market means to achieve interaction and complementation among the government, the market and the society, so as to improve the efficiency of the supply of public products and services. Comrade Xi Jinping pointed out, "The government must increase its input in the public welfare cultural programs, but it is necessary to adopt the reforming line of thought and mode, apply the market mechanism, enhance capital operations, give full scope to the guiding and driving role of fiscal input, introduce the financial transfer payment system and the system of government procurement of cultural products and services which support cultural projects and gradually achieve a transformation from general input in cultural units and their staff to the input in cultural projects, from 'supporting the headcount' to promoting the cause".[18] This new philosophy for the development of the public welfare cultural programs in a market economy was fully reflected in the *Decision of the Party Committee of Zhejiang Province on Accelerating the Building of a Culturally Large Province*, made when comrade Xi Jinping served as the Secretary of the Party Committee of Zhejiang Province. The Decision called for giving full play to the supporting role of public finance, and exploring a new pattern for the development of cultural programs in which the government plays the leading role with social participation and market operations. Since the beginning of the 21st century, especially since the implementation of the "Eight-Eight Strategies", local authorities in Zhejiang have made active attempts and experiments in optimizing the structure for the governance of public cultural services, especially in applying the market mechanism and introducing social forces in the process of promoting the development of public culture to enable diversified cooperation, interaction and complementation among the government, the market and the society; they have accumulated a great deal of experience, which conforms to the market economy, in bringing about innovations to the mode of input in the field of public cultural services and the management and operational mechanism.

---

[18]Xi (2006), pp. 329–330.

5.4.1 Bringing About Innovations to the Input Mechanism Involving the Building of the Public Cultural Service System

As mentioned above, since the beginning of the 21st century, especially since the implementation of the "Eight-Eight Strategies", with a gradual improvement in public finances, Zhejiang has increased its fiscal input to culture year by year. It is more worth noting that local authorities in Zhejiang have brought about innovations to the input and supply mode concerning public cultural services, and have greatly changed the philosophy of building them up; in particular, many authorities in Zhejiang have attempted to establish a cooperative partnership among the government, the market and the society regarding public cultural services, strengthen the effectiveness of, the incentives for and the guiding role of fiscal input. The practice of Zhejiang's local innovation to the mode of input in public culture shows that an inevitable trend in building up the public cultural service system under the condition of a market economy was that the single responsibility system in which the government solely carries out cultural programs under the conventional mode shifted to a diversified pattern in which government security plays the leading role with the participation of the government, enterprises, the third parties, and individuals.

5.4.1.1 From Direct Appropriation to Replacement of Appropriation by Rewards

For a long time, China made fiscal input into cultural programs basically through direct appropriation, in other words, allocating "headcount" funds according to the permanent staff of units so that these staff provided public cultural products and services. In the period of the planned economy, the cultural public institutions were small, fiscal expenditure was limited, the administrative allocation mode was then effective to a certain extent in China. However, that mode led to overstaffing and inefficiency.

Since the beginning of the 21st century, especially since the implementation of the "Eight-Eight Strategies", some authorities and departments in Zhejiang have started the change from "supporting staff" and "supporting institutions" to "supporting programs". "Supporting programs" means that the service charge is measured by the amount of service needed by the public from public institutions, namely, the charge is determined by the programs, so that public institutions are driven to determine staff and overcome the long-standing problems concerning overstaffing and inefficiency, and thus effective breakthroughs have been made in the mode under which cultural programs were supported solely by the government's direct appropriation under the planned economic system. In order to achieve the change from "supporting staff through money" and "supporting institutions through money" to "supporting programs through money" and "supporting projects through money", enhance the effectiveness, the incentive and guiding role of fiscal input in the public cultural service projects, and increase the financial input in the building of the public cultural service system, some local governments in Zhejiang have adopted such modes as "replacement of appropriation by rewards", "subsidies" and "project applications".

Besides "replacement of appropriation by rewards", "subsidy" is also a manner of government input in the field of public cultural services within a market economy, but this mode is totally different from the previous mode of public financial input under which the government solely carried out relevant programs. In the modern society, "subsidy" is an economic policy commonly adopted by many countries around the world; it is an economic lever through which the government regulates economic operations and coordinates various relations of interest distribution; it is also an important means for leveraging the public finance function as incentive. During the transformation of mode of the public cultural service development, "subsidy" is a valuable economic measure. As mentioned by scholars, the mode under which the government builds cultural facilities and provides a certain subsidy for commercial operations is conducive to cultivating the market of cultural consumption, while low ticket prices arising out of government subsidies also encourage some people to consume cultural products and services.[19]

During the period of the 12th Five-Year Plan, the central government would allocate 7 billion yuan to subsidize the building of public libraries, cultural centers and museums at the level of prefecture cities. Subsidizing the development of public culture has become a common practice adopted by the governments at various levels across the country, while Zhejiang is one of the provinces which adopted this practice early on. During the period 2001–2005, each year, 50 million yuan in a special subsidy fund was allocated from provincial finance to support the primary-level cultural development, the protection of national and folk art and the development of the cultural industry; the special subsidy fund for the protection of cultural relics was raised from 4.90 million yuan in 2001 to 15 million yuan in 2005. Since the implementation of the "Eight-Eight Strategies", many cities (prefecture-level cities) and counties (county-level cities) in Zhejiang have provided subsidies. Apparently, these subsidies and allowances are in striking contrast to the previous mode of "supporting staff through money" and "supporting institutions through money", they reflect the principle of "supporting programs through money" and "supporting projects through money", and thus bring into play the effectiveness, the incentive and the guiding role of fiscal input.

Since the turn of the century, "project application", as a cultural input mode, has been increasingly adopted in various parts of Zhejiang. As from 2006, Hangzhou introduced the project initiation examination and approval system combining expert evaluation with administrative decision-making for the cultural industry supporting projects—as from 2008, it was renamed the special fund for the creative cultural industry; it should be noted that these projects were called cultural industry supporting projects, but in fact they also included the public cultural facility supporting projects. From 2006 to 2014, Hangzhou carried out this system for nine consecutive years; with project initiation examination and approval, a large number of key high-quality

---

[19]Zhang (2007), p. 231.

projects with potential were supported, thus vigorously promoting the development of the creative cultural industry and the construction of public cultural facilities in Hangzhou.

The practice of some local governments of Zhejiang in the "replacement of appropriation by rewards" and "project application" is an active attempt at bringing innovations to the fiscal input mode and represents an effective breakthrough in the government's direct appropriation for cultural programs under the planned economic system. The significance of "replacement of appropriation by rewards", "subsidy" and "project application" lies in breaking the conventional pattern in which the superior governments solely made fiscal input in culture. They stimulated multiple forces to participate in the building of the public cultural service system and enhanced the efficiency of government fund utilization.

5.4.1.2 Public Cultural Products: From Direct Production by the Government to Procurement

Government procurement of the public welfare cultural products and services is an important innovation to the mode of government input against the general background of a market economy. Under the conventional system of cultural programs, most public cultural products and services tended to be supplied within units. Such a supply mode often lacked a practical basis and a strategic consideration, caused repeated construction and left facilities unused, increased the wasting of public financial funds and the burden on public finance. Furthermore, the use of fiscal funds was excessively scattered and lacked transparency, it was easy to generate rent-seeking. Government procurement is an important way of overcoming these drawbacks in public financial input. At present, each year the government purchases a number of key projects from the society and provides them to the public at low prices or free of charge, and this has become a relatively common practice in various parts of the province. Practice shows that the public cultural product procurement system is dominated by competitive procurement, under the procurement system, open tendering or competitive inquiry, competitive invitation is carried out to attract suppliers for bidding, so that the buyer's market favorable for the government is formed, the government obtains better public cultural products or services at relatively preferential prices, the efficiency of public expenditure is improved. This indicates that government procurement of the public welfare cultural products effectively plays a guiding role. The public welfare cultural projects covered by government procurement are often of high artistic quality, so enterprises and other social forces can be attracted to make joint investments, the multi-win outcome beneficial for multiple parties can be achieved. Obviously, government procurement of the public cultural products and introduction of the market mechanism help improve the efficiency of public cultural input and the quality of supply.

5.4.1.3   Public Cultural Services: From Single Input to Diversified Input

As fiscal revenue served as the single fund source for the building of the public cultural service system, two drawbacks often occurred: First, the single input by the government was too limited to meet the increasing needs for public cultural services; second, it was hard to monitor the efficiency and effects of the single input by the government. In order to make up for the deficiency in the single investment mode, since the beginning of the 21st century, especially since the implementation of the "Eight-Eight Strategies", some local authorities in Zhejiang have attempted multiple financing channels and modes, and have experimented with new modes under which the government and non-governmental forces cooperate in developing the public cultural programs. In Ningbo City, a number of private museums and art galleries, including the newly built Shili Hongzhuang Museum in Ninghai, the Jinlun Art Gallery in Cixi, the Zilin Wenfang Workshop, and the Zhangdehe Bamboo Root Carving Art Gallery in Xiangshan, have been open to the public for free or with a low charge; all of them are built through diversified input with a combination of state support, private operations and individual investments.

In particular, since the beginning of the 21st century, and especially since the implementation of the "Eight-Eight Strategies", local authorities in Zhejiang have actively guided and stimulated social forces to financially support the public cultural programs, thus producing marked effects on the transformation from single input in public cultural services to diversified input. As a large province with a private economy in China, Zhejiang has sufficient conditions for mobilizing social forces to financially support the public welfare cultural programs. Since the beginning of the 21st century, and especially since the implementation of the "Eight-Eight Strategies", Zhejiang has encouraged social forces to support the public cultural programs, making breakthroughs. In this regard, Cixi City, Funchun City, Shaoxing County and Haining City are representatives.[20]

5.4.2   Bringing About Innovations to the Operational Mechanism for Public Cultural Facilities and Services

The public cultural programs must embody the principle of public welfare—free of charge or low charge, but their operational cost is an issue which is hard to avoid. In China, many local authorities have been trapped in the vicious cycle that the construction of a facility adds a burden. Obviously, in order to overcome this difficulty, it is necessary to explore a new mode of construction, operation and management of public cultural facilities under the market mechanism, enhance the self-development function of public cultural facilities, and improve their operating efficiency. Since the beginning of the 21st century, and especially since the implementation of the "Eight-Eight Strategies", some local authorities in Zhejiang have made meaningful attempts in these respects.

---

[20]Luo (2009).

5.4.2.1 State-Owned, Privately Operated and State-Supported and Privately Run: Innovations to the Public Cultural Facility Operational Mechanism

In Zhejiang, a province as a forerunner in the market economy, some government departments realized early on the drawbacks in the conventional operational mechanism of the public cultural facilities, and put forward some ideas for reform concerning the public cultural facility construction and operational mechanism consistent with the law of a market economy. Since the beginning of the 21st century, and especially since the implementation of the "Eight-Eight Strategies", more and more local governments in Zhejiang have adopted some market and socialized means to innovate the public cultural facility operational mechanism, gradually attempting to get out of the vicious cycle in which the construction of a facility adds a burden. Apparently, these experiments have offered beneficial experience and inspirations for the rest of the country in overcoming the difficulties in the operation and management of public cultural facilities and services.

1. Cultural facility owners perform enterprise-oriented operations

For instance, the Redstar Theatre was restructured to establish the Hangzhou Redstar Culture Co., Ltd.; the Ningbo Grand Theatre sets up an operating limited company with the goal of "enterprise-oriented management and market-oriented operations" to vigorously exploit the art performance market. These moves are the attempts and experiments in the mode by which cultural facility owners carry out enterprise-oriented operations. In this regard, the experiment made by the Hangzhou Redstar Culture Co., Ltd. is representative to a great extent. It is a company established according to the modern enterprise system, its main building is Hangzhou Redstar Culture Tower built with 130 million yuan in investments from the municipal government and 40 million yuan in investments from the municipal culture bureau. The Hangzhou Redstar Culture Co., Ltd. endeavors to cultivate the Redstar brand, become large and strong on the cultural market, and take the new path of the market-oriented operation of state-owned cultural and sports venues.

2. Specialized companies are entrusted to carry out management, or private enterprises are entrusted to perform operations

Under the planned economic system, large domestic cultural and sports venues were basically invested in by the government and operated by the units affiliated to the cultural and sports department. Such a mode combining "running cultural affairs" with "managing cultural affairs" often led to a shortage of funds, poor management and difficulties in sustaining operations. Since the beginning of the 21st century, and especially since the implementation of the "Eight-Eight Strategies", some local governments in Zhejiang have followed the principle of separating ownership from management, they have attempted to entrust the public welfare cultural facilities to specialized companies for management or to private enterprises for operations, thus successfully overcoming the above difficulties. Entrusting operations and management to others means that the production and supply of the public cultural services can be entrusted to the private sector, the government is no longer the direct producer and supplier, and becomes purchaser, trustor and supervisor; it means that the government's function of "steering" can be separated from the function of "paddling", the government can break way from the role of the direct producer and supplier of public cultural products and services.

It is worth mentioning the Tiantianyan People-oriented Cultural Project in Yinzhou District. In 2009, with open tendering, the Government of Yinzhou District and Ningbo Hesheng Cultural Performance Development Co., Ltd. cooperated in carrying out the Tiantianyan People-oriented Cultural Project, in which the government is responsible for purchasing and supervision, the outsourcing company arranges performances and is responsible for distribution and implementation, with a view to giving free touring performances for the public. Tiantianyan has become a typical mode for outsourcing the government's public cultural services.[21]

(1) Government-led efforts. In the operations of Tiantianyan, the philosophy that the government is the entity responsible for the public cultural services has been clearly embodied. The Department of Publicity under the Party Committee of Yinzhou District and the Bureau of Culture of Yinzhou District have always played the role of the responsible entity; they are the builders of the outsourced service platform and the investors of the outsourced services, and they also supervise and evaluate the outsourced services. Unlike the conventional practice in which the public cultural services were carried out solely by the government, with the public cultural services outsourced, the government's administrative departments have gradually changed from "a combination of management and running" to "separation between management and running", from "running cultural affairs" to "managing cultural affairs".

(2) Company-oriented operations. The greatest innovation in the Tiantianyan mode lies in introducing the outsourcing undertaker Ningbo Hesheng Cultural Performance Development Co., Ltd.. Hesheng is a joint-stock company with a registered capital of 5 million yuan—the private company Raymond Cultural Sports Development Co., Ltd., Yinzhou Urban Construction Investment Development Co., Ltd. under the district government, Haishu Hemei Cultural Co., Ltd. and individuals contribute 51, 30, 10 and 9% of the capital, respectively. The company undertakes service outsourcing from the district government and is responsible for the connection between supply and demand, product purchasing, distribution and whole-process supervision. It is natural that an independent market entity makes profits, so there is no exception for Hesheng. Subject to completing the Tiantianyan government procurement contract, Hesheng strives to reduce procurement and operating costs as much as possible to make certain operating profits, basically guaranteeing the company's daily operations. On this basis, the company actively exploits the market, develops and grows.

(3) Specialized production. Specialized production is another characteristic of the Tiantianyan operational mechanism. Tiantianyan's procurement is conducted across the country so that the people can enjoy more performance services

---

[21] Hong and Hu (2010).

which are highly professional, while in the past, products were supplied more by state-owned cultural units and local cultural groups. With Tiantianyan, a large number of excellent performance resources have been introduced, fundamentally changing the situation in which the rural performance market is dominated by the performances of folk troupes, so it is widely welcomed and recognized by the primary-level people.

(4) Public participation. From the selection of the purchasing team, repertoire and performers to the appraisal of the performance quality, public opinions are valued, and the people have a higher degree of participation and a higher sense of belonging. In the era of a shortage of public cultural services, the people basically had no choice regarding cultural products and services; the government performed all of the public cultural services, public participation was low, the connection between supply and demand was not sufficient, even if a great deal of money was spent, the people were not necessarily satisfied. The Tiantianyan mode has effectively guaranteed the people's rights to participate in, enjoy, choose and evaluate the public cultural services.

For a long time, how to effectively and rationally utilize the public cultural facilities and resources was an issue which severely beset China's public cultural programs. Under the conventional system of local and industrial segmentation, the limited cultural resources were not utilized rationally and fully. Under the conventional mode with all cultural services performed by the government, the public cultural facilities and resources often lacked the function of self-development, the service function was low, and social benefits were poor; as a result, on the one hand, the public cultural needs could not be effectively satisfied; on the other hand, some public cultural facilities and resources were unused and wasted for a long time. Zhejiang's practice shows that the introduction of a market economic means can effectively promote the utilization of public cultural facilities and resources to a higher level, and enhance the function of self-development and operating efficiency of the public cultural facilities and resources.

5.4.2.2 Marketing: Improving the Operating Efficiency of the Public Cultural Facilities

For the cultural industry, the marketing strategy must be adopted because the cultural industry consists of the enterprise groups which produce and operate cultural products and services and pursue maximum profits. Should the marketing strategy be adopted for the public cultural services under the general environment of a market economy? In this regard, Francois Colbert gave an affirmative answer: "Such cultural institutions as museums, concert halls, public libraries or universities produce cultural goods or cultural products; now all of these institutions have realized that they have to compete in attracting the attention of consumers and in the national resources shared by them, in other words, they also encounter the issue of marketing."[22]

---

[22]Colbert (2002), p. 18.

In this regard, Zhejiang, a province as a forerunner in the market economy, has made beneficial attempts in many respects, thus improving the operating efficiency of the public cultural facilities. For instance, Xiaoshan District of Hangzhou City stresses that as the district's iconic public welfare cultural venue, Xiaoshan Theater should, during operations, adopt the philosophy of "making the theatre accessible to more people, bringing more food for the mind to the theatre". The theater adopts flexible and diverse means to actively organize and plan various types of marketing activities; at the level of performance operations, it integrates venue renting, self-operation with joint operation, combines elegant excellent art with mass culture and it takes multiple paths; it actively organizes and plans such activities as product promotion, enterprise celebration and festival carnivals for large enterprises; it energetically holds a variety of large meetings, special lectures, academic reports and large open classes. In the meantime, it makes efforts to combine indoor activities with outdoor square activities to gain popularity and foster an atmosphere. These measures promote diversification of theater operations and create a larger margin of profit, they also draw attention from more citizens so that the Xiaoshan Theater gradually becomes an important venue indispensable for citizens to enjoy leisure, entertainment and a cultural life, thus vigorously boosting the formation of a cultural atmosphere in the Xiaoshan New Area and improving the cultural quality.[23]

Enterprise title sponsorship is a way of enterprise promotion and also a means adopted by some public cultural facilities in Zhejiang to enhance the function of self-development. Enterprise naming can make enterprise names receive a great deal of attention and greatly increase the exposure of enterprises; this is a very good way for enterprises to promote themselves and build a good image among the public. Therefore, enterprise naming can effectively encourage enterprises to participate in the development of public cultural programs.

5.4.2.3 Social Composite Subject: An Innovation in the Construction of Public Cultural Facilities and in the Operational Mechanism

Since the beginning of the 21st century, Hangzhou has made large-scale efforts at comprehensive protection and improvement in the West Lake area, and park attractions accounting for 70% of the West Lake have been open for free. This move is first embodied in the principle of putting social benefits first. With this move, the Party Committee and the People's Government of Hangzhou City have honored the commitment of "returning the lake and the green spaces to the people", and the West Lake really becomes a public cultural facility beneficial to the people of Hangzhou and to visitors. More importantly, free admission to the West Lake reflects more support for the vulnerable groups in reform, and makes it possible for rural migrant

---

[23] See the Department of Publicity under the Party Committee of Xiaoshan District, the Xiaoshan Theater Explores the New Path of Becoming a State-run Privately Operated Theater, in: the Office of the Leading Group of Hangzhou City for the Reform of the Cultural System, *A Review of the Reform of the Cultural System in Hangzhou City*, Hangzhou Publishing House, 2007.

workers and low-income households to visit most scenic spots in the West Lake for free during their spare time. Free admission to the West Lake is not a conventional non-economic public welfare behavior, it makes the West Lake become the preferred leisure and sightseeing place for the local people and the people in the surrounding areas, so visitors have greatly increased in number year by year; the total amount of Hangzhou's revenue from tourism far exceeds the costs for sustaining free admission to the West Lake. Moreover, in the past, several parks in the West Lake were divided into different blocks, making it difficult for visitors to fully experience the charm of the West Lake; if admission tickets are bought, it is hard to make the people regard it as a paradise on earth. With massive protection and improvements, the West Lake holistically appears before the people free of charge; this greatly improves Hangzhou's image, and the resulting indirect economic benefits are inestimable.[24] Since the beginning of the 21st century, Hangzhou has also carried out the projects for comprehensive protection of the Beijing-Hangzhou Grand Canal and the Xixi National Wetland Park, and other major projects, delivering significant social and economic benefits.

In a sense, the projects for comprehensive protection of the West Lake, the Beijing-Hangzhou Grand Canal and the Xixi National Wetland Park can be considered as large public cultural facility construction and management projects. The success of these projects is attributable to the new operational mechanism involving public cultural facility construction and management in which the government plays the leading role with market-oriented operations and social participation. In Hangzhou, the operational mechanism in which the government plays the leading role with market-oriented operations and social participation has been summarized as the "social composite subject" operational mechanism with interaction among the Party and government circles, the intellectual circles, the industrial circles and the media circles. Such a "social composite subject" has the following five characteristics[25]: First, a multi-level and composite structure and diversified participation. The Party and government circles, the intellectual circles, the industrial circles and the media circles participate in the process, there is an interactive operation, interconnection and mutual support. Second, complementation among functions and characteristics, connection and integration of functions. The functions include guidance, coordination, management, entrepreneurship, development, operations, research, planning, design, publicity, promotion and display; functions are performed separately and are also complementary and interconnected. Third, full-time and part-time personnel, diverse roles and identities. There are full-time and part-time personnel, they perform functions at posts, and also consult each other and work together on an equal footing. Fourth, being program and project-driven; a flexible and well-regulated mechanism. Given that culture, knowledge-based industries or projects are flexible and open and project construction is staged, the flexible organizational structure and operational mode have been built. Fifth, being social public welfare-led; sustained operations. It strives to promote the development of programs and social projects

---

[24]Zhang (2007).
[25]Wang (2009).

and knowledge-based entrepreneurship, it has the nature of program development and gives prominence to public welfare; it can be operated and does not rely on the extension of power or administrative examination and approval rights; it is under enterprise-oriented and socialized operations, has the function of self-development and can achieve sustainable development.

The composite social subject is a main entrepreneurial player which is based on social diversification and stratification, has the function of interpenetration and integration, can arouse the creativity of individuals to the greatest extent and can also pool resources to do great things. In this sense, the social composite subject can be understood as a community for a cause. In striking contrast to the hierarchical structure of traditional units and organizations under which things are established or abandoned in light of staffing, the social composite subject can arrange work and personnel focusing on projects and programs according to the goal of doing things and accomplishing something, pushing forward social projects, knowledge-based entrepreneurship and program development. In this sense, the social composite subject can be considered as a thing-oriented community. Within the social composite subject, the players in different social entities or units have different interest appeals, but there is a high degree of interest correlation or common interest. Both respects constitute the basic interest relationship within the social composite subject and are also the starting point and ultimate goal of coordinating the interest relations among different social players.

As shown by the above practice, the public cultural service mode in a market economy is totally different from the developmental mode with all cultural programs carried out by the government in a planned economy. When the market economy becomes a basic economic system, not only the cultural industry but also the public welfare public cultural programs must perform their functions in light of market advantages and defects. In a market economy, in order to better safeguard the people's basic cultural rights and interests, subject to upholding the public welfare principle of the public cultural services, it is essential to introduce the market mechanism and private capital to optimize the micro players in the public cultural services, promote the reform and transformation of the mechanism of state-owned cultural public institutions, so as to solve government problems in the field of public culture, including insufficient input, poor operations, inefficiency and the wasting of resources. The introduction of an economic mechanism and social forces is aimed at making the government better assume the responsibility for developing public cultural programs rather than abandon that responsibility. Under the new mechanism, the government's responsibility lies in observing and applying the law of the market economy to develop public cultural programs, and the government's task consists of organizing and coordinating various forces to make joint efforts, namely, changing from the operator of public cultural products and services to organizational manager. This can solve the problem of rigid and excessive control in the development of public cultural programs, and make the government concentrate more of its energy on managing public cultural programs, thus improving the working efficiency and better performing its function in the building of the public cultural service system.

References

Action Plan for Ensuring Equal Access to Basic Public Services (2008–2012), *Zhejiang Economy*, 2008(19).

Francois Colbert, *Marketing Culture and the Arts*, trans. by Gao Fujin et al, Shanghai People's Publishing House, Canada, 2002, p. 18.

Fu Caiwu, et al, A Survey on the Current Cultural Life of Rural Migrant Workers and a Study of Countermeasures, in: Zhang Jiangang, Yin Changlong, and Zhang Xiaoming, *Annual Report on China's Public Cultural Service Development (2007)*, Social Sciences Academic Press, 2007.

Hong Xianxing, Hu Huahong, A Survey and Line of Thought of Yinzhou's Tiantianyan Public Cultural Service Outsourcing, *Zhengce Liaowang*, 2010(11).

Li Jianxin, Luo Yingjie, Transferring the Cultural Consumption Option to the People: Inspirations from Ningbo's Activity of "Showing Films on 10,000 Occasions and Staging 1,000 Performances" in Rural Areas, *Zhejiang Daily*, April 25, 2005.

Liu Chan, Chain Distribution, Integration and Activation, Two-wheel Drive, *China Culture Daily*, May 22, 2013.

Luo Wei, The Building of Zhejiang's Rural Public Cultural Service System, in: Chen Lixu, Pan Jiejun, et al, Rural Customs: the Construction of the New Countryside – A Study Based on Zhejiang's Practice, Science Press, 2009.

Wang Feng, The Development of Zhejiang's Rural Cultural Programs and Its Inspirations, *Xi'an Social Science*, December 15, 2009.

Wang Guoping, *A Study of and Practice in the Cultivation of the Social Composite Subject*, Hangzhou Publishing House, 2009, pp. 8–11.

Wang Quanji, Zhou Hang, *A Survey on the Cultural Life of the New Generation of Rural Migrant Workers in Zhejiang*, Zhejiang Literature & Art Publishing House, 2012.

Xi Jinping, *Carrying out Concrete Work to Stay Ahead – Line of Thought and Practice in Promoting New Development in Zhejiang*, The Party School of the CPC Central Committee Press, 2006.

Yang Jianhua, Ge Licheng, *Blue Book of Zhejiang's Economic and Social Development in 1998–1999*, China International Radio Press, 1999, pp. 200–201.

Zhang Jiangang, The Public Cultural Service System: The rebuilding under the Condition of a Market Economy, in: Li Jingyuan, Zhang Xiaoming, *The Zhejiang Experience and Its Implication for the Development of China (Culture Volume)*, Social Sciences Academic Press, 2007, pp. 202–213.

Zhao Xiaoming, The Cultural System Reform: the Key to Emancipating and Developing the Productive Cultural Forces, in: Li Jingyuan, Zhang Xiaoming, *The Zhejiang Experience and Its Implication for the Development of China (Culture Volume)*, Social Sciences Academic Press, 2007, p. 135.

Chapter 6
Intensifying the Reform of the Cultural System to Promote Vigorous Development of the Cultural Industry

Jie Li

In the international competition in the 21st century, the cultural industry has increasingly become an important means for various countries to prevail in both ideological and economic competition. Since the beginning of the 21st century, China has given unprecedented importance to the cultural industry. The *Recommendations of the Central Committee of the Communist Party of China for the 10th Five-Year Plan for Economic and Social Development of the People's Republic of China*, issued in 2000, and *the 10th Five-Year Plan for Economic and Social Development of the People's Republic of China*, issued in 2001, called for improving the policy regarding the cultural industry, strengthening the development and management of the cultural market, and promoting the development of the relevant cultural industry. The cultural industry was written into the central document for the first time. The cultural industry became a key for China to further overcome the structural contradictions and institutional barriers in economic development. The report delivered at the 16th National Congress of the Communist Party of China drew a distinction between the two different concepts—"cultural program" and "cultural industry", providing the necessary theoretical support for earnestly developing the cultural industry.

Against such a background, Zhejiang keenly realized the big role of developing the cultural industry in economic and social development, and took "developing the cultural industry and building a culturally large province" as an important part of the "Eight-Eight Strategies". On July 18, 2003, comrade Xi Jinping attended the meeting of Zhejiang Province on the reform of the cultural system and the building of a culturally large province, and identified the direction for the reform of Zhejiang's cultural system and development of the cultural industry; he pointed out, "culture is of a clear ideological nature, thus the reform of the cultural system must be conducted by taking into full account China's national conditions, focusing on managing the direction, introducing a flexible mechanism, making management result-oriented and improving the quality of management". When raising requirements for

J. Li (✉)
The Zhejiang Academy of Social Sciences, Hangzhou, China

© Social Sciences Academic Press and Springer Nature Singapore Pte Ltd. 2019
D. Xie and Y. Chen (eds.), *Chinese Dream and Practice in Zhejiang – Culture*,
Research Series on the Chinese Dream and China's Development Path,
https://doi.org/10.1007/978-981-13-7216-2_6

Zhejiang's development of the cultural industry, he put the cultural market players and the cultural market system in the same important position, and stressed, "to cultivate the cultural market players, it is necessary to intensify the reform of the state-owned cultural units, reshape a number of state-owned or state-owned holding cultural enterprises, leverage the advantages of Zhejiang's private economy, develop a number of private cultural enterprises, fully utilize the favorable conditions from China's accession to the WTO and introduce a number of foreign-funded cultural enterprises or cultural joint ventures, form a cultural industrial pattern in which public ownership is the mainstay and multiple forms of ownership develop side by side. Given Zhejiang's reality, the difficulty and breakthrough in nurturing the cultural market players lie in reforming state-owned cultural units, and the bright spot is the development of private cultural enterprises".[1]

In more than ten years, Zhejiang actively explored and promoted the path of reforming and bringing about innovations to the cultural system and mechanism, emancipated and developed the cultural productive forces, established a cultural system capable of arousing the enthusiasm and creativity of millions upon millions of people, leveraged Zhejiang's humanistic advantages and the advantages of Zhejiang's private cultural enterprises, and took the cultural industry as an important engine for cultivating core values, building consensus on reform, and promoting economic transformation and upgrading, thus vigorously simulating Zhejiang to move from an economically large province to a culturally large province.

6.1 Zhejiang's Theories and Practice in the Reform of the Cultural System

At the beginning of implementing the "Eight-Eight Strategies" in 2003, the then Secretary of the Party Committee of Zhejiang Province, comrade Xi Jinping, put forward the task of becoming the first to establish the system and mechanism capable of arousing the enthusiasm of millions upon millions of people, and pointed out, "Culture without a market is certainly not advanced culture".[2] Energetically promoting the reform of the cultural system is an important force for driving the sound and rapid development of Zhejiang's cultural industry.

Since the reform and opening-up, especially since the implementation of the strategy for the building of a culturally large province, Zhejiang has actively explored and steadily promoted the reform of the cultural system and accumulated a great deal of successful experience. Since the 16th National Congress of the Communist Party of China, Zhejiang has been designated as the pilot province for promoting the comprehensive reform of the cultural system, increased the scope of reform and the pilot areas for reform , expanded the content of reform, and comprehensively pushed

---

[1] Xi (2006), pp. 326–328.
[2] Xi (2006), p. 332.

forward the reform of the cultural system in the press, publications, radio, film and television, and cultural and artistic performances from points to plane, at stages and in batches across the province, producing marked effects.

6.1.1 The Formation and Development of Zhejiang's Theories Concerning the Reform of the Cultural System

6.1.1.1 The Formation of Zhejiang's Line of Thought Regarding the Reform of the Cultural System

Since 1992, in parallel to the reform of the economic system, Zhejiang has also explored and pushed forward the reform of the cultural system. Before 2000, Zhejiang started exploring the change of the functions of the competent department for cultural affairs, achieved the change from "running cultural affairs" to "managing cultural affairs", and promoted the reform of the cultural and artistic system focusing on the reform of cultural and artistic performance groups; Zhejiang also established a new mechanism consistent with the requirements of cultural and ethical development, the law of artistic creation and the market demand, enhanced the developmental vitality of cultural programs, and built multiple operational channels.

However, the Party Committee and the People's Government of Zhejiang Province were also keenly aware that the reform of Zhejiang's cultural system lagged behind the reforms in other fields including that of the economic system. "Subject to the restrictions from the underdeveloped social security mechanism, capital input mechanism and cultural economic policy, the ongoing reform of the cultural system is nothing but local reform, the breakthroughs in some aspects have not yet been made in an all-round way; Zhejiang's macro cultural management system and operational mechanism suitable for the socialist market economic system has not yet been fully established, overstaffing and excessive burden on the state still exist. The channels for cultural investments are not sufficiently smooth, a benign input mechanism in which government input is dominant and social capital is extensively absorbed has not yet really taken shape; the policy measures in the field of cultural economics still need to be further improved and implemented, and cultural industrialization still needs to be accelerated".[3]

The *Plan of Zhejiang Province for the Building of a Culturally Large Province (2001–2020)*, unveiled in 2000, fully expounded the direction, goals and methods for the reform of Zhejiang's cultural system for the first time. Some details in the Plan represent the embryonic form of the subsequent national reform of the cultural system, such as "vigorously promoting innovations to the cultural system, establishing the scientific, rational, flexible and efficient operational mechanism for the system

---

[3]The Research Group of "A Study of Zhejiang's Current Social Development and Countermeasures", *Zhejiang's Social Development during the Period 1992–1996*, Zhejiang People's Publishing House, 1997, p. 111.

of management and the production of cultural products; further transforming government functions, rationalizing relationships, really achieving separation between the government and enterprises, between enterprises and public institutions, between management and running, giving full scope to the basic role of the market in resource allocation, pushing forward the rational flow of various cultural resources and cultural elements and actively promoting enterprise-oriented restructuring of the for-profit cultural public institutions".

In May, 2002, the Party Committee and the People's Government of Zhejiang Province held a provincial working conference on cultural affairs, further identifying the strategic significance of building a culturally large province and becoming the first nationwide to put forward the new proposition of "a cultural economy", which marked Zhejiang's deepening understanding of the development of cultural economics and the reform of the cultural system. The *Several Opinions on Intensifying the Reform of the Cultural System and Accelerating the Development of the Cultural Industry*, issued during the conference, specified the measures for speeding up the group-oriented development of the cultural industry, enhancing the competitiveness of the cultural industry, conducting enterprise-oriented restructuring, intensifying the reform of state-owned cultural units, nurturing the market-oriented operators, relaxing control to enhance vitality, vigorously developing the private cultural industry, and shaping a great pattern in which multiple social forces run cultural affairs, thus creating a loose policy environment for building a culturally large province. This series of measures for the reform of the cultural system marked the basic formation of Zhejiang's line of thought regarding the reform of the cultural system.

6.1.1.2   The Deepening of Zhejiang's Line of Thought Regarding the Reform of the Cultural System

In the first half of 2003, Zhejiang and Guangdong were designated as the national pilot provinces for the comprehensive reform of the cultural system, and the significance of Zhejiang's experiments on the reform of the cultural system ahead of the rest of the country was further identified. In the provincial conference on publicity and ideological work in 2004, the then Secretary of the Party Committee of Zhejiang Province, comrade Xi Jinping, pointed out, "Intensifying the reform of the cultural system is an important part of efforts at carrying out the decision made during the 3rd Plenary Session of the 16th Central Committee of the Communist Party of China and the decision made during the 5th Plenary Session of the 11th Party Committee of Zhejiang Province, and also an important part of efforts at improving the socialist market economic system, as well as an urgent task for more rapidly building a culturally large province."

On July 18, 2003, when delivering his important lengthy speech during the meeting of Zhejiang Province on intensifying the reform of the cultural system and promoting the building of a culturally large province, the then Secretary of the Party Committee of Zhejiang Province, comrade Xi Jinping, expounded the guiding line of thought, main goal, basic principle of and the policy for the reform of Zhejiang's cultural system, and made arrangements for the reform of Zhejiang's cultural system. In his speech, comrade Xi Jinping stressed, "The reform of the cultural system focuses on making people- and market-oriented innovations to institutions and mechanisms, gradually establishing the cultural management system and operational mechanism conducive to arousing the enthusiasm of cultural workers, promoting cultural innovation, producing more excellent works and talents"[4]; he also arranged three main tasks: developing the public welfare cultural programs, reforming the for-profit cultural industry, developing and nurturing the cultural market players and intensifying the reform of state-owned cultural enterprises and units, and developing private cultural enterprises.

After the *Master Plan of Zhejiang Province for the Pilot Reform of the Comprehensive Cultural System* was approved by the Central Committee of the Communist Party of China in August, 2003, the leading group of Zhejiang Province for the reform of the cultural system quickly approved the pilot plans of six provincial pilot departments, including the Department of Culture, the Press and Publication Bureau, the Radio and Television Bureau of Zhejiang Province, the Zhejiang Daily Press Group, the Zhejiang Publishing United Group, the Zhejiang Radio & TV Group, and two cities, including Hangzhou and Ningbo, fully initiating the pilot work on the reform of Zhejiang's cultural system. In 2005, the reform of Zhejiang's pilot cultural system expanded from the provincial level, Hangzhou and Ningbo, to 11 cities across the province, and the provincial pilot work expanded from 30 units to 80–100 key units.

In the process of promoting the reform of the cultural system, the Party Committee of Zhejiang Province vowed to address the following six issues: First, stressing the ideological attribute and industrial attribute of culture, preventing excessive emphasis on the ideological attribute of culture and complete disregard of its industrial attribute, preventing the tendency of neglecting the ideological attribute of cultural products and upholding complete marketization as well as fostering the market-oriented philosophy and strengthening the awareness about resources, commodities, market and benefits, being market-oriented and people-oriented. Second, achieving two goals: enhancing the controlling force and competitiveness. In the reform of the cultural system, it is necessary to enhance the vitality and competitiveness of the cultural enterprises and public institutions, expand and publicize the strength of cultural programs by bringing about innovations to systems and mechanisms in a market-oriented way, enhance the controlling force of the Party in the cultural field by conducting reforms to improve the Party's leadership over the cultural publicity, firmly establishing the guiding role of Marxism in the ideological field, guaranteeing "four powers" and "changelessness in four respects" and combining the enhancing of the controlling force with improving the competitiveness. Third, drawing a distinction between two types that are the public welfare cultural programs and the for-profit cultural industry, placing equal emphasis on developing and strengthening the public welfare cultural programs and the for-profit cultural industry. Fourth, focusing on two levels, namely, the reform of the macro management system and the reform of the mechanism of micro operations. At the macro level, exploring

---

[4]Xi (2006), p. 326.

and establishing a macro management system under which the Party committee exercises a vigorous kind of leadership, the government performs effective management, moderate regulation and orderly operation are carried out, and personnel, matters and assets are managed. At the micro level, invigorating the internal mechanism, intensifying the reform of internal systems involving cadres, personnel, labor and distribution, establishing the micro operational mechanism in which the guidance of public opinion is correct, operations are vibrant and competitive advantages are obvious. Fifth, leveraging two forces—the state and the private sector—to run cultural affairs, intensifying the reform of state-owned cultural units, steadily promoting group-oriented development, building a number of socially influential and economically competitive cultural enterprises and public institutions, thus giving full scope to the leading role of the state in running cultural affairs in the cultural market. In the meantime, fully leveraging the advantages of Zhejiang's developed private economy to strengthen the cooperation between state-owned cultural enterprises and private enterprises, and to the extent permitted by national policy, increasing the areas for allowing access, developing supportive policies, energetically developing the private cultural enterprises and making the private cultural enterprises a bright spot in Zhejiang's development of the cultural industry. Sixth, improving two systems, including the policy and regulations system and the cultural market system, improving the supporting reform measures and the economic policies for the development of cultural programs and the cultural industry, guaranteeing smooth reform and speeding up the development of cultural laws and regulations to provide the necessary legal guarantee for cultural development. In the meantime, improving the cultural market system, promoting comprehensive law enforcement within the cultural market, reforming the means and mode of the cultural market supervision, vigorously cultivating the specialized markets of cultural goods and the cultural industrial element markets, and energetically nurturing market players to boost the prosperity of the cultural market.

In July, 2005, the 8th Plenary Session of the 11th Party Committee of Zhejiang Province adopted the *Decision of the Party Committee of Zhejiang Province on Accelerating the Building of a Culturally Large Province*, further deepening and improving the *Plan of Zhejiang Province for the Building of a Culturally Large Province (2001–2020)*, unveiled five years ago, in terms of the line of thought regarding the reform of the cultural system, which marked the formation of Zhejiang's line of thought regarding the reform of the cultural system. The Decision took the reform of the cultural system as the main part of the goal of "emancipating and developing the cultural productive forces", and called for further intensifying that reform, actively promoting innovations to cultural philosophy, content, system, science and technology, resolutely breaking the mindsets which impede development, firmly changing the practices and rules which hinder development, resolutely removing the institutional drawbacks which affect development, respecting the people's pioneering spirit, fully arousing the enthusiasm of cultural workers, fostering a good environment for cultural development, carrying out the reform of the cultural system, speeding up the development of cultural programs, bringing forth more excellent works, talents and results to meet the people's increasing cultural needs as well as accelerating the development of the cultural industry, enhancing the overall strength and competitiveness of the cultural industry and developing the cultural industry into a new economic growth point and a pillar industry.

In July, 2006, the Department of Publicity under the Party Committee of Zhejiang Province organized the main provincial news media, including Party newspapers, TV and radio stations and news websites, to carry out the themed publicity and recommend 50 models of reform and development from various areas for intensive publicity and reporting, and continued encouraging the competent department for publicity and cultural affairs to go deep into the primary level and practice, summarize and discover a number of typical cases in the front line of reform and development, thus providing models for promoting extensive reform.

In 2011, given the new situation, in the *Decision of the Party Committee of Zhejiang Province on Earnestly Carrying Out the Guiding Principles Adopted during the 6th Plenary Session of the 17th Central Committee of the Communist Party of China and Actively Promoting the Building of a Culturally Strong Province,* Zhejiang put forward the new task of promoting the reform of and innovations to the cultural system and mechanism, and called for concentrating on intensifying the reform of state-owned cultural units, pushing forward the reform of the cultural management system and innovating the mode of making culture go global.

With respect to intensifying the reform of state-owned cultural units, efforts focused on accelerating the reform of for-profit cultural units across the province, establishing a modern enterprise system, nurturing the qualified cultural market players, and building a number of powerful and competitive state-owned cultural enterprises. Large state-owned cultural groups, including film and performance groups, were built. Actions were taken to reform publication, distribution, film and television enterprises, speed up the reform of the systems of corporation and joint-stock, improve the structure of corporate governance, and form a manner of operation and management of the cultural enterprises consistent with the requirements of a modern enterprise system. Subject to the requirements of carrying out differential treatment, providing classified guidance and progressively promoting relevant work, steps were taken to conduct enterprise-oriented restructuring of general state-owned artistic troupes, non-current politics newspaper and periodical offices, news websites, to promote the reform of the Party newspaper distribution system and the reform involving separation between production and broadcasting of movie and television plays, and to deepen the integrative development of a radio and television cable network which features "one network in one province". Prominence was given to the attribute of public welfare, measures were taken to enhance service functions and developmental vitality, comprehensively push forward the reform of the labor personnel, income distribution and social security systems involving public cultural institutions, develop service specification, strengthen performance evaluation and explore and establish the corporate governance structure of public institutions. The management and operational mechanism involving Party newspapers and periodicals and radio and TV stations was further improved. Efforts were made to promote the enterprise-oriented management of artistic troupes with the public institution system retained and the general current politics newspaper and periodical offices.

With regard to promoting the reform of the cultural management system, emphasis was placed on accelerating the change of government functions, rationalizing the relationship between the government and cultural public institutions, achieve separation between the government and enterprises, between enterprises and public institutions, between management and running, thus better performing the functions of policy regulation, market supervision, social management and public services. Actions were taken to expand the achievements in comprehensive law enforcement on the cultural market, continue to intensify the reform involving the operational mechanism of municipal and county-level cultural, radio, television, press and publication bureaus, and bringing about innovations to the comprehensive law enforcement mode and to the supervisory mode on the cultural market. Subject to the requirements of managing personnel, matters, assets and guidance, actions were taken to improve the evaluation of performance and other managerial systems involving state-owned cultural groups and really strengthen the management of state-owned cultural assets. Policy measures for the guarantee of public cultural services, cultural industry revitalization and cultural market management were developed; the legal, administrative, economic, scientific and technological means were adopted to make cultural development more scientific and to promote the rule of law in cultural development.

On the front of innovating the way to make culture go global, efforts concentrated on implementing the external cultural development plan, engaging in multi-channel, multi-mode and multi-level external cultural exchanges, thus intensifying the exportation of cultural products and services, promoting Zhejiang's culture to the world. Efforts were made to further build external cultural exchange brands, including Connect Zhejiang, and the Zhejiang Culture Week (Festival). Actions were made to actively promote the building of the overseas fronts of Zhejiang's mainstream media and to encourage cooperation and exchange with overseas media. Full scope was given to the resource advantages of academic organizations and artistic organizations in external cultural exchanges. The provincial external cultural exchange fund was established to support Zhejiang's major external cultural exchange activities and to encourage people-to-people external cultural exchanges. Intensified efforts were made to build the international marketing networks involving film, television, animation, publication and artistic performances, to expand cooperation with international performances, exhibitions, publication intermediary bodies and brokers, to support the cultural enterprises dealing with the production of content and services with various types of ownership to set up branches and distribution bodies overseas. The policies for supporting cultural exportation were developed and introduced; the *Catalogue of Zhejiang's Key Cultural Export Enterprises and Projects* was established, emphasis was placed on cultivating a number of outward-looking cultural export enterprises and production bases; moreover, cultural enterprises were encouraged to exploit the international market by various means including holding shares, mergers and acquisitions; and a number of well-known international cultural enterprise brands were built. Actions were taken to enhance cooperation on cultural exchanges with Hong Kong and Macao as well as cultural exchanges with Taiwan.

Since 2011, the Party Committee of Zhejiang Province has held standing committee meetings and special meetings on many occasions to study and arrange key work on cultural reform and development. The leading group of Zhejiang Province for the reform of the cultural system has held meetings, making arrangements for the special coordination meetings on the provincial radio and television network—"one network in one province"—and the reform of provincial artistic troupes, the institutional reform of the non-current politics-type newspaper and publication units, and coordinating efforts to develop the plan for promoting reform and relevant supporting policies.

6.1.2 Zhejiang's Measures for the Reform of the Cultural System

6.1.2.1 Carrying Out the Reform for Rationalizing the System of Cultural Management

In April, 2006, Zhejiang unveiled the *Report of Zhejiang Province on the Pilot Work on the Comprehensive Reform of the Cultural System* in coordination with the *Several Opinions of the Central Committee of the Communist Party of China and the State Council on Intensifying the Reform of the Cultural System*. Zhejiang established a macro management system under which the Party committee exercises leadership, the government performs management, the industry practices self-discipline, and enterprises and public institutions operate according to laws, it carried out macro management in the cultural field, promoted separation between the government and public institutions, between management and running, and it speeded up the change in government functions.

The key work on macro management in the cultural field consists of strengthening the guidance of planning, policy guarantees and asset management. Based on the line of thought of the guidance of planning, Zhejiang developed the *"Four-batch" Plan of Zhejiang Province for Cultural Development* focusing on the development of the cultural industry, which put forward a line of thought regarding development and presented a layout planning, in the form of a plan for the first time, for building a batch of key cultural facilities, developing a batch of key cultural sectors, cultivating a number of key industrial blocks, creating a batch of key cultural enterprises; Zhejiang developed the investment guide for cultural industrial projects. The plan for accelerating the building of a culturally large province, unveiled in 2005, also identified eight projects for cultural development. According to the line of thought regarding the guarantee of policies, in order to carry out the policies of the reform of the cultural system developed by the Central Committee of the Communist Party of China, Zhejiang introduced a slew of policies for supporting the reform of the cultural system and cultural development so as to provide a policy guarantee for institutional reform.

The priority for the work on promoting separation between the government and public institutions, between management and running lies in achieving separation between the government and public institutions, between the government and enterprises, between management and running, a change from "running cultural affairs" to "managing cultural affairs" and from "micro management" to "macro management". When the separation between management and running had not yet been made in the national radio and television circles and most provinces and municipalities, the Radio and Television Bureau of Zhejiang Province explored the separation between management and running and the separated establishment of bodies. The leading Party group of the Radio and Television Bureau of Zhejiang Province put forward the guiding line of thought of "sufficiently advancing and retreating" in administrative management and the working policy of "intensifying management and promoting development", they vowed to resolutely and vigorously manage the fields which fall within the scope of management, unceasingly explore new management modes and firmly and thoroughly get out of the fields which fall outside the scope of management; they ensured that management did not go beyond the specified limits, and was not in the wrong position and that it was not absent when it was needed; they also speeded up coordinated and sustainable development of the province's radio, film and television industry and comprehensively and impartially carried out the administrative management of the radio, film and television industry.

With respect to accelerating the transformation of government functions, relevant work focused on taking the comprehensive law enforcement in the cultural market as an opportunity to achieve establishment, merger and separation. As early as late October, 2004, Zhejiang developed and issued the *Implementation Opinions on Establishing the Comprehensive Law Enforcement Agency for the Cultural Market*, putting forward the work in three aspects, including establishment, merger and separation, and requiring all cities and counties across the province—including Hangzhou and Ningbo not subject to requirements from the Central Committee of the Communist Party of China as they are two sub-provincial cities—to set up the administrative management agency for culture, radio, television, press and publication through adjustment and merger; these Implementing Opinions also required all cities and counties across the province to establish a unified comprehensive law enforcement agency for the cultural market and they required the radio and TV stations in all cities and counties across the province to be separated from the administrative agency for radio and television under the principle of separation between the government and public institutions, between management and running.

6.1.2.2 Nurturing the Cultural Market Players

Since the strategy for the building of a culturally large province was implemented, in particular, Zhejiang has been designated as the national pilot province for the reform of the cultural system, Zhejiang has actively built and nurtured new-type market players according to the overall line of thought of "bringing forth a batch of main players through change, bringing forth a batch of main players through restructuring, bringing forth a batch of main players by relaxing control, and supporting a batch of main players".

The specific content of the above "four batches" is as follows:

First, bringing forth a batch of main players through change. State-owned cultural public institutions intensify the reform of the internal cadre and personnel system and of the distribution system, change the mechanism to enhance vitality so as to build an enterprise-oriented method of management which is consistent with development requirements.

Second, bringing forth a batch of main players through restructuring. With clarification of property rights, restructuring and transformation efforts, some state-owned cultural units undergo the restructuring of public institutions into enterprises, the units where conditions permit are restructured into well-regulated modern enterprises.

Third, bringing forth a batch of main players by relaxing control. To the extent permitted by policy, the industrial policy is improved and the service environment is optimized to allow private capital to enter the cultural field, thus giving birth to a batch of private cultural enterprises.

Fourth, supporting a batch of main players. The leading cultural industrial groups and key public welfare cultural units are supported. Among the above four batches of main layers, there are the public welfare cultural public institutions and the for-profit cultural industrial institutions.

The *Report of Zhejiang Province on the Pilot Work on the Comprehensive Reform of the Cultural System*, unveiled in April, 2006, further calling for dealing with different types of market players in different ways: "conducting restructuring into enterprises", "separating the publicity service of the news media from operations", "intensifying the reform of artistic troupes", "building state-owned cultural groups" and "guiding the private cultural industry".

6.1.2.3   Promoting the Reform of State-Owned Cultural Units

Regarding the reform of state-owned cultural units, with the goal of "increasing input, transforming the mechanism, enhancing vitality, improving services", Zhejiang intensified the reform of the internal management system and operational mechanism, a series of reforms in personnel, distribution and incentives in public welfare cultural public institutions. Actions were taken to comprehensively carry out the all-staff appointment system, the cadre appointment system, expand development channels, increase the service level and more extensively and effectively serve the public. For the for-profit cultural industrial institutions, according to the basic direction of "innovating the system, transforming the mechanism, and being market-oriented to enhance vitality", Zhejiang restructured a batch of pilot for-profit state-owned cultural units into enterprises in a classified and step-by-step way according to the requirement of "transforming the nature of units, labor relations and property rights structure".

From 2002 to now, Zhejiang has built 8 state-owned cultural enterprise groups. The Zhejiang Radio & TV Group is one of the units which early on successfully underwent group-oriented restructuring. Under the principle of "making coordinated planning, separate arrangement, stressing respective characteristics and sharing resources", the

Group comprehensively reorganized its channel resources to build a multifunctional, three-dimensional, serialized new-type radio and television channel system which presents the overall unified image and features a rational division of work in which Zhejiang TV plays the leading role, while two main channels—the radio and news channel and a comprehensive channel—and 13 specialized channels of the Group serve as two wings. The operating system with two-level management and channel-specific operations was built; the macro management function was centralized at the group level; all channels were under the director responsibility system.

Zhejiang also actively explored a separation between news publicity service and operations, it identified 9 units, including radio and television units, as the pilot units for that separation, it stripped operations to build relatively independent operating companies and it introduced social capital to companies.

6.1.2.4   Guiding Private Investments, Cultivating Private Cultural Enterprises as the Main Players

Besides energetically promoting the reform of state-owned cultural units, Zhejiang also actively improved the industrial policy, optimized the service environment, and encouraged private capital to enter the cultural field, thus preliminarily shaping a pattern in which multiple social forces run cultural affairs, effectively guiding the development of private cultural enterprises as the main players. In Zhejiang, private enterprises have become the main players in economic activities; this is an advantage and a characteristic of Zhejiang's development. With more than 30 years of development since the reform and opening-up, Zhejiang has accumulated massive private capital. In the meantime, Zhejiang's private cultural industry has developed rapidly. Relying on the incremental impetus from the private cultural industry, building market players and increasing the controlling force of the state-owned cultural economy is an outstanding characteristic of the reform of Zhejiang's cultural system.

In the meeting on the reform of the cultural system and the building of a culturally large province in July, 2003, comrade Xi Jinping pointed out, "Developing private cultural enterprises is essential for the development of Zhejiang's cultural industry, and is also a characteristic and an advantage of Zhejiang's cultural reform and development; it is conducive to forming a pattern of cultural development which caters to Zhejiang's pattern with the development of the economy with different types of ownership", "it is necessary to, like supporting the development of the private economy, further relax control in order to enhance vitality, break the institutional bottleneck in the development of the cultural industry, open the door for the development of the cultural industry, seize the opportunities for developing the cultural industry and vigorously developing private cultural enterprises".[5] In the process of piloting the reform of the cultural system, Zhejiang has always leveraged its realistic advantage—private capital, and put forward the working line of thought of taking "developing the private cultural industry" as the bright spot in the reform of Zhejiang's pilot cultural system,

---

[5]Xi (2006), p. 327.

taking "upholding the correct political direction and active reform" as the important guiding thought, and working on these three main tasks: cultivating a number of key private cultural enterprises, encouraging participation in the reform of state-owned cultural units, and optimizing the developmental environment for the development of the private cultural industry. Zhejiang has encouraged private capital to enter the for-profit cultural industry, actively guided and encouraged private cultural enterprises to participate in the reform and development of state-owned cultural units, supported key industry bases and developed characteristic industries.

6.2 The "Eight-Eight Strategies" and the Overall Layout of Zhejiang's Cultural Industry

After 2000, the elements of development and the market environment for Zhejiang's economy and society changed greatly; Zhejiang's economy entered a stage of highly industrialized development, and Zhejiang became the first nationwide to enter the period of economic change. In July, 2003, during the 4th Plenary Session of the 11th Party Committee of Zhejiang Province, the then Secretary of the Party Committee of Zhejiang Province, comrade Xi Jinping, completely and systematically put forward the "Eight-Eight Strategies" on behalf of the Party Committee of Zhejiang Province, and based on summarizing Zhejiang's experience, gave answers to overcome new problems, new contrasts and address new challenges, presented the path for Zhejiang's economic and social development and also identified the direction for building Zhejiang into a culturally large province and developing Zhejiang's cultural industry.

6.2.1 The Current Development of Zhejiang's Cultural Industry and Three Growth Peaks

In the ten years from 2003 to 2012, Zhejiang's cultural industry grew by an average of 17.9%, higher than the level of the national average and much higher than the average rate of Zhejiang's national economic growth; the cultural industry became an important engine for stimulating Zhejiang's economic and social development. At present, Zhejiang's cultural industry shows a good momentum of rapid growth and presents the following five characteristics.

6.2.1.1 The Scale of the Aggregate has Increased Significantly

The added value realized by Zhejiang's cultural industry reached 188.04 billion yuan in 2013, up 18.9% compared with the previous year, accounting for 5.0% of the GDP;

the cultural industry became the pillar industry in Zhejiang's national economy (see Table 6.1). According to statistics, in Zhejiang, there were 85,683 cultural enterprises, 3,690 key enterprises above the designated size—the enterprises relating to industry, trade and service above the designated size—and 81,993 enterprises below the designated size. According to the *Annual Report on the Development Index of China's Cultural Industry 2013* released by the National Cultural Industry Innovation & Development Research Base of Shanghai Jiao Tong University and the China Cultural Development Index Research Center, Zhejiang ranked no. 3 nationwide in cultural development indicators.

6.2.1.2   The Advantageous Sectors have Developed Rapidly

The advantageous position of Zhejiang's press, publication, film, television, animation and cultural tourism sectors in the country has been further established. In 2014, the Zhejiang Daily Press Group realized 3.5 billion yuan in operating income and 520 million yuan in profits, up more than 30%; the Zhejiang Radio & TV Group realized 8.52 billion yuan in main business income and 2.07 billion yuan in profits, each of them grew by 20%. Each of the total sales, main business income and total assets of the Zhejiang Publishing United Group exceeded 10 billion yuan, making the group one of the publishing groups across the country with 10 billion yuan in three aspects.

The operating income relating to radio, film and television in Zhejiang was 40,388 million yuan in 2014, up 30.86% compared with the previous year, among which the advertising income, cable TV network income, and sales income of radio and TV programs were 11,343 million yuan, 6.29 billion yuan and 8.18 billion yuan, respectively. In 2014, Zhejiang ranked no. 2, no. 2 and no. 1 in the advertising income, cable TV network income, and sales income of radio and TV programs, respectively.

In 2014, 62 TV plays (2,717 episodes) were produced, ranking Zhejiang no. 3 nationwide in output; 51 animated films (25,388 min) were produced, including 41 animated films (19,020 min) that had been granted distribution permits, ranking Zhejiang no. 2 nationwide in output.

6.2.1.3   The Emerging Forms of Business Have Risen Rapidly

In 2014, 48 enterprises were granted the qualification of online publishing, 45 online audio-visual program units were established in Zhejiang, ranking Zhejiang no. 3 nationwide in quantity. Hangzhou National Digital Publication Industry Base delivered 8,425 million yuan in operating income, up 12.0% compared with the previous year, among which the China Mobile Reading Base and the China Telecom E-surfing Reading Base delivered 6,208 million yuan and 235 million yuan in operating income, respectively. In 2013, the Hangzhou National Digital Publication

Table 6.1 The added value of the cultural industry in Zhejiang province, 2003–2013. Unit: 100 million yuan

	2003	2004	2005	2006	2007	2008	2009	2010	2011	2012
The added value of the cultural industry	312	377.61	442.24	501.72	595.93	735.4	807.96	1056.09	1290.01	1581.72
#The manufacturing of cultural products		213.35	247.29	276.00	331.82	385.59	406.23	524.98	638.79	706.30
Wholesale and retail of cultural products		61.59	71.52	79.52	92.73	85.20	100.42	133.06	150.01	160.73
Proportion of the cultural service industry in the GDP (%)		102.67	123.43	146.21	171.38	264.65	301.31	398.05	501.21	714.69
	3.3	3.2	3.3	3.2	3.2	3.4	3.5	3.8	4.0	4.6

Note The data for the year 2003 cover sports and the data for the year 2012 are statistical data based on the new national classification of cultural and related industries and sectors

Industry Base ranked no. 5, no. 6 and no. 2 among national digital publication bases in the operating income, total assets and total profits, respectively.

At present, there are 14,997,100 cable TV subscribers in Zhejiang, including 14,426,200 digital TV subscribers. In 2014, the task of digital development was fully finished, the overall digital TV conversion rate and the rate of bidirectional transformation of cable network reached 99% in urban areas across the province.

6.2.1.4 The Level of Intensive and Professional Development has Increased Rapidly

The cultural industry parks have entered the stage of rapid development. As of 2012, there were 115 cultural industry parks (bases) of various types in Zhejiang, including 16 with plates conferred by relevant departments of the central government, accounting for 13.91%. The combined effect of the China International Cartoon & Animation Festival, the China (Yiwu) Cultural Products Trade Fair and other cultural trade fair brands has been further improved. In 2014, the volume of trading at the 10th China International Cartoon & Animation Festival totaled 14,846 million yuan.

6.2.1.5 The Development of the Cultural Industry has Generally Accelerated in Various Areas

The regional central cities, including Hangzhou, Jinhua and Ningbo, have witnessed prominent advantages in the development of the cultural industry. As of 2012, the added value of the cultural industry in these three cities reached 92,041 million yuan, accounting for about 58% of the total added value of Zhejiang's cultural industry. The added value of the cultural industry in Hangzhou and Jinhua accounted for more than 6% of the GDP, suggesting further advancement in building it into an important pillar industry; Ningbo's cultural industry achieved leapfrog development, in 2012, the added value of the cultural industry in Ningbo grew by 16.2% and accounted for 4.16% of the GDP. In Huzhou, Shaoxing, Lishui and Zhoushan, the cultural industry developed rapidly at a rate above 20%.

As shown by the development of Zhejiang's cultural industry in more than ten years, as from the implementation of the "Eight-Eight Strategies" by Zhejiang in 2003, Zhejiang's cultural industry has noticeably shown three growth peaks: The first peak occurred during the period 2003–2004 and was 21.03%, suggesting a substantive improvement in mindsets made by the series of measures for the building of Zhejiang into a culturally large province and the "Eight-Eight Strategies"; the second peak occurred during the global financial crisis during the period 2007–2008 and was 23.40%, and during this period China underwent economic adjustment, the cultural industry grew against the trend and was vibrant; the third peak occurred during the period 2009–2010 after a strategic adjustment of the cultural industry and reached 30.71%; as of 2013, the added value of the cultural industry accounted for 5% of the GDP, the cultural industry became the pillar industry in the national economy. This represented the effects from Zhejiang's efforts at intensifying the reform of the cultural system and further carrying out relevant policies regarding the cultural industry. The three developmental peaks corresponded to the transformation of the cultural mindset, the upgrading of the strategy of the cultural industry and the intensification of the reform of the cultural system during Zhejiang's implementation of the "Eight-Eight Strategies"; this indicates that mindset change, upgrading of the strategy and institutional reform are three factors which aided in the acceleration of the development of Zhejiang's cultural industry.

6.2.2 Mindset Improvement and Three Adjustments of Zhejiang's Strategy for the Development of the Cultural Industry

As early as 1999, Zhejiang, a forerunner in China's reform and opening-up and economic development, put forward the strategic goal of building a culturally large province. In 2000, Zhejiang developed and unveiled the *Plan of Zhejiang Province for the Building of a Culturally Large Province (2001–2020)*. In 2001, Zhejiang issued the *Opinions of the People's Government of Zhejiang Province on Several Cultural Economic Policies Concerning the Building of a Culturally Large Province*. In 2002, Zhejiang held the provincial working conference on cultural affairs and developed the *Several Opinions on Intensifying the Reform of the Cultural System and Accelerating the Development of the Cultural Industry*. In 2003, Zhejiang was designated by the Central Committee of the Communist Party of China as the pilot province for the comprehensive reform of the cultural system. In 2005, the 8th Plenary Session of the 11th Party Committee of Zhejiang Province specially arranged the building of a culturally large province and made the *Decision of the Party Committee of Zhejiang Province on Accelerating the Building of a Culturally Large Province*, calling for comprehensively carrying out eight projects for cultural development including the cultural industry promotion project. In 2006, the People's Government of Zhejiang Province developed and issued the *"Four-batch" Plan of Zhejiang Province for Cultural Development (2005–2010)*, specifying the goals and developmental priorities for Zhejiang's cultural development in the subsequent five years; the Department of Publicity under the Party Committee of Zhejiang Province and the Zhejiang Provincial Development and Reform Commission developed the investment guide for cultural industry projects, providing guidance for the people from various sectors of the society to invest in the cultural industry. In 2007, the People's Government of Zhejiang Province held the provincial working conference on rural cultural affairs and issued the *Implementation Opinions on Further Strengthening Rural Cultural Development*; the 12th Party Congress of Zhejiang Province put forward the overall strategy of "making the people rich by starting businesses and of building a strong province through innovation" and took cultural development as an important support for and an important part of entrepreneurship and innovation, vowed to make careful arrangements and promote vigorous implementation. To push forward the reform of the cultural system and the development of the cultural industry, the General Office of the People's Government of Zhejiang Province issued the *Several Opinions on Supporting the Pilot Reform of Provincial State-owned Cultural Units and the Development of the Cultural Industry*. On this basis, the Department of Finance, the National Tax Bureau and the Local Tax Bureau of Zhejiang Province jointly issued the *Circular Concerning Several Tax Policy Issues in the Reform of the Cultural System*, specifying the preferential tax policy.

As shown by this series of strategic policies, there were the following three obvious improvements in the mindset and some strategic adjustments in the development of Zhejiang's cultural industry.

6.2.2.1 Development Plan: Increasing the Strength of the Cultural Industry Becomes an Important Part of Efforts in Building a Culturally Large Province

The building of a culturally large province is a grand systematic project for comprehensively promoting socialist modernization in Zhejiang during the 21st century. Earnestly developing the cultural industry is an important part of efforts at building Zhejiang into a culturally large province. The *Plan of Zhejiang Province for the Building of a Culturally Large Province (2001–2020)*, developed in 2000, stressed, "the cultural industry is part of the national economy, cultural products have the attribute of commodities, so it is essential to give a high value to the economic benefits of cultural products subject to delivering social benefits, and to achieve an optimal combination of both benefits".

The *Plan of Zhejiang Province for the Building of a Culturally Large Province (2001–2020)* put forward the goal of building Zhejiang into a culturally large province which witnesses a high quality of the entire population, social progress, developed science and education and which stays ahead nationwide in the main indicators concerning cultural development, the overall level of cultural programs and the strength of the cultural industry; the plan took "increasing the strength of the cultural industry" as an important part of efforts at building a culturally large province. The *Opinions Concerning Several Cultural Economic Policies for the Building of a Culturally Large Province* issued in 2001 and the *Several Opinions on Intensifying the Reform of the Cultural System and Accelerating the Development of the Cultural Industry* developed during the provincial working conference on cultural affairs in 2002 put into practice that goal, and also enriched and concretized that strategic goal.

The *Plan of Zhejiang Province for the Building of a Culturally Large Province (2001–2020)* put forward the basic principle of "being based on developing the education of science and technology and starting with developing the cultural industry, advancing on the whole and making breakthroughs in key points to prosper the socialist culture in an all-round way", and took "more rapidly shaping the cultural pattern of industrial development that is suitable for the drive towards modernization" as an important task for developing the cultural industry. The Plan called for actively adjusting the structure of the cultural industry, more quickly bringing into being the emerging clusters of cultural industries focusing on audio-visual publishing, electronic CDs, arts and crafts, tourism and sightseeing and physical fitness. Actions were taken to intensify scientific and technological innovations, greatly introduce advanced technical equipment, management experience, talent and intellectual resources to increase the technological content in the cultural industry and to upgrade cultural products, enhance the competitive advantage of the leading cultural industry in the country, and promote the transformation of resource advantages into industrial economic advantages.

6.2.2.2   The "Eight-Eight Strategies": Fully Leveraging Zhejiang's Advantages of Its Economic and Humanistic Resources to Promote the Development of the Cultural Industry

As the "Eight-Eight Strategies" were put forward in 2003, Zhejiang's strategy for cultural development was upgraded as follows: further leveraging Zhejiang's advantages to shape Zhejiang's characteristics of the cultural industry, making Zhejiang rely on the advantages in economic development and humanistic resources, further expanding the mindsets in Zhejiang's cultural industry, and working out an important path for the characteristic development of Zhejiang's cultural industry.

Comrade Xi Jinping pointed out, "Developing the cultural industry is first of all an essential part of cultural development; the contemporary cultural competition largely depends upon the competition in the cultural industry; soft power and cultural power are certainly a part of it through the competitive strength of the cultural industry. In the meantime, this is also the significance of promoting adjustment of the economic structure and changing the growth mode."[6] The abundant cultural deposits and humanistic resources in Zhejiang are inexhaustible mineral resources just as raw materials are for Zhejiang's cultural development; more importantly, the blood of the people of Zhejiang always contains cultural genes and inherits the Zhejiang Spirit of advancing with the times, and giving shape to the humanistic advantages peculiar to Zhejiang. The profound humanistic deposits offer abundant advantages of resources for the development of the cultural industry.

The rapid rise of Zhejiang's film and television industry is largely the successful model of fully tapping the abundant and distinctive cultural resources in Zhejiang and transforming cultural resources into cultural capital. The *Legend of Entrepreneurship*, a TV series jointly produced by the Zhejiang Radio & TV Group, the Zhejiang Film & TV Group, the Wenzhou Radio Television System and CCTV, presents the epic history of reform and opening-up in 30 years, the journey of entrepreneurship for the people of Wenzhou and the change of the times over a period of 30 years by describing the history of grassroots entrepreneurial efforts made by an ordinary household in Wenzhou.

---

[6]Xi (2006), p. 331.

6.2.2.3 The Decision on Building a Culturally Strong Province: The Cultural Industry Becomes an Important Guarantee for Building a Culturally Strong Province

The *Decision of the Party Committee of Zhejiang Province on Earnestly Carrying Out the Guiding Principles Adopted during the 6th Plenary Session of the 17th Central Committee of the Communist Party of China and Vigorously Promoting the Building of a Culturally Strong Province* ("the Decision"), made in November, 2011, newly adjusted and upgraded Zhejiang's strategy for the development of the cultural industry.

The Decision stressed that the 17th Plenary Session of the 17th Central Committee of the Communist Party of China would make the great strategic arrangement for upholding the path of the development of socialism with Chinese characteristics and building a culturally strong socialist province, which presented the direction for Zhejiang's cultural reform and development. The Decision called for solving the problems in Zhejiang's cultural industry—the scale is small, the structure is irrational, and strength and competitiveness still need to be further improved—and promoting vigorous cultural development and great cultural prosperity, making sure that the people enjoy a rich material life and a healthy and rich cultural life.

The Decision identified the position of Zhejiang's cultural industry in building a culturally strong province and called for intensifying efforts to implement the plan for developing cyberculture and modern media and the cultural industry doubling plan while continuously deepening the building of the system of development of the cultural industry. The Decision presented the following goal: By 2015, the added value of Zhejiang's cultural industry in 2010 should be doubled and its added value should account for 7% of Zhejiang's GDP. Based on this goal, the Decision provided the optimized layout of Zhejiang's cultural industry and called for focusing on implementing the "122" project for the development of the cultural industry, namely, cultivating 100 key cultural enterprises, 20 key bases for cultural industry parks, and boosting the listing of 20 cultural enterprises, building a number of characteristic cultural sectors, increasing the level of the cultural industry, strengthening the development of the cultural market, making the cultural industry larger, more intensive and professional and actively cultivating national first-class cultural industrial centers.

6.2.3 The 12th Five-Year Layout of Zhejiang's Cultural Industry is Based on Zhejiang's Advantageous Location

The overall line of thought of the "Eight-Eight Strategies" contains the whole organic concept of cultural, economic and social development. Taking cultural development as an integral part having an interrelation and a relation of mutual support with economic, social and ecological development and the rule of law was an important theoretical experiment and the first-ever practical basis before the 3rd Plenary

Session of the 18th Central Committee of the Communist Party of China put forward the overall layout of economic, political, cultural, social and ecological development in the socialist cause with Chinese characteristics. The line of thought, in the "Eight-Eight Strategies", of leveraging local advantages and massive characteristic advantages and valuing the marine economy and the land-sea interaction has laid the foundation for the overall layout of the development of Zhejiang's cultural industry.

According to the policy, in the "Eight-Eight Strategies", of further leveraging Zhejiang's advantage of a good location, the advantages of massive characteristic industries and mountain and sea resources and vigorously developing the marine economy, the *Plan of Zhejiang Province for the Development of the Cultural Industry (2010-2015)* planned the overall layout of Zhejiang's cultural industry which features one core, three poles, seven centers and four belts.

6.2.3.1 One Core: Hangzhou

Based on the unique status of the provincial capital as the political and cultural center, the scale of the creative cultural industry which has risen rapidly in Hangzhou in recent years, Hangzhou's brand effect of the Capital of Animation, the Capital of Leisure and the Capital of Creativity, the resource advantages of large provincial groups of cultural industries and the highly agglomerated high-end talents in the cultural industry are leveraged to turn Hangzhou into the province's comprehensive cultural industry development center and the national first-class creative cultural industry center.

6.2.3.2 Three Poles: Ningbo, Wenzhou and the City Group in Central Zhejiang with Jinhua, Yiwu and Dongyang as the Main Parts

The institutional advantage of Ningbo City as the sub-provincial city and the city specifically designated in the state plan is leveraged, and the status of Ningbo City as the province's important industrial center and international port city is relied upon to turn Ningbo City into the province's growth pole for its important cultural industry and the important national cultural industry base. The advantages and foundation of Wenzhou's existing printing, cultural product manufacturing, creative design and cultural tourism industries are relied upon to encourage the development of the creative cultural industry for promoting the transformation and upgrading of the manufacturing industry, consolidate and enhance the cluster advantage of the printing industry, support the formation of the province's growth poles for its important cultural industry and the base for the domestically and internationally famous printing industry. In the city group in central Zhejiang with Jinhua, Yiwu and Dongyang as the main part, it is necessary to utilize the existing commercial, trade, film and television cultural foundation to further develop such sectors as film and television production, online games, cultural tourism, brand exhibitions, cultural product circulation, further consolidate the leading position in national industrial development and shape the province's important growth pole for the cultural industry.

6.2.3.3   Seven Centers: Huzhou, Jiaxing, Shaoxing, Quzhou, Zhoushan, Taizhou, Lishui

Under the principle of characteristic advantageous development, actions are taken to guide the formation of seven major characteristic cultural industrial agglomeration centers in the province, including the Characteristic Huzhou Lake Taihu Creative Cultural Center, the Characteristic Jiaxing Jiangnan Creative Cultural Center, the Characteristic Shaoxing Light Textile and Pearl Creative Cultural Center, the Characteristic Quzhou Confucius and Chess Creative Cultural Center, the Characteristic Zhoushan Marine Creative Cultural Center, the Characteristic Taizhou Industrial Product Design Center, and the Characteristic Lishui Ecological Craft Cultural Center.

6.2.3.4   Four Belts: Northern Zhejiang, Central Zhejiang, Eastern Zhejiang, Southwestern Zhejiang

Based on the existing massive economic pattern in Zhejiang, the original cultural industry's developmental resources and common characteristics in various areas, actions are taken to guide the formation of four belts of development of the cultural industry basically covering the whole province.

First, the creative cultural industry belt in northern Zhejiang. With the Shanghai–Hangzhou-Ningbo Expressway as the overall axis, the profound cultural deposits in the region of rivers and lakes in eastern Hangzhou, northern Ningbo, Jiaxing, Huzhou, northern Shaoxing and other areas around Hangzhou Bay in northern Zhejiang, the advantages from these areas' proximity to such culturally innovative resource agglomeration centers as Shanghai are leveraged to guide the development of advantageous industries, promote the development of the emerging forms of cultural services, strengthen the role of culture in enhancing and stimulating the development of other industries, and build the creative cultural industry belt with a strong sense of modern culture in northern Zhejiang.

Second, the cultural industry belt of film, television and circulation. With the Hangzhou-Jinhua-Quzhou Expressway as the overall axis, the cultural product commerce, trade, circulation foundation in such areas as Jinhua, southern Shaoxing, central Quzhou, northern Lishui, and the famous film and television brand in Hengdian, Dongyang are utilized to build the cultural industry belt of film, television and circulation with a strong sense of traditional culture in central Zhejiang.

Third, the marine cultural industry belt in eastern Zhejiang. With the Ningbo-Taizhou-Wenzhou Expressway as the overall axis, the marine cultural industry belt with a strong sense of marine culture in eastern Zhejiang is built by relying on the unique marine culture in Wenzhou, Taizhou, eastern Ningbo, Zhoushan and other coastal areas and islands, the foundation of advanced manufacturing of daily necessities, light products, stationery and sporting goods, and by seizing the favorable opportunity from the province's efforts at promoting the development of the marine economy.

Fourth, the ecological cultural industry belt in southwestern Zhejiang. With the mountainous region extension line in southwestern Zhejiang as the overall axis, the resources presented by ecological leisure tourism and the traditional characteristic cultural advantages in such areas as western Hangzhou, Quzhou, southern Lishui and southern Wenzhou are leveraged to guide the development of such advantageous industries as ecological cultural tourism, artistic production and the manufacturing of traditional artwork.

6.2.4 The Cultural Industry is the Engine for Economic Transformation and Upgrading

In 2003, comrade Xi Jinping expounded the significance of "developing the cultural industry" for promoting the adjustment of the economic structure and the transformation of the growth mode, and vowed to take "the development of the cultural industry" as an important breakthrough in building a culturally large province, and make the cultural industry an important support for building a culturally large province and an important growth point for Zhejiang's economic development.[7] Zhejiang's experience in developing the cultural industry shows that with respect to economic transformation and upgrading, the cultural industry really serves as the engine for promoting the transformation of the growth mode, opening new space for growth and enhancing the people's capability for innovation.

Zhijiang Creative Cultural Park in Hangzhou is a vivid example in which economic transformation is achieved through culture, and the regional landscape is changed through creative efforts; it very vividly indicates the role of the cultural industry as the engine for economic transformation. Zhijiang Creative Cultural Park is one of the ten creative cultural industry parks in Hangzhou and also an important branch of the famous China International Cartoon & Animation Festival. However, in the past, farmers built cement plants, and massively exploited cement minerals; they obtained great economic benefits, but their acts caused damage to the environment.

In order to protect Hangzhou's lush mountains and clean, clear waters, the provincial and municipal governments decidedly stopped this unsustainable manner of economic development. With the building of the new campus of the China Academy of Arts and the establishment of Zhijiang Creative Cultural Park near the mountains and by the river and with the exotic style of small towns, strong artistic atmosphere, the original cement plants have been turned into the key cultural creative parks focusing on four main characteristic industries, including new media, animation and games, modern design and artwork, adding a new cultural landmark to Hangzhou.

---

[7]Xi (2006), p. 331.

Ten years later, the 4th Plenary Session of the 13th Party Committee of Zhejiang Province brought forth a further connection with and development of the "Eight-Eight Strategies", and made a clear roadmap for Zhejiang to comprehensively intensify the reforms. The plenary session vowed to make the market play the decisive role in resource allocation, promote structural adjustment and industrial upgrading, foster the new advantages of an open economy, push forward urban and rural integration and the building of a strong marine province, reach a new realm of cultural development, boost social fairness and justice, and build a beautiful Zhejiang. The plenary session called for further leveraging advantages, intensifying the reforms and innovating measures to make sure that the development of the cultural industry is consistent with the economic, social, political and ecological development, and make the building of a culturally strong province and the realization of the Chinese dream constitute a whole.

6.3 "122" Project: Three Characteristics of the Zhejiang Model for the Cultural Industry

The "122" project for the cultural industry, put forward in the *Decision of the Party Committee of Zhejiang Province on Earnestly Carrying Out the Guiding Principles Adopted during the 6th Plenary Session of the 17th Central Committee of the Communist Party of China and Vigorously Promoting the Building of a Culturally Strong Province,* mainly covers three aspects: First, the top 100 revitalization plans—making selections from across the province to intensively cultivate 100 cultural enterprises, supporting these enterprises to become strong and better, develop into the "leading wild geese" for guiding the development of Zhejiang's cultural industry; second, the key park development plan—choosing and cultivating 20 key cultural industry parks, promoting these parks to open new spaces and to become large and strong; third, the boosting plan for listing—by three-year cultivation and support efforts to make 20 cultural enterprises with great potential for growth and development to be listed or enter the period of pre-listing.

The "122" project is a great initiative aimed at exploring the Zhejiang Model for the cultural industry and it is taken in light of the situation of global development and the national strategy during the period of the 12th Five-Year Plan as a crucial period for national economic and social development; it reflects the strategic characteristics of the line of thought of Zhejiang's cultural industry regarding its positioning, layout and brand.

6.3.1 Positioning: "Soul" and "Engine"

All of the cultural enterprises covered by the top 100 revitalization plans in Zhejiang's "122" project are the for-profit enterprises engaged in the creative design of cultural products, production, sales and cultural services; the objective is to put into practice the orientation of the plan for the development of Zhejiang's cultural industry and that of the relevant national industrial policy, develop the advanced culture and combine economic benefits with social benefits. Such a line of thought regarding the policy gives more prominence to the dual role of the cultural industry as the "soul" and "engine". "Soul" means that the cultural industry first lies in culture and its value is its soul. "Engine" means that the cultural industry plays an important role in increasing the GDP and also serves as an engine for stimulating economic change and upgrading.

6.3.2   Layout: Strategic Vision for Super City Groups

The "parks" under the key park development plan in the "122" project are the particular spatial areas in which a certain number of cultural enterprises and related industries gather together to carry out research, development, production and sales of cultural industrial resources for creating certain economic and social benefits. For the parks covered by the plan, their integrated plan should comply with national standards regarding land, fire protection, safety, energy conservation, environmental protection and health, and enterprises within these parks are required to mainly engage in eight main categories of the cultural industry which Zhejiang gives priority for development; these parks should have distinctive features of the cultural industry and have brought together a certain number of cultural enterprises, and they should enjoy significant economic and social benefits. This is a great bright spot, in the "122" project, for putting in practice Zhejiang's 12th five-year plan for the development of the cultural industry—based on the characteristics of Zhejiang's massive economy and the strategic line of thought for super city groups, as well as Zhejiang's regional functions in global economic culture, giving shape to the momentum for agglomeration and regional characteristics of the cultural industry.

Zhejiang's 12th five-year plan for the development of the cultural industry presented the overall layout for the development of the cultural industry which features one core, three poles, seven centers and four belts; it is an upgraded layout of the cultural industry which breaks away from the early developmental mode with administrative division as a boundary; it shows clear characteristics of the strategic line of thought for super city groups.

As of late 2008, Zhejiang had been home to more than 70 cultural industry agglomeration areas of various types with Hangzhou and Ningbo as the main agglomeration areas, producing an increasing number of demonstration and driving effects. Film and television production, animation and games, publication and printing, stationery production, and artwork become the sectors with the most prominent industrial agglomeration effect.

6.3.3 Brand: A Great Key to Making the Cultural Industry Strong

The boosting plan for listing in the "122" project focuses on supporting the cultural enterprises which are under a good operational management plan and enjoy a good credit standing and are mainly engaged in creative cultural design, film and television services, modern media, digital contents and animation, cultural tourism, advertising and exhibitions, performance and entertainment, artwork, manufacturing and the circulation of cultural products.

More rapidly pushing forward the brand strategy for the cultural industry is an inevitable choice in order for China to develop from a large country of cultural resources to a powerful country of the cultural industry. As Zhejiang has given full scope to the role of private enterprises and private capital, and has fostered an awareness of brand competition of private entrepreneurs, Zhejiang has found a distinctive path for China to carry forward the brand strategy for the cultural industry.

So far, Zhejiang's private cultural industry has risen: there are more than 40,000 private cultural enterprises above the designated size,[8] and the total scale of investment has exceeded 130 billion yuan. Seven enterprises have been listed on the market. The Songcheng Group, Huace Film and Television, and Huayi Brothers are the important cultural brands created by Zhejiang in recent years and that are becoming the fresh forces in China's brand strategy for the cultural industry.

6.4 Zhejiang's Matrix of Modern News Media Groups

Subject to dual pressure from global economic culture and the development of digital technology, the production of news content and its communication modes are undergoing profound changes; bringing about innovations and changes is essential for the further development of the traditional press media. The leap of the traditional news media industry to the cultural industry is a great historical evolution in the contemporary news communication circles; such an evolution will profoundly change the direction of China's media ecology and media development.

Zhejiang has stayed ahead nationwide in the comprehensive strength of the press, publications, radio, film and television industry. In 2014, the operating income, total output and the added value of Zhejiang's press and publication industry were 150,392 million yuan, 152,952 million yuan and 40,808 million yuan, respectively; the operating income of Zhejiang's radio, film and television industry exceeded 34 billion yuan,

---

[8]"The enterprise above the designated size" is a statistical term. The State develops different requirements for the scale of enterprises in different industries; generally, annual output is taken as the standard for enterprise scale; the enterprises which reach the standard are called the enterprises above the designated size; the enterprises above the designated size are divided into several categories, such as extra-large enterprises, large enterprises, medium-sized enterprises, and small enterprises. The State generally compiles statistical data on the enterprises above the designated size.

up more than 10% compared with the previous year—box office income exceeded 2.3 billion yuan, up about 28% compared with the previous year.

The Zhejiang Publishing United Group, the Zhejiang Daily Press Group, the Hangzhou Daily Press Group, the Zhejiang Xinhua Bookstore Group and Zhejiang Printing Group Co., Ltd. have been listed among the top ten under the same category across the country in the comprehensive evaluation concerning the total economic scale at the group level; Zhejiang Education Publishing House has ranked No. 3 in national comprehensive evaluation concerning the total economic scale of local book publishing houses. Each of total assets and sales of Zhejiang Publishing United Group has reached 10 billion yuan.

However, the most important characteristic of Zhejiang's news media industry does not lie in staying ahead regarding the economic scale but it is the intensive development based on transformation, innovation and change. Based on unremitting experiments and efforts for many years since 2003, with the "Eight-Eight Strategies" as a guide, the people in Zhejiang's press media industry responded to the competition of "seeking changes through innovations" by courageously blazing new trails and acting in a realistic and pragmatic way, and they have made gratifying achievements in press transformation, upgrading and its innovative development, they have built Zhejiang's media matrix characterized by modern media groups and have achieved deep integration between the core competitiveness of the press and the technology for the transmission of information via networks.

6.4.1 Relying on the Capital Platform to Move Towards the Double-100 Goal

"News media have a distinctive ideological nature; it is necessary to ensure that the nature of the mouthpiece of the Party and the people remains unchanged, that the Party supervises the media, that cadres are placed under party supervision and that the correct guidance of public opinion is unchanged; it is essential to, under this premise, establish an organizational structure in which publicity services and operations are relatively independent, to separate the operating segment so as to establish independent enterprises, and to more rapidly restructure them into well-regulated modern enterprises".[9] Since 2010, the Zhejiang Daily Press Group (Zhejiang Daily Media) has relied on the capital platform to make three decisive steps in marching towards the double-100 goal.

First, building the capital operational platform. Under the condition that the Party supervises the media, the Zhejiang Daily Media has practiced the philosophy that the media control the capital and the capital expands the media; the Zhejiang Daily Media has been successfully listed on the Shanghai Stock Exchange and it became the first listed state-owned cultural enterprise group in Zhejiang and the first press group with a listing of the entire operating assets among the media in China.

---

[9]Xi (2006), p. 327.

Second, building a platform for technology research and development. The Zhejiang Daily Media has established the group's new media center and built the Zhejiang Daily "Media Dreamworks", the first new media incubation base in China. In the project, the gene of combining traditional media with the Internet was utilized, the operational mode covering new media content and technology application was adopted to carve out an innovative path of press transformation and Internet integration, making it become an iconic brand in China's new media industry.

Third, building a platform for user aggregation. With the listing-based capital platform, the Zhejiang Daily Media acquired the Winger and CGA online platform under Shanda with the consideration of 3.19 billion yuan to obtain 300 million registered users and 20 million active users, thus building the first large autonomous online user platform controlled by state-owned capital, offering a successful mode for fusion between traditional mainstream media and emerging media. With merger and acquisition, the Zhejiang Daily Media has built another "Zhejiang Daily Media" by diluting less than 15% of the shares; it reached another record high on the capital market, with market capitalization soaring from 5.26 billion yuan on the day of listing to 28.9 billion yuan.

The Zhejiang Daily Press Group was successfully listed among the World's Top 500 Media of the Year 2013, reflecting Zhejiang Daily's high speed in the leap of China's press to the cultural industry. Thanks to the successful listing of the Zhejiang Daily Media, it has achieved connection with the capital market, and that connection has further promoted the reform of institutions and mechanisms as well as innovation. The Zhejiang Daily Media has completed market-oriented reform to shape the "3 + 1" developmental pattern covering news media, entertainment interaction, film and television production plus the platform for strategic investment in the cultural industry.

6.4.2   Digital Media Revolution: Leap from Traditional Media to the Modern Cultural Industry

The combination of science, technology and culture is the basic quality of a modern cultural industry. In the global competition of media innovation, winners are often the people who have changed from traditional media to the cultural industry through the combination of science, technology and culture. The people of Zhejiang's press have an exceptionally keen insight into the digital revolution of the cultural industry in the Internet era, and they have great enthusiasm for the application of new digital technology in the media field.

At present, internationally, there are increasingly high requirements for energy conservation, consumption reduction, emission reduction, green development and safety in the printing industry. Green printing reflects the scientific and technological level of the developed European countries and the USA and is also an important tool for acquiring a green mindset and establishing a green barrier in industrial competition. Developing green printing has become the main direction for the development of China's printing industry during the period of the 12th Five-Year Plan. Against such a background, the following fact is of particular significance: Shengyuan Printing Co., Ltd. under the Hangzhou Daily Press Group has passed the national certification of green printing. With this green revolution, Shengyuan Printing Co., Ltd. has become the only printing enterprise among China's press and the first printing enterprise in Zhejiang, which has passed that certification; this suggests that Zhejiang's press has entered a new era of reaching the international standard in the quality of printing and has opened the channel for cooperating with the top 500 worldwide companies.

It is difficult to achieve a coherent connection between traditional paper media and dynamic digital media, thus restricting the new media change of the press for a long time. At present, with the application of QR code technology, it is expected that this problem will be solved to a certain extent. The *Daily Business* under the Hangzhou Daily Press Group adopts BOBO code technology to make breakthroughs in system compatibility and the technology of video connection, having achieved a smooth connection between paper media and digital media and sharpened the competitive edge through revolutionary technical changes.

6.4.3 Omnimedia Interaction: Press and Internet Fusion in the Internet Era

Technically, one of the important parts of press transformation and upgrading lies in changing the channel of distribution from single paper media to diversified omnimedia; fusion between traditional media and new media has been achieved to carry out the strategy of omnimedia. Therefore, press transformation cannot be achieved without the development of technical software and hardware and the integration of resources based on the new technical platform.

The Zhejiang Daily Media has more rapidly built the basic platform for technical facilities, a system and mechanism of integration to provide strong support for the integrative development of the media. First, bringing about innovations to the organizational structure for integrative development. The Zhejiang Daily Media has specially established the group's digital collection and editing center, in which the collecting and editing personnel from the Zhejiang Daily and Zhejiang Online play the leading role, and the group's news resources are coordinated to guide the group's the collection and editing of the news and technical support for cross-platform integrative communication. Second, building up the procedure for omnimedia news production. With the group's digital collection and editing center as the core, a multi-media collection and editing platform for unified command and dispatching has been built. Third, exploring a sustainable business model which supports news communication. The Zhejiang Daily Press Group has actively explored the mode for the integrative development of news communication and Internet information and cultural services, and has made significant achievements in promoting the integrative development of news and cultural services. Fourth, building a domestic platform for the integration of leading information. With a focus on utilizing big data and cloud computing technology for the production of news, based on an in-depth feasibility study, the Zhejiang Daily Press Group is more quickly building a platform for intelligent information services for omnimedia fusion, and it is conducting big data mining and analysis to greatly enhance the guidance level and the capability for service of news reporting.

Against the background of more rapidly developing the cultural industry, the industrial attribute of the press has been valued. The Zhejiang Daily Media and Alibaba have engaged in cross-industry cooperation to jointly launch the *Taobao World Media*. It targets the e-commerce groups who are not covered by the media market, and relies on online and offline channels to make paper media e-commerce profitable, so it becomes the most widely circulated Chinese language weekly magazine in China; it delivered more than 100 million yuan in advertising sales in two months and has been rated as the best yearly magazine by *New Weekly* and *Media*.

The omnimedia integrated marketing of tourism is a great attempt made by the Zhejiang Daily Media for carrying out the omnimedia strategy in 2013. With integrative promotion through newspapers, the Internet, magazines and outdoor and mobile terminals, it has engaged in strategic cooperation with dozens of tourism departments across the country to carry out omnimedia and full-service tourism marketing, making great breakthroughs in the publicity of tourism brands and inbound marketing at scenic spots.

6.4.4 Media Community: Innovating the Building of a Network of Urban Communities

As the center of cultural and economic activities, a city plays an important role in cultural communication and the establishment of relationships. The change from traditional media to new media is accompanied by changes in the relationships of urban social networks. How to bring about innovations to the urban media system in the Internet era and build new-type relationships of urban communities has become an important issue in the development of changes in urban media. In this regard, 19lou Media under the Hangzhou Daily Press Group provides us with a successful case.

19lou Media under the Hangzhou Daily Press Group introduces an innovative business model of an urban community website, making Zhejiang the forerunner in urban community websites. 19lou Media is based in Zhejiang and covers the whole country. With the inter-city duplication of a new business model, the development and application of the SBS platform, the establishment of the C2B business model, strategic investments and resource integration, it has made milestone achievements in moving towards the goal of building 100 active urban communities in five years.

Moreover, the Hangzhou Daily Press Group has utilized a distribution network to perform intra-city distribution services and integrate the resources of newspaper delivery teams, self-owned e-commerce platforms and physical chains to provide customers with a package of services covering the making of bills of lading, commodity purchasing, ordering by customers, home delivery service and the recovery of bills of lading; this has not only put the strategy of diversified development into practice, but it has also increased the level of intra-city distribution services.

6.5   Film, Television and New Media: Zhejiang's Cultural Industry Based on Digital Technology

Zhejiang's meeting on the reform of the cultural system and the building of a culturally large province, held on July 18, 2003, put forward the developmental strategy for developing the cultural industry in a market-oriented way by seeking support from science and technology, building up connections with the existing related industries, and making the cultural industry an important pillar industry in Zhejiang's economy. During the meeting, the then Secretary of the Party Committee of Zhejiang Province, comrade Xi Jinping, pointed out, "It is necessary to adapt to the market needs, bring about continuous innovations in the cultural industry; in particular, it is essential to adopt new and high technology to actively promote integration between the information industry and the cultural industry, continuously increase the technological content, and transform the cultural industry from a labor-intensive one to a technology-intensive one, from a low value-added one to a high value-added one and from an extensive one to a quality-based one".[10]

Following such a guiding thought, Zhejiang's cultural industry has relied on modern new and high technology to venture down a characteristic "culture + N" path. Take the Wasu Digital TV Media Group as an example, "N" means digital technology, namely, going down the "culture + technology" path towards development.

6.5.1   "Culture + Technology" Cultural Industry Group

According to the arrangements made by the Party Committee of Zhejiang Province for the "Eight-Eight Strategies", with support from new and high technology, the Wasu Group has integrated market development players, fully leveraged Zhejiang's advantageous institutions and mechanisms, brought about innovations and practiced the philosophy of "technology + culture integration" to build an innovative developmental mode which combines cultural media with information services and features coordinated and benign win-win development", and it has promoted industrial development "supported by new media, new networks, culture and technology" to extend

---

[10]Xi (2006), p. 331.

the development of the information service industry. With many years of development, Wasu has become a large state-owned cultural media industry group established by the Zhejiang Radio & TV Group, the Hangzhou Cultural, Radio & TV Group, and the Ningbo Radio & TV Group; it is the largest interactive TV, 3G mobile TV and Internet TV integrated digital content operator and provider in China, and has received commendations and rewards from the Department of Publicity under the Central Committee of the Communist Party of China, the Ministry of Science and Technology, the State Administration of the Press, Publications, Radio, Film and Television, the Zhejiang Province and Hangzhou City on many occasions.

For a long time, Zhejiang's radio and cable TV network was in a state of segmentation, making it fail to address the requirements of new media and the integration of the three networks. According to the requirements from the Central Committee of the Communist Party of China, under the correct guidance of the Party Committee and the People's Government of Zhejiang Province, as the provincial platform for cable digital TV development and the market player for cable network integration, Wasu has actively experimented with bringing about innovations to promote the integration of the provincial radio and television network which features "one network in one province". At present, the Wasu Group owns the national integrated operation licenses of IPTV, 3G mobile TV and Internet TV; it is part of the first camp involving new media and the integration of three networks across the country, and is also currently the largest cable network operator under cross-regional operations in China; more than 20 million households have subscribed to its cable TV service; its Wasu Media is the listed company with the highest market capitalization in China's radio and television industry.

Zhejiang's mode of integration is unique in China. Under its mode of integration, the government neither spends money nor imposes administrative orders to force integration; Zhejiang mainly relies on the market, enterprises, capital and interest orientation to push forward integration, and fully mobilizes the initiative and enthusiasm of the radio and television departments at various levels in the province. The advantages of such a mode of integration will certainly become evident in its subsequent development. The cable TV subscribers across the province will enjoy high speed and convenience from Zhejiang's new mode which features "one network in one province".

In such fields as animation, games, digital music and digital reading, Zhejiang's cultural enterprises and cultural parks have actively explored the "culture + technology" mode, and probed the new forms of cultural services based on emerging science and technology through collaborative innovations among the government, industries, universities and research. The (Zhejiang) National Digital Entertainment Industry Park has actively promoted the building of a regional service platform for the sharing of digital entertainment technology, building a technical service platform to achieve connection between the cultural industry and new and high technology. Under the guidance of the guiding group for the project for a regional service platform for the sharing of digital entertainment technology, this technical service platform has undergone basic work including a feasibility study of platform building, enterprise surveys, site planning, equipment selection and the building of an operating mechanism, playing a certain role in promoting cooperation among industries, universities and research in the enterprises within the park. For instance, it has helped Hangzhou Huihuang Shidai Animation Production Co., Ltd. to successfully research and develop the industry-leading project "Research on the Three-dimensional Animation Production Technology that is Locally Reused in the Development of a Model, a Motion and a System"; the platform for talent cultivation, internship and communication among the enterprises within the park and the institutions of higher learning has been built to provide reserve talent support for enterprises.

6.5.2 Developmental Mode: Cultural Innovation and Technology Exportation

The path for the development of Zhejiang's cultural industry is a path of continuous exploration, intensifying of reform and innovation. Wasu adopted the then advanced Ethernet IP network technology in 2001, and relied on Hangzhou's cable TV network resources to build a network which featured the highest speed, the latest technology, a large scale, the widest application and the greatest bandwidth at that time, breaking new ground in the integration of radio, television and cable networks ("three networks"). After Wasu successfully initiated the new digital TV mode—interactive TV in 2004, Wasu was dedicated to innovative digital development across networks, applications, terminals and media, and it built a new segment of the media industry with the development of interactive TV, 3G mobile TV and Internet TV across the country. As from 2005, with capital as the bond, Wasu established the entities involving cable TV network operations and digital development in Jiaxing, Jinhua, Huzhou, Lishui and Xinchang in Zhejiang, and became the main platform for local digital and information development, actively pushing forward the joint development of radio and television networks across the province. In 2008, Wasu extensively conducted wireless digital urban construction in Hangzhou and built connections with a wired broadband network to achieve "integrated sky-earth" coverage by broadband networks in Hangzhou. In 2010, based on the resource advantages of the Wasu Group and Taobao, the online trading platform for cultural goods was built to enable online trading and the distribution of cultural goods, online trading of related cultural copyrights, and to perform industrialized operations. With the digital TV payment platform, e-commerce was developed in interactive TV. In 2011, Wasu promoted the CCMTS-based access solution and media cloud construction. In 2012, Wasu pushed forward a cross-generation network and cloud service construction.

In the process of promoting the digital development of cable TV, Wasu brought about innovations to the digital TV development mode, became the first nationwide to initiate the application of interactive digital TV and information, it extended digital TV to the field of digital industrial development covering new networks, new communications, new media and new information applications, thus fostering comprehensive advantages in innovations involving technology, applications and business models and establishing the Hangzhou Model of digital TV development in the industry. Wasu rapidly promoted integrated digital conversion of cable TV in Hangzhou, became the first nationwide to make the number of integrated conversion-related subscribers exceed 1 million in late 2006, delivering good social and economic benefits. With close attention paid to the people's needs, Wasu conducted product packaging and professional consumption guidance with respect to video services, and pioneered high-definition video on demand in China, thoroughly changed the passive watching mode in conventional cable TV, provided the people with a new digital TV platform which contains mass content and supports on-demand operations. Wasu has established a cooperation mechanism open to the whole society and extensively built an urban information service platform covering various aspects of the society, politics, the economy and life, including education, financial and economic affairs, games, government affairs and communities; it has provided citizens and the society with application services concerning financial and economic affairs, education, games and entertainment, and the 96345 city information service, the Jiayintong online payment platform, e-commerce applications, Party member distance education, an industry window, rural information and digital home integrated services, so that the conventional mode of "watching TV" has been changed to the mode of "using TV", and the quality of the people's life regarding the obtaining of information has been greatly improved.

The regional service for the sharing of digital entertainment technology is the first characteristic of the (Zhejiang) National Digital Entertainment Industry Park. The park has cooperated with the neural communication team from the School of Media and International Culture of Zhejiang University to cultivate and promote the project called "Optimization of Neuroscience-based Animation and Game Products and Technology Development"; the park has worked with the College of Computer Science & Technology of Zhejiang University of Technology to build the regional service platfrom for the sharing of digital entertainment technology and the key laboratory of Zhejiang Province for research on intelligent processing technology for visual media, providing cultural enterprises across the country with high-end equipment services, new and hi-tech services and innovative talent cultivation services, thus promoting the transformation of scientific and technological achievements and the cultivation of innovative and entrepreneurial talents.

6.5.3 The Export of Capital and Models

According to the developmental strategy of "being based on Zhejiang and seeking development across the country", Wasu exported its business model to promote cross-region business development. At present, Wasu's new media service covers the radio and television network in 30 provinces and more than 150 cities and tens of millions of Internet TV terminals across the country. It has full access to three main telecom operators including China Mobile, China Telecom and China Unicom, and enjoys more than 65% of the Internet TV market share. Wasu has built the cable network at the highest level of operational service and with the greatest growth potential covering nearly 20 million cable TV subscribers throughout Zhejiang and the rest of the country, which is the largest one in China; Wasu has become an integrated new media information service provider offering full services involving cross-generation networks, cloud platforms and multiple terminals. Wasu has built the digital content repository in the new media industry, which is the largest one in China and contains 1-million-hour digital media content resources; it has the full service qualification covering cable TV, interactive TV, mobile TV and Internet TV. Wasu has kept a foothold in Hangzhou and has actively expanded to other cities in China; it has built a network of content delivery and a service system covering more than 20 provinces in China. At present, Wasu is building an Internet-based system for the delivery of digital media content, thus giving shape to a novel new media developmental mode with full service qualification, full network coverage and full terminal penetration.

With the expansion of the service platform for the digital entertainment industry, the (Zhejiang) National Digital Entertainment Industry Park has strengthened the function of commercial exchanges of the chambers of commerce and the industrial service platform. Since their inception, the Xihu District Chamber of Commerce for the Digital Entertainment (Animation and Game) Industry and the Service Platform for the National Digital Entertainment Industry have produced marked effects in promoting industrial exchanges and helping the enterprises within the park go global. For instance, recommending the animation products of the enterprises within the park to the peers from Japan and South Korea at the Tokyo Animation Fair, the Japan Media Arts Festival, and the China-South Korea Forum on the Future Development of the Digital Content Industry in 2008, holding the 2nd China-Japan-South Korea Industry-Government-University Animation Exchange Meeting, and the Animation Industry Development (Hangzhou) High-level Forum 2008.

6.5.4 Building the Whole Chain of the Film and Television Industry, Promoting Omnimedia Fusion

At present, the (Zhejiang) National Digital Entertainment Industry Park has established a one-park multi-point pattern of development and is one of the largest areas of digital entertainment industrial agglomeration in Zhejiang; it mainly provides business incubation, policy and technical support and other services to the enterprises along the chain of the digital entertainment industry, promotes the transformation of scientific and technological achievements, and cultivates the new and hi-tech enterprises and the research and development bodies; it adopts the strategic line of thought of "building a public platform, mobilizing social resources, applying the market mechanism, enhancing the core competitiveness and promoting industrial development" to attract the digital entertainment enterprises within and outside the province to the park for development.

With a focus on the production, distribution, circulation and consumption of digital media content, Wasu has played a driving and integrative role in the industrial chain, while relevant partners have developed into strong performers in the domestic digital media service field, the whole industrial chain from points to plane and from plane to lines has taken shape. Currently, the Wasu Group has nine bases and open platforms, mainly including a viewing screen base, a games base, a publication base, a shopping base, an information base, a music base, a payment base, a communication base and an original creation base. Each base is supported by rich contents, for instance, the video base cooperates with more than 360 copyright providers in the world, owns a 1-million-hour program content, more than 200 production lines and a planning and publicity team of more than 600 people.

With respect to promoting omnimedia fusion, Waus has actively tracked the technical hot spots concerning an ultra-wide band, cloud computing and the Internet of Things. Based on the developmental needs and technical advantages of its own radio and television service, Wasu has endeavored to promote omnimedia fusion and new media development, and has occupied the new front of public opinion and publicity, fully utilized information technology to build new media which integrate interactive TV, mobile TV and Internet TV, and is a leader of the new trend in the services concerning the integration of three networks; it has become the leading enterprise in the national new media industry. Wasu enjoys the advantage of an "integrated sky-earth" wired and wireless transmission network, and has established a fusion of a supporting network consisting of a wired broadband network, a wireless broadband network, a cable digital TV network and a mobile digital TV network; it has built a number of service supporting platforms, including a digital TV interactive portal platform, a content management platform, an application management platform, a certification platform, and a billing and operation supporting system.

6.6 Four Main Creative Cultural Platforms Promote Four Main Cultural Sectors

The creative cultural platforms are an important support for integrating relevant resources and achieving collaborative innovation; they are an important means for making breakthroughs in stimulating intensive, large-scale and professional development of the cultural industry. Making efforts to improve the large creative cultural platforms is a task with priority in Zhejiang's relevant functional departments and is also a great bright spot in Zhejiang's creative cultural industry. Four distinctive creative cultural platforms, including the animation culture communication and trading platform, the film and television creative industry platform, the platform for cultural tourism and the creative media platform, show four different directions for experimentation for Zhejiang's cultural industry in building creative platforms.

6.6.1 The International Cartoon & Animation Festival Promotes the Rapid Development of the Animation Industry

Animation and games is an important category in the development of Zhejiang's cultural industry. With nearly ten years of development, Zhejiang has become a center for the animation and games industry which is highly influential in China. In 2012, 46 animated films (a total of 26,375 min) were created and produced in Zhejiang, ranking Zhejiang no. 3 nationwide in output. As the Capital of Animation, Hangzhou has held the international cartoon and animation festival for 11 consecutive years; this festival is famous in the domestic and foreign animation circles, promoting the development of the animation industry of Zhejiang, and even that of China itself.

The China International Cartoon & Animation Festival—sponsored by the State Administration of Radio, Film, and Television and the People's Government of Zhejiang Province and organized by the People's Government of Hangzhou City, the Radio, Film and Television Bureau of Zhejiang Province and the Zhejiang Radio & TV Group—is currently the only national-level festival dedicated to animation and also currently the largest, most popular and most influential animation fair in China. It has been listed as the cultural exhibition project that is intensively supported in the *National 12th Five-Year Plan for Cultural Reform and Development* and serves as an important platform for making the Chinese culture go global.

With the purpose of becoming the "Animation Fair, the People's Festival", the China International Cartoon & Animation Festival attracted a large number of visitors for more than 10 million person-times in the ten years that it has been held. During the 10th China International Cartoon & Animation Festival in 2014, the China COSPLAY Super Gala activity alone attracted more than 700 teams from home and abroad to participate in the contest and more than 40,000 participants. The China COSPLAY Super Gala also had contests in seven foreign countries including the USA, the Netherlands and Japan. Hangzhou initiated and established the World COSPLAY Alliance.

In order to ensure participation of a greater number of ordinary people, the animation festival also featured other activities, including an animation symphony concert, an animation voice contest, the "Ten-Year Animation · Hangzhou Story" citizen's photographic exhibition, and the autographed copy sale by animation masters, with ten activity venues located in Hangzhou, Tonglu and Jiande, which fostered a strong atmosphere of an animation carnival for all.

With a ten-year animation journey, Hangzhou sets out again. At present, the Executive Committee of the China International Cartoon & Animation Festival in Hangzhou is a carefully summarizing experience, further emancipating the mind and innovating philosophies, as well as endeavoring to turn the animation festival into an international leader, Asia's first-class and the national no. 1 animation fair, thus making a greater contribution to the development of the animation industry.

6.6.2 "Hengllywood" Film and Television Experimental Area Promotes the Active Development of the Film and Television Industry

The Hengdian Film and Television Industry Experimental Area, built in 2004, is reputed as China's Hollywood. Initially, Hengdian adopted the operational mode of a film and television platform of "bringing scripts, taking away films". Now Hengdian strives to become a large omnimedia platform for "bringing scripts, taking away the box office", vividly embodying the pursuit on the part of Zhejiang's cultural enterprises of the global cultural industry and the integrated film and television creative service platform.

The then Secretary of the Party Committee of Zhejiang Province, comrade Xi Jinping, inspected Hengdian twice to guide the development of the film and television cultural industry, earnestly promoting the rapid development and growth of Hengdian's film and television cultural industry. In response to the problems in Zhejiang's economic development, comrade Xi Jinping put forward the "two bird" strategy—"achieving the rebirth of the phoenix amidst fire" and "vacating the cage to change birds"—to explain the economic structural adjustment, and advocated the "cultivation of good 'birds' which eat less, lay more eggs and fly high", thus requiring Zhejiang's enterprises to play their roles in industrial upgrading. Hengdian's practice proves that Hengdian's film and television cultural industry is a "good bird".

So far, Hengdian's cultural industry for film and television has stayed ahead nationwide with respect to the base scale, the building of the industrial chain, policy development and the building of the service system; it has become the largest service platform for the film and television industry in China.

6.6.3 The Cultural Tourism Platform Stimulates Cultural Consumption

On December 9, 2010, the Hangzhou Songcheng Tourism Development Co., Ltd. ("The Songcheng Group") was listed on the Shenzhen Stock Exchange and it became the first shares in China's cultural performance industry. For more than ten years, the Songcheng Group relied on Zhejiang's unique cultural deposits and advantageous tourism resources to build the platform for cultural tourism consumption, and it adopted a mode dominated by theme parks and cultural performances to successfully build the brands "Songcheng" and "The Romance of the Song Dynasty". It has been rated as the National Advanced Unit for the Reform of the Cultural System and one of China's Top Ten Most Influential Cultural Industry Demonstration Bases. It is the only enterprise granted the title of "One of China's Top 30 Cultural Enterprises" for four consecutive times in China.

Hangzhou is a world-famous tourist city. Cultural tourism has always been an important pillar industry in Hangzhou. At present, Hangzhou has nearly 20 large performance venues, in which a variety of performances, covering music, dance and song, cross talk and comedy show, were staged more than 1,000 times. In order to upgrade the general trend of cultural leisure consumption in Hangzhou, the Songcheng Group has built the Songcheng · Chinese Showbiz Valley, a platform for cultural tourism consumption under the theme of performance culture and with a new lifestyle as a consequential connotation.

The successful birth and development of the Songcheng Group is closely related to Zhejiang's policies and measures for cultivating a creative cultural environment. As from 2008, based on introducing a raft of policies for promoting the development of the creative cultural industry, Hangzhou launched the "creative fairs" with a view to developing the people's habits regarding the consumption of cultural products and services. The West Lake Creative Fair and the Xiling Yiyuan Holiday Fair—Walk Street are the representative projects.

6.6.4 The Internet Platform Boosts the New Forms of Cultural Services

Zhejiang's platforms for the creative cultural industry have relied on the Internet to unleash the energy of organizations from enterprises as isolated points and put them in their ecosystem to form a business ecosystem. The integration between cultural enterprises and their social ecological network has internalized social responsibility as the internal impetus for enterprises, thus extending business ecology to the entire social ecology. Founded in 1999, the Alibaba Group is currently the largest e-commerce group in China and also the representative of creative cultural platforms and new forms of cultural services in the digital media era.

6.6.4.1 Making It Easy to Do Business Everywhere: "The Greatest Fair in the World"

The business platform built by Alibaba has successfully communicated with consumers, merchants and other participants. The open, collaborative and prosperous ecological chain of business built by Alibaba makes it possible for relevant sectors to fully participate in different parts of commercial activities and reap benefits from them. Alibaba's Taobao and Tmall have been hailed as "the greatest fair in the world" by the British magazine *The Economist*.

6.6.4.2 Pan Media: The Cultural Service Market for the Exchange of Values

Alibaba's e-commerce platform is a business platform for the trading of goods and it is also a communication platform for the exchange of information. With its "pan media" characteristics that are unlike the conventional mass media, it creatively provides a new market for cultural services and a new form of service in the cultural industry.

As an internet company connecting the most extensive social elements, Alibaba naturally has the attribute of being a media. Besides the e-commerce field, Alibaba has also been engaged in logistics (rrs.com), finance (Yu'E Bao, Zhongan Insurance), group purchasing (Meituan, Juhuasuan), games (Alibaba Mobile Games Platform), education (xue.taotao.com), tourism (Alitrip), medical services (CITIC 21CN), sports (Guangzhou Evergrande Taobao Football Club), digital TV (Wasu), cloud computing (Aliyun), social media (Laiwang), and culture (China Vision Media Group). With the characteristic of communication—"connection in four aspects", the pan media platforms represented by Alibaba reflect, to a certain extent, some characteristics of the future creative cultural work and communication.

First, building connection between online and offline transactions, between buyers and sellers and becoming the media for business communication. Each store at taobao.com is wemedia. In a meeting on the economic situation with the participation of Taobao's founder Jack Ma, Chinese Premier Li Keqiang said that he once visited taobao.com and was moved by the messages left by store owners. He encouraged young people to start businesses, and further develop e-commerce on the basis of guaranteeing quality and fair competition.[11]

Second, building a connection between financial products and investors, thus becoming the media for financial circulation. The financial products represented by Yu'E Bao jointly launched by Alibaba and the Tian Hong Fund have been well received on the market and have absorbed massive idle private capital.

Third, building a connection between culture and consumption, creating a shopping festival as the time node of consumption. Since 2009, on November 11, originally an ordinary day, this day has become a day that is now well-known for the Double 11 Shopping Carnival.

Fourth, building a connection between social media and businesses, making it possible for businesses to become rooted in daily life. When WeChat had occupied almost all smartphone screens, Alibaba launched a mobile social app called Laiwang. In 2013, Alibaba became a shareholder of the Sina microblog with more than 500 million users. One is a highly influential social media platform, and the other is a tremendously influential e-commerce platform. There are more than 500 million registered users on the Sina microblog, while the Taobao and Tmall platforms also have more than 500 million registered users. More than 40% of the users are the users of both sides. After Alibaba became a shareholder of the Sina microblog, under the Article "Data Exchange" in the strategic agreement, the commercial value behind the "footprint" of 500 million registered users of the Sina microblog on the Sina microblog will be mined by Alibaba through big data technology.[12]

---

[11] Feng (2013).
[12] Yu (2013).

6.6.5 "Cultivating Both Entrepreneurs and Thinkers": Culture Unleashes the Creative Vitality of Private Enterprises

As early as 2003, comrade Xi Jinping pointed out, "Developing private cultural enterprises is essential for the development of Zhejiang's cultural industry and it is also the characteristic and advantage of Zhejiang's cultural reform and development". In Zhejiang's practice in the development of the cultural industry, a number of cultural enterprises and cultural people in the business circles which/who have led the tendencies of the times and have the courage to remold the spirit of the times have emerged. After Lu Guanqiu and Zong Qinghou, Jack Ma, an advocate of the new business civilization, has become the new model of Zhejiang merchants; he is hailed as the Godfather of China's E-commerce. The rise of Chinese Internet enterprises, represented by Alibaba, originates from the great practice of China's reform and opening-up in more than 30 years and it is also rooted in Zhejiang's profound cultural soil.

6.6.5.1 The Enterprise Culture of Seeking Win-Win Outcomes and Bravely Assuming Responsibilities

The values of the new-type cultural enterprises represented by Alibaba contain the distinctive style of Zhejiang's private enterprises. The name Alibaba means "open sesame", in other words, opening the door to the world market. Valuing the cooperation on business ecosystem and the interests of small and medium-sized enterprises is the first tenet in Alibaba's culture. "Alibaba's values can be summarized as: CUSTOMER FIRST, the interests of our community of consumers, merchants and enterprises must be our first priority; TEAMWORK, we believe teamwork enables ordinary people to achieve extraordinary things; EMBRACE CHANGE, in this fast-changing world, we must be flexible, innovative and ready to adapt to new business conditions in order to maintain sustainability and vitality in our business; INTEGRITY, we expect our people to uphold the highest standards of honesty and to deliver on their commitments; PASSION, we expect our people to approach everything with fire in their bellies and never give up on doing what they believe is right; COMMITMENT, employees who demonstrate perseverance and excellence are richly rewarded, nothing should be taken for granted as we encourage our people to work happily and live seriously."[13]

---

[13]http://www.alibabagroup.com/cn/about/culture, last accessed: September 28, 2014.

Alibaba attaches great importance to the social responsibility of an enterprise. As stressed by Jack Ma, Alibaba is an idealist company, social responsibility is Alibaba's integral intrinsic gene, and the people at Alibaba always take great pride in this country and the times and have a sincere thankful heart.[14]

6.6.5.2   The Penetration of Business Culture into Daily Interaction

The new forms of business based on digital media have changed the people's habits in business, daily life and social interaction, and they have also exerted an impact on the people's daily habits regarding language and popular psychology. With the increasing popularity of Taobao, the word "dear" used between buyer and seller at Taobao has gone viral, for instance, government departments adopt the style of Taobao to change their image—orthodox and inflexible, and become lively, which is considered by the people as approachable for the people. The cyberculture represented by Alibaba has brought refreshing changes to the conventional manner of communication; it is the typical penetration of business culture into social culture and it is sufficient to serve as the window for observing the current changes in popular culture.

References

Feng Yue, In a Dialogue with Jack Ma, Li Keqiang Talked about the Development of E-commerce, and Said That He Once Visited Taobao and Was Moved by the Messages Left by Store Owners, www.cnr.cn, 2013-11-09, http://china.cnr.cn/xwwgf/201311/t20131109_514084368.shtml, last accessed: 2014-09-28.
Xi Jinping, *Carrying out Concrete Work to Stay Ahead – Line of Thought and Practice in Promoting New Development in Zhejiang*, The Party School of the CPC Central Committee Press, 2006.
Yu Fenghui, The Alliance between Alibaba and Sina Microblog Targets "Data", *Beijing News*, May 2, 2013, p. B02.

---

[14]CEO's Message, http://view.1688.com/cms/shichang/csr/ceo.html?spm=b26101.29865.0.0, last accessed: September 28, 2014.

Chapter 7
Excellent Cultural Products: Inspiring the Spirit of the Times

Jing Zhou

On June 1, 2005, during the meeting of Zhejiang Province on surveying the cultural publicity circles, comrade Xi Jinping pointed out, "Excellent cultural products are important signs of the level of cultural development in a country, a territory and an era, and the most important and most basic elements for writing the cultural history". "In order to further bring about glory in Zhejiang's culture, it is essential to create and produce a number of excellent cultural products which combine thought with artistry, a number of the enduring works which can withstand the test of history, and a number of excellent works which reflect the characteristics of the times, represent the national level and embody Zhejiang's characteristics; make them become the important symbols of Zhejiang as a culturally large province".[1]

7.1 The Excellent People-Oriented Cultural Products Bring into Being Symbols of Zhejiang

On September 10, 2004, the 7th China Arts Festival, sponsored by the Ministry of Culture and organized by the People's Government of Zhejiang Province, was inaugurated in Hangzhou. During the opening ceremony at the Zhejiang Dragon Sports Centre, comrade Xi Jinping, the then Secretary of the Party Committee of Zhejiang Province, Chairman of the Standing Committee of the People's Congress of Zhejiang Province, specially invited a 90-year-old person and a 5-year-old child to strike a gong for the opening, suggesting that he earnestly interpreted the purpose of holding an "Artistic Pageant, the People's Festival".

---

[1] Xi (2006), p. 330.

J. Zhou (✉)
The Zhejiang Academy of Social Sciences, Hangzhou, China

© Social Sciences Academic Press and Springer Nature Singapore Pte Ltd. 2019
D. Xie and Y. Chen (eds.), *Chinese Dream and Practice in Zhejiang – Culture*,
Research Series on the Chinese Dream and China's Development Path,
https://doi.org/10.1007/978-981-13-7216-2_7

7.1.1   2001–2005: Major Cultural and Artistic Awards Make Excellent Cultural Products Stand Out

During the 7th China Arts Festival, the first batch of excellent cultural products made after Zhejiang vowed to build a culturally large province were reviewed. It was the largest national-level artistic pageant at the highest level in Zhejiang and also the new starting point for a massive emergence of Zhejiang's excellent cultural products.

The competitive strength of Zhejiang's excellent artistic works was fully demonstrated at the 7th China Art Festival. In the appraisal and selection for the 11th Splendor Award, 7 excellent dramatic works from Zhejiang were selected, fully showing that the enduring cultural works, the award-winning works and the iconic works mushroomed after Zhejiang put forward the goal of building a culturally large province.

The 7th China Arts Festival was a sign that the environment for Zhejiang's cultural and artistic creations had become the first to be open to the outside world. For the creation of excellent cultural and artistic works, Zhejiang has taken an innovative path of "introducing a batch of experts, opening the door to one world", while the starting point was the creation and performance of a number of excellent stage works stimulated by the 7th China Art Festival in 2004. Almost seven award-winning operas were jointly created by the most outstanding Chinese artists. During their creation, Zhejiang provided a loose experimental environment and good creative conditions for artists. The Ningbo opera *The Pawned Wife* was given a number of awards, including the Cao Yu Drama Award during the 8th China Drama Festival, and the Chinese Opera Society Award in 2004. The Ningbo opera, a local opera with a history of nearly 200 years, became vibrant again thanks to this wonderful show.

The 7th China Arts Festival won more applause from audiences, especially young audiences, for its "expert operas" and its "operas for appraisal in deciding on awards", which highly tallied with Zhejiang's characteristic that the people run cultural and artistic affairs. The 7th China Arts Festival integrated the China Arts Festival Award, the Splendor Award, the Galaxy Award, and the Suqin Awards for the first time, showing the clear direction for artistic creation in contemporary China: Creation should showcase the deposits of the Chinese culture, be close to the people's life, focus on the theme of the times, and should bring works to more people through various carriers. During the 7th China Arts Festival, the stage masterpieces from the provinces across the country competed in Hangzhou, Ningbo, Wenzhou, Jiaxing and Shaoxing; 51 operas involved in appraisal for granting the 11th Splendor Award were performed on 102 occasions nationwide; 41 operas for congratulatory exhibition and performance were performed on nearly 130 occasions within and outside the province, in Hong Kong, Macao, Taiwan and some foreign countries.

With the 7th China Arts Festival, Zhejiang was given 449 national-level awards by the Department of Publicity under the Central Committee of the Communist Party of China, the Ministry of Culture, the State Administration of Radio Film and Television, the China Federation of Literary and Art Circles, and literature and art associations during the period 2001–2005. Zhejiang's writers published more than 400 full-length novels and reportages, more than 1,600 literary works of other genres, and more than 70 monographs on literary theory. The full-length novel *The Sun Comes Up in the East* was granted the national Five-Ones Project award by the Department of Publicity under the Central Committee of the Communist Party of China. The children's literary work *Gourmet Hunting* was given the 5th National Excellent Children's Literary Work Award. *Chasing the Sun* and the *Full Story of the Stupid Cat* were given the 6th National Excellent Children's Literary Work Award.

During the period 2001–2005, Zhejiang's television artists created, shot and produced more than 100 TV plays (more than 2,000 episodes), and more than 18,000 episodes of other TV art programs. The TV plays *Supreme Interests, My Dear Motherland* and the opera TV play *Dream of the Red Chamber* were given the Five-Ones Project award by the Department of Publicity under the Central Committee of the Communist Party of China; 15 TV plays were given the National TV Play Flying Apsaras Award; 41 works (columns) were given the National Television, Literature and Art Starlight Award; 48 works were given the China TV Golden Eagle Award. The musical dance film *Hanhao Bird* was given the 12th Chinese Film Child Cow Award of the Excellent Feature Film Award; after the scripts *Ribbons in the Sky, Deng Xiaoping 1928* were made into films, they were given the Five-Ones Project award by the Department of Publicity under the Central Committee of the Communist Party of China and the China Ornamental Column Awards.

"People-oriented cultural communication" has become a brand in the popularization and work of philosophy and social science in Zhejiang. In April, 2005, the Zhejiang Federation of Humanities and Social Sciences Circles and the *Qianjiang Evening News* jointly launched the Zhejiang Humanities Lectures, which, with the general public, great masters and great learning as the call, focused on historical and cultural traditions, the philosophy of life and social hot spots, and adopted the communication mode with lecture-media interaction; it was given on each Saturday, and the essence of the lecture was published on a full page of the *Qianjiang Evening News* on Monday. A large number of famous scholars and social celebrities—including He Zhenliang, Wu Jianmin, Yu Qiuyu, Han Meilin, Wei Jie, Jing Yidan, Yu Dan, Liu Xinwu, Hu Angang, Zhou Guoping, and Yu Hua—were invited to the lectures, exerting a huge social impact. The Xinhua News Agency published articles twice to highly praise the Zhejiang Humanities Lectures to open a new channel for popularizing the humanities. In 2006, the Humanities Lectures were rated by Hangzhou citizens by means of a vote as one of the top ten events for improving the quality of life in Hangzhou.

With respect to the awards given to excellent cultural and artistic works, during the 10th National Fine Arts Exhibition, Zhejiang was given 3 gold awards, 7 silver awards, 20 bronze awards and 21 excellence awards, ranking Zhejiang continuously no. 1 nationwide in the number of awards and the number of selected works. Zhejiang's calligraphers submitted 624 works to participate in the national calligraphy and seal cutting exhibition, 49 people were granted awards, 10 works were given a gold award or the first award; Zhejiang ranked No. 1 nationwide in the number of selected works many times, and stayed ahead nationwide in the overall performance of calligraphy. During the 20th and the 21st National Photographic Art Exhibition,

106 works from Zhejiang were selected, 7 awards were given to Zhejiang, ranking Zhejiang no. 2 nationwide in total scores. During the 9th and 10th International Photographic Art Exhibition, 85 works from Zhejiang were selected, 4 silver awards and 7 bronze awards were given to Zhejiang. In the appraisal and selection for the 4th, 5th and 6th China Photography Golden Statue Award, 5 photographers from Zhejiang were given awards.

With regard to such performing arts as drama, music, dance and Chinese folk art, Zhejiang was given 56 created repertoire awards and other single awards. The singers, concert performers and art performance troupes from Zhejiang were given 8 gold awards, 4 silver awards and 6 bronze awards in national and international vocal music and instrumental performance contests. Regarding choreographic performances, more than 40 choreographic works participated in national dance contests.[2]

7.1.2   2006–2010: Film, Television and Animation Became the Main Fronts for Creating Excellent Works

The creation of excellent cultural works certainly keeps up with the reformation in mindset, carrier and communication mode. Since the 21st century, cultural consumption has increasingly become an important dimension of cultural competitiveness, and has been given the new connotation that creation is people-oriented. The most vivid example is that film and television works fully surpassed stage works in cultural communication and influence, they became one of the most active literary and artistic styles, the most thriving cultural sectors, the most popular literary and artistic works, the most mainstream literary and artistic creations and the hottest social issues; they also started the change from the mechanism of single award incentive evaluation to the mechanism of market-oriented, diversified incentive evaluation.

In 2006, with the purpose of "repaying the audiences and the society", the Zhejiang Radio & TV Group became the first nationwide to hold the China Zhejiang TV Audience Festival, focusing on a series of large themed activities and characteristic cultural and artistic performances, giving prominence to the basic characteristics—participatory, lively, recreational and open, including the Radio & TV Group Open Day, the Interactive Get-together, Intra-city Audience Day, the Audience Carnival, the Passion Theme Evening Party, the Qiantang Gala, and Ten Major Play Presentations. Each time, the TV Audience Festival changed, in a novel and creative manner, the way in which the people participated in and analyzed the public culture relating to radio and television, and created a unique rule regarding media communication.

In 2010, 121 film and television companies were newly registered in Zhejiang; 43 plays (1,500 episodes) were produced, accounting for 1/10 of the national

---

[2]The data materials on Zhejiang's excellent cultural and artistic works over the years come from the Report in the 6th Congress of Zhejiang Federation of Literary and Art Circles (2005) and the Report in the 7th Congress of Zhejiang Federation of Literary and Art Circles (2010).

output of TV plays; there was participation in producing 33 films. Zhejiang's excellent film and TV works have always based value orientation on explicit national mainstream ideology and focused on realistic, revolutionary and historical themes. *The Gate of Sea* was given the national Five-Ones Project award for cultural and ethical development in 2007.

The TV plays produced in Zhejiang in the same period were also frequently given awards in the appraisal and selection for government awards. The TV play *The Great Craftsman*, shown in 2007, was given the national Five-Ones Project award for cultural and ethical development. The TV play *The Wind from the North*, shown in 2008, was given the 11th national Five-Ones Project award for cultural and ethical development and a number of single TV play awards. *The Memories In China* was given the excellent TV play Golden Eagle Award and an award from the Seoul International Drama Awards; the animated film *Zhenghe's Travelling to the West* was given the national Five-Ones Project award for cultural and ethical development.

The film *Super Typhoon*, shown in October, 2008, was jointly shot by the Department of Publicity under the Party Committee of Zhejiang Province, the Department of Publicity under the Party Committee of Wenzhou City, the Department of Publicity under the Party Committee of Taizhou City, the Zhejiang Radio & TV Group and the Zhejiang Film & TV Group, and it was directed by Feng Xiaoning; it was shortlisted at the Tokyo International Film Festival and contended for the Gold Kirin Award in 2008. In 2009, the *Super Typhoon* was given the 11th national Five-Ones Project award for cultural and ethical development and was included in the list of films nominated for excellent films under the Ornamental Column Awards.

The rise of animation, creative and other digital content works served as a connecting link in the transformation of Zhejiang's production of excellent cultural works from the separate operation of single content carriers to a fusion among content media. The earliest base camp for Zhejiang's creation of animation products was Hangzhou. Hangzhou, which strives to become the Paradise Silicon Valley, is the national pilot city for information development, the pilot city for e-commerce, the pilot city for e-government, the pilot city for digital TV and a national software industrialization base and a base for the industrialization of integrated circuit design. The rise of Hangzhou's animation industry also relied on creative talents from the China Academy of Arts, Zhejiang University, Zhejiang University of Media and Communications and other institutions of higher learning. In 2003, the Zhejiang Zoland Group was established, indicating that Zhejiang can compete with Beijing, Guangzhou, Changsha and Shanghai in animation creation.

During the period 2006–2010, Zhejiang's creation of excellent cultural works fully reached a new level amidst the rapid rise of the Zhejiang Film and Television Phenomenon and Zhejiang's animation bases. In the appraisal and selection for the 10th national Five-Ones Project award for cultural and ethical development, 9 works from Zhejiang were selected. At that time, Zhejiang witnessed the largest number of works selected in the appraisal and selection for the national Five-Ones Project award after 1991. The Department of Publicity under the Party Committee of Zhejiang Province was thus given the first prize for its organizational work.

With respect to operas, the Kun opera called *The Public Grandson* was given the Splendor Award; the Yue opera *Five Daughters Offering Felicitation* was given the first excellent repertoire award by the Ministry of Culture; the Kun opera *The Public Grandson* and the Yue opera *The Butterfly Lovers* were included in the Top Ten Excellent Repertoires under the National Project for Excellent Stage Art Works. At the 11th National Fine Arts Exhibition, 260 works from Zhejiang were selected. At the 21st, 22nd and 23rd National Photographic Art Exhibitions and the 12th and 13th International Photographic Art Exhibition, 6 works were given gold awards, and 3 people were granted the 7th China Photography Golden Eagle Award. Regarding Chinese folk art (Quyi), five China Quyi Peony Awards were given.

7.1.3 After 2011: Cyberculture Generated New Creations and a New Dissemination of Digital Content

Creative ideas make sure that cultural creation wins. In about 2011, as a new cultural form, cyberculture gave rise to a huge and complicated social system in which information technology serves as the precursor, the new space-time view and worldview constitute the framework, putting the key and difficult points in the development and management of socialist culture before managers. At this time node, the necessity and urgency for addressing the development of cyberculture in the creation of excellent cultural works was on the rise. With the persistent development of film and television culture for 20 years, the existing pattern of cultural development was subject to adjustment; cyberculture brought about great changes in cultural expression, communication, carrying and fusion, and also showed a great capacity for integration, resulting in a cultural blue ocean with huge potential.

The first factor for building the "new Zhejiang force" for Zhejiang's cyberculture was the creation of online literature in Zhejiang. As a traditional large province of literature, Zhejiang started early in the creation of online literature and has witnessed its rapid development, a large number of people engaged in that creation and a great influence of online literature. According to the incomplete statistics from the Zhejiang Writers Association, at present, nearly 1,000 online literature writers who are natives of Zhejiang are active on major online literature websites, and their creations almost cover the major categories of online literature. In 2008, the (Online) Committee for the Types of Literary Creation of the Zhejiang Writers Association was established, and a creation base which is aimed at cultivating online literature and types of literature, and that covers the whole province was set up. These measures fully reflected keen cultural and artistic organizations and a flexible management structure in Zhejiang and Zhejiang's regional character of blazing new trails and capability for innovation.

Zhejiang's new media products established the benchmark for Zhejiang's creation of excellent works relating to cyberculture. As from the first half of 2013, Internet mobile client resources were arranged rapidly, a new round of online public opinion and the competition for a platform of cultural communication was extremely fierce.

In November, with study and discussions by the Standing Committee of the Party Committee of Zhejiang Province, the New Red Media Construction Project, for which the Zhejiang Daily Press Group is responsible, was initiated; the digital collection and editing center and the core body for the project were established to undertake the group's heavy task of researching and developing new media products and driving the group's integrative development of the media.

On June 16, 2014, two core products in the new media matrix of the Zhejiang Daily Press Group—the Zhejiang News mobile client and Zhejiang Mobile Newspaper (updated version) debuted. The Zhejiang News mobile client is Zhejiang's only authoritative mobile media studied, discussed and unanimously adopted by the Standing Committee of the Party Committee of Zhejiang Province; after it was put into operation, it became the first to release authoritative provincial information; it is an important channel through which Zhejiang can release information on major policies, personnel appointments and removals and respond to emergencies. As the no. 1 platform for Zhejiang's political and economic news, each day, the Zhejiang News mobile client provides the reports on the activities of the main leaders of the Party Committee and the People's Government of Zhejiang Province, and information on the major political, financial, economic and cultural affairs as well as sports within and outside the province; it conveys the Party's voice at the mobile terminal and occupies the commanding height in online public opinion. The Zhejiang Mobile Newspaper is the first provincial-level mobile newspaper in China; after upgrading and revision, the Zhejiang Mobile Newspaper focuses on publicizing the central work of the Party Committee and the People's Government of Zhejiang Province, and is more focused on adopting the elements that are more suitable for mobile reading habits, such as videos, thus greatly enhancing the readability and appeal, and more effectively guiding the dissemination of news and public opinion for mobile phone users.

Another innovative project for Zhejiang's cyberculture platform is the service platform for intelligent information regarding omnimedia fusion which is being promoted by the Zhejiang Daily Press Group. This platform is made up of three main parts: First, a 50-milllion-level user data warehouse, including 6-million reader database resources, 560 million online registered users and more than 40 million active user resources of the Zhejiang Daily Press Group; they are the service objects of the group's full Internet-based integrative development and also the targets of the group's omnimedia product matrix. Second, a specialized content data warehouse, including mass data from the group's omnimedia dynamic collection and an editing resource pool, the omnimedia historical resource pool, the whole-network resource pool (including websites, microblogs, WeChat). Third, the omnimedia intelligent information service platform, including omnimedia intelligent monitoring analyses and clues discovery, the omnimedia fusion collection and editing system, omnimedia fusion release system, covering the open platforms of new media cloud services such as WeChat, e-commerce, microsite APP template service, and such subsystems as application evaluation and the analysis of user behavior. The platform can carry out structured and template-based development of new media applications, and also provides effective guidance and support for new media production within and outside the group.

The project "service platform for intelligent information regarding omnimedia fusion " is planned to be completed within three years. At present, the application for seeking support from the national special fund for culture is being filed for the project. Some experts point out that it is currently the most comprehensive major scientific research project which is addressed by the most profound thinking and planning of a domestic media group for promoting media fusion.

7.2 The Government-Led Cultural Projects Lead Mainstream Values

"A period of great change, great transition, vigorous development and a great leap is a period of new creation, new experiences and new achievements and also a period during which new situations, new problems and new contrasts pop up."[3] This is a sign of social progress and poses new issues and new challenges for literary and art workers.

On November 7, 2005, comrade Xi Jinping attended the 6th Congress of the Zhejiang Federation of Literary and Art Circles, and briefly introduced the great era for contemporary literary and artistic creation. Before stressing the direction that literature and art should take to serve the people and socialism, and the policy of letting all flowers bloom together and a hundred schools of thought contend, he clearly and vigorously set the goal, which features firmer confidence, a deeper and wider vision and a broader mind, for literary and artistic creation: "It is necessary to uphold the guiding role of Marxism in the ideological field, consolidate the common ideological basis for the whole society, the leading values of the state and the cultural and ethical pillar for the nation, uphold the unitarity of the guiding thought and the leading values while recognizing and developing pluralism and diversity, seek the leading role amidst pluralism, form the main body amidst diversity and strive to become the mainstream among multiple choices."[4]

Comrade Xi Jinping required the Party committees and governments at various levels across the province to always uphold and comprehensively carry out the Party's policy for cultural and art work, take the perspective of "enhancing the Party's governance capacity" to deeply understand the important position of "prospering and developing the cultural and artistic cause" in accelerating the building of a culturally large province, and carry out eight projects for cultural development to promote cultural and artistic prosperity and development in Zhejiang.

---

[3]Ren (2004).

[4]Xi (2006), p. 333.

7.2.1   A Great Deal of Attention from the Party Committee and the People's Government of Zhejiang Province Provided Vigorous Support for the Production of Excellent Cultural Works

On September 13, 2014, the result of appraisal and selection for the 13th Five-Ones Project award for cultural and ethical development was unveiled, and 10 works from Zhejiang were given the award, reaching an all-time high. Zhejiang's experience and practices in taking multiple measures to prosper cultural and artistic creation cover the following five respects: First, providing a guidance to creation, strengthening the guiding role of values; second, making scientific plans, intensifying efforts to push forward projects; third, cultivating main players, enhancing market vitality; fourth, promoting team building and increasing talent support; fifth, providing vigorous policy support and strengthening input guarantee.

Since "accelerating the building of a culturally large province" was incorporated into Zhejiang's overall strategy for economic and social development, the Party Committee and the People's Government of Zhejiang Province and the departments at various levels have increased their input into the cultural field, and the whole society has actively participated in cultural development, thus providing important support for Zhejiang's production of excellent cultural works. In recent years, the annual 50 million yuan in a special fund for cultural development has been established through provincial finance; each year, Zhejiang has arranged 15 million yuan for supporting projects of provincial excellent cultural works, 8 million yuan for supporting stage art creation and production of provincial troupes, 10 million yuan for supporting the creation and production of excellent film, television and animation works, and 500,000 yuan for supporting two excellent works projects for literature. Each year, the Zhejiang Radio & TV Group has invested 30 million yuan in film and television creation and production; each year, Hangzhou City (the municipal level) has allocated 30 million yuan from public finance for supporting and rewarding literary and artistic creations. There has been unprecedented enthusiasm from private capital in the creation and production of cultural products; with the reform of the cultural system and the development of the cultural industry, a mechanism for diversified input in the creation and production of cultural products has taken shape. The Party committees and governments at various levels have dedicated more resources to promoting the creation of excellent works, providing a financial guarantee for further pushing forward the creation and development of excellent works.

Based on increasing financial input in major literary and artistic projects, in order to further make the appraisal and selection for literary and artistic awards produce demonstration and incentive effects, Zhejiang has established provincial literary and artistic awards mainly including: the Lu Xun Literature and Art Award, the highest award in Zhejiang's literary and art circles, the Five-Ones Project award under the charge of the Department of Publicity under the Party Committee of Zhejiang Province, the Zhejiang Opera Festival, the Zhejiang Folk Art & Acrobatics Festival, and the Zhejiang Music & Dance Festival under the charge of the Department of

Culture of Zhejiang Province, the TV Program Technology Quality Award under the charge of the Radio and Television Bureau of Zhejiang Province, the Zhejiang Fine Arts Award, the Zhejiang Calligraphy Award, the Zhejiang Photography Golden Statue Award, the Zhejiang TV Peony Award, the Zhejiang Film Phoenix Award, the Zhejiang Drama Award · Jingui Performance Award, the Zhejiang Dance Award, and the Zhejiang Folk Literature and Art Yingshanhong Award under the charge of literature and arts associations within the Zhejiang Federation of Literary and Art Circles, and the Yu Dafu Fiction Award and literature star appraisal and selection under the charge of the Zhejiang Writers Association. These awards have played an active role in the creation of literary and art works and have been gradually valued and supported by various sectors.

With respect to policy support, Zhejiang has continuously adjusted relevant supporting policies in light of actual needs, developed and implemented a number of policy measures, including the *Implementation Measures of Zhejiang for the Excellent Literary and Art Works Support Project*, the *Supporting Incentive Measures of Zhejiang Province for the Five-Ones Project Award*, the *Incentive Measures of Zhejiang Province for the Broadcasting of Excellent TV Plays*, and the *Incentive Measures of Zhejiang Province for Creative Achievements in Literary Periodicals*. Zhejiang has stayed ahead nationwide in the policy concerning humanities and social science. Zhejiang developed the *11th Five-Year Development Plan for Philosophy and Social Science of Zhejiang Province*, and incorporated it into the 11th five-year master plan of Zhejiang Province for development; the *Measures of Zhejiang Province for the Popularization of Science and Technology*, which had been issued and implemented, officially incorporated social science in parallel to science and technology.

7.2.2 The Excellent Cultural Works Support Project Led the Guidance of Creation and Offered the Innovative Platform for Organizational Management

The Excellent Cultural Works Project, initiated in May, 2005, was the project which was launched at the earliest among the "eight projects" for accelerating the building of a culturally large province; the project led the guidance of creation and gathered the resources for creation in a project-based way and offered a supporting platform for generating masterpieces.

The Project of Zhejiang Province for Fine Arts Creation under Major Themes, implemented during the period 2006–2009, is a typical case in which the People's Government of Zhejiang Province made outstanding achievements in financially supporting major projects for the creation of excellent cultural works through government procurement. The project was among the first batch of the intensively supported projects under the Excellent Cultural Works Project of Zhejiang Province. As the main source of funds for the project, the Excellent Cultural Works Project of Zhejiang Province provided 45 million yuan for seeking creators through open tendering in the society; this occurred for the first time among the provinces across the country. In June, 2008, more than 80 huge completed works were observed, examined and approved by the project organizing committee, the arts committee and the group of experts for the National Project for Fine Arts Creation under Major Themes at the Giant-Long art gallery on the Xiangshan Campus of the China Academy of Arts. Among the 100 signed works under the National Project for Fine Arts Creations under Major Historical Themes, 15 works under the Project of Zhejiang Province for Fine Arts Creations under Major Themes were selected, ranking Zhejiang no. 1 among the provinces (autonomous regions, municipalities) across the country in the number of selected works.

During the period 2006–2012, the Excellent Cultural Works Project of Zhejiang Province received more than 900 project applications; with expert review, more than 140 creative projects in 7 batches were supported; they have become important brands for Zhejiang's cultural development. The Excellent Cultural Works Project supported ten categories in five batches, including drama, film, TV plays, radio plays, animated films, literature, music, fine arts and photography; the supported operas included the Yue opera, the Kun opera, the Wu opera, the Shao opera, the dance opera, the acrobatic opera and farce; the financially supported TV plays were created in diverse styles, including epic, realism and romanticism; the supported film creations covered the films produced with high input and on a large scale and TV films produced at low costs and on a small scale; it also supported a number of animated films for TV and brought forth many original animation images; it also financially supported the creation of some animated films; the financially supported projects for literary creations were mostly full-length novels and reportages under revolutionary, historical and realistic themes, and also included collections of poems and collections of essays. The intensively supported Project of Zhejiang Province for Fine Arts Creations under Major Themes delivered spectacular performances in traditional Chinese paintings and oil paintings. The above facts fully reflected the diversity of the Excellent Cultural Works Project in genre, style and form.

Under the Excellent Cultural Works Project, investors in creations were diverse; they included the Zhejiang Radio & TV Group, the Zhejiang Federation of Literary and Art Circles, the institutions of higher learning relating to the arts, the Zhejiang College of Arts, provincial state-owned troupes and other state-owned cultural units, which became the main forces in the Excellent Cultural Works Project. A number of private cultural companies—including the Zhejiang Great Wall Movie and Television Co., Ltd., Zhejiang Huace Film and Television, Hangzhou Southern Pictures Co., Ltd., Zhejiang HG Entertainment, and the Zhejiang Zoland Group—were increasingly passionate about filing applications under the Excellent Cultural Works Project year by year. Individual applications for literary types were also filed in large quantities. For the areas involved in the applications under the Excellent Cultural Works Project, Hangzhou and Ningbo were neck-and-neck and became a highland of creations. Under the Excellent Cultural Works Project, equal treatment was given to state-owned, private and individual applicants, the boundary between the inside and outside of the system was broken, an open, fair and impartial support mode was built, and the possibility to apply was open to the whole society, thus greatly arousing enthusiasm for creation on the part of private enterprises and social individuals.

7.2.3 The Cultural Research Project Became the Top-Level Planning Platform for Promoting Social Science Research in Zhejiang

The Cultural Research Project, separately initiated in the building of a culturally large province in 2005, is a great characteristic of Zhejiang's cultural development. At the provincial level across the country, it was the only large cultural project focusing on academic research at that time. The current achievements in the project prove the great affection of the policymakers of the time regarding the homeland because the successive leading groups carried out concrete work, and Zhejiang's cultural research was elevated to the national level of cultural research,

Zhejiang's Cultural Research Project is one of the important parts of the "eight projects" for Zhejiang's cultural development advocated by comrade Xi Jinping; it is also currently the largest local cultural research project in China. When the project was initiated, he served as the chairman of the steering committee of the project and called for further arousing the infinite wisdom and great creativity of the people of Zhejiang and promoting sound and rapid development in Zhejiang by carrying out Zhejiang's Cultural Research Project. He guided the initial planning for the project, and called for first gaining a better understanding of Zhejiang's culture, then researching the work carried out by comrade Mao Zedong in Zhejiang and its great impact on China's process, and the history of the Republic of China (1912–1949)—half of the history occurred in Zhejiang. He also pointed out that Zhejiang's academic circles should have Zhejiang's style.

As a provincial overarching integrated platform for the philosophy and social science research projects, Zhejiang's Cultural Research Project is aimed at taking the perspective of philosophy and social science to conduct systematic research on Zhejiang's historical culture and contemporary development, and providing the cultural and ethical impetus and intellectual support for further rapid economic and social development in Zhejiang. As a cultural developmental work platform for integrating the power of governments at various levels and the social science research force, it is designed to efficiently mobilize the cultural development resources of governments at various levels and, to the greatest extent, stimulate the humanities and social science groups in various parts of the provinces and from various sectors to conduct scientific research, become a high-level planning platform for building the high-end humanistic research forces within the province.

Zhejiang's Cultural Research Project is fully provided with the function of top-level planning for provincial humanistic and social science research and covers four segments concerning research on Zhejiang's culture—"contemporary issues, ancient times, the people, historical documents"—separately corresponding to the research on the issues concerning Zhejiang's contemporary development, special research on Zhejiang's historical culture, the research on Zhejiang's celebrities, and the reorganization of Zhejiang's historical documents. Regarding the content of the research, actions were taken to tap Zhejiang's cultural deposits, systematically analyze the internal structure of Zhejiang's historical culture, its changing laws and regional characteristics and uphold and develop the Zhejiang Spirit; there were also actions taken to do research on the similarities and differences between Zhejiang's culture and the culture in other areas, clarify the position of Zhejiang's culture within Chinese culture and their interplay and proceed from the vivid contemporary practice in Zhejiang to deeply analyze the Zhejiang Phenomenon, summarize the Zhejiang Experience and guide Zhejiang's development.

The project contained a number of subjects for research involving major theories and countermeasures for realistic problems in Zhejiang's social development; after initiation in 2005, the tendering for provincial major research subjects relating to social science was conducted to carry out surveys on the realistic problems with Zhejiang's characteristics concerning social development, social policy and social management; each year, several topics were chosen, prominence was given to the characteristics of Zhejiang's development, careful surveys were conducted with respect to major issues and social developments which were of great referential significance for national development, thus providing theoretical support for the Party Committee and the People's Government of Zhejiang Province to make great decisions and continue staying ahead nationwide.

The research achievements in the research on and inheritance of traditional culture are prominent. In December, 2005, *The General History of Zhejiang* (12 Volumes) was published by Zhejiang People's Publishing House. With more than 5.80 million words, the book systematically and comprehensively narrates, for the first time, Zhejiang's history and civilization covering about 7,000 years from the Jiande people in the Neolithic Age, especially the Hemudu Culture, to the founding of the People's Republic of China. During its writing, many departments worked together, a number of scholars conducted key research, the experts and scholars, within and outside the province, in history, economics, sociology, culturology, archaeology, geography and the reorganization of historical documents participated in writing and reviewing the book, while local departments of research on historical material at various levels, libraries, museums, relevant departments and forces involving chorography and from various sectors of the society across the province assisted with the work. *The General History of Zhejiang* was given the special award—the 15th Zhejiang Shuren Publication Award in the year of publication and the 1st China Publication Government Award (National Book Award) in 2007.

The Collection of Zhejiang's Literature is currently the largest publication project regarding local literature and reorganization in China; it contains a rich range of content, covers extensive fields and has a long period of research; it results from efforts from a large number of participants. In April, 2006, the People's Government of Zhejiang Province officially approved the inclusion of the Zhejiang Literature Integration and Compilation Center into the Key Humanities and Social Science

Research Base of Zhejiang Province for the management of the project. In the meantime, 18 literature reorganization projects undertaken by the Zhejiang Literature Integration and Compilation Center—including the *Complete Works of Hu Yinglin*, the *Complete Works of Yu Dafu*, the *Complete Works of Zhang Xuecheng*, and the *Complete Works of Chen Wangdao*—were identified as projects. The Zhejiang Literature Integration and Compilation Center at Zhejiang University is the subplatform for the segment—reorganization of Zhejiang's historical documents, and it made joint efforts to develop and release the annual list of selected topics, carry out integrated planning and unified publication. Thanks to the working structure of the Zhejiang Literature Reorganization and Publication Project and the Literature Compilation Center, the overall advantages from the disciplines, talents and external academic influence of Zhejiang University were actively leveraged; the research characteristics of teaching and scientific research units, famous colleges and universities, functional departments and various areas within the province were brought together; the intellectual resources of scholars within and outside the province, at home and abroad were fully utilized; the mechanism of the management of scientific research, the working mechanism and the talent operations mechanism which were more consistent with the law of the development of social science were established.

In nine years since the initiation of Zhejiang's Cultural Research Project, the leaders of the Party Committee and the People's Government of Zhejiang Province have given great importance to the cultural research project, the main leaders of the Party Committee of Zhejiang Province served as the chairman of the steering committee successively, and gave important instructions about the formulation and implementation of the plan for the cultural research project on many occasions. The cultural research project is so far the largest social science research plan in Zhejiang, a total of 60 million yuan was planned to be allocated from provincial finances, stimulating teaching and scientific research institutions, cities and counties to mobilize more than 60 million yuan, so the actual expenditure was more than 52 million yuan. Zhejiang's Cultural Research Project also produced strong demonstration and driving effects, the cities (counties) reorganized, tapped and researched regional culture accordingly, Wenzhou, Ningbo, Jinhua and Yiwu reorganized and published local historical documents. The project execution exerted an active impact within and outside the province, and Beijing, Guangdong, Yunnan and Shandong all drew upon experience from Zhejiang.

The implementation of the cultural research project established the orientation of values for Zhejiang's cultural development, so that learning and drawing upon excellent cultural achievements in ancient and modern times, at home and abroad, extensive cultural research became a main part of efforts in promoting Zhejiang's cultural development. The execution of the project expanded the working pattern of Zhejiang's cultural development and further strengthened the master plan, resource integration and system development for Zhejiang's philosophy and social science research; it also pushed forward and led to the establishment of a system of management and a working mechanism consistent with the law of philosophy and social science development; it expanded and upgraded Zhejiang's philosophy and social science research, gave rise to a number of academic achievements with significant academic influence and good social benefits, an academic echelon with high-caliber academic leaders, a number of key disciplines and academic brands concerning philosophy and social science with Zhejiang's characteristics, thus prospering and developing Zhejiang's philosophy and social sciences and enhancing Zhejiang's cultural soft power.

7.3 Being Market-Oriented, Building a Connection Between Cultural Programs and the Cultural Industry

On July 18, 2003, when attending the meeting of Zhejiang Province on the reform of the cultural system and the building of a culturally large province, comrade Xi Jinping pointed out, "In order to build a culturally large province, it is necessary to fully leverage the advantages of the socialist economic system, create and produce the cultural products close to the reality, life and the people, catering to the needs of the drive towards modernization, of the world and of the future, so as to occupy the market, win the people over, and continuously consolidate and expand the socialist ideological front".[5] Under the new situation of the reform of the cultural program and the development of the cultural industry, he raised higher requirements for Zhejiang's creation of excellent literary and artistic works: "The ideological attribute of cultural products is consistent with the industrial attribute, the occupation of the market is consistent with that of the front, and social benefits are consistent with economic benefits."[6]

The reform of the cultural system is aimed at building a connection between cultural programs and the cultural industry, clarifying the boundary between the government and the market in cultural development and promoting the institutional reform in state-owned cultural units to make them serve as the backbone force in the protection of excellent cultural works.

7.3.1 The State-Owned Cultural Enterprises Became the Main Forces for Creating Excellent Works Within the Market

The restructured state-owned cultural enterprises led the way in creating excellent works of Zhejiang's plays to deliver win-win outcomes in the appraisal and selection for awards and the market. In December, 2004, the Zhejiang Film & TV Group, wholly owned and operated by the Zhejiang Radio & TV Group, was founded. In a decade, with the production of excellent film and TV works featuring a grand pattern

---

[5]Xi (2006), p. 332.
[6]Xi (2006), p. 332.

and a great vision, the Zhejiang Film & TV Group obtained both social and economic benefits.

The TV play series *China 1921* is regarded as the model for which "red plays become popular"; it is another excellent work of Zhejiang's plays produced at the major festivals and historical hubs of the Party and the state, following *The Rebirth of Zhejiang Businesses amidst a Crisis*. In 2011, CCTV purchased the right to premiere *China 1921* across the country at a price of 1 million yuan and broadcast it as the first gift to the 90th anniversary of the founding of the CPC. On the first day of broadcasting, it ranked no. 1 in audience rating among all satellite channels in the same period of time. The Zhejiang Film & TV Group is a model of Zhejiang's state-owned cultural enterprises in proactively and consciously disseminating culture, producing excellent film and TV works, and assuming social responsibilities.

In 2003, the Zhejiang United Publishing Group was designated as the national pilot unit for the reform of the cultural system. In late 2006, the Zhejiang United Publishing Group became the first among 25 provincial-level publishing groups nationwide to complete overall restructuring; it ranked no. 2 nationwide in total assets, net assets and sales revenue. As of late 2013, the Group's assets totaled 13.9 billion yuan, its total sales volume reached 15.8 billion yuan, and its main business income was 10.7 billion yuan; it published more than 8,300 types of books, and reached new levels in various operational indicators.

Since the period of the 12th Five-Year Plan, the series of books on intangible cultural heritage, *The Cambridge History of Africa* introduced by the Zhejiang People's Publishing House was incorporated into the national 12th five-year plan for the publication of key books; the *Album of National Rejuvenation under the Leadership of the Communist Party of China* was chosen as one of the key topics for greeting the 18th National Congress of the Communist Party of China; the *Mass Line and Intra-party Educational Activity* was chosen as one of the key publication topics for publicizing and carrying out the guiding principles adopted during the 18th National Congress of the Communist Party of China; the *Dictionary of Mao Zedong's Works* was given the nomination award of the 4th Chinese Excellent Publication Award, and the 3rd China Publication Government Award. The *Complete Works of Chinese Printing* (30 volumes) and the *Complete Works of Chinese Folk Fine Arts*, jointly published by the Zhejiang People's Fine Arts Publishing House and the Cultural Relics Publishing House, were given the national book award's honorary award; the *Complete Works of Huang Binhong* (10 volumes), published in cooperation with the Shandong Fine Arts Publishing House, was given the 1st China Publication Government Award; the publication of the *Complete Works of Lu Yanshao* (6 volumes) and the *Complete Works of Pan Tianshou* (6 volumes) improved the publication system of the complete works type of the group of excellent works. Four projects (involving 44 books) published by the Zhejiang Juvenile and Children's Publishing House, including the *Shen Shixi Legendary Stories of Endangered Animals*, were included in the national 12th five-year plan; the *Seed of Faith* was chosen by the State Administration of Press, Publication, Radio, Film and Television as of one of the key publication topics under the guiding principles adopted during the 18th National Congress of the Communist Party of China; two types of books, including the *Modern History of China (Drawing*

Book), were included in the 100 excellent books recommended to juveniles across the country by the Department of Publicity under the Communist Party of China, the Ministry of Education and the Central Committee of the Communist Young League; the *I Become an Invisible Man* was given the book nomination award of the 3rd China Publication Government Awards; three types of books, including the *Good! My First Set of Inspirational Books*, were included in the 100 excellent books recommended to juveniles across the country by the State Administration of Press, Publication, Radio, Film and Television. A number of series published by the Zhejiang Literature & Art Publishing House, including the *Complete Series of Poetic Prose from Chinese Modern Writers of Classics*, the *Collected Translations of Classic Impressions*, the *Series of Scholarly Prose*, and the *A Collection of Centurial Papers*, were the best-selling excellent works for building up literature and arts publications. Key books published by the Zhejiang Ancient Books Publishing House—including the *Complete Works of Huang Zongxi*, the *Complete Works of Li Yu*, the *Collected Works of Ma Yifu*, the *Collected Works of Xia Chengtao*, the *Complete Works of Song Lian*, the *Dictionary of the Names and Aliases of Chinese Figures in Modern Times*, the *History of Chinese Printing*, the *Le Sac du Palais d'Eté*, the *Series of Works from Writers in Zhejiang and Jiangsu*, and the *Series of Books on the History of Chinese Fiction*—have built up a strong market influence and professional influence. The Group, the Juvenile and Children's Publishing House, the Education Publishing House, the Zhejiang Xinhua Bookstore Group and Huashuo Co., Ltd. were identified as the national key cultural export enterprises by six ministries, including the Department of Publicity under the Communist Party of China, the Ministry of Commerce and the General Administration of Press and Publications.

Thanks to embodying the national level and ethnic characteristics, the Zhejiang Xiaobaihua Yue Opera Troupe became the only state-owned cultural and arts troupe in China's Yue Opera circles. In 2013, the Zhejiang Xiaobaihua Yue Opera Troupe was listed among 39 key national troupes for local opera creations and performances; it is the only troupe given such a laurel in the Yue Opera circles.

7.3.2 The Private Cultural Enterprises Became the Surfers in the Production of Excellent Cultural Works

The Hengdian Group is the forerunner engaged in the cultural industry among Zhejiang's private enterprises. As Zhejiang was identified as the national pilot province for the reform of the cultural system in late 2003, the Hengdian Group started its journey of transformation to build the Hengdian Film and Television Industry Experimental Area which is in the charge of a government department and focuses on enterprise development, and to achieve leapfrog development from a film and television base, a film and television cultural tourism enterprise to a film and television platform for factor agglomeration. In ten years, many famous film and television enterprises, including Huayi Brothers, Enlight Media, and Hong Kong Chinese Movie, entered the Experimental Area; it is reputed as China's Hollywood.

With nearly ten years of development, as one of Zhejiang's private film and television cultural enterprises, the Zhejiang Huace Film and Television Co., Ltd., which emerged in October, 2005, has come out on top in the production and exportation of excellent film and television works. In 2010, Zhejiang Huace Film and Television was successfully listed on the Shenzhen GEM; it has become a leading enterprise with the greatest brand influence which has ranked no. 1 in the annual film and television output and market share in the domestic film and television industry. It has been rated as the national key cultural export enterprise four consecutive times.

Zhejiang's market platform for creating excellent film and television works achieved leapfrog development in 2013. China (Hangzhou) TV Play Autumn Fair was moved from Beijing to Hangzhou for the first time, attracting more than 1,200 participants—including those from more than 300 domestic and foreign TV play production bodies, including Huace Film and Television, China Film Group Corporation, Huayi Brothers, Enlight Media, Galloping Horse, Hong Kong TVB, Now TV, from 125 TV stations (channels), new media, and the leaders at various levels from relevant departments, scriptwriters, directors, scholars and experts, elites from the production and broadcasting industries, and audience representatives, with an exhibition of 17,700 episodes. It reached new levels in meeting the scale and the number of copyright transactions. The 1st International Professional Film Festival in Zhejiang was held during this fair, drawing a great deal of attention from the industry and media; it has become the new symbol of Zhejiang's cultural brand value and influence.

7.4 Pooling Talents, Building the "Zhejiang Force" in the Cultural Industry

On October 19, 2005, at the ceremony of awarding certificates to the first batch of more than 30 special-class experts in Zhejiang, comrade Xi Jinping pointed out, "It was necessary to more rapidly cultivate a high-caliber expert group, promote the building of high-level talents, further foster an atmosphere of respecting four aspects, enhance Zhejiang's ability to attract and gather various types of talents, and give full scope to the role of high-level talents, providing human resources and intellectual support for Zhejiang in doing concrete work and staying ahead."[7]

On November, 7, when attending the 6th Congress of the Zhejiang Federation of Literary and Art Circles, comrade Xi Jinping once again paid attention to talent work by calling for cultivating Zhejiang's literary and art celebrities and building the "Zhejiang literary and artistic force" in the literary and art circles. He said, "An outstanding literary and artistic force is the foundation for achieving the prosperity and

---

[7]The Ceremony of Awarding Certificates to Special-class Experts in Zhejiang Was Held in Hangzhou, *Zhejiang Daily*, October 20, 2005, p. 1.

development of literature and art". Pursuing both professional excellence and moral integrity is the scientific summary of the path for all outstanding artists to achieve success and also the expectation and requirement of the Party and the country for literary and artistic workers. We should pay close attention to the reality of Zhejiang's literary and arts development, bring about innovations to the working method, explore the new ways to performing industrial services and practicing industrial self-discipline, vigorously advocate both professional excellence and moral integrity, cultivate a number of nationally influential literary and artistic celebrities and great masters, and build the "Zhejiang literary and artistic force" which contains young, middle-aged and old artists, professionals and amateurs, and various types of literary and artistic talents".[8]

7.4.1 Building a Number of High-Level Leading Figures and Teams in the Cultural Field

In 2005, the "five-batch" talent project was initiated in Zhejiang's cultural publicity circles. The project focused on choosing and cultivating a batch of theoretical experts who have an overall grasp of the Deng Xiaoping Theory, the Important Thought of Three Represents, enjoy high academic attainments and attach importance to the reality, a batch of famous journalists, editors and hosts who uphold the correct direction, go deep into life and are popular among the people, a batch of publication experts who are familiar with the Party and the country's policies, have a strong sense of social responsibility and are proficient in professional work, a batch of writers and artists who closely follow the pace of the times, love the country and the people and are at a high artistic level, and a batch of cultural operational and managerial experts who know the law of the development of cultural publicity and the law of market operations. The project was mainly aimed at cultivating and supporting the young and middle-aged backbone literary and artistic talents below the age of 50; since its implementation in 2005, appraisal and selection has been conducted every two years, it has led to the selection and cultivation of 279 leading figures and backbone talents in the press, publications, literature, art, social science and in the management of cultural operations in four batches, and they have made active contributions to Zhejiang's cultural publicity work through their posts.

Zhejiang started the building of key teams for innovation (of the cultural innovation type) in 2009, with a focus on enhancing the capability for cultural innovation in four respects including talents, platforms, projects and the environment. Zhejiang has selected teams of cultural innovation from the institutions of higher learning, social science research, creative culture, press and publication, and public cultural service bodies across the country, and has endeavored to build and support a number of domestic first-class teams with an agglomeration of innovative talents, a flexible mechanism for innovation, a strong capability for sustained innovation and apparent

---

[8]Xi (2006), p. 335.

innovative performances. Each year, 15 teams of cultural innovation are selected, the period is three years, and 65 teams of cultural innovation have been selected. Certain funds from Zhejiang's provincial finance have been provided for the selected teams and have been used to support talent cultivation within the teams and surveys, research, project research and development, platform building and academic exchanges in the main directions. The teams for innovation generally carry out work with the leading figures as the core on the basis of teamwork, certain platforms and projects according to the clear goals and tasks of innovation.

7.4.2 The Young Talent Development Series of Projects with Zhejiang's Distinctive Characteristics

Zhejiang's young talent development series of projects focus on strengthening the strategic development of talents, enhancing Zhejiang's future talent competitiveness, continuously intensifying the cultivation of young cultural artistic talents, and reinforcing the development of young cultural artistic talents on the basis of continuing to implement the Zhijiang Young Scholar Cultivation Plan, the Xinsong Plan for Young Artistic Talents and to standardize the appraisal and selection of Young Literary Stars. Each year, Zhejiang has chosen and nurtured young talents below the age of 35 with a great potential for development in the field of cultural publicity.

The appraisal and selection of the Zhejiang Young Literary Stars by the Zhejiang Writers Association was conducted early on; it is the highest honor for young writers in Zhejiang. Since its initiation in 2009, it has been carried out once a year, and a young literary star has been selected every time. In 16 years, 16 Zhejiang Young Literary Stars were selected through appraisal; most of them have become active forces in China's literary circles and the backbone forces in Zhejiang's literary circles.

Regarding the cultivation of artistic talents, the Xinsong Plan for cultivating young artistic talents in Zhejiang, carried out by the Department of Culture of Zhejiang Province, has always been very active and has produced extraordinary effects. Since 2005, each year 2 million yuan in special funds have been allocated to cultivate and support nearly 200 young creators and performers, and a certain number of effects have been produced. So far, Zhejiang's outstanding artistic talents have been given the Splendor Award by the Ministry of Culture 74 times and the China Plum Blossom Award for Drama 27 times.

The Zhijiang Action Plan for Young Social Science Scholars taken by Zhejiang is Zhejiang's innovative practice in cultivating young talents in research on humanities and social science. Since its implementation in 2011, according to the *Implementation Scheme for the Zhijiang Action Plan for Young Social Science Scholars (2011–2015)* developed by the Zhejiang Federation of Humanities and Social Sciences Circles, the appraisal and selection of Zhijiang Young Social Science Scholars and Teams has been carried out twice, with each period being three years. For Zhijiang Young Social Science Scholars and Teams, the Zhejiang Federation of Humanities and

Social Sciences Circles has developed the cultivation supporting strategies for project research, learning and research, academic exchanges, tutoring, and it has specially organized a variety of academic discussion, exchange training and survey activities, while relevant units have provided 1:1 subject research funds, offered support in scientific research conditions and a time guarantee, and it has organized and held the Youth Academic Forum on a regular basis.

During the period 2011–2012, the Department of Publicity under the Party Committee of Zhejiang Province, in conjunction with the Department of Human Resources and Social Security of Zhejiang Province, and the Zhejiang Federation of Literary and Art Circles, carried out an activity of provincial appraisal, selection and commendation for the young and middle-aged professionally and artistically excellent workers. The activity is conducted every two years and not more than 20 workers are selected through appraisal every time.

7.4.3 Fully Mobilizing Various Forces to Participate in Selecting Folk Literary and Artistic Talents

To intensify the cultivation and support of the talents outside the system, as from 2009, Zhejiang has carried out the *Provincial Administrative Measures for the Cultivation of Folk Literary and Artistic Talents*, calling for cultivating and supporting the outstanding folk artists who master certain cultural skills, have professional attainments, are widely recognized in the industry, socially influential and have the spirit of dedication, the representative inheritors of intangible cultural heritage and the popular literary and artistic workers with outstanding contributions. A batch of these personages are selected and supported every 2–3 years, with each batch including about 1,000 personages; the number of the selected personages is expected to reach about 3,000 by 2015. At present, the selection of the first batch of 988 outstanding folk literary and artistic talents and the second batch of 949 have been completed. For the selected personages, the provincial information archives for outstanding folk literary and artistic talents have been established, a one-time cultural allowance has been provided, a platform has been built, and folk artists have been cultivated through professional teaching and institutional inheritance. A large number of outstanding nationally influential folk artistic talents have been received as provincial-level talents.

7.4.4 A Flexible Plan for the Introduction of Talents

The introduction of talents relies on the strength and appeal of cities. For Zhejiang's introduction of cultural talents, Hangzhou, the capital of Zhejiang Province, is the most popular; it has introduced two famous writers, Yu Hua and Mai Jia. Hangzhou introduces talents in a flexible way, talents can settle in Hangzhou, or stay in Hangzhou for a short time, or engage in project cooperation. During the period 2007–2010, Hangzhou set up studios for Yu Hua, Mai Jia and Liu Heng, and provided special housing for literary and artistic talents; the government also allocated tens of millions of yuan in special funds for introducing and rewarding literary and artistic talents and as a settling-in allowance for literary and artistic talents. With the implementation of these policies, Yu Hua has returned to and settled in Hangzhou, his native place, and has become a professional writer of the Hangzhou Federation of Literary and Art Circles; Ma Jia has settled in Hangzhou; Han Meilin has built the Han Meilin Art Museum in Hangzhou and donated about 1,000 artistic works to Hangzhou. Besides introducing artists, Hangzhou has also carried out the Young Literary and Artistic Talent Discovery Plan, and established the special discovery fund; each year, Hangzhou has assigned 5–8 people to foreign countries for further study and 10–15 people for taking temporary posts at the primary level.

7.5 Making Culture Go Global to Demonstrate the Zhejiang Style of Zhejiang's Culture

In order to bring innovations to the mode of making culture go global, it is first necessary to have a very conscious awareness of cultural themes; only in this way can cultural products be really attractive and can soft power be formed in international cultural competition. Leveraging diplomatic activities and economic and trade fairs is a traditional effective way to showcasing the regional cultural landscape.

On May 9, 2006, the 2006 U.S. China Zhejiang Week activity was inaugurated in New York; in the opening ceremony, comrade Xi Jinping delivered the keynote speech entitled "Sharing Opportunities, Jointly Seeking Development"; he expounded Zhejiang's relatively developed market economic system, its advantageous location in opening-up, great industrial advantages, apparent environmental advantage, and the advantage in coordinated urban and rural development, as well as its unique humanistic advantage. These advantages have laid a good foundation for Zhejiang's development and have also provided opportunities, platforms and made a way for expanding the mutually beneficial cooperation between and the common development of China and the USA. In the opening ceremony, 63 investment projects were signed, with a total investment of USD 2.49 billion and a contractual foreign investment of USD 1.02 billion. During the Zhejiang Week, 20 cooperation agreements covering tourism, education, finance and transportation were signed, and the U.S. China Zhejiang Cultural Week activity was also carried out, a series of activities including special acrobatic performances, photographic picture shows, and TV exhibition shows were carried out.[9]

---

[9]The U.S. China Zhejiang Week Activity Was Inaugurated in New York, *Zhejiang Daily*, May 11, 2006, p. 1.

7.5.1 The Formation of the Basic Framework for Making Zhejiang's Culture Go Global

As from 2007, the Department of Commerce of Zhejiang Province added the content of "supporting the development of trade in services, expanding cultural exportations" to the foreign trade and economic promotion policy system, and provided financial support to the key cultural export enterprises for expanding the international market. In 2008, the Ministry of Commerce officially arranged a special fund for cultural exportations, which is used to support different areas in expanding the exportation of cultural products and services; four projects in Zhejiang were approved and supported by the Ministry of Commerce.

With nearly ten years of development, the pattern and working mechanism of cultural trading with the government playing the leading role and social participation has basically taken shape in Zhejiang. With the leading forces of the provincial and local governments, Zhejiang has actively created a number of excellent external cultural works with Chinese characteristics at the international level, and has built up an impetus for making culture go global.

With efforts in intensifying the reform of the cultural system, Zhejiang has focused on supporting a number of the emerging cultural sectors and key cultural export enterprises, developed and issued the *Several Opinions on Further Improving the Cultural Economic Policy and Promoting the Building of a Culturally Large Province*, and the *Administrative Measures of Zhejiang Province for the Guiding Catalogue for the Exportation of Cultural Products at Commercial Performance Exhibitions*.

7.5.2 "Delivering" Culture to the Outside World: "Connect Zhejiang" and the Zhejiang Cultural Week Offer Inter-governmental Platforms

"Connect Zhejiang" is a brand carefully built up by Zhejiang for external news and cultural exchanges and as a means of external publicity; it is aimed at creating a channel for disseminating Zhejiang's culture to the outside world, which tallies with Zhejiang's developmental reality, the needs and the thinking habit of foreign audiences. "Connect Zhejiang" is jointly held by the Office of External Publicity under the Party Committee of Zhejiang Province and the Foreign Affairs Office of Zhejiang Province; since 1999, each year, it has invited the mainstream personages from the foreign press and cultural circles to Zhejiang to carry out field inspection and interviews, engaging in interaction and exchanges, and experiencing the changes in Zhejiang's economic and social development. In the meantime, with guests as the communication channels, Zhejiang has showcased its tremendous achievements in reform, opening-up and economic development and it has built a good image.

Initiated in 2005, the Zhejiang Cultural Festival is the leading project for further international exchanges and demonstrations of Zhejiang's culture. In 2009, the Zhejiang Cultural Festival entered Latin America for the first time; it was sponsored by the Government of Baja California, Mexico and the People's Government of Zhejiang Province, organized by the Department of Culture of Baja California, Mexico and the Department of Culture of Zhejiang Province and co-organized by the China National Silk Museum. The Cultural Festival consisted of a silk exhibition, the Zhejiang Folk Photographic Exhibition, a painting and calligraphy exhibition and a variety show dominated by acrobatics and magic. Zhejiang and Baja California assigned a large number of journalists for news coverage of the event. The cultural demonstrations mainly covered Chinese paper cutting, Hangzhou's embroidery, boxwood carvings, Dongyang's bamboo weaving, Pujiang's wheat straw patchwork, West Lake silk parasols, silk brocade, Xiaoshan's lace, Wangxingji's fans, Xiangshan's bamboo root carving, Longquan's treasured swords, Wenzhou's powder molding, Wenzhou's figured silk fabrics and other intangible cultural heritages from Zhejiang.

7.5.3 "Selling" Culture to the Outside World: The Country's Leadership in the Exportation of Cultural Products and Services

According to the statistics in a relevant catalogue of cultural products and services, the total amount of Zhejiang's exports of cultural products and services was USD 1 billion in 2002, it reached USD 2,741 million in 2006 and increased to USD 4.1 billion in 2008, an average annual increase of 26.8%; they were exported to more than 180 countries and territories around the world. Seventeen enterprises and 28 projects in Zhejiang were included in the national key cultural export enterprises and key cultural export projects during the period 2009–2010, accounting for 8.1% and 12.4% of the national ones, respectively.

First, the Zhejiang Publishing Group was the absolute main force in book exportation and copyright trade. In 2013, the Zhejiang Publishing Group exported 300 types of copyrights, delivering USD 6 million in income. The Oriental Publishing House, a publishing organ in France, preliminarily began to shape the scale of publication and publication characteristics. The Tokyo branch of the Group started operations. The British branch of the Oriental Publishing House prepared to be built. The overseas website and chain of Bookuu Book Mall were developed in an orderly fashion, which had laid a good foundation in the USA and Taiwan and had started to explore business in Africa and South America. For co-publishing in Africa, two series—African agriculture and healthcare—had covered four languages, with cooperation in 10–20 countries including Mali, Namibia, Tanzania, Kenya, Rwanda, Sierra Leone, Ethiopia, Sudan, Zimbabwe, Equatorial Guinea, Nigeria and South Africa. The scientific teaching materials concerning middle schools were exported to Malaysia and entered full-time middle schools. The mathematics teaching material involving middle schools entered Hong Kong, while that concerning primary schools was published in French for Africa. The Group made breakthroughs in B2C sales on global mainstream e-book platforms, B2B sales at overseas digital libraries and e-book sales on overseas wireless operator platforms. Intense cooperation with U.S. Amazon continued to be promoted rapidly, and cartoons entered the Japanese mainstream mobile reading platforms.

Based on a year-by-year increase in Zhejiang's foreign copyright trade, the new cooperation mode under which domestic and foreign publishing houses jointly planned topics, worked together in editing, processing and distribution also emerged. In 2013, the English edition of *The History of Chinese Printing* debuted at the Gutenberg Printing Museum. For the series of Mai Jia's works, 24 types of copyrights had been exported, arousing a strong reaction on the European and U.S. markets and in the mainstream media.

Second, significant progress was made in the overseas launch of TV programs, the overseas distribution of digital newspapers, and the exportation of film, TV and animation products. For instance, the overseas center of the Zhejiang Radio & TV Group launched international channels in Europe and the USA, with monthly fixed broadcasting of about 550 min self-produced overseas radio and TV programs. Zhejiang's film and television production organizations and animation enterprises endeavored to exploit the overseas market, with total sales surpassing USD 4 million, bringing Zhejiang to the forefront nationwide.

Third, overseas commercial literary and artistic exhibition shows were started regularly. The Zhejiang Folk Art & Acrobatics General Troupe performed such programs as *The Story of Hangzhou*, *The Stitching of Happiness*, and the *Exotic Paradise* on more than 400 occasions in Europe and the USA, with audiences for more than 700,000 person-times.[10]

Fourth, the building of a super-large trading platform was the country's leading project. Established in 2006, the China Yiwu Cultural Products Expo was rated as the most influential cultural industry exposition brand in China in 2008; in 2010, it was upgraded to be the only national-level foreign trade-oriented exposition in the cultural and sports industry organized by the Ministry of Culture and the People's Government of Zhejiang Province and co-organized by the Department of Culture of Zhejiang Province and the People's Government of Yiwu City; it was identified by the Ministry of Culture as one of the exposition brands intensively supported during the period of the 12th Five-Year Plan. In 2014, the 9th China Yiwu Cultural Products Expo was held by identifying the China Council for Promotion of International Trade as an additional organizer and the expo was officially renamed the China (Yiwu) Cultural Products Trade Fair; it has become an important platform for the trading of Chinese cultural products, an important window for Sino-foreign cultural exchanges, making contributions to promoting the development of the cultural industry and making Chinese culture go global.

---

[10]Zhang and Zhao (2009).

References

Ren Zhongping, On Closeness in Three Respects – Being Close to Reality, Life and the People, *People's Daily*, December 17, 2004, p. 1.

Xi Jinping, *Carrying out Concrete Work to Stay Ahead – Line of Thought and Practice in Promoting New Development in Zhejiang*, The Party School of the CPC Central Committee Press, 2006.

Zhang Qianjiang, Zhao Zhizhan, Foreign Cultural Trade: a New Strategic Engine – Some Thinking of Zhejiang's Strategy for the Development of Foreign Cultural Trade, *Zhejiang Economy*, 2009(21).

Chapter 8
Folk Culture: Cultural Belongingness and the Source of Impetus for Social Cohesion

Xibiao Wu and Junjie Wei

As a Chinese saying goes, southeastern China abounds in wealth, Zhejiang and Jiangsu boast a galaxy of talents. It demonstrates the advantages of the region of Jiangsu and Zhejiang in the economic, cultural and other areas since the Song Dynasty (960–1279). Since the reform and opening-up, Zhejiang has been economically developed and culturally prosperous, and has become a culturally large province and a culturally strong province in China. The prosperity and development of folk culture in nearly ten years shows the brilliant achievements in building Zhejiang into a culturally large province and a culturally strong province.

When delivering a speech during the meeting held by the Zhejiang Federation of Literary and Art Circles in 2005, comrade Xi Jinping pointed out, "In an effort to make Zhejiang's literature and art prosper and develop, it is essential to be close to the reality, life and the people, this is the call of the times and the people's needs; the reality is the foundation, life is the source, the people are the starting point and the ultimate goal; the reality, life and the people are always the vitality, charm, value and significance of excellent works". The leaders of the Party committees and governments at various levels in Zhejiang have carefully carried out the principles expounded in the speeches delivered by comrade Xi Jinping, they have paid attention to the reality to incessantly meet the people's cultural and living needs, they have endeavored to promote the prosperity and development of folk culture, achieve active inheritance of intangible cultural heritages, give shape to a variety of folk cultural organizations, and conduct various mass cultural activities. In the general preface to *A Series of Books on the Achievements in Zhejiang's Cultural Research Project*, comrade Xi Jinping said, "Culture offers the norms, ways and environment for the people's life, culture plays the basic role in social progress through inheritance, cultural can promote or inhibit the development of the economy, and even of the society; the power of culture has been deeply rooted in the vitality, creativity and cohesive force of the nation."

X. Wu (✉) · J. Wei
Quzhou College, Quzhou, China

© Social Sciences Academic Press and Springer Nature Singapore Pte Ltd. 2019
D. Xie and Y. Chen (eds.), *Chinese Dream and Practice in Zhejiang – Culture*,
Research Series on the Chinese Dream and China's Development Path,
https://doi.org/10.1007/978-981-13-7216-2_8

8.1 Active Inheritance of Intangible Cultural Heritages

Protecting and inheriting the historical and cultural heritages is an important part of General Secretary Xi Jinping's cultural developmental thoughts and also the indispensable important practice in realizing the Chinese dream. When working in Zhejiang, comrade Xi Jinping expounded this important thought early on, and this thought was practiced feasibly. In early 2005, comrade Xi Jinping gave five important instructions concerning strengthening the protection of Zhejiang's intangible cultural heritages, suggesting the high degree of attention that he gave to the protection of intangible cultural heritages. On June 10, 2006—the Cultural Heritage Day—comrade Xi Jinping further gave a clear instruction, calling for strengthening the protection of Zhejiang's cultural heritages and the inheritance of fine cultural traditions. With the ambitious goal of building Zhejiang into a culturally large province, Zhejiang's cultural circle has more rapidly protected and inherited intangible cultural heritages and has always stayed ahead nationwide in list building, policy formulation, team building and other fields. The reasons why Zhejiang can stay ahead nationwide in protecting and inheriting intangible cultural heritages are as follows: First, the successive Party committees and governments of Zhejiang Province, represented by comrade Xi Jinping, gave a great deal of importance to their protection and inheritance; second, a scientific and effective mechanism for protecting intangible cultural heritages took shape; third, the people of Zhejiang gradually participated more and more in protecting intangible cultural heritages.

8.1.1 The Government-Led Mechanism for the Protection of Intangible Cultural Heritage

In October, 2003, UNESCO adopted the *Convention for the Safeguarding of Intangible Cultural Heritage*; the expression "intangible cultural heritage" began to be used in the international community. On March 26, 2005, the General Office of the State Council issued the *Opinions of the General Office of the State Council on Strengthening the Protection of China's Intangible Cultural Heritages*; since then, China has adopted the expression "intangible cultural heritage". The *Circular of the State Council Concerning Strengthening the Protection of Intangible Cultural Heritages*, issued in August, 2005, defines the "intangible cultural heritage" as follows: Intangible cultural heritage refers to the traditional forms of cultural expression which exist in an intangible state, are closely related to the people's life and are passed down from generation to generation, and these include oral traditions, traditional performing arts, folk activities, rituals and festivals, the folk traditional knowledge and practice relating to nature and the universe, traditional handicrafts and skills, and the cultural spaces relating to the above forms of traditional cultural expressions. The Circular also specifies the principle and policy for the work on intangible cultural heritages: intangible cultural heritages should be protected according to the policy of "mainly stressing protection, putting saving first, rationally utilizing, inheriting and developing intangible cultural heritages". For the protection of cultural heritages, when conducting surveys on the Cultural Heritage Day in 2006, comrade Xi Jinping pointed out, "We have a clear boundary for intensifying the reform of the cultural system: differentiating the cause from industry, cultural heritage should be protected by mainly taking it as a cause and then utilized from an industrial perspective; emphasis should be placed mainly on protection and rescue, more consideration should be given to spending money rather than making money, and this issue should be properly addressed at the institutional level." This provides a scientific orientation for the protection of Zhejiang's intangible cultural heritages and identifies the direction for specific work.

Intangible cultural heritages mainly exist in the folk society; as they are highly ethnic and regional and are inherited by particular personnel, they easily fail to be handed down with the changes in the social environment and lifestyle and the passing of inheritors. Early on, Zhejiang started work on intangible cultural heritages and has established a well-developed mechanism for the protection of its intangible cultural heritage in the work on protecting intangible cultural heritages.

8.1.1.1   Sound Organization

The protection of intangible cultural heritages is a government-led task, so the specialized organizations are needed to help safeguard and protect those heritages. Zhejiang became the first nationwide to protect intangible cultural heritages at the provincial, municipal and county levels. With more and more protection of intangible cultural heritages, in 2009, the Department of Culture of Zhejiang Province established the Division of Intangible Cultural Heritages responsible for making regulations, policies and developmental plans for the protection of intangible cultural heritages, undertaking and reviewing the applications for the projects in the provincial list of intangible cultural heritages, organizing and carrying out inheritance, publicity and display of intangible cultural heritages. Afterwards, the centers of intangible cultural heritages and the leading groups for the task were set up at the municipal and county levels, which are provided with full-time personnel for protection. The organizations for intangible cultural heritages at various levels provide a strong organizational guarantee for Zhejiang's work on the protection of intangible cultural heritages.

8.1.1.2   Well-Functioning System of Laws and Regulations

To concretely and effectively protect intangible cultural heritages, Zhejiang continuously improved relevant regulations and worked out developmental plans, made active experiments and practice in rendering that protection scientific and regular and promoting the rule of law in the protection it provided. In this regard, comrade Xi Jinping gave an important instruction in 2006: "It is necessary to really strengthen the leadership over the protection of cultural heritages, intensify legislation and guarantees, and rationalize the working mechanism for the protection of cultural heritages." Inheriting and protecting intangible cultural heritages is an important part of efforts in building Zhejiang into a culturally large province and also the consensus built among various sectors of the society. The *Plan of Zhejiang Province for the Building of a Culturally Large Province (2001–2020)* issued by the Party Committee and the People's Government of Zhejiang Province, the *Decision of the Party Committee of Zhejiang Province on Accelerating the Building of a Culturally Large Province*, and the "Eight-Eight Strategies" have created a good policy environment for the protection of intangible cultural heritages. The *Circular Concerning Strengthening the Protection of National Folk Art* issued by the General Office of the People's Government of Zhejiang Province in March, 2004 has made comprehensive in-depth arrangements for the protection of national folk art. In 2006, Zhejiang issued the *Interim Measures of Zhejiang Province for the Management of a Special Fund for the Protection of Intangible Cultural Heritages*, specifying the detailed rules for the use and management of the special fund. During the months of February–May, 2007, Zhejiang issued the *Measures of Zhejiang Province for the Application and Identification Concerning the Representative Inheritors of Intangible Cultural Heritages*, the *Rules of Zhejiang Province for Review Work on the List of Intangible Cultural Heritages (Trial)*, the *Work Plan of Zhejiang Province for a Pilot General Survey on Intangible Cultural Heritages*, and the *Interim Measures of Zhejiang Province for the Protection and Management of the Representative Works of Intangible Cultural Heritages*. The above measures actively promote and standardize Zhejiang's protection of intangible cultural heritages.

8.1.1.3 Protection Fund

Putting in place a special fund is an important guarantee for smoothly, persistently and effectively protecting intangible cultural heritages. In this regard, when delivering a speech during his survey on the Cultural Heritage Day, comrade Xi Jinping expressed a very clear attitude saying that it was necessary to spend money rather than make money and to increase input in the protection of cultural heritages. The Department of Culture and the Department of Finance of Zhejiang Province made active efforts, and allocated 20 million yuan to rescue and protect national folk art and cultivate folk art talents during the years 2002–2005. As from 2006, each year, 15 million yuan in a special fund from provincial finance was arranged for rescuing and protecting intangible cultural heritages. In the same year, the Department of Culture and the Department of Finance of Zhejiang Province jointly developed the administrative measures for the special fund for intangible cultural heritages. The cities, counties (city-level counties, districts) set up special funds for protecting intangible cultural heritages. Zhejiang was rare nationwide in offering financial support for the protection of intangible cultural heritages and provided a solid material guarantee for comprehensively protecting those heritages.

8.1.1.4 Expanding the General Survey

As the intangible cultural heritages are deeply stored in the folk society, if there is no general survey conducted in an extensive and in-depth way, it is impossible to establish a relatively complete list of intangible cultural heritages, systematically and effectively inherit and protect them. Zhejiang became the first nationwide to initiate a general survey on intangible cultural heritages. Zhejiang's general survey on those heritages was started in the second half of 2003 and fully completed in 2008; the general survey covered five years. With the general survey, Zhejiang gained a systematic and full understanding of the types, stock and distribution of the resources of Zhejiang's intangible cultural heritages, the environment for their existence and the status quo of their inheritance. The in-depth and solid general survey laid a comprehensive and reliable foundation of information for tapping, reorganizing, protecting, inheriting and developing the resources for Zhejiang's intangible cultural heritages.

8.1.1.5 The Release of the Intangible Cultural Heritage List

Establishing the system of listing intangible cultural heritages is the core of efforts in protecting intangible cultural heritages. Based on the results of the general survey on the resources for intangible cultural heritages, Zhejiang determined the list of intangible cultural heritages to be rescued and protected, and gradually established the system of listing intangible cultural heritages covering the municipal, municipal and county levels, and laying a solid foundation for inheriting and protecting those heritages.

8.1.2 The Cause of the Protection of Intangible Cultural Heritage with Public Participation

To ensure the healthy development of intangible cultural heritages, the government should improve the protection mechanism and the people should consciously participate in the protection of intangible cultural heritages. The intangible cultural heritages are the quintessence of folk culture, so they should be protected and inherited mainly by the people. Therefore, the protection and inheritance of those heritages must be deeply rooted in the folk society and be based on continuously increasing the degree of public participation; only in this way can active inheritance of intangible cultural heritages be promoted.

8.1.2.1 The Degree of Public Participation has Increased in the Bases of Intangible Cultural Heritages

The bases for inheritance are the important venues for protecting and inheriting intangible cultural heritages. In nearly ten years, Zhejiang earnestly developed various types of bases for the inheritance of intangible cultural heritages, providing spaces and conveniences for the cultivation of the inheritors of intangible cultural heritages and for public participation. As of 2013, the Department of Culture of Zhejiang Province, in conjunction with the Department of Education of Zhejiang Province, announced 131 inheritance and teaching bases for provincial-level intangible cultural heritages; the Department of Culture of Zhejiang Province announced 46 inheritance bases for provincial-level intangible cultural heritages, 20 bases for the protection of provincial-level national traditional festivals, 50 bases for the publicity and demonstration of provincial-level intangible cultural heritages, 55 provincial-level bases for the productive protection of intangible cultural heritages, 9 experimental areas for the protection of intangible cultural heritages and 8 institutions of higher learning as the provincial-level intangible cultural heritage research bases. Nevertheless, various types of intangible cultural heritage demonstration halls have also been built in various parts of Zhejiang; local authorities in Zhejiang have given great importance to the construction of demonstration halls and learning centers for intangible cultural heritage as well as other infrastructures for the dissemination and demonstration of intangible cultural heritages, providing important carriers for the people to participate in the protection and inheritance of intangible cultural heritages in a wider scope and at a higher level.

8.1.2.2 The Inheritors of Intangible Cultural Heritages have Grown Amidst Cultivation

The intangible cultural heritages appear in an active state, their inheritance carriers are the people. The inheritors are the important carriers of intangible cultural heritages, thus strengthening the protection of inheritors is naturally a key task for the protection of intangible cultural heritages. One of the priorities of the task of the protection of intangible cultural heritages lies in protecting the inheritors, expanding the force of the inheritors, intensifying the management and protection of those inheritors. In this regard, Zhejiang has taken many active measures. First, for the representative inheritors of the projects on the intangible cultural heritage list, Zhejiang has developed the measures for application and identification accordingly, established the list, provided the venues for their inheritance and learning, financially supported them to carry out such activities as teaching apprentices and imparting art, teaching and exchanges; Zhejiang has commended and rewarded the representative inheritors with outstanding contributions to inheritance. Second, Zhejiang has offered assistance and scholarships to those who want to learn artistic skills, so as to nurture more talents. With various financial support policies, Zhejiang has gradually built a force of inheritors on a certain scale. As of 2013, Zhejiang had 122 representative inheritors of the national-level intangible cultural heritage projects, and 738 representative inheritors of the provincial-level intangible cultural heritage projects. Moreover, these inheritors have also exerted active influence nationwide. Five people from Zhejiang were given the Chinese Intangible Cultural Heritage Inheritor Award in 2012; Zhejiang was the province with the largest number of inheritors given that award nationwide.

8.1.2.3   The Knowledge About Intangible Cultural Heritages has been Popularized Among the People in Making Cultural Achievements

In order to better put the achievements regarding intangible cultural heritages on show and protect them, expand the ways to inherit and spread intangible cultural heritages, and popularize the achievements in intangible cultural heritages among the people, Zhejiang organized relevant forces to compile and publish a series of books, including the *A Collection of National Folk Formative Arts in Zhejiang Province*, the *Addendum to a Collection of National Folk Performing Arts in Zhejiang Province*, and the *Series of the Representative Works of Intangible Cultural Heritages in Zhejiang Province*. Local authorities also compiled a local series of books on intangible cultural heritages accordingly; for instance, Jinhua has 21 series of books on intangible cultural heritages, including the *Series of the Representative Works of Intangible Cultural Heritages in Zhejiang Province*, the *Magnificent Spectacle of Intangible Cultural Heritages in Jinhua,* the *Ten-year Picture Album on Intangible Cultural Heritages in Jinhua* and the *Legend of Huang Daxian*. Local authorities in Zhejiang also promoted the building of intangible cultural heritage data banks and databases; for instance, Hangzhou's system of databases for intangible cultural heritage consists of an integrated application platform, four databases and six systems. These series of books on intangible cultural heritages, relevant data banks and databases have made it greatly convenient for the people to understand and access the achievements in intangible cultural heritages, and they have helped effectively build and develop the ways to disseminate intangible cultural heritages, so that the knowledge about those heritages is popularized among the people.

8.1.2.4   The People's Awareness About the Protection of Intangible Cultural Heritages has been Enhanced Through Media Publicity

When conducting surveys on the Cultural Heritage Day in 2006, comrade Xi Jinping stressed the importance of the publicity about intangible cultural heritages. He called for conducting a series of publicity activities, utilizing various channels to publicize the protection of intangible cultural heritages; carrying out—through various media including demonstrations, performances and media—the publicity and education concerning the protection of intangible cultural heritages among the people, especially juveniles; advocating the behavior of treasuring cultural heritages, enhancing the people's understanding of cultural heritages and fostering a good atmosphere in which the people in the whole society participate in protecting cultural heritages. According to the important instructions from comrade Xi Jinping and specific arrangements made by the Party Committee and the People's Government of Zhejiang Province, the Department of Culture of Zhejiang Province actively publicized the work on protecting intangible cultural heritages through mass media including radio, films, television, newspapers, periodicals and the Internet. Media publicity has made the people understand intangible cultural heritages and it has also enhanced the people's awareness about the protection of intangible cultural heritages and greatly expanded the influence of intangible cultural heritages, thus laying a good base among the masses for the people to spontaneously protect and inherit intangible cultural heritages.

8.1.2.5 Social Forces have Spontaneously Participated in the Development of Intangible Cultural Heritages

Comrade Xi Jinping gained insights into mobilizing extensive social forces to protect intangible cultural heritages; he called for actively guiding and encouraging social forces to participate in the protection of cultural heritages, and guiding private capital to protect and develop them under the condition that government input plays the leading role. The spontaneous participation of social forces has further promoted the protection and inheritance of intangible cultural heritages. For instance, the People's Government of Taizhou City has worked with enterprises to allocate 2.6 million yuan to establish the Taizhou Haidongfang Luantan Troupe, a private troupe—each of the five promoters annually earmarks 200,000 yuan to support the troupe's operations. The participation of social forces, especially the injection of social funds, has brought new vitality into the protection and inheritance of intangible cultural heritages; this is also an important innovation in Zhejiang's working mechanism for intangible cultural heritages. Moreover, Zhejiang has also built up voluntary service teams for the protection of intangible cultural heritages in order to make the ordinary people spontaneously participate in the protection of those heritages. At present, 230,000 volunteers in various areas participate in the general survey on and protection of intangible cultural heritages. The extensive participation of volunteers has opened extensive spaces for conducting various types of intangible cultural heritage activities, protecting and inheriting intangible cultural heritages.

8.1.2.6 The Cultural Activities Relating to Intangible Cultural Heritages have been Integrated into the People's Life

Integrating intangible cultural heritages into a variety of cultural activities is an effective way of spreading those heritages. In various parts of the province, various types of activities have been conducted to publicize intangible cultural heritages so as to enhance the people's awareness about the protection and inheritance of those heritages. A wide range of cultural activities focusing on them have attracted the people in various areas and have greatly extended intangible cultural heritages to more audiences, so that those heritages have entered the ordinary households and are being actively inherited in Zhejiang.

8.2   A Variety of Non-governmental Cultural Organizations

The non-governmental organization is the general term that refers to social groups and private non-enterprise units. The former is the non-profit social organization which is generally organized by citizens of their own accord for achieving a common vision and conducts activities according to the articles of association. The non-governmental organizations involved in this section mainly refer to the social groups and organizations similar to the former. In August, 2005, when conducting a survey in the Department of Civil Affairs of Zhejiang Province, comrade Xi Jinping pointed out, "A law-based government is a limited government, the government cannot perform functions in every aspect of social life; in an effort to strengthen social management, the government should also give play to the role of social organizations"; he stressed, "Both history and reality prove that excessively strict management of social organizations is unfavorable for achieving social harmony and arousing social vitality; on the contrary, lack of management of social organizations is unfavorable for maintaining social stability and social order"; on this basis, he called for properly dealing with the relations between organizational leadership and political leadership, between control and guidance, and between management and service.[1] This remark made by comrade Xi Jinping fully affirmed the role of non-governmental cultural organizations in organizing, coordinating and promoting the people's cultural life on the one hand, and identified a correct direction for the development of non-governmental organizations in the new period on the other hand. The *Measures for Qualifying Examination of Private Social Science Research Organizations*, implemented by the Zhejiang Federation of Humanities and Social Sciences Circles as from 2008, have actively encouraged social forces to build social science research organizations and have strengthened the guidance and supervision of private social science research organizations to promote their well-regulated operations and healthy development.

8.2.1   Vigorous Development of Non-governmental Cultural Organizations

8.2.1.1   The Basic Characteristics of Non-governmental Cultural Organizations

There are a great variety of non-governmental organizations; they are widely distributed in various industries and fields, and their functions are diverse. It is hard to accurately determine the number of non-governmental organizations officially registered with the departments of civil affairs at various levels in a certain period of time, let alone a large number of social organizations not registered with the departments of civil affairs in sub-districts (towns), communities and other fields. According to relevant surveys, among the social groups known by the Department of Civil Affairs

---

[1] Xi (2006), pp. 329–330.

of Zhejiang Province, the number of the groups which are really of a cultural nature is not large; the provincial social cultural groups are engaged more in the extensive and macro work. In fact, the non-governmental organizations really having close connections with the cultural life of the people at the primary level are the following two types of non-governmental organizations: First, the primary-level social groups below the municipal level, especially those at the level of county (county-level city, district), organize and conduct a great variety of activities closely related to the social life and cultural activities of the people at the primary level, and have the important characteristic of combining guidance with participation; second, the grassroots non-governmental cultural organizations which are not registered with the departments of civil affairs and are widely distributed in sub-districts (towns), communities, and even in rural areas.

In a general sense, the grassroots non-governmental cultural organizations often have the following characteristics: They are highly spontaneous, they have a large number of participants, they better cater to the people's needs, the activities are frequent, there is great appeal, and their influence is extensive. All of these characteristics are closely related to the characteristics of the members of non-governmental cultural organizations—primary-level, grassroots. The members of non-governmental cultural organizations live at, come from and are active at the primary level, they often have skills, common aspirations and tastes, so it is easy for them to spontaneously get together; they have no clear interests and goals, they stay together mainly for the purpose of creating entertainment for and by themselves, their activities are not subject to restrictions on time, place and form, thus they fully reflect the characteristics of non-governmental cultural organizations: spontaneous, unrestrained and voluntary.

8.2.1.2 The Self-development of Non-governmental Cultural Organizations

The primary-level, grassroots non-governmental cultural organizations play an important role in enriching the cultural life of the people at the primary level and enhancing the quality of the people's life. First, they build large platforms for greatly enriching the people's cultural life; second, they foster a healthy and harmonious humanistic environment amidst a variety of cultural activities, they pool positive social energy and enhance social cohesion.

The non-governmental cultural organizations have changed from the traditional cultural artistic form to a modern cultural lifestyle. On the one hand, the traditional folk cultural activities are enduring; on the other hand, the modern cultural lifestyle has greatly aroused the people's cultural creativity, and new modes of cultural activity have emerged in large quantities.

8.2.1.3   The Main Characteristics of the Development of Non-governmental Cultural Organizations

In 2005, the Zhejiang Non-governmental Organization Research Society finished a major project under Zhejiang's key science and technology program and conducted a systematic survey on the issues concerning the province's non-governmental organizations. The research achievements divided non-governmental organizations into three categories: First, the non-governmental organizations built in a top-down way according to the requirements of the government's functional departments, such as the senior citizen associations and the associations for the handicapped; second, the people's organizations which are built in a down-top way in light of residents' actual needs and mainly conduct the fellowship, recreational, physical fitness and correct safeguarding activities, such as amateur performer groups, the groups doing exercise and senior citizens' cultural and artistic groups; third, the non-profit entities which provide convenient services to residents, such as community service centers, community health and medical institutions. As shown by the development of Zhejiang's non-governmental organizations in a period of nearly ten years, we can summarize the following main characteristics of non-governmental organizations: First, they have developed rapidly, their number is large. Second, they are widely distributed in a variety of industries, urban areas, sub-districts (towns), communities, and even in rural areas. Third, their functions are diverse and include resource integration, services, management, culture and education. Fourth, the base among the masses is wide; for instance, the New Era Cultural, Entertainment and Physical Fitness Club, established in Wangma Community in Xiacheng District, Hangzhou City in June, 2003, includes 10 cultural and artistic groups, and it acquired more than 700 members in a very short time. Fifth, they are mainly spontaneous, unrestrained and voluntary; this really embodies the non-governmental nature.

8.2.2   The Great Vitality of Non-governmental Cultural Organizations

8.2.2.1   The Vitality of Non-governmental Cultural Organizations

The non-governmental cultural organizations play the role which cannot be replaced by the government, the most important reason for this being that they come from and are active in the folk society, they are close to the primary level and the people, and they are approachable. Such approachability fully demonstrates the vitality of non-governmental cultural organizations and makes them highly capable of uniting and inspiring. As the people are served by these organizations, a sense of cultural identity and a sense of belonging have emerged.

8.2.2.2 The Brand-Building of Non-governmental Cultural Organizations

With the vigorous development of non-governmental cultural organizations, it is particularly important to increase the support for them, managing them in a well-regulated way and enhancing their quality; this plays an important role in building the brands of folk culture and social influence. Under the principle that the government plays the leading role and the people carry out autonomous management, Hangzhou actively supported the building of the mass cultural and artistic groups and guided those groups to regularly conduct cultural activities. First, fostering models, in 2008, 13 cities, counties (county-level cities) designated 46 mass cultural groups as the municipal-level mass cultural demonstration groups; second, building platforms, carrying out characteristic cultural square activities, and 100-troupe and 100-occasion cultural performance activities; third, providing financial support, each year offering 5,000 yuan in subsidies for the municipal-level mass cultural demonstration groups. With actions taken to foster models, build platforms and provide financial support, the groups' initiative has been fully aroused, and the professional quality of groups has been improved greatly. In the meantime, towns also strengthened the management of non-governmental cultural organizations through active experiments and practice.

8.3 The Colorful Cultural Life of the People

In nearly ten years, the people's cultural activities in various parts of Zhejiang were diverse in form, new in content, positive and healthy in style; the people's subjectivity and enthusiasm for participation in cultural activities and cultural development were fully aroused; the positive energy of nourishing and cultivating the people through culture took shape; full scope was given to the role of folk culture in ensuring cultural ownership and social cohesion. During this process, the cultural development among the people of Zhejiang featured a pattern of interaction with the active participation of the people, extensive involvement of non-governmental forces and active leading role played by government departments; the people's cultural life underwent a series of major changes from pure cultural entertainment to a leisure culture combining culture with sports, from the traditional mode of cultural activity to the modern cultural lifestyle, and from individual cultural enjoyment to the improvement of the quality of group culture.

8.3.1 The People's Cultural Life from Folk Vitality

8.3.1.1 The Folk Enthusiasm About Culture has been Fully Aroused

In the spring of 2013, a real farmers' art festival was held in Jindong District, Jinhua City, in which 12 towns produced, directed and staged one 40 min cultural and artistic performance in more than 20 days; in the farmers' culture contest, 12 performances and 80 programs lasted from 8:30 a.m. to 5:00 p.m., the performances with a combination of foreign culture and local culture made farmers happy and presented the great vitality of Zhejiang's rural culture. This was an ideal event in which the people's cultural self-consciousness was activated and their cultural enthusiasm was ignited.

The Red Tourism Festival launched in Ou'hai District, Wenzhou in July, 2009 attracted visitors from various parts of the country to Wenzhou to visit the Jingde Temple—the former site of negotiations on peaceful liberation, and the Liaoyuan Producers' Cooperative where the reform of fixing farm output quotas for each household was initiated. The towns in Ou'hai District utilized local resources, and the people showed an unprecedented enthusiasm for participation in cultural activities. The Spring Flower Festival in Li'ao, the Lantern Festival in Zhou'ao, the February 1 Fair in Zhaixi, the Reading Festival in Wutian, the Green Cultural Festival in Xianyan, the Chashan Ecological Waxberry Cultural Tourism Festival and other folk cultural activities were held one after another. The government departments provided guidance and services, while the main participants were the people at the primary level. As "there are festivals each month", the cultural vitality in the folk society was fully aroused. In Shaoxing City, there were a wealth of cultural and artistic talents, the cultural atmosphere was strong, more than 500 groups involving balls, fan dances and waist drums were developed; cultural activities were conducted as if seeds were sown across Shaoxing.

8.3.1.2 The Folk Cultural Resources have been Effectively Integrated

With an increasing material living standard, the people actively took part in various cultural activities and extensively participated in various activities for cultural development. According to the report from the *Zhejiang Daily* on March 15, 2014, the first folk lantern culture museum in Wenzhou, built with more than 3 million yuan of investments from Zhang Jincheng, a native of Wenzhou and a collection for many years, was open for free. Zhang Jincheng hoped that the museum could play the role of education. Zhang Jincheng's practice was supported by the people from various sectors of the society and the local government, and stimulated the government to attract more private resources to support the development of public culture. The Government of Ou'hai District took advantage of this situation to plan the large museum education theme parks, including five theme museums—the Cultural Museum, the Wenzhou Tanghe Cultural Life Museum, the Wenzhou Stone Carving Statue Museum, the Wenzhou Old Trade Experience Museum, and the Wenzhou

Ou Kiln Museum—and one Blue Lamp Old-style Academy. As support for the construction of public cultural facilities, folk running of culture has effectively integrated social resources, promoted the development of cultural programs, and presented the vitality of folk culture, thus better meeting the people's cultural needs and largely covering the shortage of government investments.

8.3.1.3   The Mass Cultural Activities have been Conducted Vigorously

The *"Four-batch" Plan of Zhejiang Province for Cultural Development (2005–2010)* called for placing equal emphasis on mass culture and the culture of excellent works, being close to the primary level, life, the people and reality, promoting the development of mass culture including characteristic community culture, campus culture and enterprise culture. In nearly ten years, the mass cultural activities were energetically carried out in various parts of Zhejiang; they gradually presented the following trends and characteristics: themes, a large scale, new carriers and widespread participation. The mass cultural activities focused on building a harmonious society and carrying out the socialist core values, and they really made folk culture become the impetus for enhancing the people's sense of cultural belonging.

1.   The community cultural activities have shown varied bright spots.

The development of community culture in various parts of Zhejiang had the following characteristics: First, giving prominence to traditions and regional characteristics, such as the historical and cultural research group at Yangming Community in Yuyao, traditional marriage custom percussion music band at Houdajie Community in Zhenhai, Ningbo; second, building communities into the places for producing and initiating local and original culture; for instance, the community groups in Jiangdong District, Ningbo produced works and staged performances with respect to local people and things; third, promoting theme brand building, new-type themed festival activities, including community culture festivals, sports meetings, reading festivals and neighbor festivals, emerged.

2.   The campus culture has led to a healthy growth of students.

For a long time, kindergartens, primary and middle schools and the institutions of higher learning in various parts of Zhejiang gave great importance to the function of nurturing the people through campus culture, and promoted the development of campus culture to lead the growth and development of students. Various types of schools at various levels proceeded from historical and regional advantages, the characteristics of specialties and disciplines; with the goal of leading the growth and development of students, they integrated the development of campus culture into various aspects of education and teaching and actively built the campus culture brands, thus obtaining fruitful achievements.

The Zhejiang Campus Culture Development Theme Forum, which was held in May, 2013 and focused on "Beauty, Happiness, Dream of Education", showcased the achievements in and characteristics of the development of campus culture at the primary and middle schools across the province in recent years. The campus culture at Zhejiang's institutions of higher learning was highly influential nationwide. Based on a high degree of attention from the institutions of higher learning to cultural development, the Educational Workers' Union under the Party Committee of Zhejiang Province actively pushed forward the building of campus culture brands at Zhejiang's institutions of higher learning. Specifically, first, identifying distinctive themes, developing a strong sense of the times. Second, giving expression to individual character and the characteristics of running schools; being close to campus, students and life, considering the characteristics of teachers and students to inherit the fine traditions and historical deposits of schools, and presenting the unique cultural landscape of schools. Third, ensuring extensive participation, stressing the demonstration effect and the role in stimulating the development of others. In the meantime, campus culture went beyond the campus to interact with communities.

3. Enterprise culture has built a cultural homeland.

Zhejiang's entrepreneurs who have stayed ahead in economic development have fully realized that the core competitiveness of enterprises depends upon not only products and services, but also on the charm of enterprise culture. Therefore, entrepreneurs have taken excellent enterprise culture as an important part of enterprise development, and so bright spots have frequently occurred in the development of enterprise culture. The development of enterprise culture has not only made enterprises successful, but it has also built the cultural homeland and pooled positive social energy. Zhejiang's entrepreneurs have built the following consensus: capability comes with responsibility.

8.3.2 *Institutional Innovations have Broken New Ground in Mass Culture*

Local authorities in Zhejiang fully realized that only a life with culture is a life of quality. As an important part of the public cultural service system, mass culture has always been the focus of attention from the Party committees and governments at various levels in Zhejiang. The *Decision of the Party Committee of Zhejiang Province on Accelerating the Building of a Culturally Large Province*, issued in 2005, called for vigorously carrying out the "eight projects" for cultural development. The section concerning the Cultural Front Project stressed that cultural front was an important carrier for developing advanced culture, and specified concrete tasks for the development of a cultural front: giving full scope to the functions of public cultural facilities including libraries, cultural centers and museums, strengthening the development of the public welfare cultural fronts at and below the county level, especially in rural areas and communities, cultivating a number of cultural model villages and cultural model communities and promoting culture in rural areas, thus routinizing and institutionalizing this effort. The Cultural Communication Project and the Cultural Talent Project provided an important institutional guarantee for promoting the development of mass culture. With a focus on delivering culture to rural areas, local authorities have actively carried out the activities of delivering culture and sowing cultural seeds, bringing about significant social benefits. Jinhua City is taken as a particular case for analysis.

With a series of activities of delivering culture and sowing cultural seeds in 1,000 towns and 10,000 villages—including "Showing Films on 10,000 Occasions in Rural Areas", the "Wu Opera Performance Season", "Staging 1,000 Performances in Rural Areas", and "Delivering 10,000 Books to Rural Areas"—as the effective carriers, Jinhua City extensively conducted a variety of activities of sowing cultural seeds, including the "sowing cultural seeds" contest in towns and villages, the "sowing cultural seeds" achievement demonstration, folk cultural activities at festivals and celebrations, exhibition shows of excellent traditional characteristic culture, and the appraisal and selection for the "sowing cultural seeds" achievements, thus greatly enriching the cultural life of the people at the primary level.

8.3.3   The Main Line for the Prosperity and Development of Zhejiang's Folk Culture

With an analysis of the course of development of Zhejiang's mass culture and its effectiveness during the period 2003–2013, we can find the following main line: in promoting the prosperity and development of Zhejiang's mass culture, the people are the main actors, the government-led efforts are the guarantee, being close to the people is the source, institutional innovations are the impetus, and the integration of folk resources is the new path.

(1) The people are the main participants in cultural creations and in activities with cultural experience.
(2) The government-led efforts and administrative promotion are the important guarantee for pushing forward the healthy and rapid development of mass culture.
(3) Being close to the people and life is the source for promoting extensive public participation.
(4) Institutional innovations are the endless impetus for promoting the prosperity and development of mass culture.
(5) The participation and integration of folk resources is the new path for promoting the prosperity and development of mass culture.

Overall, in an effort to promote the development of mass culture and enrich the people's life, local authorities in Zhejiang made active experiments and took practical actions, acted in a top-down and down-top way, combined activity with inertia—combining cultural activities with the construction of cultural infrastructures—and promoted the integrative development of high culture, the culture of excellent works and mass culture, thus really integrating the Chinese dream about the building of a culturally powerful country into the people's daily life.

Reference

Xi Jinping, *Carrying out Concrete Work to Stay Ahead – Line of Thought and Practice in Promoting New Development in Zhejiang*, The Party School of the CPC Central Committee Press, 2006.

Chapter 9
The Inspirations from Zhejiang's Cultural Development: Exploring the Local Path for Cultural Governance

Xiaoming Zhang and Chunming Zu

When reviewing the practical achievements in the more than ten years of Zhejiang's cultural development, we increasingly realize that a breakthrough with important significance is being made in that development; this breakthrough may represent the future developmental trend of Chinese culture, and it presents the future path for China's cultural revival and also suggests that the soft power support for realizing the Chinese dream is gradually taking shape.

9.1 The Zhejiang Example of a Cultural Strategy: From a Culturally Large Province to a Culturally Strong Province

After the 6th Plenary Session of the 17th Central Committee of the Communist Party of China put forward the concept of "a culturally powerful country", the concept of "a culturally strong province" was increasingly valued by the Party committees and people's governments of various provinces. The 10th Plenary Session of the 12th Party Committee of Zhejiang Province, convened in 2011, further issued the *Decision on Carrying Out the Principles Adopted during the 6th Plenary Session of the 17th Central Committee of the Communist Party of China and Promoting the Building of a Culturally Strong Province*, identifying the goal of building a culturally strong province as follows: the humanistic spirit is lofty, cultural programs are prosperous, the cultural industry becomes developed, the cultural atmosphere is strong and the cultural image is distinctive.

A culturally strong province is a developmental goal which has been put forward by more than half of the provinces across the country. What are the differences between Zhejiang's strategy for building a culturally strong province and that in

X. Zhang (✉) · C. Zu
The Chinese Academy of Social Sciences, Beijing, People's Republic of China

© Social Sciences Academic Press and Springer Nature Singapore Pte Ltd. 2019
D. Xie and Y. Chen (eds.), *Chinese Dream and Practice in Zhejiang – Culture*,
Research Series on the Chinese Dream and China's Development Path,
https://doi.org/10.1007/978-981-13-7216-2_9

other areas? How does the strategy stimulate Zhejiang to take an unusual "local path" for cultural development? Our views are as follows:

First, a kind of moral development that is suitable for Zhejiang's economic development is the soul for building Zhejiang into a culturally strong province.

Moral development is the soul of cultural development, and in Zhejiang, moral development is reflected in the great amount of attention given to the change from Zhejiang's business culture to modern market ethics. In the early period of Zhejiang's economic development, the traditional interpersonal relationship with blood ties, marriage and geography as bonds exerted an important impact on economic development, and the formation of the massive economy peculiar to Zhejiang's economy was closely related to the culture of impartation, help, assistance and guidance in such an interpersonal relationship. However, when the economy develops to a certain stage, Zhejiang's enterprises need to address greater challenges from domestic and international markets, the limitations from business ethics based on the acquaintance society loom large. On the one hand, it restricts the expansion and growth of enterprises based on the general market credit; on the other hand, the mutual guarantee within small circles will lead to the binding of enterprises in case of financial risk, so if the financial risks for enterprises increase drastically, it would be very easy to incur systemic risks. After the financial crisis broke out, the owners of some enterprises in Zhejiang ran away to dodge debts, and that act is related to those kinds of immature business ethics.

For special historical reasons, Zhejiang's private economy generally features governance by able persons and patriarch-based management; this imposes great restrictions on Zhejiang's economy in reaching a higher level and embarking on a broader stage. After the outbreak of the financial crisis, the able-person economy and patriarch-based management mode were subject to huge challenges, the Party Committee and the People's Government of Zhejiang Province seized opportunities and actively guided private enterprises to push forward the building of a modern system of enterprise governance, including shareholding socialization, specialized operations and professional management, and made further improvements to modern ethics across the province. Thanks to the long-term and unremitting building of the social credit system and of modern business ethics, the awareness of the enterprises in Zhejiang about market integrity and market ethics was enhanced greatly; the enterprises in Zhejiang have progressively advanced within the world's economic arena, and they have become a strong force as China's economy moves towards the world.

When summarizing the Zhejiang Spirit, Zhejiang's scholars gained this valuable understanding: "In order to build a modern Zhejiang, it is necessary to form two new cultural factors: competitive and well-regulated."[1] They have summarized two cultural factors from Zhejiang's developmental practice, combined two ethical principles including efficiency and equity—which are characterized by the concepts "competitive" and "well-regulated", respectively—to carve out the new dimension for research on the ethics of China's market economy.

---

[1]Lixu (2013).

Second, high cultural self-consciousness is the inexhaustible impetus for building Zhejiang into a culturally strong province.

High cultural self-consciousness is the prominent impression left to us by Zhejiang's cultural development. The government, enterprises and the folk society have passionately promoted cultural development, bringing about an endless driving force for building a culturally strong province. The open regional ethos and the local tradition of highly valuing cultural education determine that cultural self-consciousness exists throughout the process of Zhejiang's development.

As from the early 21st century, the cultural strategy for Zhejiang's development has experienced three leaps, and cultural self-consciousness has been on the rise. The *Plan of Zhejiang Province for the Building of a Culturally Large Province (2001–2020)*, unveiled in 2000, fully showed that Zhejiang, a province which preliminarily became affluent and stayed ahead nationwide in economic development, had a deep understanding about the importance of and necessity for cultural development, and marked a new starting point for Zhejiang's self-consciousness in cultural development. The *Decision of the Party Committee of Zhejiang Province on Accelerating the Building of a Culturally Large Province*, issued in 2005, incorporated cultural development into the "Eight-Eight Strategies" for Zhejiang's all-round development, and suggested the path of self-consciousness for Zhejiang's cultural development. The *Decision of the Party Committee of Zhejiang Province on Earnestly Carrying Out the Guiding Principles Adopted during the 6th Plenary Session of the 17th Central Committee of the Communist Party of China and Vigorously Promoting the Building of a Culturally Strong Province*, issued in 2011, called for deeply promoting the building of a system of values with a socialist core, a system of public cultural services and the development of a cultural industry, and it also called for focusing on carrying out the plan for popularization of the socialist theoretical system with Chinese characteristics, the plan for the development of civic morals, the plan for the creation of excellent cultural and artistic works, the plan for the development of cyberculture and modern media, a plan for the construction of major cultural facilities, a plan for the improvement of basic public cultural services, the plan for the inheritance of cultural heritage, the plan for doubling cultural industries, the plan for the development of external culture and the plan for the development of cultural celebrities; it indicated that the path of self-consciousness for Zhejiang's cultural development would become more mature and clearer, and the strategic goal for cultural development would become more explicit. The report at the 13th Party Congress of Zhejiang Province in 2012 specified the strategic goal of building a modern socialist Zhejiang which is materially affluent and culturally advanced, and called for further stressing co-building and sharing, social harmony, a combination of material modernization and the people's modernization, making it possible for all the people across the province to share the achievements of modernization, thus truly ensuring that the people across the province have a stronger sense of pride in development, of happiness in life, and of belonging and of a social identity; it suggested that the original self-consciousness regarding cultural development was coming to Zhejiang. The original self-consciousness regarding cultural development means that it is necessary to make culture serve development, turn the supporting role of culture in development into the main role of culture in development, make sure that culture itself becomes the highest goal of development, and make culture really serve the people's well-rounded development, so that there is a richer cultural connotation in the people's life.

Finally, the formation of a pattern of cultural development for all-round innovation is a sign of success in building a culturally strong province.

As from the time when the building of a culturally large province was established, Zhejiang incorporated all-round innovation into various aspects of cultural development. In the field of public cultural services, in order to promote the construction of the primary-level public cultural service facilities, Zhejiang creatively put forward the East Sea Pearl project, promoted the construction of town and village-level public cultural service venues according to the requirements that were noticeably higher than national standards, so that Zhejiang fully stayed ahead nationwide in province-wide construction of the primary-level public cultural service infrastructures. In recent years, in response to the new needs for the development of the primary-level public cultural services, Zhejiang has focused on building rural cultural auditoriums, and comprehensively enhancing the quality of rural public cultural services through resource integration, functional upgrading and self-management, thus providing the Zhejiang Experience to improve the performance of the primary-level public cultural services across the country. Moreover, Zhejiang has carried out the activity of appraisal and selection for the Innovation Award concerning the primary-level public cultural services. Zhejiang has become the first nationwide to allow free admission to public museums and the whole 5A West Lake scenic spot; Hangzhou has pioneered the adoption of an all-purpose card for public libraries, and has become the first nationwide to introduce the mode of borrowing books from and returning books to public libraries at the municipal-county, district-sub-district, town-village levels; Hangzhou has incorporated the external population and rural migrant workers into the scope of service objects, subversively changing the service mode and philosophy of China's public libraries; local authorities in Zhejiang have also developed a number of public cultural service philosophies and modes—including the "15 min Cultural Circle", the cultural green card for rural migrant workers, "sowing cultural seeds" in 1,000 towns and 10,000 villages, the "mobile cultural station", the "1% Cultural Program", "One Product in One Village", and the "Four-season Tour for Enriching the People through Culture"—to enrich the connotation of public cultural services. In the field of the cultural industry, the people of Zhejiang have developed new forms of business and a new boundary in China's cultural industry with their unique business acumen and awareness of innovation. Zhejiang is home to the Hengdian Film and Television Industry Experimental Area, the largest film and television shooting and production base in Asia, the China (Yiwu) Cultural Products Trade Fair, the bellwether of global trade in cultural goods, Huace Film and Television, the largest private film and television producer in China, Songcheng, the no. 1 share in China's performance circle, Huayi Brothers, the no. 1 share in China's film industry and Shunwang Technology, the no. 1 share in the Internet bar software industry. The market success of these cultural enterprises comes from successful innovations to the business model and cultural content. More than ten years ago, comrade Xi Jinping said, "In a sense, the history of Zhejiang's reform and opening-up for more than 20 years is a vivid history of innovation".[2] In Zhejiang, cultural innovation has become a habit. The history of Zhejiang's cultural development is a history of the continuous innovation in cultural development that the people of Zhejiang have carried out.

Zhejiang's strategy for building a culturally strong province reflects Zhejiang's confidence in its achievements in building a culturally large province; it also embodies Zhejiang's self-consciousness in its future cultural development; it suggests that Zhejiang has consciously realized that cultural development should always be people-oriented, cultural development should tally with social and economic development, economic transformation and upgrading and industrial renovation and upgrading should rely on unleashing and arousing cultural creativity. More importantly, in the process of transforming Zhejiang from a culturally large province to a culturally strong province, it is necessary to venture down a new cultural developmental path with Chinese characteristics, the features of the times and Zhejiang's characteristics.[3]

9.2 Zhejiang's Choice for Cultural Development: Exploring the Local Path for Cultural Development

The building of a culturally strong province is a strategic choice made by Zhejiang on the basis of seizing upon the situation and looking to the future, and exploring the local path for cultural development is key to building a culturally strong province.

We have mentioned, in Chapter One, some innovative practices adopted by Zhejiang for cultural development. This section will mainly analyze how Zhejiang proceeds from the potential of its primary-level social resources in urban and rural areas to arouse the people's cultural creativity and promote the role of culture in economic and social change, and to especially discuss some innovative practices adopted by Zhejiang in the field of public cultural services; this is because public cultural services most directly act upon individuals and are most likely to act upon everyone.

There have been many discussions about the role of culture in economic and social transformation, the people have also gradually realized that culture is an important factor for competition in comprehensive national strength and the intellectual support for economic and social development; however, how culture plays these roles and how local authorities should develop measures according to local conditions in order to guarantee the roles of culture remain issues which deserve further attention. The Zhejiang experience serves as a good example for us to consider these issues.

First, conducting such activities as "sowing cultural seeds", the building of rural cultural auditoriums, to actively cultivate the awareness of citizens as the main actors and their self-organization capability.

---

[2]Xi (2006).

[3]See the *Decision of the Party Committee of Zhejiang Province on Earnestly Carrying Out the Guiding Principles Adopted during the 6th Plenary Session of the 17th Central Committee of the Communist Party of China and Vigorously Promoting the Building of a Culturally Strong Province.*

In the present age, it is necessary for us to have a creative culture, while such a culture cannot be cultivated without extensive public participation. If the people do not have the enthusiasm for and initiative in cultural participation, there is no source for the creativity of culture. Therefore, the key lies in mobilizing and arousing the people's enthusiasm about participating and turning their sense of participation into a sense of entitlement.

In order to root culture among the people at the primary level and give shape to the intrinsic and sustainable autogenous mechanism, Zhejiang has actively cultivated local cultural and artistic personnel inside the towns, and has extensively carried out the activity of "sowing cultural seeds", which has produced marked effects. In recent years, Zhejiang has extensively conducted the activity of building cultural auditoriums in rural areas, and this has become an effective means to integrating the public cultural service systems in towns and villages; the rural cultural auditoriums, whether newly built or renovated, have increasingly become the regular venues in which local residents can carry out a variety of cultural activities. At these cultural auditoriums, villagers have organized a wide range of cultural and artistic activities, and most of these activities are based on local cultural resources and the artistic forms most familiar to local people; for instance, "A Bowl of Dachen Noodles" at Dachen Village is a village song created according to local folk customs; it is very popular among local people, and almost everyone in Dachen Village can sing the song.

Second, guiding local people to develop the micro cultural industry in villages by taking the diversified cultural development path which features "one product in one county" and "one characteristic in one auditorium".

We generally believe that it is very hard to develop the cultural industry in the areas below the county level, but our surveys in Zhejiang show that the micro cultural industry in villages in Zhejiang is gradually taking shape, and it has become an important path for cultural development.

Zhejiang has always stressed in cultural development that local cultural resources should be relied upon to promote diversified and characteristic cultural development, and make sure that there is "one product in one county" and "one characteristic in one village" as far as possible. This is favorable for putting to use the local cultural resources; moreover, the people have an increasing amount of enthusiasm about participation in cultural development, the traditional skills and arts which were only used by local people for the recreational purpose in the past have gradually become the cultural resources which can be utilized for industrial development.

Third, mobilizing social forces to participate in cultural development in order to actively cultivate social organizations.

An important aspect of intensifying the reform of the cultural system is that the government should further streamline administration and delegate powers to the lower levels. Who are the recipients of the powers so delegated? If the powers are fully delegated to the market, in case of market failure, universality and equity cannot be guaranteed. Therefore, the decision made by the 3rd Plenary Session of the 18th Central Committee of the Communist Party of China vowed, for the first time, to cultivate the non-profit cultural organizations, and stressed that the things which the government cannot do, cannot conveniently do or do better should be undertaken by the non-profit cultural organizations, so that they serve as a bridge and a bond between the government and the market.

Zhejiang has always given importance to mobilizing social forces to participate in cultural development, and their social organizations are available in large quantities. At present, in the cultural field, there are more than 1,300 groups that show films, more than 500 folk opera troupes, more than 10,000 amateur groups for the protection of cultural relics, nearly 25,000 amateur cultural and sports groups, and more than 500,000 amateur cultural and sports personages in Zhejiang's rural areas.

In order to really respect the people's choices, interests and rights, it is necessary to consider their situation and feelings, and judge whether they live with dignity. This can be considered as an important step from cultural development to cultural governance. Overall, Zhejiang has actively explored the local path for cultivating the creative culture to promote economic and social transformation; such a path focuses on cultural governance.

9.3 Zhejiang's Breakthroughs in Cultural Development: From a Local Path to Cultural Governance

The cultural governance mentioned here is not cultural governance in the traditional sense, but it is modern cultural governance. In the traditional system of social management, culture is generally considered as the governance object and the governance tool for regulating morality and ethics, behaviors and lifestyles at the primary social level; this is the common function of culture: social edification. Modern cultural governance is a kind of modern national governance; it reflects the fundamental change in the government's cultural function from traditional cultural management to modern governance. Such a change is closely associated with the change in governmental functions and the cultivation of a civic society.

In order to achieve cultural governance, besides the change in governmental functions, the following conditions also need to be satisfied at the same time: (1) cultural enterprises should be vibrant; (2) social organizations should be efficient; (3) the ordinary people should show a keen interest. "Cultural enterprises should be vibrant" means that it is necessary to fully arouse the capability for creation and innovation of cultural enterprises, to produce diverse high-quality cultural products to make the cultural market prosperous, and adopt the administrative, tax and other means to encourage enterprises to participate in the cultural development of public welfare. "Social organizations should be efficient" means that it is necessary to thoroughly change the pattern in which social organizations excessively rely on the government and are inefficient, so that they are really organized, take actions, perform their functions of coordinating government governance and make up for market failure. "The ordinary people should show a keen interest" means that it is necessary to thoroughly change the situation in which the people passively accept, skimp and show indifference to public cultural activities, so that they are willing, pleased to participate in and actively take part in public cultural activities, and fully arouse the people's initiative and creativity in participating in cultural governance.

With a review of the local path for Zhejiang's cultural development, we can find that many practices in it make way for cultural governance and make it possible for cultural governance to be ultimately achieved.

First, there are many cultural enterprises and diverse cultural products, and the cultural market is brisk in Zhejiang. Many enterprises are willing to take and have taken actions to participate in the cultural development of public welfare. For instance, in 2006, the Zhejiang Radio & TV Group became the first nationwide to hold the China Zhejiang TV Audience Festival under the theme of "repaying the audiences and the society"; in 2007, China Sanke Electrical Co., Ltd. established the Sanke Intangible Cultural Heritage Museum in Yueqing, Zhejiang, which is dedicated to collecting Yueqing's boxwood carvings and excellent products of fine-grained papercutting. These particular cases show that enterprises in Zhejiang have great enthusiasm and a high sense of social responsibility for participating in the cultural development of public welfare.

Second, Zhejiang's social organizations are available in large quantities and are active. Take the above-mentioned Kecheng District, Quzhou City as an example; in recent years, Kecheng District has carried out the developmental activity called the "Volunteers' Homeland · Loving Heart for Realizing Dreams", giving shape to the three-level network of volunteer service organizations covering the whole district, including the volunteers federation, branches of the volunteers federation, and volunteer service stations (volunteers' homeland). At present, there are more than 50 characteristic volunteer groups, more than 10,000 volunteers and volunteer services have been performed 20,000 times in Kecheng District.

Third, local people of Zhejiang have a very high degree of cultural participation; that degree of participation is reflected in the enthusiasm for participating in cultural and sports activities and presents a sense of responsibility for cultural inheritance and development. When visiting the rural auditorium at Lizhang Village in Yantou Town, Pujiang County, Jinhua City, a famous calligraphy and painting village, we found that several elderly local people voluntarily taught local children calligraphy and painting. Some of these people were more than 80 years old, but they still taught students at the auditorium or their homes every day; they considered this their responsibility, and believed that they were duty-bound to pass down the local calligraphy and painting tradition to the younger generations.

Overall, cultural governance is a new attempt for China, so much preparatory work is needed; as Zhejiang has consciously experimented the local path for cultural development, such experimentations have laid the necessary foundation for Zhejiang's transformation from cultural development to cultural governance. Nevertheless, there is still a long way to go before really achieving cultural governance, and even before evolving from cultural governance to the mode of civilization; this should also be the future path for Zhejiang's cultural development.

9.4   Zhejiang's Vision for the Cultural Dream: From Cultural Governance to a Model of Civilization

For a long time in history, China has represented a model of civilization and the Chinese civilization circle thus took shape. However, the course of modernization has deconstructed the traditional structure and mode of governance of rural social organizations in China, the Chinese civilization circle and the significance of Chinese civilization as a model. With its unique local path, Zhejiang's cultural development has presented to us the Zhejiang Model for a cultural dream: from modern cultural governance to a new model of civilization.

China's modernization has lasted for about 100 years and has entered its peak in the past ten years. With the increasing rate of urbanization, China's traditional rural society has disintegrated rapidly, and the traditional social organization and mode of governance has left daily life accordingly. This has made us become a generation without roots or nostalgia. The people have started to think about the meaning of life and consider whether a model cultural lifestyle can be rebuilt and if so, the way to rebuild it; this has a vital bearing on the success in China's social, economic and cultural transformation, and the realization of the vision that the Chinese nation once again can contribute a model of civilization to the world.

As shown by the Zhejiang experience, a reasonable path for fostering a model lifestyle during modernization is cultural governance. A kind of cultural governance rooted in the primary-level society is of an important significance for rebuilding the rural society and the society of an urban community, and it essentially represents the rebuilding of the overall lifestyle of the Chinese people in the era following the building of a moderately prosperous society in all respects, while such a lifestyle may lead to a new model of civilization.

First, cultural governance further enlightens the people and enhances their civic awareness. In a modern society, there are no gentlemen and authority, the people should learn to practice self-governance; this is the first step for fostering a culturally advanced model lifestyle. In order to ensure that the Chinese people achieve the transformation from "managed objects" to becoming the "main players in governance", the cultivation of civic awareness is crucial.

In the process of Zhejiang's cultural governance, the people's sense of participation and entitlement has been enhanced effectively. They have organized various types of amateur cultural and artistic groups, volunteer organizations and non-profit cultural organizations; they have also gradually learnt to keep checks and balances and provide coordination in building bodies and groups. This is because all bodies, whether large or small, involve the issue of cooperation with others, while that cooperation should be achieved under the condition of equality among the members. In essence, each social organization is similar to a civic society; the people get familiar with the rules and ways of a civic society by participating in social organizations. More importantly, the people are apt to have public needs and build consensus on public affairs during their participation in cultural governance.

Second, with cultural governance, the relationship between the government and the people gets better, and thus the society becomes more harmonious. In cultural governance, the people are no longer the "managed objects", but they serve as the main actors in governance, like the government, to participate in cultural development. Take the building of the rural cultural auditoriums as an example; our surveys show that many village secretaries or village directors take charge of cultural auditoriums and are the organizers of cultural activities, they even sing and dance together with local people, thus they establish a closer relationship with the people. When the people encounter difficulties and problems, they will take the initiative to seek help from village cadres, so matters, large or small, are handled within villages in Zhejiang.

Third, with cultural governance, the tradition of mutual assistance has been rebuilt in the rural society. The people in the modern society become indifferent due to rational calculations, while the tradition of strong mutual assistance in Zhejiang may be a good solution to this problem.

Overall, as the lifestyle in China's traditional rural society comes to an end, that lifestyle characterized by equilibrium and harmony necessary for the modern society which is in the making. As we observe, in Zhejiang, there are some characteristics which should exist in such a new lifestyle; for instance, citizens have the awareness of self-governance and subject consciousness, the relationship between the government and the people has changed from management to joint governance based on consultation; furthermore, the people do not lose tender feelings because of rational calculations.

Of course, "what lifestyle should exist in the modern society" is always a question at issue. However, undeniably, after the people become well-off in material life, they have the reason and right to live a life with more dignity. In the meantime, the sense of entitlement, being treated equally, and being followed with interest by groups are the important indicators for judging whether the people live a life with dignity. The sign that the people live a life with dignity is an important sign for judging whether a nation or a society is culturally advanced.

9.5   Conclusions: The Zhejiang Experience and the Chinese Dream

General Secretary Xi Jinping put forward the concept of the Chinese dream at the beginning of his governance. It should not be merely considered as a political slogan and catchword; it should be regarded as the confidence in China's current achievements and the expectation about the future development; it should not be considered as a whim which occurred after he became the core of the new generation of leadership; it can be tracked from the thoughts and practice during his governance of Zhejiang.

In history, China once had glory demonstrated by the fact that a host of states paid tribute to China and China enjoyed the commanding height in the universe. Huntington even regarded the Chinese civilization circle with China as the core country as the only surviving ancient civilization. However, since modern times, the Chinese empire has declined, the people have been ridiculed as the Sick Man of East Asia, and the vassal states which once took the initiative to be sinicized sought de-sinicization to varying degrees. With more than 30 years of reform and opening-up, China's GDP has surpassed that of Japan to become no. 2 in the world, and China has become a military power which can be compared to the USA and Russia. However, have we realized the Chinese dream? The extent to which the Chinese nation can restore its past glory depends on the country's ability to regain its phenomenal cultural appeal.

If the Chinese dream is only considered as the enhancement of hard power, we can say with pride that we have reached the shore of realizing the dream; however, in fact, if China only has a great economic and military strength without cultural appeal, the rise of China will only lead to fear, even hostility, from other countries.

Therefore, China's ability to once again contribute a model of civilization to the world and provide an attractive lifestyle and model of development to the world should be an expectation within the Chinese dream, in the two centenary goals, even an expectation from the world about the peaceful rise of China. Then how can the Chinese dream which contains such an expectation be realized?

We believe that the practice, in the cultural field, of the pattern of social organization and the mode of governance reestablished by the national governance system and modernization of the capacity for governance will further contribute a model of civilization to the world. Cultural governance will be the important way and foundation to modernizing the national system of governance and the capacity for governance. With a review of the Zhejiang experience, we have reason to believe that General Secretary Xi Jinping outlined the realization of the Chinese dream through cultural governance during his governance of Zhejiang; only in this way can Zhejiang carry through one blueprint in cultural development and change from cultural development to cultural governance.

As indicated, the path for Zhejiang's future cultural development should be that Zhejiang continuously strengthens, under the guidance of the Chinese dream, the change from cultural development to cultural governance and thus continues to stay ahead nationwide in a new round of the system of national governance and the modernization of the capacity for governance.

On this basis, we suggest that Zhejiang should strengthen its work in the following aspects:

First, further intensifying the reform of the cultural system, transforming the administrative department for cultural affairs from cultural management to cultural governance. In the conventional system of cultural management, the administrative department for cultural affairs ran cultural affairs. Since the reform of the cultural system, the cases of adopting such a practice have decreased markedly and there has been a gradual change to cultural management. However, this is not enough, it is necessary to further change from cultural management to cultural governance; in other words, the administrative department for cultural affairs should focus on the goal of developing its primary-level ability for self-organization and further delegate its powers of cultural management to the lower levels, and transfer the part which needs to be managed by it, but cannot be better managed by it to social organizations or to the people for management.

Second, further strengthening the software development of public cultural services. In recent years, with increasing input in public cultural services in China, hardware facilities have become fairly complete, but the rate of utilization of these facilities is generally low, so currently there is an urgent need to reinforce the software development of public cultural services.

Although Zhejiang has made certain achievements in this regard, given the requirements of cultural governance, it is also necessary to further connect the development of public cultural services with local cultural resources. Only in this way can local people be more willing to participate in public cultural affairs, and achieve sustainable development and utilization of local cultural resources.

Third, further arousing the enthusiasm of enterprises, especially private cultural enterprises, about participation in the cultural activities of public welfare. Enterprises are not only the main forces for rendering the cultural market prosperous, but also the main actors in cultural governance. In Zhejiang, there is a sound system of a market economy, the private economy has developed well, and private cultural enterprises are largely active in participating in the cultural activities for public welfare. Therefore, the government should innovatively develop the public system of cultural services and it should especially adopt the market means such as government procurement to attract private cultural enterprises to participate in providing public cultural services. In the meantime, it is necessary to further intensify the execution of traditional means, such as tax exemption and reduction or preferential policies, to encourage cultural enterprises, especially private cultural enterprises, to participate in the cultural activities for public welfare and cultural governance.

Four, further strengthening the cultivation of social organizations to make them become the main actors in cultural governance. Chinese citizens have less public awareness and lack the experience and foundation for establishing social organizations, China's social organizations have always been underdeveloped, and the number of social organizations with high executive ability is small. However, social organizations are very important for cultural governance, thus it is necessary to actively cultivate them by reducing the examination and approval procedures, lowering the access threshold, providing necessary policy guidance, and improve the system of laws and regulations and reinforce supervision to ensure the normal and orderly activities of social organizations.

Overall, further contributing a model of civilization to the world is the essential part of the Chinese dream, while cultural governance is an important way to achieve a model of civilization. In cultural practice, Zhejiang is changing from cultural development to cultural governance. As long as Zhejiang promotes cultural development in this direction, it will certainly provide the Zhejiang Example which deserves to be imitated for realizing the Chinese dream.

References

Chen Lixu, Building a Culturally Strong Province: A Review Based on the Strategic Goal of Building a Modern Zhejiang, in: Chen Ye, *Annual Report on Zhejiang's Development 2013 (Culture Volume)*, Hangzhou Publishing House, 2013, p. 65.

Xi Jinping, *Carrying out Concrete Work to Stay Ahead – Line of Thought and Practice in Promoting New Development in Zhejiang*, The Party School of the CPC Central Committee Press, 2006, p. 79.

Postscript

On March 21, 2014, the Zhejiang Academy of Social Sciences convened a meeting with the participation of relevant personnel from the Academy to officially arrange the work on building the research groups for various volumes concerning the major program "The Chinese Dream and Zhejiang's Practice", and designate the research fellow Chen Ye, the Editor in Chief of the Editorial Department of the Academy's *Think Tank Report* to serve as the deputy leader of the Culture Group. During the period of April 9–12, the members of the Research Group who came from Zhejiang's side intensively studied the two works of comrade Xi Jinping—*Carrying Out Concrete Work to Stay Ahead—Thinking and Practice in Promoting New Development in Zhejiang, Zhijiang Xinyu*, and his series of important speeches since the 18th National Congress of the Communist Party of China. The research fellow Chen Ye—a member of the Culture Group, and the associate research fellow Zhou Jing—the editor of the Academy's *Think Tank Report*, attended this meeting. In the charge of the research fellow Ge Licheng, a vice president of the Academy responsible for the work, the research fellow Chen Ye worked out the first draft of the outline for writing the Culture Volume, which was delivered to the Research Group for discussion on April 11.

On April 22, the first plenary meeting of the Research Group of "The Chinese Dream and Zhejiang's Practice" was held in Hangzhou. The research fellow Xie Dikun, the leader of the Culture Group and the Director of the Institute of Philosophy at the Chinese Academy of Social Sciences, the research fellow Zhang Xiaoming, the Executive Deputy Director of the Cultural Research Center of the Chinese Academy of Social Sciences, the research fellow Jia Xudong, the Deputy Director of the Cultural Research Center of the Chinese Academy of Social Sciences, the research fellow Chen Ye, an expert from Zhejiang's side, professor Chen Lixu, the Director of Education at the Zhejiang Party School of C.P.C (the then Director of the Teaching and Research Office for Sociology and Culturology), Wang Zheng, the Deputy Director of the Office of the Zhejiang Academy of Social Sciences, and the associate research fellow Chen Jing convened the first meeting of the Culture Group, discussing the composition of members, tasks, the first draft of

© Social Sciences Academic Press and Springer Nature Singapore Pte Ltd. 2019
D. Xie and Y. Chen (eds.), *Chinese Dream and Practice in Zhejiang – Culture*,
Research Series on the Chinese Dream and China's Development Path,
https://doi.org/10.1007/978-981-13-7216-2

writing an outline and the plan for field surveys. Afterwards, repeated consultation and exchanges were conducted between Beijing and Zhejiang with respect to relevant matters. During this period, professor Li Jie, the Vice Dean of the College of Media and International Culture, Zhejiang University, associate professor Zhang Hongling from the Teaching and Research Office for Sociology and Culturology at the Zhejiang Party School of the C.P.C and other experts from Zhejiang's side joined the Culture Group. On June 3, the writing of the outline was finished.

On the morning of June 11, the Research Group convened the review meeting on the writing of the outline for the Culture Volume, with participation of the research fellow Chen Ye, professor Li Jie and the associate research fellow Zhou Jing from the Culture Group, who were the experts from Zhejiang's side. The reviewing experts Hu Jian, Zhang Weibin, Jin Yanfeng, Mao Yue, Shao Qing, Ma Lihong, and Sheng Shihao put forward pertinent and detailed suggestions about revision on the basis of basically affirming the outline. According to expert opinions, the Culture Group adjusted and revised the outline. Thus the outline was basically finalized on the basis of having been revised more than ten times.

After the Research Group of "The Chinese Dream and Zhejiang's Practice" convened the first plenary meeting, entrusted by the research fellow Xie Dikun, the research fellow Zhang Xiaoming organized the pre-survey preparatory work of the experts from Beijing's side, and convened a meeting to discuss the issues concerning the survey in Zhejiang, preliminarily determine the members of the Research Group according to the objective and requirements of the survey, identify the survey priorities and direction, and arrange the work on collecting and reorganizing the preliminary materials.

During the period of June 23–28, the Culture Group conducted field surveys in such counties, county-level cities (districts) as Hangzhou, Quzhou, Jinhua, Jiangshan, Kecheng, Longyou, Dongyang and Pujiang, and the provincial cultural publicity circles, while the research fellow Chen Ye and the Deputy Director Wang Zheng organized the preparatory and concrete work on field surveys. The research fellow Zhang Xiaoming; the editor and reviewer Wu Shangming, the Deputy Director of the Cultural Research Center of the Chinese Academy of Social Sciences, the research fellow Chen Ye, professor Chen Lixu, professor Li Jie, the Deputy Director Wang Zheng, the associate research fellow Hui Ming, the assistant to the Director of the Cultural Research Center of the Chinese Academy of Social Sciences, the associate research fellow Zhou Jing and the assistant research fellow Zu Chunming from the Cultural Research Center of the Chinese Academy of Social Sciences participated in survey activities. The survey activities were actively supported and assisted by the leaders and experts from relevant areas and departments. During the surveys in Quzhou, Jinhua and Hangzhou, the Culture Group held talks with the representatives from the departments of publicity under local municipal Party committees, the departments directly under these Party committees, the cultural publicity circles in the counties (city-level cities, districts), conducted the activities of inspecting, visiting and interviewing. In the surveys in the provincial cultural publicity circles, the personnel in charge of relevant divisions in the Department of Publicity under the Party Committee of Zhejiang Province, the

Civilization Office of Zhejiang Province, the Department of Culture, the Press, Publication, Radio and Television Bureau, the Bureau of Statistics of Zhejiang Province, the Zhejiang Writers Association, the Zhejiang Federation of Literary and Artistic Circles, the Zhejiang Daily Press Group, the Zhejiang Radio & TV Group, the Zhejiang United Publishing Group, and the Zhejiang Culture Center introduced to the Culture Group the progress in various fields of Zhejiang's cultural development in recent years, and provided abundant materials and cases.

During the surveys, the Culture Group held two meetings. The first meeting focused on the outlines of various chapters to determine the framework for the writing, and identify the survey priorities concerning various chapters and the requirements for staged progress. The second meeting focused on discussing the primary-level cultural development and the work on rural cultural auditoriums in Zhejiang in light of surveys, and exchanged views, clarified the train of thought and requirements for further revising and substantiating the outline of the writing. With arrangements made by Director Xie Dikun, professor Wu Xibiao, the Head of the Scientific Research Division at Quzhou University, associate professor Wei Junjie and others joined the Culture Group. Thus the personnel of the Culture Group were fully put in place.

After surveys, based on fully analyzing survey materials, in the charge of the research fellow Zhang Xiaoming, the Research Group on Beijing's side—including the research fellow Li He from the Cultural Research Center of the Chinese Academy of Social Sciences, the editor and reviewer Wu Shangmin, the associate research fellow Hui Ming, the assistant research fellow Zu Chunming and others— carried out repeated discussions and in-depth studies to basically develop the Introduction and the outline of the writing for Chap. 9, and determined the writing tasks and scheduling. During the writing, they exchanged views on problems by telephone, email and other means on many occasions to improve the train of thought on the writing.

On Zhejiang's side, in the charge of the research fellow Chen Ye, the Research Group held many discussions and consultations about the division of work, the train of thought, rules of style, the collection of material, the selection of the content, and the summarization of the points of view. Chen Lixu, Li Jie, Wu Xibiao, Zhou Jing, Zhang Hongling, and Wei Junjie undertook the research and writing tasks for Chaps. 2–8.

The experts from Beijing and Zhejiang worked closely, exchanged views, and supplemented materials and data, basically finishing the first draft in the middle of October. The research fellows Zhang Xiaoming and Chen Ye reviewed the first draft many times, and put forward revision opinions on style, content, materials, data and points of view. The authors actively cooperated and made repeated revisions, and they also made many great adjustments and revisions to some chapters to work out the second draft.

In November, the Culture Group received the review opinions and feedback from the reviewing experts including Hu Jian, Jin Yanfeng, Lian Xiaoming, and Chen Xianchun. On the morning of November 29, the research fellow Chen Ye organized the experts from Zhejiang's side to hold discussions, further improve the main line of writing, discuss the revision opinions and suggestions from the experts on a chapter-by-chapter basis, and to identify the revision requirements. With careful revisions by the authors, the third draft was finished.

During the period of December 5–8, the Research Group convened a meeting on the final compilation and editing of various volumes, the research fellow Chen Ye dealt with overlaps and repetitions, supplemented content and materials, deleted and pruned the texts, checked the data, and carried out other final compilation and editing work on the third draft of the Culture Volume, feeding back some matters to authors for revision. The associate research fellow Zhou Jing provided assistance and coordination, and carried out much of the work. After final compilation and editing, the fourth draft was finished.

As the writing of the Culture Volume is finished and the Culture Volume is about to be published, we hereby express our heartfelt thanks to the leaders of relevant departments—including the Chinese Academy of Social Sciences, the Department of Publicity under the Party Committee of Zhejiang Province, and the Zhejiang Academy of Social Sciences—who provided great support to us during the research on the subject, and the above leaders, experts and scholars who provided direct guidance to us, as well as all of the personnel who helped us in research but are not mentioned due to a limitation of space.

The authors of various chapters of the Culture Volume are as follows:

Chapter 1, Xiaoming Zhang, Ming Hui (The Chinese Academy of Social Sciences);
Chapter 2, Jing Zhou (The Zhejiang Academy of Social Sciences);
Chapter 3, Ye Chen (The Zhejiang Academy of Social Sciences);
Chapter 4, Hongling Zhang, Ye Chen (The Party School of the Zhejiang Provincial Party Committee, the Zhejiang Academy of Social Sciences);
Chapter 5, Lixu Chen (The Party School of the Zhejiang Provincial Party Committee);
Chapter 6, Jie Li (Zhejiang University);
Chapter 7, Jing Zhou (The Zhejiang Academy of Social Sciences);
Chapter 8, Xibiao Wu, Junjie Wei (Quzhou College);
Chapter 9, Xiaoming Zhang, Chunming Zu (The Chinese Academy of Social Sciences).

The Research Group of the Chinese Dream
and Zhejiang's Practice Culture Volume
December 8, 2014

Bibliography

Chen Lixu, *The Power of Culture*, Zhejiang University Press, 2008.

Chen Wei, *A Study of the Public Cultural Service System*, The Publishing House of Shenzhen Press Group, 2006.

Chen Ye (ed.), Zhejiang Blue Book: Zhejiang Development Report 2008 (Culture Volume), Hangzhou Publishing House, 2008.

Chen Yao, *Public Cultural Services: Institutions and Model*, Zhejiang University Press, 2012.

Department of Publicity under the Party Committee of Zhejiang Province, *The Zhejiang Spirit of Advancing with the Times*, Zhejiang People's Publishing House, 2005.

(Britain) Elaine Baldwin et al., *Introducing Cultural Studies*, trans. by Tao Dongfeng, Higher Education Press, 2004.

Guo Jianning, *The Interpretation of the Basic Content of the Socialist Core Values*, People's Publishing House, 2014.

Huang Chuanxin et al., *A Study of the Appeal and Cohesive Force of Socialist Ideology*, Xue Xi Chu Ban She, 2012.

Huang Kunming, *The Reader of the Chinese Ancient Civilization for the Leading Cadres*, Zhejiang Ancient Books Publishing House, 2010.

Jiang Yihua, *The Foundation of the Chinese Civilization – the Core Value of National Rejuvenation*, Shanghai People's Publishing House, 2012.

(Britain) Jim McGuigan, *Rethinking Cultural Policy*, trans. by He Daokuan, China Renmin University Press, 2010.

Jin Pusen, Chen Shengyong, *The General History of Zhejiang*, Zhejiang People's Publishing House, 2005.

Li Jingyuan, Zhang Xiaoming, *The Zhejiang Experience and Its Implication for the Development of China (Culture Volume)*, Social Sciences Academic Press, 2007.

Lin Lvjian (ed.), Zhejiang Blue Book: Zhejiang Development Report 2009 (Culture Volume), Hangzhou Publishing House, 2009.

Lin Lvjian (ed.), Zhejiang Blue Book: Zhejiang Development Report 2010 (Culture Volume), Hangzhou Publishing House, 2010.

Lin Lvjian (ed.), Zhejiang Blue Book: Zhejiang Development Report 2011 (Culture Volume), Hangzhou Publishing House, 2011.

Lin Lvjian (ed.), Zhejiang Blue Book: Zhejiang Development Report 2012 (Culture Volume), Hangzhou Publishing House, 2012.

Li Qiang, *Building a Modern Zhejiang Which is Materially Affluent and Culturally Advanced*, Zhejiang People's Publishing House, 2012.

© Social Sciences Academic Press and Springer Nature Singapore Pte Ltd. 2019
D. Xie and Y. Chen (eds.), *Chinese Dream and Practice in Zhejiang – Culture*,
Research Series on the Chinese Dream and China's Development Path,
https://doi.org/10.1007/978-981-13-7216-2

Lu Yingchuan, Wan Pengfei et al., *The Organization and Management of Innovative Public Services*, People's Publishing House, 2007.

People's Publishing House, Studying General Secretary Xi Jinping's Important Address on August 19, People's Publishing House, 2013.

Song Junhua, A Study of the Protection of Intangible Cultural Heritage, Sun Yat-Sen University Press, 2013.

The *Decision of the Central Committee of the Communist Party of China on S.* ssues *Concerning Building a Moderately Prosperous Society in All Respect*s, adopted during e 6th Plenary Session of the 16th Central Committee of the Communist Party of China on O ober 11, 2006.

The *Decision of the Central Committee of the Communist Party of China on Some Major Issues Concerning Intensifying the Reform of the Cultural System and Promoting Vigorous Development and Great Prosperity of the Socialist Culture*, adopted during the 6th Plenary Session of the 17th Central Committee of the Communist Party of China on October 18, 2011.

The *Decision of the Central Committee of the Communist Party of China on Some Major Issues Concerning Comprehensively Intensifying the Reform*, adopted during the 3rd Plenary Session of the 18th Central Committee of the Communist Party of China on November 12, 2013.

The Department of Publicity under the Party Committee of Hangzhou City, *Moving towards the Cultural Highland: "Our Values" Themed Practical Activity*, Hangzhou Publishing House, 2012a.

The Department of Publicity under the Party Committee of Hangzhou City, *Hangzhou's Practice in Making the Core Values Popular*, Hangzhou Publishing House, 2012b.

The Department of Publicity under the Central Committee of the Communist Party of China, *The Reader of General Secretary Xi Jinping's Important Addresses*, Xue Xi Chu Ban She, People's Publishing House, 2014.

The Office of the Reform and Development of the Cultural System of the Department of Publicity under the Central Committee of the Communist Party of China, the Bureau of External Cultural Relations under the Ministry of Culture, *The Report on International Cultural Development*, The Commercial Press, 2005.

The Office of the Leading Group of Hangzhou City for Reform of the Cultural System, *A Review of the Reform of the Cultural System in Hangzhou City*, Hangzhou Publishing House, 2007.

The Party Literature Research Center of the CPC Central Committee, *Excerpts of Xi Jinping's Remarks on Realizing the Chinese Dream of National Rejuvenation*, Central Party Literature Press, 2013.

The Party Literature Research Center of the CPC Central Committee, *Excerpts of Xi Jinping's Remarks on Comprehensively Intensifying the Reform*, Central Party Literature Press, 2014.

Wan Bin (ed.), Zhejiang Blue Book: Zhejiang Development Report 2005 (Culture Volume), Hangzhou Publishing House, 2005.

Wan Bin (ed.), Zhejiang Blue Book: Zhejiang Development Report 2006 (Culture Volume), Hangzhou Publishing House, 2006.

Wan Bin (ed.), Zhejiang Blue Book: Zhejiang Development Report 2007 (Culture Volume), Hangzhou Publishing House, 2007.

Weng Weijun, *Our Values*, Hangzhou Publishing House, 2014.

Zhang Renshou et al., *A Study of the Zhejiang Phenomenon*, Zhejiang People's Publishing House, 2006.

Zhang Weibin, *The Reader of Zhejiang's History and Humanities*, Zhejiang People's Publishing House, 2013a.

Zhang Weibin (ed.), Zhejiang Blue Book: Zhejiang Development Report 2013 (Culture Volume), Hangzhou Publishing House, 2013b.

Zhang Weibin (ed.), Zhejiang Blue Book: Zhejiang Development Report 2014 (Culture Volume), Hangzhou Publishing House, 2014.

Zhu Yingyuan, *A Multi-dimensional Study of the Socialist Core Values*, People's Publishing House, 2013.